AF754429
WITHDRAWN

SOCIAL PHOBIA: ETIOLOGY, DIAGNOSIS AND TREATMENT

SOCIAL PHOBIA: ETIOLOGY, DIAGNOSIS AND TREATMENT

CLAYTON P. AXELBY
EDITOR

Nova Biomedical Books
New York

Copyright © 2009 by Nova Science Publishers, Inc.

All rights reserved. No part of this book may be reproduced, stored in a retrieval system or transmitted in any form or by any means: electronic, electrostatic, magnetic, tape, mechanical photocopying, recording or otherwise without the written permission of the Publisher.

For permission to use material from this book please contact us:
Telephone 631-231-7269; Fax 631-231-8175
Web Site: http://www.novapublishers.com

NOTICE TO THE READER

The Publisher has taken reasonable care in the preparation of this book, but makes no expressed or implied warranty of any kind and assumes no responsibility for any errors or omissions. No liability is assumed for incidental or consequential damages in connection with or arising out of information contained in this book. The Publisher shall not be liable for any special, consequential, or exemplary damages resulting, in whole or in part, from the readers' use of, or reliance upon, this material. Any parts of this book based on government reports are so indicated and copyright is claimed for those parts to the extent applicable to compilations of such works.

Independent verification should be sought for any data, advice or recommendations contained in this book. In addition, no responsibility is assumed by the publisher for any injury and/or damage to persons or property arising from any methods, products, instructions, ideas or otherwise contained in this publication.

This publication is designed to provide accurate and authoritative information with regard to the subject matter covered herein. It is sold with the clear understanding that the Publisher is not engaged in rendering legal or any other professional services. If legal or any other expert assistance is required, the services of a competent person should be sought. FROM A DECLARATION OF PARTICIPANTS JOINTLY ADOPTED BY A COMMITTEE OF THE AMERICAN BAR ASSOCIATION AND A COMMITTEE OF PUBLISHERS.

LIBRARY OF CONGRESS CATALOGING-IN-PUBLICATION DATA

Social phobia : etiology, diagnosis, and treatment / [edited by] Clayton P. Axelby.
p. ; cm.
Includes bibliographical references and index.
ISBN 978-1-60692-159-3 (hardcover)
1. Social phobia. I. Axelby, Clayton P.
[DNLM: 1. Phobic Disorders. 2. Shyness. WM 178 S6779 2009]
RC552.S62S654 2009
616.85'22--dc22

2008035223

Published by Nova Science Publishers, Inc. ✦ New York

Contents

PREFACE

Social phobia (DSM-IV 300.23), also known as social anxiety disorder (DSM-IV 300.23) is a diagnosis within psychiatry and other mental health professions referring to excessive social anxiety (anxiety in social situations)[citation needed] causing abnormally considerable distress and impaired ability to function in at least some areas of daily life. The diagnosis can be of a specific disorder (when only some particular situations are feared) or a generalized disorder. Generalized social anxiety disorder typically involves a persistent, intense, and chronic fear of being judged by others and of potentially being embarrassed or humiliated by one's own actions. These fears can be triggered by perceived or actual scrutiny by others. While the fear of social interaction may be recognized by the person as excessive or unreasonable, considerable difficulty can be encountered overcoming it. Approximately 13.3 percent of the general population may meet criteria for social anxiety disorder at some point in their lifetime, according to the highest survey estimate, with the male to female ratio being 1:1.5. This book presents new and important research in the field.

Chapter I - Social phobia (SP) is an under-recognized and sub-diagnosed clinical condition even though it is the most frequent anxiety disorder, which responds to drug and psychotherapeutic treatment. The early and correct identification of this disorder is considered to be of extreme importance, minimizing suffering and preventing the development of psychiatric co-morbidities, which are associated with a poorer prognosis. It is within this context that instruments for evaluation can make a potential contribution.

Many instruments are currently available in the international literature for the evaluation of SP, including self-applicable scales, hetero-evaluation scales, scales for the evaluation of non-generalized SP, scales for the evaluation of the functional impairments associated with SP, and scales for the evaluation of other specific aspects of SP. Some scales have already been translated for use in different cultural contexts and have been extensively studied in terms of their psychometric qualities. The applicability of some of these scales has been confirmed in the clinical context and in empirical studies related to SP, while others still need further investigation.

The objectives of this chapter are to: a) to present a critical review of the literature about the main instruments used for the evaluation of SP, focusing on their objectives, major characteristics and psychometric qualities, and b) to present results of unpublished psychometric studies carried out by our research group in Brazil on samples of clinical and non-clinical subjects with SP using the following instruments: Social Phobia Inventory (SPIN), Mini-SPIN (MS), Brief Social Phobia Scale (BSPS), Self Statements During Public Speaking Scale (SSPS- trait and state version), Liebowitz Social Anxiety Scale- self-applied version, (LSAS), Liebowitz Self-Rated Disability Scale (LSRDS), The Disability Profile (DP), Social Interaction and Performance Anxiety and Avoidance Scale (SIPAAS), and Social Thoughts and Beliefs Scale (STABS).

This analysis, based on the literature and on empirical data, is considered to provide a tool for researchers and clinicians in the choice of instruments for the evaluation of SP that will be adequate for empirical investigations and for support in clinical practice.

Chapter II - Behavioral biologists and psychologists of various stripes have an interest in identifying the relation of social phobia to factors such as genetic contributions, early experiences, and neurological functions. The phenotypic expression of social phobia bears some relation to extreme shyness. Whether the conditions exist on the same plane is debatable among clinicians, however support exists for the notion that the two are related. Exploring the biological factors underlying extreme shyness may therefore help in understanding aspects of social phobia. An initial discovery in a literature review is that neuroscientists using animals in their research seldom use the DSM term of social phobia. On the other hand, there are scores of published papers with animal models on behavioral traits that we will make the case are closely linked to the human condition. Terms used by behavioral neuroscientists include behavioral inhibition, neophobia, social fear, timidity, social anxiety, and our preference, shyness. Many of these empirical reports are not specific to social interactions but our literature review will focus on shyness in social settings. In addition, field biologists have identified shy individuals in animal species ranging from rainbow trout to bighorn sheep. One outcome of these data and subsequent discussions is a renewed interest in biology for individual differences in "personality" of conspecifics. Another outcome has been to posit the existence of a shyness-boldness behavioral axis in the same mold as the five axes of personality traits (extraversion - introversion, neuroticism etc) suggested for humans. Implications for evolution of behavior are notable. The goals of this chapter will be to review the existing literature using animals models relevant to social phobia and discuss how the results compare to findings in human studies, and to point future research in directions that appear to be fruitful for a better understanding of the condition and for developing new treatment possibilities.

Chapter III - Individuals suffering from social phobia are excessively concerned about being negatively evaluated by others. Etiological models suggest that information processing biases and hypersensitivity to signals of social threat play a central role for the development and maintenance of the disorder. Indeed, it has been shown that individuals with SP display an increased sensitivity towards social cues of disapproval by others. Consistent with this notion, functional imaging studies have repeatedly revealed enhanced neural activity to negative facial expressions. Furthermore, new studies extended these findings to the domain of verbal stimuli and of emotional prosody expressed by the human voice. For these classes of social stimuli, socially phobic subjects show also remarkably altered brain activation, as compared to healthy subjects. In this chapter, recent findings concerning neural correlates of the processing of phobia-related stimuli in patients suffering from social phobia are reviewed and the implications for the understanding of altered information processing in social phobia are discussed.

Chapter IV - Inherited temperamental variables such as behavioral inhibition are important in the pathogenesis of social anxiety disorder (SAD). However, research suggests that early interpersonal experiences influence temperamental variables and interact with them in later development of social avoidance and shyness. In this chapter, the authors will describe the research on the role of stressful life events (SLE) in the pathogenesis of SAD.

The studies in the field show that individuals with SAD report parental conflicts (Magee et al, 1999) and also frequent history of physical and sexual abuse. Individuals with SAD also describe experiences of peer neglect and rejection, as well as harassment, teasing and bullying.

It is not clear whether these experiences have a causal effect on SAD or are either non-disorder specific or a result of behavioral inhibition and excessive submission. However, a vicious cycle has been described by Rubin & Burgess (2001) and by Gazelle & Ladd (2003), in which youngsters with a biological vulnerability to overreact in social situations, perhaps also influenced by parental overprotection, withdraw from peers. This withdrawal leads to a lack of sufficient peer interactions, which precludes development of appropriate social skills and positive relationships. This in turn leads to increased social anxiety and feelings of inferiority.

At present, our knowledge about SAD's etiology is far from conclusive. Clearly, further research about SLE and their role in the development of SAD is important and should use prospective studies that assess both temperament and SLE. The elucidation of these important factors might allow us to develop more targeted interventions in the prevention and treatment of SAD.

Chapter V - *Introduction:* The chapter was designed to describe the association between social phobia and alcohol or other psychoactive substance abuse. It aims to determine the frequency of social phobia among drug addicts and to describe the influence of this anxiety disorder on the occurrence of relapses and on adherence to treatment for substance use disorders, such as Alcoholics Anonymous (AA) and psychotherapy.

Methods: A literature review will be carried out of articles published for the last 20 years using the following databases: Medline, Cochrane, Lilacs and Scielo. The keywords chosen were: “social phobia”, “drug abuse”, “drug dependence”, “alcohol abuse”, “alcohol dependence”, “co-morbidity”, ” drug use treatment”, “alcoholics anonymous”, and “narcotics anonymous’. The text is focused on topics related to prevalence of drug use, chronological and causal relationship between social phobia and alcohol or other drug use, diagnosis of the co-morbidity and impact of co-morbidity on drug abstinence and treatments adherence.

Results: Social phobia is highly frequent among drug addicts, being observed at a higher frequency than in the general population. Nevertheless, it is underdiagnosed and, hence, undertreated. The adherence to such groups as Alcoholics Anonymous and Narcotic Anonymous tends to be weaker among social phobic drug users. Not all studies indicate that social phobia increases the relapse rates.

Discussion: Although social phobia is a frequent co-morbidity, it is underdiagnosed among alcohol or other psychoactive substance dependents, which can lead to nonadherence to drug use treatment and may potentially increase relapses, and a worse clinical progress.

Only if both disorders are properly evaluated and treated the cycle of social phobia and drug abuse can be broken. Early identification of social phobia and appropriate interventions are needed to improve treatment response and the quality of life of the alcohol or other psychoactive substance-dependent patients.

Chapter VI - *Objectives:* To determine if social anxiety and other specific child characteristics predict cognitive behavioral therapy (CBT) outcomes in anxious children, and if these characteristics improve with CBT. High social anxiety was hypothesized to have an adverse effect on outcome.

Method: Children with anxiety disorders (n=110) ages 8 to 12 years and their mothers completed measures of children's general level of anxiety, social anxiety, depression, negative self-statements, self-esteem, locus of control, coping style and social skills pre- and post-CBT. Outcome measures were clinician-rated child functioning and child- and parent-rated child anxiety.

Results: Low initial social anxiety predicted child- and mother-rated improvement in anxiety. Initial use of active coping predicted clinician-rated improvement in functioning. Several child characteristics including social anxiety improved with CBT though they were not targeted directly.

Conclusion: In anxious children specific child characteristics, particularly social anxiety, predict less favorable response to CBT. Tailored treatments for children with these characteristics merit investigation.

Chapter VII - The purpose of this chapter is to review the current state of literature on *social phobia* in children and adolescents as well as identify areas for future research on this understudied disorder. The chapter begins with a brief overview of the clinical characteristics of the disorder. The next section covers the up to date empirical literature on the epidemiology and comorbidity followed by risk factors and correlates of *social phobia* in children and adolescents. The developmental course of the disorder is described next. The final section reports on the evidence-based status of the treatment approaches for social phobia in the child and the youth.

Chapter VIII - *Objective*: Depression is often associated with social phobia. Several previous studies have reported that there are differences by sex in the risk factors for negative behavior, such as a suicide attempt. This study focused on the relationship between depression and impulsivity, a personality trait associated with negative behaviors, such as suicide, and possible sex differences on the relationship.

Method: 120 students from Hokkaido University and 20 psychiatric patients from Hokkaido University Hospital were included in the present study.

Results: The correlation between depressive tendency and self-reported impulsivity was higher in males than in females, and the correlation was significant only in male students.

Conclusion: Impulsivity may be a predictor of suicidal behavior. The results from the present study showed a strong correlation between depressive tendency and impulsivity only in males. Furthermore depressive tendency correlated with the sub-fators of impulsivity – *Attentional Impulsiveness* and *Nonplanning Impulsiveness*. It is possible that in males, depression leads to quick decisions being made (*Attentional Impulsiveness*), and a "present orientation" or a lack of "future consideration" (*Nonplanning Impulsiveness*), then results in committing a suicidal behavior. Further studies are needed.

Chapter IX - Behavioral inhibition is defined as a consistent style of responding toward novel situations, individuals, and objects with wariness, distress and avoidance and is experienced by about 10% of typically developing children. Although behavioral inhibition is a normal variant of behavioral style, research has shown that behaviorally inhibited children are at an increased risk for a variety of internalizing problems, including anxiety disorders. In this chapter, the authors provide a review of the studies conducted to date that have investigated the role of behavioral inhibition in the development of anxiety disorders, with a specific focus on social phobia. The authors review studies that have used both clinical and non-clinical samples as well as a variety of methods and designs, including retrospective, cross-sectional and longitudinal. They suggest that behavioral inhibition by itself is not sufficient for the development of social phobia. Rather, it is the interaction of behavioral inhibition and environmental factors such as social stressors, parenting, and attachment that place an individual at an increased risk for developing social phobia. The authors propose a diathesis-stress model for the role of behavioral inhibition in the development of social phobia, with a need for future research to further investigate the stressors and protective factors that interact with behavioral inhibition. They conclude the chapter with a discussion of clinical implications.

Chapter X - Social anxiety disorder (SAD; also called social phobia) is characterized by an intense and persistent fear of one or more social or performance situations (e.g., public speaking, dating situations). People with SAD typically present with significant levels of distress and impairment, and greatly fear being judged negatively by others, or acting in a way that might be embarrassing. SAD has the lowest overall remission rate of all the major anxiety disorders, and is the fourth most common psychiatric disorder. The purpose of this chapter is to provide an overview of the clinical features of SAD, and to highlight issues related to assessment and treatment. First, the authors discuss diagnostic and descriptive characteristics of SAD, including a discussion on the epidemiology and course of the disorder. Second, they review etiological factors contributing to SAD, with a specific focus on environmental, genetic, and cognitive and behavioural processes. Third, they discuss assessment instruments and strategies, including information on clinical interviews and self-report measures. Fourth, the authors review empirically-supported treatments (e.g., cognitive-behavioural therapy) for SAD. Fifth, the authors note emerging trends in relatively unexplored issues pertaining to SAD. The authors conclude with a summary and a brief outline of issues that warrant future research attention.

Chapter XI - Social anxiety disorders or social phobia are irrational, disabling fears of humiliation in social situations. This disorder is defined as an overwhelming and disabling fear of scripting, and embarrassment in social situations, which leads to the avoidance of potentially pleasurable and meaningful activities. Usually, studies show an incidence rate of 14.4%. Although this disorder affects 1 to 18% of the general population in France, few clinical epidemiologic studies have been conducted on social phobia in France.

Social phobias are marked by extreme anxiety, fear and avoidance of social situations which involve social interactions with other people, or performance and evaluation such as speaking or eating in front of others.

Among the situations avoided by people with such phobia, we find: being teased or criticized, being the centre of attention, being watched or observed while doing something, having to speak in public, meeting people with authority, eating, talking or making phone calls in public.

People with social anxiety disorders usually recognize that their fears are irrational, but they cannot help feeling fearful and allowing their fears to affect the way they conduct their lives; social phobia can start during childhood when children avoid eye contact, speak inaudibly or fidget and tremble and often do not want to go to school. However, we will discuss this disorder in adults only.

In a study in France involving 952 psychiatric in- or out-patients with a primary diagnosis of social phobia, according to DSM-IV criteria, the average duration of social anxiety disorders was shown to be 12 years. A major depressive disorder was found in 47.7% of the sample, the prevalence of agoraphobia was even higher (49,2%), alcohol-dependence affected 10,6% of the patients and substance abuse 12,7%. About 15% of the patients with a history of suicide attempts and suicide risk were present.

The psychosocial impact and the alteration of quality of life was high, and the quality of life was found to be poorer than in other anxiety disorders, with respect to childhood, friends, partner and health.

Social learning within the family environment appears to be related to the presence of anxiety disorders. Temperamental factors were involved.

People with this disorder have a tendency to negatively evaluate aspects of their own performance, or to interpret the response of others as a form of criticism.

Biased information processing contributes to the aetiology and maintenance of social anxiety.

The risk in social anxiety disorders is often associated with alcohol use disorders and cannabis dependence, whereas other anxiety and mood disorders do not, according to a study made with 1709 adolescents who were followed for 30 years. In adolescents, social phobias were associated with the subsequent regular and hazardous use of alcohol, in a 4-year follow-up.

Chapter XII - Several studies have described high rates of comorbidity between the anxiety disorders and schizophrenia. Social anxiety disorder (SAD) also known as social phobia is arguably the anxiety disorder that occurs with the highest frequency among patients with schizophrenia. Despite this correlation, the connection between the two disorders remains poorly studied in the literature. This brief review will examine the current literature and attempt to clarify the hypotheses regarding how social anxiety and schizophrenia are related. The connection may be a primary one, relating to a biological/genetic or phenomenological connection between schizophrenia/psychotic symptoms and social phobia, or a secondary one, relating to a psychological connection where social phobia develops in response to the damaging consequences of coping with schizophrenia and its social sequelae. There may also be a connection to prodromal symptoms of schizophrenia and its own social sequelae during childhood and adolescence. Treatments such as anti-anxiety pharmacology and CBT that target this particular comorbidity have shown good efficacy in preliminary studies. Neurobiological studies of SAD and schizophrenia both examine the dopaminergic system of the brain and may show some connection in terms of its relationship to perceptions of social behavior and interpersonal threat and judgment and even paranoia. More studies are warranted to clarify the timing and nature of the relationship between the two disorders over the full course of schizophrenia.

Chapter XIII - Japan is well-known as the country of taijin kyofusho (TKS), but it remains unclear whether TKS rather than social anxiety disorder (SAD) is still predominant, even in clinical settings. Subjects consisted of 11 responders to a newspaper advertisement (ad-responders) and 103 self-referrals with SAD. All subjects underwent SCID-I and II (Structured Clinical Interview-DSM-IIIR Axis I Disorders and Personality Disorders) in addition to evaluation of basic background demographics. Ad-responders were significantly older and more likely to have finished university, be married, have better occupational (academic) function, to have later a onset of SAD and they were less likely to have lifetime comorbidity of major depression than self-referrals. In addition, ad-responders tended to be less likely to have TKS offensive subtype than self-referrals. Although limited by the small sample size, the results suggested the hidden presence of untreated and undiagnosed middle-aged patients with SAD, and that the presence of TKS offensive subtype might be skewed.

Chapter XIV - Disfiguring physical diseases like acne, psoriasis, essential tremor, cervical dystonia, hemifacial spasm, stuttering etc. may cause significant social embarrassment which leads to social avoidance and decreases the quality of life. Previous research on social anxiety secondary to chronic medical diseases clearly demonstrates the importance of this condition, since the rates they reported were considerably higher than the rates of primary social anxiety disorder in general population. However, previous research mainly examined the prevalance of secondary social anxiety and clinical characteristics or the treatment of secondary social anxiety were not clearly identified. This chapter reviews previous literature about social anxiety secondary to disfiguring diseases like hyperkinesias, stuttering and dermatological diseases.

In: Social Phobia: Etiology, Diagnosis and Treatment
Editor: Clayton P. Axelby
ISBN 978-1-60692-159-3
© 2009 Nova Science Publishers, Inc.

Chapter I

Instruments for the Evaluation of Social Phobia

Flávia de Lima Osório, José Alexandre de Souza Crippa and Sonia Regina Loureiro
Faculdade de Medicina de Ribeirão Preto – Universidade de São Paulo, Brazil.

Abstract

Social phobia (SP) is an under-recognized and sub-diagnosed clinical condition even though it is the most frequent anxiety disorder, which responds to drug and psychotherapeutic treatment. The early and correct identification of this disorder is considered to be of extreme importance, minimizing suffering and preventing the development of psychiatric co-morbidities, which are associated with a poorer prognosis. It is within this context that instruments for evaluation can make a potential contribution.

Many instruments are currently available in the international literature for the evaluation of SP, including self-applicable scales, hetero-evaluation scales, scales for the evaluation of non-generalized SP, scales for the evaluation of the functional impairments associated with SP, and scales for the evaluation of other specific aspects of SP. Some scales have already been translated for use in different cultural contexts and have been extensively studied in terms of their psychometric qualities. The applicability of some of these scales has been confirmed in the clinical context and in empirical studies related to SP, while others still need further investigation.

The objectives of this chapter were: a) to present a critical review of the literature about the main instruments used for the evaluation of SP, focusing on their objectives, major characteristics and psychometric qualities, and b) to present results of unpublished psychometric studies carried out by our research group in Brazil on samples of clinical and non-clinical subjects with SP using the following instruments: Social Phobia Inventory (SPIN), Mini-SPIN (MS), Brief Social Phobia Scale (BSPS), Self Statements During Public Speaking Scale (SSPS- trait and state version), Liebowitz Social Anxiety Scale- self-applied version, (LSAS), Liebowitz Self-Rated Disability Scale (LSRDS),

The Disability Profile (DP), Social Interaction and Performance Anxiety and Avoidance Scale (SIPAAS), and Social Thoughts and Beliefs Scale (STABS).

This analysis, based on the literature and on empirical data, is considered to provide a tool for researchers and clinicians in the choice of instruments for the evaluation of SP that will be adequate for empirical investigations and for support in clinical practice.

Social Phobia- Clinical and Diagnostic Aspects

According to the DSM-IV (APA, 1994), social anxiety disorder or social phobia (SP) is characterized by persistent fear of one or more situations in which an individual is exposed to possible evaluation by others, such as eating, drinking, speaking in public, being the center of attention, interacting with the opposite sex, being afraid to do something, or behaving in a humiliating or embarrassing manner. Avoidance of these situations is frequent, but when these situations are unavoidable, important manifestations of anxiety occur, frequently accompanied by autonomic symptoms.

Although SP is the most frequent anxiety disorder and responds to drug medication and psychotherapy, few people seek treatment and the condition is often underestimated and under-recognized by clinicians (Pollack, 2001; Martín-Santos and Crippa, 2003). Thus, an early and correct identification of this disorder is considered to be extremely important in order to minimize suffering and to prevent the development of co-morbidities with are usually associated with a poorer prognosis. It is within this diagnostic context that structured diagnostic interviews and scales of symptom assessment and measurement can make a potential contribution.

The objective of structured clinical interviews is to collect clinical and diagnostic data in a precise and exhaustive manner, especially within the context of research. Their use for the improvement of the reliability of psychiatric diagnoses is also of unquestionable importance. Among these interviews, particular important are the Structured Clinical Interview for DSM-IV (SCID-IV, First et al., 1997), the Composite International Diagnostic Interview (CIDI, Word Health Organization, 1980), the Anxiety Disorder Interview Schedule (ADIS, Di Nardo et al., 1983), and the Mini International Neuropsychiatric Interview (MINI, Amorin, 2000).

Scales for the evaluation and measurement of symptoms can be very valuable as an aid for a systematic diagnosis in Psychiatry, representing an excellent resource for the characterization of clinical signs and symptoms, prognosis, prediction of the response to treatment, and measurement of disorder severity, both within clinical and research contexts (Ito & Ramos, 2000; Vilela, 2000). Their use permits the characterization and quantitation of subjective states, insuring an uniform assessment of the profile and levels of the symptoms. It also allows the use of a common and standardized language by a wide variety of observers in diverse situations, in addition to permitting the translation of clinical phenomena into objective quantitative information that can be compared and submitted to statistical treatment (Vilela, 2000).

Many instruments are currently available in the international literature for the evaluation of SP, including self-applicable scales, hetero-evaluation scales, scales for the evaluation of non-generalized SP, scales for the evaluation of the functional impairments associated with

SP, and scales for the evaluation of other specific aspects of SP (Clark et al., 1997; Tharwani & Davidson, 2001; Osório et al., 2005). Chart 1 lists the principal scales for the assessment of different aspects of SP, which will be described in detail below regarding their characteristics and psychometric qualities.

Chart 1. Principal scales for the evaluation of Social Phobia (modified from Clark et al, 1997; Tharwani & Davidson, 2001 and Osório et al, 2005)

Self-evaluation scales
• Fears of Negative Evaluation – FNE (Watson & Friend 1969) • Brief Fears of Negative Evaluation- BFNE (Leary, 1983) • Social Avoidance and Distress Scale - SADS (Watson & Friend 1969) • Fear Questionnaire – FQ (Marks & Mathews, 1979) • Social Interaction and Self-Statement – SISST (Glass et al 1982) • Social Phobia Scale – SPS (Heimberg et al 1992) • Social Interaction Anxiety Scale – SIAS (Heimberg et al 1992) • Social Phobia and Anxiety Inventory- SPAI (Turner et al 1995) • Social Phobia and Anxiety Inventory for Children – SPAI-C (Beidel et al 1995) • Situational Social Avoidance Scale - SSAS (Ishiyama, 1999) • Social Phobia Inventory – SPIN (Connor et al 2000) • Social Phobia Inventory – reduced version – MINI-SPIN (Connor et al 2001) • Social Anxiety Spectrum – SCI- SHY (Del'Osso et al 2002) • Social Phobia Diagnostic Questionnaire – SPDQ (Newman et al 2003) • Social Interaction and Performance Anxiety and Avoidance Scale –SIPPAS (Pinto-Gouveia et al 2003)
Hetero-evaluation scales
• Liebowitz Social Anxiety Scale – LSAS (Liebowitz, 1987) • Brief Social Phobia Scale – BSPS (Davidson et al 1991)
Scales for the evaluation of non-generalized SAD
• Personal Report of Confidence as a Speaker Questionnaire – PRCS (Paul, 1966) • Personal Report of Communication Apprehension – PRCA (McCroskey, 1997) • Self Statements During Public Speaking Scale –SSPS (Hofmann & DiBartolo, 2000) • Speech Anxiety Thoughts Inventory – SATI (Cho et al, 2004)
Scales for the evaluation of functional impairment associated with SAD
• Liebowitz Self- Rated Disability Scales- LSRDS (Liebowitz, 1987) • The Disability Profile- DP (Schneier et al 1994)
Scales for the evaluation of specific aspects of SAD
• Social Phobia Safety Behaviours Scale - SPSAS (Pinto-Gouveia et al 2003) • Social Thoughts and Beliefs Scale – STABS (Turner at al 2003)

Some scales have already been translated for use in different cultural contexts and have been extensively studied in terms of their psychometric qualities. The applicability of some of these rating scales has been confirmed in the clinical context and in empirical studies related to SP, while others still need further investigation.

The objectives of this chapter were: a) to present a critical review of the literature about the main instruments used for the evaluation of SP, focusing on their objectives, major characteristics and psychometric qualities, and b) to present results of unpublished psychometric studies carried out by our research group in Brazil on samples of clinical and non-clinical subjects with SP.

The description of the instruments and the psychometric data reported in the various studies cited will first be presented, followed by the most important data obtained by our research group in Brazil in relation to eight instruments studied.

Main Instruments for the Assessment of Social Phobia

1. Structured Clinical Interviews

1.1. Structured Clinical Interview for DSM-IV (SCID-IV)

The SCID-IV was proposed in 1997 by First et al. It is an instrument used for the elaboration of clinical psychiatric diagnoses based on the DSM-IV. It consists of a total of ten modules that can be applied in an independent or combined manner according to the desired objectives. Module F is the one used for the assessment of anxiety disorders in general, and SP, in particular.

In the study of the Brazilian version of the SCID-IV, translated and adapted by Del-Ben et al. (2001), the rate of inter-rater reliability of this instrument for the assessment of anxiety disorders was 0.61. In a study conducted by our research group in Brazil, the inter-rater reliability for the diagnosis of SP in a "face-to-face" interview was 87%, with a Kappa of 0.80. When the reliability of the "live" interview and a telephone interview for this diagnosis was compared, a value of 87% was detected, with a Kappa of 0.85, demonstrating the high correlation between these two forms of assessment of SP symptoms (Crippa et al., 2008).

1.2. Composite International Diagnostic Interview (CIDI)

The Composite International Diagnostic Interview (CIDI) is a fully standardized, structured interview that provides a psychiatric diagnosis through computerized algorithms according to the International Classification of Diseases, 10th edition (ICD-10), and the DSM-IV. The CIDI was developed in 1980 by the World Health Organization (WHO) in collaboration with the former US Alcohol, Drug Abuse and Mental Health Administration (ADMHA) as a Joint Project for the Diagnosis and Classification of Mental Disorders, and Alcohol- and Drug-Related Problems. Its greatest appeal is that it was designed to be administered by trained lay interviewers in epidemiological studies, clinical trials and research centers. It can be administered to individuals aged above 18 years, regardless of their social, economic and cultural status, and does not depend on the patients' literacy.

The CIDI is available in paper-and-pencil and computer-administered forms (self-administered) with a diagnostic coverage for both lifetime (Core version) and 12-month assessment. The average time to administer the questionnaire is 75 minutes. The questions are explicit and positive answers are further explored by a specified probing system, the Probe Flow Chart (PFC). The PFC leads the interviewer to a standardized decision tree (algorithm) that will determine if the symptom was present but was not important enough for the individual to seek assistance (code 2); if the symptom occurred but was due to the use of medication, drugs, alcohol, or caused by trauma or a physical disorder (codes 3 and 4) or, finally, if it is a psychiatric symptom (code 5). The CIDI comprises 288 symptom questions distributed throughout 14 sections, 10 of which are for diagnostic purposes and 4 are non-diagnostic. Module D (Phobic, Anxiety and Panic Disorders) is the one that comprises the diagnosis of SP. Training for the use of the CIDI should follow the norms and regulations established by the WHO. The CIDI is available in many languages and is supported by ten centers around the world, which conduct regular training programs for interviews.

In general, the studies that assessed the validity and reliability of the CIDI indicated that it was adequate in the different sessions (Andrews & Peters, 1998). Specifically regarding the assessment of SP, a study conducted by Komit et al. (2001) concluded that the agreement between clinicians and the CIDI-auto ranged poor for SP (Kappa <0.30). Means-Christensen et al (2003) also indicated difficulties in the use of CIDI-auto for the diagnosis of SP and of panic disorder, suggesting a modification of the decision rules used to assign or rule out diagnoses of panic disorder and SP. Another study about the validity of the CIDI was carried out in Brazil by Quintana et al. (2007). In contrast to the findings cited above, this study revealed an adequate agreement between the diagnosis made with the CIDI and the medical diagnosis made by a psychiatrist, which was adopted as the gold standard (Kappa = 0.70). The study also revealed acceptable indicators of sensitivity (80.6%) and specificity (93.5%) for the diagnosis of SP.

1.3. Anxiety Disorders Interview Schedule (ADIS)

The Anxiety Disorders Interview Schedule was proposed by Di Nardo et al. (1983). It is a semistructured diagnostic interview that was developed to facilitate reliable diagnosis of DSM anxiety disorders. It also includes diagnostic criteria for selected DSM mood disorders, such as major depressive episode and dysthymia, and screening questions for Axis I bipolar and psychotic disorders.

The ADIS requires the interviewer to make a severity rating for each diagnosis given. The severity rating is made on a 0 through 8 scale that indicates the level of distress and/or functional impairment associated with the diagnosis in the interviewer's judgment (0 = absent/none – 8 = severe/very severely disturbing/disabling). A severity rating of 4 or greater is, by convention at the Center for Stress and Anxiety Disorders, regarded as indicative of clinically significant impairment.

The inter-rater reliability of the CIDI for the diagnosis of SP was assessed and found to be excellent in two studies, with a Kappa ranging from 0.77 to 0.79 (Di Nardo et al. 1983; Di Nardo et al., 1993).

1.4. Mini International Neuropsychiatric Interview (MINI)

The MINI is a standardized brief diagnostic instrument (3 to 15 minutes for application) compatible with the criteria of the DSM-III-R, DSM-IV and CID-10 and usually employed in clinical practice and in research on primary care and in psychiatry. It was developed by researchers at the Hospital Pitié-Salpêtrière de Paris and at the hospital of the University of Florida (Amorin, 2000). It is organized into independent diagnostic models elaborated in order to optimize the sensitivity of the instrument, and its scoring is dichotomous (Yes/No). Two versions of the MINI have been developed: the first is destined in particular to use for primary care and in clinical assays and consists of 19 modules that explore 17 disorders of axis I of the DSM-IV (including SP), in addition to risk for suicide and antisocial personality disorder. The second version, more adequate for in-depth evaluation of life-long mental disorders, has been named MINI-plus and systematically explores all the inclusion and exclusion criteria and the chronology of 23 diagnostic categories of the DSM-IV, also including SP. As is the case for the SCID, its modules can be used jointly or separately.

According to Amorim (2000), studies conducted in France and in the US have evaluated the reliability of the MINI and its validation in relation to the CIDI, SCID-IV and the psychiatric diagnosis made by clinicians. A test-retest reliability higher than 0.75 was detected for all the diagnoses, including SP. The study of concurrent validity indicated a correlation of 0.51 to 0.60 between the MINI and SCID-IV, of 0.54 between the MINI and CIDI, and of 0.66 between the MINI and a psychiatric diagnosis by clinicians, all of these values being relatively adequate. The sensitivity of the MINI was estimated at 0.72 to 0.81, specificity at 0.86 to 0.90, the positive predictive value at 0.46 to 0.57, the negative predictive value at 0.94 to 0.97, and the diagnostic efficacy at 0.72 to 0.87.

2. Scales for the Assessment and Measurement of Symptoms

2.1. Self-assessment Scales

2.1.1. Fear of Negative Evaluation (FNE) and Brief Fear of Negative Evaluation (BFNE)

The Fear of Negative Evolution (FNE) scale was proposed by Watson and Friend in 1969 for the evaluation of aspects associated with SP, althoug such diagnosis was not yet a formally recognized psychiatric disorder.

The objective of the scale is to assess the aspects involved in situations of negative evaluation on the part of others, such as expectations, avoidance and level of apprehension. It is composed of 30 items scored as true or false, with one point being attributed to each true reply. The total score is the sum of the points and can range from 0 to 30. Some items of this instruments are mentioned here as examples: *"If someone is evaluating me I tend to expect the worst"; "I am afraid that others will not approve of me"; " I am usually worried about what kind of impression I make".*

The first psychometric study carried out with the FNE was published by Watson and Friend (1969) using a sample of college students (N = 80). The mean score for this population was 15.5 (SD = 16.0), the internal consistency was 0.94 (Cronbach alpha), the test-retest reliability (one week) was 0.78 to 0.94, and the convergent validity with the Social Approval subscale of Jackson's Personality Research Form was 0.77. Factorial analysis indicated the presence of a single factor, demonstrating the unidimensionality of the scale. These indicators demonstrated the adequacy of the FNE for the assessment of the fear of negative evaluation construct.

Other psychometric studies have been carried out ever since in order to improve the validity and reliability of the FNE. Some of these studies are discussed below.

Tuner et al (1987) assessed the discriminative capacity of the FNE in a sample of patients with different psychiatric disorders (N = 206) and concluded that the instrument is not sensitive enough to differentiate subjects with SP from subjects with other disorders, except for subjects with simple phobia. These investigators also studied the validity of the instrument in relation to the Stait-Trait Anxiety Inventory (STAI = 0.56-0.62), the Beck Depression Inventory (BDI = 0.55), and General Symptom Index SCL-90 (0.55), and concluded that the instrument had little specificity for the evaluation of situations typical of SP, with emphasis on this point as a limitation of the instrument.

Heimberg et al. (1988) agreed with Tuner et al. (1987) regarding the low specificity of the FNE, but pointed out the importance of this scale for the evaluation of aspects related to social anxiety, underscoring the need for more psychometric studies in order to demonstrate the potential of the FNE.

In this respect, Oie et al.. (1991) obtained adequate results about the discriminative validity of the FNE since in their study the scale was able to discriminate between SP subjects and subjects with other psychiatric disorders and also between subjects with generalized SP and subjects with specific SP. Cox et al. (1998) demonstrated the convergent validity of the FNE with general measures of anxiety, depression and general worry. Other studies demonstrated the predictive validity of the FNE (Beidel et al.. 1993; Heimberg 1990).

When analyzing all of these studies and the diagnostic criteria established for SP since its introduction into the DSM-III as a psychiatric disorder, it can be seen that the FNE indeed is not an instrument that can be used for the evaluation and measurement of the different symptoms of SP. This was highlighted as the FNE is foused in only one of the dimension of this disorder, i.e., the fear to be evaluated negatively. However, in view of its pioneering nature, despite these limitations, the FNE has been and continues to be extensively used, especially as a parameter for the psychometric study of instruments developed later. Thus, the FNE was consolidated as a measure for the evaluation of the cognitive symptoms associated with the cognitive model of SP, a fact that stimulated its use in empirical studies, especially those aiming at the evaluation of the efficacy of treatments based on cognitive-behavioral theories and therapies of exposure and cognitive restructuring in particular (Cox et al., 1998; Heimberg 1990).

Few recent studies on the FNE were detected in the literature. Among them is the validation of the French version of the FNE performed by Musa et al (2004) with samples of clinical and non-clinical subjects (N = 168). The major findings were: 0.94 internal consistency, adequate discriminative validity to differentiate SP cases from non-cases, and convergent validity with the Liebowitz Social Anxiety Scale (LSAS) (0.55), BDI (0.48) and STAI-T (0.47). As observed in the original study, factorial analysis showed the unidimensionality of the FNE. Thus, it was concluded that the French version of the FNE was adequate.

Another feature of more current interest is the study of the reduced version of the FNE, proposed by Leary (1983). This proposal was based not only on the advantages of dealing with a smaller instrument of easier and faster application and correction, but also on the fact that the form of scoring of the FNE (dichotomous) did not permit the assessment of different grading levels of fear of negative evaluation. Thus, this version of the instrument, denoted Brief Fear of Negative Evaluation (BFNE) consisted of items of the original instrument that obtained a satisfactory item-total correlation, with values between 0.43 and 0.75. Twelve items were selected, which were scored on a five-point Likert scale (1 = not at all characteristic of me; 5 = extremely characteristic of me). Eight of these 12 items described the presence of fears and concerns (straightforwardly worded items) and four described their absence (reverse worded items).

The initial study of the psychometric qualities of the BFNE was also carried out by Leary (1983) on a sample of college students and demonstrated adequacy of the scale regarding internal consistency (0.90-0.91), test-retest reliability (4 weeks: 0.75), and convergent validity with the FNE (0.96). Later studies were conducted in order to confirm the validity of the BFNE in other population samples, but mainly in order to evaluate the factorial constitution of the instrument and its form of presentation/constitution. It was mainly done because the division of the BFNE into straightforwardly worded items e reversed worded items was a matter of divergence and questioning regarding its adequacy in view of the possibility of reversed worded items to be erroneously interpreted by the subjects.

For example, Taylor et al (1993), in a study of the structure of fundamental fears, proposed that the BFNE should be modified so that the items written in a negative form (reversed worded items) would be written in an affirmative manner, thus becoming straightforwardly worded items (example: "*Other people's opinions of me do not bother me*" → "*I am concerned about other people's opinions of me*"). This modified version was called BFNE-II, but was not appreciated with respect to its psychometric qualities in the cited study. Rodebaugh et al (2004) suggested the use of only the eight straightforwardly worded items. Weeks (2005) proposed that the original version should be maintained but that the reversed worded items should not be computed for the final scoring, in agreement with Rodebaugh et al (2004).

These studies, as well as the remaining ones that evaluated the different psychometric qualities of the BFNE, are listed in Table 1, which presents their main results.

Analysis of the studies listed in Table 1 reveals that, in general, the original version of the BFNE presented good psychometric indicators when applied to clinical and non-clinical samples in different cultural contexts. It seems to be more indicated than the FNE for the evaluation of aspects related to fear of negative evaluation, especially because of its scoring forms, which favors discriminative validity. However, compared to the BFNE-total, the BFNE-S (BFNE-straightforwardly worded items) seems to be psychometrically more adequate and is preferentially used. Thus the proposals of Taylor et al (1993), Rodebaugh et al (2004) and Weeks et al (2005) obtained theoretical support regarding factorial analysis and the remaining studies conducted with the BFNE. There is consensus about the fact that items of the BFNE-R (BFNE-reversed worded items) interfere negatively with the validity of the instrument, and how to administer them is still an open question. Three possibilities have been studied thus far: a) to invert the reversed worded items to straightforwardly worded items; b) to apply the reversed worded items without scoring them; c) to exclude the reversed worded items. Carleton et al. (2006) conducted the only study that evaluated comparatively these possibilities and concluded that the change proposed by Taylor et al. (1993), to invert the written form of the reversed worded items, is the most adequate. The authors found that by discarding the four reversed worded items, the total number of items and, theoretically, the sensitivity of the scale are reduced. The authors also stated that, in a scale consisting of only twelve items, reversing items in order to detect acquiescent response biases does not seem to be necessary. Future studies about these question appear to be necessary.

Table 1. Main psychometric studies conducted with the reduced version of the FNE: Brief Fear of Negative Evaluation (BFNE) and psychometric qualities demonstrated

Study	Sample	Objective	Main results/conclusions
Taylor 1993 (USA)	----	To assess the structure of fundamental fears	-Proposition of the adapted version: BFNE-II
Rodebaugh et al., 2004 (USA)	N = 1049 college students	To assess the factorial structure of the BFNE and its discriminative capacity	-Solution 2 factors better than 1 factor; Factor 1: BFNE-S – straightforwardly worded items (8 items, α = 0.94) Factor 2: BFNE-R – reversed worded items (4 items, α = 0.71) -Straightforwardly worded items: better reliability, concurrent and discriminative validity than reversed worded items
Weeks et al., 2005 (USA)	N = 165 SP adults	To assess the psychometric properties of the BFNE in a clinical sample	-Solution 2 factors better than 1 factor; -internal consistency: BFNE = 0.67-0.89; BFNE-S = 0.90-0.96; BFNE-S = 0.67-0.85; -discriminative validity: SP score > NSP score; -convergent validity: LSAS: 0.26-0.59; SIAS = 0.07-0.46; SPS: 0.11-0.40; FQ = 0.11 to 0.40; -divergent validity: ASI: 0.16-0.27; BDI: 0.15-0.32; PSWQ: 0.31-0.51; -predictive validity: pre-treatment score > post-treatment score - BFNE and BFNE-S: better indicators, especially for subjects with low schooling; -BFNE-R: questionable adequacy
Collins et al., 2005 (Canada)	N = 181 SP NSP OAD adults	To assess the psychometric properties of the BFNE-II	- 1 factor; eigenhvalue = 8.83; 74% variance - concurrent validity: FQ: 0.56; BAI: 0.16 - divergent validity: PAQR: 0.02; ASI: 0.13; BDI: 0.32 - discriminative validity: SP score > panic score > NSP score; S = 74%; Sp = 67%; pre-treatment score > post-treatment score - internal consistency: α = 0.97 - T/R (2 weeks) = 0.94
Duke et al., 2006 (USA)	N = 355 NSP adults	To assess the psychometric qualities of the BFNE as proposed by Taylor et al (1993): BFNE-II	- Solution 2 factors better than 1 factor (BFNE-S/BFNE-R) -internal consistency: BFNE: α = 0.80; BFNE-S: α = 0.93; BFNE-R: α = 0.72 -divergent validity: BDI: 0.30; UCLA: 0.30 - data confirm the better adequacy of the BFNE-II version: positive scored items perform better - they are less confusing to participants
Carleton et al., 2006 (Canada)	N = 385 college students	To assess the propositions of Taylor et al (1993); Rodeubach et al (2004) and Weeks et al (2005)	- BFNE: solution 2 factors better than 1 factor (BFNE-S/BFNE-R) - BFNE-II: 1 factor - BFNE-II score > BFNE score -internal consistency: BFNE: α = 0.89; BFNE-II: α = 0.95 item- total score correlation: BFNE-II > BFNE - better adequacy of the BFNE-II according to Taylor et al (1993)
Carleton et al., 2007 (Canada)	N = 322 college students	To assess the psychometric qualities of the BFNE-II	- factorial analysis: 1 factor - internal consistency: α = 0. 97 - convergent validity: SPS: 0.60; ASI: 0.55; SIAS: 0.64 - divergent validity: RSES: 0.48; ISI: 0.29 – 0.38

Table 1. (Continued)

Study	Sample	Objective	Main results/conclusions
Koydemir & Demir, 2007 (Turkey)	N = 250 college students	To assess the psychometric qualities of the Turkish version of the BFNE	- factorial analysis: 2 factors (BFNE-S/BFNE-R) – 61% variance -concurrent validity: RCBSS: 0.33; RSES: 0.21 -internal consistency: BFNE: α =0.94; BFNE-S: α = 0.91; BFNE-R: α = 0.87 - BFNE-R: more adequate

ASI = Anxiety Sensitivity Index; BAI = Beck Anxiety Inventory; BDI = Beck Depression Inventory; BFNE = Brief Fear Negative Evaluation; BFNE-S = Brief Fear Negative Evaluation -straightforwardly worded items; BFNE-R = Brief Fear Negative Evaluation-reversed worded items; BFNE-II = Brief Fear of Negative Evaluation (Taylor at al, 1993); FQ = Fear Questionnaire; ISI = Illness/Injury Sensitivity Index; LSAS = Liebowitz Social Anxiety Scale; N = number of subjects; NSP = subjects without social phobia; OAD = subjects with other anxiety disorders; PAQR = Panic Attack Questionnaire Revised; PSWQ = Penn State Worry Questionnaire; RCBSS = Revised Cheek and Buss Shyness Scale; RSES = Rosenberg Self-Esteem Scale; S = sensitivity; SIAS = Social Interaction Anxiety Scale; SP = subjects with social phobia; Sp = specificity; SPS = Social Phobia Scale; T/R = test-retest reliability; UCLA = UCLA Loneliness Scale; α = Cronbach alpha.

2.1.2. Social Avoidance and Distress Scale (SADS)

The Social Avoidance and Distress Scale (SADS) was developed together with the FNE by the same authors, Watson & Friend, in 1969. The objective of this instrument is to evaluate social avoidance and subjective distress by means of 28 items scored on a dichotomous true and false scale. Its maximum total score is 28 points and, the higher the score, the lower the level of avoidance and distress. To illustrate, we emphasize two of its items: "*I often find social occasions upsetting*"; "*I tend to withdraw from people*".

The psychometric qualities of the instrument were initially studied in a sample of students (N = 80) by Watson & Friend (1969), who detected a mean score of 9.1, an internal consistency of 0.77 (Cronbach alpha), and a test-retest reliability of 0.68 to 0.79. Concurrent validity was studied in relation to the Social Approval subscale of Jackson's Personality Research Form, and to SADS, and the instrument was found not to be significantly correlated with the latter. However, as is the case for the FNE, the SADS has also been extensively used to support the psychometric studies of new instruments for the evaluation of the different aspects of SP, and has been found to be strongly correlated with the SPAI at the 0.77 level (Davidson et al., 1991), a fact confirming its convergent validity with measurements of anxiety.

Tuner et al. (1987) conducted a new psychometric study of the SADS using a sample of 206 patients with different anxiety disorders. The authors detected moderate correlations with measures of general anxiety (STAI = 0.50 and 0.63) and of depression (BDI = 0.42) and concluded that the SADS had a low discriminant capacity since it could not discriminate between SP subjects and patients with obsessive compulsive disorder, panic and agoraphobia. These findings were confirmed by Gelernter et al. (1992) in a study in which the SADS was also found not to be sufficiently sensitive to discriminate subjects with different anxiety disorders.

However, the results of another psychometric study conducted by Oie et al. (1991) indicated discriminative capacity of the SADS, which was found to be able to discriminate between SP patients and patients with panic and simple phobia. Also important was another psychometric study recently conducted with the SADS by Chun et al. (2003), who determined the internal consistency (0.85) and test-retest reliability (0.76) of the instrument in 857 Chinese high school and university students, indicating the validity of the instrument in this cultural context.

It can be seen that lately the SADS is being less studied than the FNE. However it is still frequently applied in empirical studies in the most varied fields of knowledge. A few examples are the study by Pinto & Phillips (2005) on body dimorphic disorder, the study by Fernandez et al. (2003) on social anxiety and anorexia, the studies by Baldwin et al. (1999) and Van Amerigen et al. (1999) on the testing of medications for the treatment of SP (paroxetine and nefazodone, respectively), and the studies by Ping et al. (2003) and Schelver & Gutsch (1983) on the effects of psychotherapy on SP.

The psychometric studies conducted with the SADS confirm, in a way, the validity and reliability of the scale, but emphasize the following critical points of the instrument: a) the scoring form which favors a reduction of sensitivity, and b) its limitation as an instrument for the screening and diagnosis of SP, in view of its specific objectives. In contrast, the empirical studies are in favor of the predictive validity of the SADS.

Finally, we emphasize the study by Hofmann et al. (2004) who pointed out an error in the instructions for scoring in the original article of Watson & Friend (1969). Item 19 ("*When my superiors want to talk with me, I talk willingly*") was incorrectly keyed "true". Thus, if participants respond with "true" to this item, one point is added to their total SADS score, increasing the rating level of social anxiety. In order to determine the impact of this error, Hofmann et al. (2004) conducted a comparative study using the version with this error and a corrected version in clinical and non-clinical samples. They observed that the incorrect version favors a higher score regarding the mean, the median and the mode compared to the corrected version in both samples, but mainly in the non-clinical one. The elimination of item 19 did not reduce the internal consistency of the instrument. The correlation of the two versions with other social anxiety scales was not statistically significant. Thus, the authors concluded that the use of the incorrect version did not reduce the psychometric properties of the SADS, but overestimated the level of social anxiety of the sample and suggested that in future studies the investigators should avoid an incorrect scoring of item 19.

2.1.3. Fear Questionnaire (FQ)

The Fear Questionnaire (FQ) was developed by Marks & Mathews in 1979, also some time before SP was recognized as an independent psychiatric diagnosis in the DSM-III. This is an instrument consisting of 15 items divided into three subscales: agoraphobia, SP and blood/injury phobia, each consisting of 5 items used to evaluate the severity of the most common phobias. The items are scored on a Likert scale ranging from 0 (would not avoid it) to 8 (always avoid it). Some examples of the items are: "*eating or drinking with other people*" (SP subscale); "*Going into crowded shops*" (agoraphobia subscale); "*Sight of blood*" (blood/injury subscale). The scale also contains five separate items that form a subscale of anxiety and depression and one item that assess phobic distress, also scored on a nine-point Likert scale (0-9). The objective of these subscales is to assess mood symptoms associated with phobic situations. The score of the total phobia scale is given by the sum of the scores of the three subscales and ranges from zero to 120, although, the subscales can be used separately.

The FQ was first studied by Marks & Mathews (1979) in a sample of phobic patients, with 0.82-0.89 test-retest reliability being detected after a one week interval. The items correlated individually with the total score with values of at least 0.50, demonstrating coherence between the items and the total scale. The predictive validity of the instrument regarding psychotherapy was also confirmed.

Later Mizer & Crawford (1986) evaluated the properties of the FQ in a sample of the general adult population (N = 572) and detected differences in the presence of phobic symptoms as a function of gender and age.

Four other studies were devoted to the evaluation of FQ validity in discriminating subjects with SP from subjects with agoraphobia. Unanimous findings were obtained, showing that these two diagnostic groups differ in the scores of specific subscales in the expected direction, i.e., social phobic subjects score higher than subjects with agoraphobia on the SP subscale, agoraphobic subjects score higher on the agoraphobia subscale than SP subjects, and both groups differ from non-cases, with higher mean scores (Mavissakalian 1986; Van-Zurren, 1988; Oei et al. 1989; Cox et al. 1991). Cox et al. (1991) demonstrated that the SP subscale correctly classified 60% of SP subjects and the agoraphobia subscale correctly classified 72% of patient with panic and agoraphobia.

In Australia, Oie et al. (1991) conducted a more extensive study about the psychometric qualities of the FQ on a sample of 251 subjects with anxiety disorder. The results showed that the best factorial solution applied to the FQ indeed is the three-factor one, supporting the division of the scale into the three subscales mentioned above. Together, these three factors explained 42% of data variance. The internal consistency of the scale was 0.83 for the total scale and 0.71 to 0.84 for the various subscales, with the items showing 0.50 to 0.60 correlation with the total score. Again, the discriminative capacity of the instrument between patients with SP, panic and agoraphobia was demonstrated, with sensitivity of about 0.65 for all the diagnostic groups. On the basis of these results, the authors recommended that the corresponding subscale be used rather than the total scale for empirical studies on specific diagnostic groups, allouring a greater predictive capacity of the instrument.

Cox et al. (1996) also performed factorial analysis of the FQ using a sample of 122 adult patients with anxiety disorders, once again reporting that the three-factor solution was the most appropriate. The internal consistency of the scale was 0.68 to 0.81. This study again demonstrated the discriminative capacity of the FQ between patients with SP and patients with panic and agoraphobia, with emphasis on the scoring differences between sexes.

Regarding more recent publications involving the FQ, no studies devoted to the analysis of its psychometric qualities were detected, perhaps because its adequacy for the evaluation of SP and agoraphobia aspects has already been fully recognized. In general, the FQ is being used more in support of the analysis of new instruments such as the Post-Traumatic Stress Disorder Scale (Yao et al., 2003) and the Albany Panic and Phobia Questionnaire (Brow et al., 2005), or in SP studies testing psychopharmaceuticals for the treatment of clinical symptoms of SP (Walker et al., 2000; Benjamin et al., 2000; Van-Amerigem et al., 2001).

2.1.4. Social Interaction and Self-Statement (SISST)

The Social Interaction and Self-Statement (SISST) was proposed by Glass et al. in 1982. It is a 30-item questionnaire that assesses the frequency of positive (facilitative) and negative (inhibitory) self-statements in heterosexual social situations. The questionnaire consists of two subscales, was originally designed to test self-statements generated during a heterosexual role-play interaction. Instructions ask subjects to rate on a 5-point scale (1 = hardly ever had the thought; 5 = very often had the thought) how frequently they had each thought. Some of the items included in the questionnaire are: *"I can usually talk to girls pretty well"; "Maybe I can put her at ease by starting things going"; "Instead of worrying I can figure out how best to get to know her"; "It would crush me if she didn't respond to me".* The gender of pronouns and references to males and females can be manipulated easily to produce appropriate forms for both men and women.

The SISST has been evaluated using several different sets of instructions in relation to the version originally proposed by Glass et al. (1982). Zweig & Brown (1985) proposed completion of the scale after the subjects read a description of a heterosocial situation and imagined themselves participating in it, with application of the questionnaire becoming easier and more viable, in contrast to the original proposition, which required the subjects to fill out the SISST immediately after live interaction with a confederate of the opposite sex or after being presented with 16 audiotaped social situations that required overt verbal responses from them. Later, Osman et al. (1992) suggested the use of the SISST with imaginal administration, favoring and facilitating even more its application. All of these proposals have been evaluated in terms of adequacy and psychometric data and were found to be appropriate, with the proposal suggested by Osman et al. (1992) being the one most extensively used today because of its practicality and rapid application.

The first psychometric study of the SISST was conducted by Glass et al. (1982) together with its proposal, demonstrating adequacy of the instrument. Other psychometric studies were conducted later using the original English version and others, such as the Korean and French versions. The main data obtained in these studies are listed in Table 2.

As observed in Table 2, the SISSTS was studied in different population samples, including social phobic subjects, subjects with other anxiety disorders, and healthy controls. The internal consistency was found to be excellent in the three studies in which it was evaluated. Concurrent validity with measures of social anxiety, avoidance behaviors and irrational beliefs was also adequate, especially for the negative thoughts subscale. Discriminative validity was also detected, with the SISSTS being able to discriminate between subjects with SP, subjects with other anxiety disorders and healthy controls. It was observed that social phobic persons tended to self-assess in a negative manner more than in a positive manner compared to subjects with no SP. Regarding the factorial composition of the scale, some divergences were observed and were explained as a function of the sociocultural context in which the scale was studied, with future studies being needed to reach a conclusion about the best factorial solution of the SISSTS. The negative subscale seems to be the most adequate and sensitive one for the assessment of the aspects proposed by the instrument.

In general, the SISSTS is a highly specific instrument that assesses only one of the feared situations experienced by subjects with SP, i.e., personal interaction with the opposite sex. The SISSTS has been extensively used in psychometric studies as a support for the evaluation of other instruments and also in empirical studies. Among them are the study by Voges & Addington (2005) who determined the associations between social anxiety and functioning during the first psychotic episode, the study by Meningaud et al. (2001), who assessed aspects of anxiety, depression and quality of life in cosmetic surgery patients, and the study by McDougall (2000), who assessed the efficacy of cognitive-behavioral therapy for the treatment of SP.

Table 2. Psychometric studies conducted using the Social Interaction Self-Statement Test (SISST) and psychometric qualities demonstrated

Study	Sample	Internal consistency	Concurrent validity	Discriminative and predictive validity	Factorial analysis	T/R Reliability
Glass et al., 1982 (USA)	N = 144 SP NSP college students	α = 0.73-0.86	SHI: P = 0.71 - 0.77 Ne = -0.57- -0.66 SADS: P = -0.52 - -0.76 Ne = 0.44-0.66 Self-evaluation (role-play) = 0.25 - 0.68 Hetero-evaluation (role-play) = 0.18 - 0.36	SP high anxiety score > SP low anxiety score	4 factors: -self-depreciation -positive anticipation -fear of negative evaluation -coping 91.5% variance	----
Zweig & Brown , 1985 (Canada)	N = 86 NSP x = 20.1 years	α = 0.85-0.91	FNE: P = -0.32; Ne = 0.58 SADS: P= -0.57; Ne= 0.74 IBT: P = -0.20; Ne = 0.37	♂ > negative thoughts and anxiety level	----	0.72 - 0.73 (2 weeks) 0.76 - 0.89 (3 weeks)
Dodge et al., 1988 (USA)	N = 28 SP adults	----	SADS: P= -0.58; Ne= 0.60 PRCS: P= -0.51; Ne = 0.52 FNE: P = -0.57; Ne = 0.62 STAI: P= -0.32; Ne = 0.40 SCS: P= -0.08 - -0.60 Ne = 0.03 - 0.48 % negative thoughts listed: P = 0.07; Ne = 0.39 % positive thoughts listed: P = -0.08; Ne = -0.18 Heart rate > Ne correlation	----	----	----
Osman et al., 1992 (USA)	N = 32 1 college students (x= 21,2 years)	α = 0.89 – 0.91	SADS: P= -0.32; Ne = 0.46 MMPI: P= -0.17; Ne= 0.25 ASSQ: P = ns; Ne = 0.67	♀ = ♂	2 factors: - positive subscale - negative subscale 44.4% variance	----

Study	Sample	Internal consistency	Concurrent validity	Discriminative and predictive validity	Factorial analysis	T/R Reliability
Cho et al., 1997 (Korea)	----	----	----	----	5 factors: -fear of negative evaluation -expectation of failure/avoidanc e -self-efficacy of social exchange -anticipation of positive consequences - rational coping	----
Yao et al., 1998 (France)	N = 182 SP NSP Adults	----	measures anxiety: adequate avoidance behaviors:adequate	P: SP< NSP Ne: SP>NSP; more sensitive	----	----
Hong & Cho, 1999 (Korea)	N = 446 university students	----	----	----	7 factors: more appropriate for this sociocultural context	----
Becker et al., 2001 (USA)	N = 277 SP NSP OAD adults	----	----	P: SP< NSP Ne: SP> NSP P: SP< OAD Ne: SP> OAD	----	----

ASSQ = Anxious Self-Statement Questionnaire; FNE = Fear of Negative Evaluation; IBT = Irrational Beliefs Test; MMPI = Minnesota Multiphasic Personality Inventory – social avoidance subscale; N = number of subjects; Ne = Social Interaction Self-Statement Test-negative subscale; NSP = subjects without social phobia; OAD = subjects with other anxiety disorders; P = Social Interaction Self-Statement Test-positive subscale; PRCS = Personal Report of Confidence as a Speaker; SADS = Social Avoidance Distress Scale; SCS = Self-Consciousness Scale; SHI = Survey of Heterosocial Interactions; SP = subjects with social phobia; STAI = State-Trait Anxiety Inventory; T/R = test-retest; ns = non-significant correlation; α = Cronbach alpha; x = mean; ♀ = women; ♂ = men.

2.1.5. Social Phobia Scale (SPS) and Social Interaction Anxiety Scale (SIAS)

The Social Phobia Scale (SPS) and the Social Interaction Anxiety Scale (SIAS) are companion scales with similar design, both developed by Mattick & Clarke (1989). The SPS was developed to measure anxiety when anticipating being observed or actually being observed by other people. The SIAS was designed to assess behavioral, cognitive, and affective responses to a variety of situations requiring social interaction in dyads or groups.

The SPS and SIAS each include 20 items. Each item is rated on a 5 point Likert scale (0 = not at all characteristic of me; 4 = extremely characteristic or true of me). Among the items included in the SIAS we may point out the following: *"I find myself worrying that I won't know what to say in social situations"; "I am tense mixing in a group"; "I tense-up if I meet an acquaintance in the street"*. As examples of items relative to SPS, we point out the following: *"I get panicky that others might see me faint, or be sick or ill"; "I can suddenly become aware of my own voice of others listening to me"; I worry I might do something to attract the attention of other people*". Total scores are derived by summing the ratings of individual items, after reversing the scores of the three positively worded items for the SIAS. For both scales, total scores range from 0 to 80.

These scales are usually applied together and were also studied jointly regarding their psychometric qualities. Many psychometric studies have been conducted using the SPS and SIAS in order to determine their adequacy for use in different samples and contexts. A brief description of the most important studies of these scales is given in Table 3.

As shown by the data presented in Table 3, the studies with the SIAS and SPS were conducted on extensive and diversified samples with different cultural contexts (USA, Australia, Germany, Spain, Japan, China, Italy). The internal consistency of the scales was assessed and found to be adequate for both. The concurrent validity was studied in terms of role-play situations and in terms of measures of social anxiety, general anxiety, avoidance, worry and control locus and was found to be fully appropriate for both scales. Conversely, the low correlation of the scales regarding measures of depression indicated their divergent validity. The SPS and SIAS also presented good divergent validity, with subjects with SP presenting higher scores than subjects with other anxiety disorders and controls. The scales were also sensitive in pointing out gender differences (women presented higher scores) and differences between subjects with generalized and non-generalized SP, in addition to having good sensitivity, specificity and diagnostic efficacy.

Studies on the factorial structure of the scales were divergent regarding the most appropriate number of factors. Most of the studies on the SIAS pointed out a unifactorial structure and those on the SPS pointed out a multifactorial structure. However, it is not possible to reach a conclusion about the best model, since sociocultural, influences are involved, varying as a function , of the version studied. The predictive validity was less studied but seems to be promising for both scales, as is also the case for the test-retest reliability.

In general, there are large numbers of studies on the SIAS and SPS and on their different versions used in different sociocultural contexts, which have shown psychometric qualities similar to those of the original English version. This permits the use of both scales in multicenter studies, guaranteeing the uniformity of the aspects evaluated.

Recent studies have used the SIAS and SPS in an empirical manner for the assessment of the effects of pharmacological or psychotherapeutic treatments of SP (Johnson, 2007) or in wider contexts focusing on shyness (Toth, 2007), abusive alcohol consumption (Popali, 2007), and eating disorders (Grahorn et al., 2006), with the scales proving to be very useful and effective instruments.

Regarding future studies, in addition to the cited need for a better exploration of the factorial components of the SPS and SIAS, an aspect concerning the form of SIAS presentation has been raised (Rodebaugh et al., 20006; Rodebaugh et al., 2007) and deserves further investigation. The point being questioned is the presence of reverse scored items. As already described for the BFNE, there are arguments against the maintenance and calculation of such items for the final score. Rodebaugh et al. (2007) assessed the role of these items in the SIAS and detected that: a) reverse scored items show consistently weaker relationships with a variety of comparison measures; b) reverse scored items may primarily assess extraversion, and c) removing the reversed scored questions generally helps rather than hinders the psychometric performance of the SIAS total score. In view of these findings, the authors suggested that investigators consider performing data analyses using only the straightforwardly worded items of the SIAS. However, this suggestion should be considered with caution and further evaluated in future studies.

Table 3. Psychometric studies conducted with the Social Interaction Anxiety Scale (SIAS) and the Social Phobia Scale (SPS) and psychometric qualities demonstrated

Study	Sample	Internal consistency	Concurrent validity	Discriminative validity	Factorial analysis Predictive validity	T/R Reliability
Heimberg et al., 1992 (USA)	N = 169 SP NSP college students x = 33.2 - 36.5 years	SIAS: α = 0.85-0.90 SPS: α = 0.87-0.93	SIAS x SPS: 0.41-0.89 *SIAS:* LSAS = 0.45 - 0.69 SADS = 0.62 - 0.74 FNE = 0.44 - 0.82 FQ = 0.36 - 0.76 SAS = 0.82 - 0.88 AAS = 0.62 - 0.68 SISST = 0.56 - 0.69 *SPS:* LSAS = 0.20 - 0.60 SADS = 0.28 - 0.43 FNE = 0.28 - 0.79 FQ = 0.59 - 0.73 SAS = 0.48 - 0.80 AAS = 0.53 - 0.71 SISST = 0.16 0.43	*SIAS and SPS:* SP score > NSP score ♀ score > ♂ score ICR: SIAS = 18% SPS = 12% SIAS: SPg> SPñg SPS: SPg = SPñg	----	SIAS = 0.91 SPS = 0.93 (3-13 weeks)
Brown et al., 1997 (USA)	N = 165 SP OAD	----	SIAS x SPS: 0.72 *SIAS:* ASI = 0.41 PSWQ = 0.43 *SPS:* ASI = 0.55 PSWQ = 0.45 -n° of interactional situations feared = SIAS -n° of performance situations feared = SPS	SIAS and SPS: SP>OAD *SIAS:* S = 86%; Sp= 70% ICR = 25% *SPS:* S = 76%; Sp= 72% ICR = 27%	----	----
Habke et al., 1997 (Germany)	N = 200 university students	----	Anxiety measures: adequate	Factor scrutiny fear: a stronger predictor of psycho-pathology, mainly for men	3 factors: ♀ =♂ -scrutiny fear - social interaction anxiety - discomfort in social interaction	----

Table 3. (Continued)

Study	Sample	Internal consistency	Concurrent validity	Discriminative validity	Factorial analysis Predictive validity	T/R Reliability
Safren et al., 1998 (USA)	N = 167 SP x = 35.9 years	α = 0.73-0.92	*Factor 1:* LSAS: 0.53 - 0.77 SADS: 0.76 FQ: 0.54 *Factor 2:* LSAS: 0.53 - 0.69 SADS: 0.50 FQ: 0.62 *Factor 3:* LSAS: 0.23 - 0.40 SADS: 0.30 FQ: 0.49	----	2 factors: inadequate 3 factors: Factor1: interaction anxiety (17 items SIAS) Factor 2: being observed by others (items SPS) Factor 3: fear that others will notice anxiety (items SPS)	----
Mattick & Clark, 1998 (Australia)	N = 1069 SP NSP OAD x = 21.6-40.8 years	SIAS: α= 0.88- 0.94 SPS: α = 0.89 – 0.94	SIAS x SPS: 0.72 *SIAS:* FNE = 0.66 SADS = 0.74 FQ = 0.66 STAI-S = 0.45 STAI-T = 0.58 LCBS = 0.30 BDI = 0.47 *SPS:* FNE = 0.60 SADS = 0.54 FQ = 0.69 STAI-S = 0.42 STAI-T = 0.57 LCBS = 0.31 BDI = 0.54	SP> NSP SP> OAD	Pre-treatment score > post-treatment score *SPS*: 3 factors 47.7% variance *SIAS*: 1 factor 43.4% variance	SIAS:0.92 SPS: 0.91-0.93 (12 weeks)
Osman et al., 1998 (USA)	N = 600 College students 17 to 43 years	high	Measures of social desirability: adequate	SIAS: more specific than SPS	2 factors: -interaction -performance	----
Ries et al., 1998 (USA)	N = 41 SP x = 30.4 years	----	SPS x SIAS = 0.66 SIAS: SPAI = 0.75 - 0.78 Time speech BAT = ns Time conversation BAT = ns SISST speech BAT = 0.36-0.53 SISST conversation BAT = 0.46 - 0.78	SPg> speech phobia group	Treatment effect sizes: SPS = 0.54 SIAS = 0.83	---

Study	**Sample**	**Internal consis-tency**	**Concurrent validity**	**Discrimina-tive validity**	**Factorial analysis Predictive validity**	**T/R Relia-bility**
Stangeir et al., 1999 (Germany)	N = 136 adults	very good	Measures of social anxiety = adequate Measures of general anxiety = low Measures of depression = low	----	----	very good
Peters 2000 (Australia)	N = 117 SP OAD Adults	----	SPS x SIAS = 0.73 SPS x SPAI = 0.72 SIAS x SPAI = 0.85	SIAS: S = 0.90; Sp = 0.60 SPS: S = 0.90; Sp = 0.70	----	----
Olivares et al., 2001 (Spain)	N = 654 university students x = 19.6 years	SPS: α = 0.90 SIAS: α = 0.89	----	SPS: ♀ > ♂ SIAS: ♀ = ♂	SIAS: 1 factor 40.1% variance SPS: 1 factor 32.4% variance	----
Novy et al., 2001 (USA)	N = 98 bilingual (English/Spanish) SP OAD 18 - 75 years Spanish and English version	SIAS: α = 0.94 - English α = 0.93 - Spanish	SIAS: APPQ = 0.84 (English) 0.81 (Spanish) FQ = 0.87 (English) 0.86 (Spanish) SIAS English x Spanish = 0.94	----	----	----
Gore et al., 2002 (USA)	N = 37 college students x = 19.8 years	----	SIAS x SPS: 0.77 *SIAS:* STAI-T = 0.65 STAI-S pre = 0.54 BAI pre = 0.47 FPSQ pre = 0.57 STAI-S post = 0.43 BAI post = 0.53 FPSQ post = 0.47 *SPS:* STAI-T = 0.75 STAI-S pre = 0.69 BAI pre = 0.57 FPSQ pre = 0.57 STAI-S post = 0.56 BAI post = 0.68 FPSQ post = 0.65	Predicts alterations in anxiety-inducing tests	Anxiety role-playing: pre score > post score	----
Heinrichs et al., 2002 (Germany)	N = 357 SP NSP OAD 15 to 72 years	good	Adequate	SP score ≠ OAD score ≠ NSP score	Factors: solution differing from the original proposal	----

Table 3. (Continued)

Study	Sample	Internal consis-tency	Concurrent validity	Discrimina-tive validity	Factorial analysis Predictive validity	T/R Relia-bility
Sakurai et al., 2005 (Japan)	N = 149 SP x = 29.6 years	----	----	----	3 factors - scrutiny fears - conversations fears - relationship fears (specific for the Japanese sample)	
Rodebaugh et al., 2006 (USA)	N = 2134 SP NSP	----	----	ICR: SP = 3% NSP = 5%	SIAS: 1 factor- it is not the best model	----
Rabung et al., 2006 (Germany)	N = 823 SP NSP OAD	adequate	Adequate	SP score ≠ OAD score ≠ NSP score	----	adequate
Zubeidat et al., 2007 (Spain)	N = 1012 NSP 13 - 19 years	SIAS: α = 0.85	SIAS: LSAS = 0.47 - 0.60 SADS = 0.49 - 0.62 FNE = 0.48	SIAS: ♀ > ♂	SIAS: 3 factors 43.9% variance -anxiety regard-ing social skills deficits -anxiety regard-ing difficulty keeping an appropriate emotional dis-tance from others - anxiety regarding discomfort caused when interacting with people	----
Ye et al., 2007 (China)	N = 1300 students	SIAS: α=0.87 SPS: α =0.90	SIAS x FNE = 0.51 SPS x FNE = 0.48	----	SIAS = 1 factor SPS = 1 factor	SIAS = 0.86 SPS = 0.84
Sica et al., 2007 (Italy)	N = 125 18 – 61 years	----	Adequate	Adequate		adequate

AAS = Avoidance Anxiousness Scale; APPQ = Albany Panic and Phobia Questionnaire; ASI = Anxiety Sensitivity Index; BAI = Beck Anxiety Inventory; BDI = Beck Depression Inventory; FNE = Fear of Negative Evaluation; FPSQ = Fear of Physical Sensations Questionnaire; FQ = Fear Questionnaire; LCBS = Locus of Control of Behaviour Scale; LSAS = Liebowitz Social Anxiety Scale; N = number of subjects; NSP = subjects without social phobia; OAD = subjects with other anxiety disorders; post = post-treatment; pre = pre-treatment; PSWQ = Penn State Worry Questionnaire; S = sensitivity; SP = subjects with social phobia; Sp = specificity; SPng = non-generalized social phobia; SPg = generalized social phobia; SADS = Social Avoidance Distress Scale; SAS = Social Anxiety Scale; SIAS = Social Interaction Anxiety Scale; SISST = Social Interaction Self-Statement; SPS = Social Phobia Scale; STAI-T = Stait Trait Anxiety Inventory-Trait; STAI-S = State Trait Anxiety Inventory-State; ICR = incorrect classification rate; T/R = test-retest α = Cronbach alpha; x = mean; ♀ = women; ♂ = men; ns = non significant correlation; n° = number.

2.1.6. Social Phobia and Anxiety Inventory (SPAI)

The Social Phobia and Anxiety Inventory (SPAI) was proposed by Turner et al. (1989a) as an instrument measuring the behavioral, physiological and cognitive aspects associated with SP, defined according to the diagnostic guidelines of the 1980 DSM-III (1980). It is an instrument consisting of two subscales: the SP scale with 32 items and the agoraphobia scale with 13 items. Twenty-one of the 32 items of the SP subscale assess the degree of distress in different social settings and require separate ratings based on the presence of four different audience groups (strangers, authority figures, opposite sex, people in general). The remaining items assess de degree to which respondents experience somatic and cognitive symptoms in anticipation of or during social situations. Some examples of the items of this subscale are: " *I feel anxious when in a small gathering with: (a) strangers, (b) authority figures, (c) opposite sex, (d) people in general*"; " *I experience the following in a social situation: (a) sweating, (b) blushing, (c) shaking, (d) frequent urge to urinate, (e) heart palpitations*".

The agoraphobia subscale assesses the extent to which respondents experience fear of panic attacks, concern about being trapped, and other agoraphobic fears, reactions which can lead to distress in social situations but which are not related to a fear of negative evaluation specific to SP. Examples of items of this subscale are: " *I feel anxious when I am home alone*" ; "*Being in large open spaces makes me feel anxious*".

All the items of the two subscales are scored on a seven-point Likert scale (1 = never to 7 = always). Scoring of the SPAI is more complex. For items with multiple components, the scores of the component questions are averaged to yield a single score for each item. The SP score is obtained by subtracting 32 from the sum of SP items, and the agoraphobia score is obtained by subtracting 13 from the sum of agoraphobia items. Scores range from 0 to 192 for the SP subscale and from 0 to 78 for the agoraphobia subscale. The SPAI total score is calculated by subtracting the agoraphobia score from the social phobia score.

Since it was first proposed, the SPAI has been extensively studied and continues to be studied in terms of its psychometric qualities. Table 4 lists the main psychometric studies conducted with the SPAI, as well as the more relevant results obtained.

Table 4 shows that both clinical and non-clinical samples of different ages, including adolescents and elderly individuals, have been used in the psychometric studies of SPAI. Studies analyzing the original English version of the instrument predominated, but the Brazilian and Spanish versions were found to be equally adequate, with psychometric qualities quite close to those of the English version.

The internal consistency of the SPAI was excellent in all studies. Its concurrent validity was studied in relation to other specific measures of social anxiety, in relation to general measures of anxiety and in relation to other measures assessing different behavioral aspects, as well as objective self-perception parameters regarding discomfort in social situations (daily recorded in diaries) and objective parameters of hetero-perception in experimental situations and in situations of observation of daily activities.

None of these studies analyzed divergent validity, whereas discriminative validity was clearly demonstrated, with the SPAI being able to differentiate between subjects with and without SP with high diagnostic efficacy. The scale was also sensitive in discriminating differences in symptoms as a function of gender, race and SP subtypes. These studies demonstrated the greater discriminatory power of the SP subscale compared to the total scale and the agoraphobia subscale.

Table 4. Psychometric studies conducted with the Social Phobia and Anxiety Scale (SPAI) and psychometric qualities demonstrated

Study	Sample	Internal consistency	Concurrent validity	Discriminative validity	Factorial analysis Predictive validity	T/R Reliability
Turner at al., 1989a (USA)	N = 225 SP NSP OAD adults	α = 0.85-0.96	----	SP score> NSP score SP score> OAD score Cut-off note 30 FN = 8.6% FP = 54%	----	0.86 (2 weeks)
Turner et al., 1989b (USA)	N = 433 SP NSP OAD	----	----	SP score ≠ OAD score ≠ NSP score	3 factors: -social anxiety - agoraphobia - mixed anxiety	
Beidel et al., 1989a (USA)	N = 182 SP NSP university students x = 19.2 years	----	- distress social situation* = 0.43 - disturbing thoughts* = 0.30 - ratings made by significant others = 0.63	SP score> NSP score ♂ score > ♀ score ICR = 25.6%	Pre-treatment score > post-treatment score	----
Beidel et al., 1989b (USA)	N = 32 SP x = 19.6 years	----	- distress social situation* = 0.43 - disturbing thoughts* = 0.52 - time remaining in activity ** = - 0.33 - mean pulse rate** = 0.43	----	----	----
Herbert et al., 1991 (USA)	N = 523 SP NSP 18 - 55 years	----	Measures of social anxiety, distress and avoidance = adequate	SP subscale: more sensitive than the total scale	----	----
Beidel et al., 1993 (USA)	N = 61 SP adults	----	HAMA = 0.27 FNE = 0.55 SADS = 0.77	----	2 factors: - social phobia - agoraphobia	----
Clark et al., 1994 (USA)	N = 223 SP NSP 12-18 years	α = 0.91 – 0.97	SPSC-R = 0.34 - 0.51 STAI-C = 0.38- 0.48 AAES = - 0.19 - -0.29	SP score > NSP score ♀ score > ♂ score ICR = 54%	2 factors: - social phobia - agoraphobia	----

Study	Sample	Internal consistency	Concurrent validity	Discriminative validity	Factorial analysis Predictive validity	T/R Reliability
Osman et al., 1995 (USA)	N = 410 college students x = 20.9 years	α = 0.85 – 0.95	SADS = 0.29 – 0.66 FQ = 0.28 – 0.51 MMPI-2-Si2 = 0.07-0.38 BSI (sensitivity) = 0.38 BSI (phobic anxiety) = 0.21	♀ score > ♂ score	2 factors: - social phobia - agoraphobia SPAI-SP = 5 factors (64.1% variance)	----
Gillis et al., 1995 (USA)	N = 261 general population 18-65 years	----	----	SPAI-SP: ♀ score = ♂ score caucasian score> black score SPAI-AS:score ♀ > ♂ age = no difference	----	----
Osman et al., 1996 (USA)	N = 385 college students 20-64 years	adequate	----	----	2 factors: - social phobia - agoraphobia	----
Olivares et al., 1999 (Spain)	N = 3160 SP NSP 14 -17 years	α = 0.83 – 0.95	----	----	2 factors: - social phobia - agoraphobia SPAI-SP = 4 factors (53.7% variance)	----
Rodebaugh et al., 2000 (USA)	N = 27 SP NSP adults	----	SAS-SR = 0.76 PSC = 0.80	SP score> NSP score	role play anxiety = 0.71 role play negative cognitions = 0.81	----
Peters 2000 (Australia)	N = 117 SP OAD adults	----	SPS = 0.72 SIAS = 0.85	AUC = 0.93 S = 0.80 E = 0.90	----	----
Garcia-Lopes et al., 2001 (Spain)	N = 303 SP NSP 14- 17 years	----	ADIS-IV-L = 0.59 – 0.78 FNE = 0.39 – 0.54 SAS-A = 0.64 – 0.73 SADS = 0.51 – 0.71 APD = 0.45 – 0.55	SP score> NSP score generalized SP score > non-generalized SP score	----	0.77 – 0.86 (10 days)
Picon et al., 2005 (Brazil)	N = 255 university students	α = 0.96	----	----	----	0.83 (2 weeks)
Picon et al., 2006 (Brazil)	N = 1014 university students	α = 0.85 – 0.96	----	----	----	----

Table 4. (Continued)

Study	Sample	Internal consistency	Concurrent validity	Discriminative validity	Factorial analysis Predictive validity	T/R Reliability
Baños et al., 2007 (Spain)	N = 270 SP NSP	A = 0.87 – 0.98	SADS = 0.42 – 0.78 FNE = 0.38 – 0.57	SP score> NSP core generalized SP score > non-generalized SP score ♀ > ♂	2 factors: - social phobia - agoraphobia (58 % variance)	----

AAES = Assertiveness Subscale of the Adolescent Assertion; ADIS-IV-L = Interview Schedule for DSM IV lifetime; APD = Avoidant Personality Disorder; AUC = area under the curve; BSI = Brief Symptom Inventory; E = specificity; FN = false-negative rate; FNE = Fear of Negative Evaluation; FP = false-positive rate; FQ = Fear Questionnaire; HAMA = Hamilton Rating Scale for Anxiety; MMPI-2-Si2 = Minnesota Multiphasic Personality Inventory – social avoidance subscale; N = number of subjects; NSP = subjects without social phobia; OAD = subjects com other anxiety disorders; PSC = Self Consciousness Scale - Public Self Consciousness Subscale; S = sensitivity; SADS = Social Avoidance Distress Scale; SAS-A = Social Anxiety Scale for Adolescents; SAS-SR = Social Adjustment Scale Self-report; SIAS = Social Interaction Anxiety Scale; SPAI-AS = Social Phobia and Anxiety Inventory- agoraphobia subscale; SPAI-SP = Social Phobia and Anxiety Inventory-Social Phobia subscale; SP = subjects with social phobia; SPS = Social Phobia Scale; SPSC-R = Fear Survey Schedule for Children; STAI- C = State Trait Anxiety Inventory for Children; ICR = incorrect classification rate; T/R = test-retest* = daily ratings; ** = during anxiety producing task; α = Cronbach alpha; x = mean; ♀ = women; ♂ = men.

Predictive validity was evaluated as a function of the response to psychotherapy and to drug treatment and also in role play situations (anxiety producing task), and was found to be adequate.

Regarding factorial analysis, the predominant evidence was that the SPAI is composed of two factors: SP and agoraphobia. Factorial analysis of the SP subscale in several studies revealed different results, varying from 4 factors (social interaction, cognitive and somatic symptoms, focus of attention, avoidance and escape) to 5 factors (individual interaction, somatic and cognitive, group interaction, avoidance, focus of attention).

The reliability of the SPAI was also determined and found to be adequate, as also were the remaining psychometric properties of the instrument.

The most recent study published about the SPAI deals with the development of the abbreviated version of the instrument following the current tendency to provide screening instruments of brief and rapid application. The study was conducted by Roberson-Nay et al in 2007 using methods based on nonparametric item response theory. The abbreviated version was denoted SPAI-23 and consisted of 16 items of the SP subscale and 7 items of the agoraphobia scale scored on a 5-point Likert scale. The initial psychometric analysis of this version of the instrument in a sample of 1607 cases and non-cases of SP revealed adequate convergent validity with the SADS (0.47-0.85 cases; 0.39-0.67 non-cases) and FNE = (0.34-0.70 cases; 0.37-0.57 non-cases), as also demonstrated for the full version of the SPAI .

However, future studies are needed to assess the remaining psychometric qualities of the SPAI-23.

The data obtained for the SPAI have demonstrated its adequacy in terms of psychometric parameters, this being a widely recognized and utilized instrument. Recent studies have used the SPAI in different contexts, such as studies on face recognition (Kolssa & Miltner, 2006), on the associations between SP and functioning in psychotic bouts (Voges and Addington, 2005) and on the associations between psychiatric disorders and cigarette smoking (Upadhyaya et al., 2003). This instrument has also supported the development of psychometric studies involving other instruments.

2.1.7. Social Phobia and Anxiety Inventory for Children (SPAI-C)

In view of the early onset of the typical symptoms of SP and of the absence of specific instruments for the evaluation of this disorder in children, Beidel et al. (1995) proposed the Social Phobia and Anxiety Inventory for Children (SPAI-C), whose theory is based on the same principles as those adopted by Turner et al. (1989a).

The instrument consists of 26 items designed to assess social anxiety in children. These items assess a range of potentially anxiety-producing situations, such as reading aloud, performing in a play, and assess physical and cognitive characteristics of social phobia as well as avoidance behaviors. Each of the 26 items is rated on a 3 point scale (0 = never or hardly ever; 1 = sometimes; 2 = most of the time, always). Nine of 26 items have subitems allowing the child to rate his or her distress based on specific characteristics of the interpersonal partner (ex: "boys and girls I know, boys and girls I don't know, adults"). Scores on the SPAI-C range from 0 to 78. Some examples of the items of this instrument are: "*If somebody asks me to do something I don't want to do, I feel scared and don't know what to say*"; "*I try to avoid social situations such as parties, school, playing with others*"; "*I am too scared to ask questions in class*".

In addition to the original study by Beidel et al. (1995), several others analyzed the psychometric properties of the SPAI-C. The principal studies are described in Table 5.

In general, studies using the SPAI-C revealed highly satisfactory psychometric properties to be used in children and adolescents aged 4 to 17 years with both clinical and non-clinical characteristics. The internal consistency of the instrument was quite adequate, as also was the test-retest reliability studied at intervals from 2 weeks to one year.

Concurrent validity was usually studied in relation to other self-assessment instruments regarding anxiety, social competence, criticism and behavior, among others, but also with respect to parental self-perception regarding the behavior of the child and hetero-assessment of behavior by professionals in role-play situations. This psychometric quality was found to be quite satisfactory in the various studies, as also observed for discriminative validity, with subjects with SP presenting a higher level of social anxiety than non-phobic subjects and subjects with other anxiety disorders in addition to a larger number of distressing events. The SPAI-C was also able to discriminate between sexes and races, indicating that girls had a higher level of symptoms than boys. The scale also showed very good sensitivity and specificity comparable to those of the SPAI.

Table 5. Psychometric studies conducted with the Social Phobia and Anxiety Scale for Children (SPAI-C) and psychometric qualities demonstrated

Study	Sample	Internal consistency	Concurrent validity	Discriminative validity	Factorial analysis Predictive validity	T/R Reliability
Beidel et al., 1995 (USA)	N = 154 SP NSP OAD 8 - 17 years	$\alpha = 0.95$	STAI-T = 0.50 STAI-S = 0.13 SPSC-R = 0.41-0.45 FCS = 0.53 CBCL-I = 0.45 CBCL-E = 0.18 CBCL-S = 0.33	SP score> NSP score ♀ score = ♂ score Cut-off note18 FN = 37% FP = 29%	3 factors (59% variance) -assertiveness and general conversation - traditional social encounters - public performance	0.86 (2 weeks) 0.63 (10 months)
Beidel et al., 1996 (USA)	N = 158 SP NSP OAD x = 9.9 - 11.4 years	$\alpha = 0.92$	No. of distressing social events = 0.50 SAM = 0.41	SP distressing events day > NSP SP days containing distressing social events > NSP SP score > NSP SP > externalizing disorders S = 0.70 Sp = 0.80	5 factors (63% variance) - assertiveness - general conversation - physical and cognitive symptoms - behavioral avoidance - public performance	----
Morris & Masia, 1998 (USA)	N = 277 NSP children	----	SASC-R = moderate	score ♀ > ♂	----	----
Melfsen et al., 1999 (Germany)	N = 481 NSP x = 12.4 - 13.8 years	----	Measures of general anxiety: adequate	----	----	adequate (2 weeks) (4 weeks)
Sppkins 2000 (USA)	N = 235 SP NSP	----	SASC-R = adequate	♀ score ≠ ♂ score ≠ age	ICR = 82%	----
Beidel et al., 2000 (USA)	N = 254 SP NSP OAD 8 - 14 years	----	- parental reports = 0.31 - independent observer ratings of behavioral skill = 0.28 - 0.37	♀ score > ♂ score SP score> OAD hispanic children > african american children	----	----

Table 5. (Continued)

Study	Sample	Internal consistency	Concurrent validity	Discriminative validity	Factorial analysis Predictive validity	T/R Reliability
Storch et al., 2004 (USA)	N = 1147 general population 13 - 17 years	α = 0.65 – 0.92	SAS-A = 0.76 FNE = 0.64 SADS = 0.63 - 0.73	score ♀ > ♂	5 factors - assertiveness -general conversation - physical and cognitive symptoms - avoidance - public performance	0.47 (12 months)
Inderbitzen et al., 2004 (USA)	N = 252 general population 13 - 17 years	----	SAS-A = 0.79	S = 61.5% Sp = 82.7%	---	---
Gauer et al., 2005 (Brazil)	N = 1871 general population 9 - 14 years	α = 0.94	----	----	4 factors (47.7% variance)	0.78 (2 weeks)

CBCL-I = Child Behavior Checklist – internalizing; CBCL-E = Child Behavior Checklist – externalizing; CBCL-S = Child Behavior Checklist – social competence; FCS = Failure Criticism Subscale; FN = false-negative rate; FNE = Fear Negative Evaluation; FP = false-positive rate; SPSC-R = Fear Survey Schedule for Children; N = number of subjects; NSP = subjects without social phobia; OAD = subjects with other anxiety disorders; S = sensitivity; SADS = Social Avoidance Distress Scale; SAM = Self- Assessment Manikin; SAS-A = Social Anxiety Scale for Adolescents; SASC-R = Social Anxiety Scale for Children- revised; SP = subjects with social phobia ; Sp = specificity; STAI-T = Stait-Trait Anxiety Scale - Trait ; STAI-S = Stait-Trait Anxiety Scale - State; ICR = incorrect classification rate; T/R = test-retest; α = Cronbach alpha; x = mean; ♀ = women; ♂ = men; nº = number.

The study of the factorial components of the SPAI-C showed variation between three and five factors, although there seems to be greater consensus about the presence of five factors, as follows: assertiveness, general conversation, physical and cognitive symptoms, behavioral avoidance and public performance.

Higa et al (2006) studied the possibility of using the SPAI-C in a version adapted to the parents, who would assess the phobic aspects of the child. This version was denoted Social Phobia and Anxiety Inventory for Children - Parent Report (SPAI-C-P). The psychometric properties of this instrument were studied in a sample of 158 students (mean age: 11.5 years), showing an important correlation between the SPAI-C-P filled out by the parents and the SPAI-C filled out by the children, as well as adequate internal consistency of the instrument.

Other studies with empirical characteristics also used the SPAI-C in different contexts. Among them were studies of the SSRIs antidepressants (escitalopram and sertraline) for the treatment of children and adolescents with SP (Isolan et al., 2007; Compton et al., 2001) and studies of the correlations between anxiety and hyperactivity (Melfsen et al. 2006), between social anxiety and peer victimization in adolescence (Storch, 2003), and between social anxiety and use of alcohol by adolescents (Smith, 2003).

Thus, the conclusion was that the SPAI-C is a valid instrument widely used for the assessment of SP and agoraphobia symptoms in children of different age ranges and in different cultural contexts. However, studies assessing its divergent validity and especially its predictive validity still seem to be necessary.

It should be pointed out that both the SPAI-C and the SPAI have been used for adolescents, with no consensus existing about which of the two instruments is the more adequate since both have shown acceptable validity and reliability for this age range.

2.1.8. Situational Social Avoidance Scale (SSAS)

The Situational Social Avoidance Scale (SSAS) was proposed by Ishiyama (1999) with the specific objective of assessing the avoidance of different social situations. It consists of 15 items scored on a 7 point Likert scale (1 = almost never; 7 = almost always), with a possible total score of 15 to 105. These items were a collection of situation- specific items found in recent research scales on shyness, social anxiety and assertiveness, as shown by the following examples: *"Asserting rights and say no to others"; "Asking questions and asking for clarification in a relative large group (over 20 people)"; "Dealing with verbally aggressive people"*.

The psychometric qualities of the scale were assessed in a sample of 407 Canadian college students and the results showed that the following three factors explain 57.3% of the variance of the data: Social Performance Avoidance; Socializing Avoidance and Self-Assertion Avoidance. Analysis of discriminative validity showed that the scale can discriminate between sexes, with women having a higher mean score, i.e., a larger number of social situations avoided. The test-retest reliability (6.5 weeks) was 0.86 and the internal consistency ranged from 0.84 to 0.85. The concurrent validity of the SSAS with other measures of social anxiety was also adequate, correlating with the SADS at the 0.34 to 0.71 level, with the Cheek Buss Shyness Scale (CBSS) at the 0.50 to 0.78 level, with the Social Anxiety Scale (SAS) at the 0.21 to 0.60 level, and with the Interaction Anxiousness Scale (IAS) at the 0.49 to 0.66 level.

The SSAS differs little in its objectives and psychometric qualities from the other scales available for the assessment of different aspects of SP and was not used in later studies at the psychometric or clinical level. This may probably be due to the universally recognized value of other instruments with the same objectives, such as the SADS, which appear to be preferred in empirical and transcultural validation studies.

2.1.9. Social Phobia Inventory (SPIN) and Mini-Social Phobia Inventory (MINI-SPIN)

The Social Phobia Inventory (SPIN), created by Connor et al.. (2000), was developed in order to provide a brief and easily applicable instrument that could also deal with the physiological symptoms of fear and avoidance related to SP. It consists of 17 items scored on a five-point Likert scale (0 = not at all; 4 = extremely), with a maximum total score of 68. The items are divided into three subscales: fear (items 1 ,3 ,5 ,10 ,14 ,15), avoidance (items 4, 6 ,8 ,9 ,11 ,12 ,16) and physiological symptoms (items 2 ,7 ,13 ,17), with the following items representing examples of each: *"Parties and social events scare me"; "I would do anything to avoid being criticized"; "Sweating in front of people causes me distress".*

The psychometric qualities of the scale were assessed in the original study for samples of individuals with SP and of healthy subjects (N = 353). Regarding the total score and the subscales, it showed adequate test-retest reliability for cases (0.78 to 0.89) and internal consistency (Cronbach alpha) ranging from 0.68 to 0.94 for cases and from 0.57 to 0.90 for non-cases. Regarding convergent validity, it demonstrated a significant correlation with the Brief Social Phobia Scale (BSPS) (0.47 to 0.82), the LSAS (0.55) and the FQ (0.42 to 0.78) for cases. However, it showed divergent validity with respect to the Medical Outcomes Study Short Form (SP36) since it did not correlate significantly with this instrument, which assesses general health and quality of life aspects, and showed a low correlation (0.33) with the Sheehan Disability Scale (SDS), an instrument that assesses the level of impairment of overall functioning. Criterion validity using the clinical interview as the "gold standard" revealed areas under the ROC curve ranging from 0.83 to 0.86, with an estimated sensitivity of 0.72 and specificity of 0.84 for a cut-off score of 19.

Factorial analysis of the instrument for the case sample pointed out five factors with self-values ranging from 5.51 to 1.06: Factor 1 - talking to strangers and social situations (items 3, 4, 8, 10); Factor 2 - criticism and embarrassment (items 5, 6, 12, 15); Factor 3 - physiological changes (items 2, 7, 13, 16); Factor 4 - authority figures (items 1, 16); Factor 5 - avoiding being the center of attention and public speaking (items 9, 11, 14). The SPIN and its subscales also demonstrated sensitivity for the identification of the effects of pharmacological treatment and psychotherapy, proving to be, in general, an excellent instrument for the quantitation of SP symptoms and of the therapeutic effects of various treatment approaches.

Other studies were later conducted using the SPIN in order to determine its psychometric qualities in different contexts. A brief description of some aspects of these studies is given in Table 6.

Table 6 shows that the studies were conducted using three versions of the instrument in addition to the English original (Brazilian, Finnish and French) on clinical and non-clinical adult populations and non-clinical adolescent populations. The internal consistency was quite adequate in all studies, with values higher than 0.69. Concurrent validity was assessed in relation to measures of social anxiety, of fear and depression and was also found to be adequate. Regarding discriminative validity, the scale was sensitive in differentiating between cases and non-cases of SP and changes caused by treatment, with highly expressive sensitivity and specificity. Test-retest reliability, assessed during a period of one to three weeks, was moderate in the various studies. In general, the values obtained for all the psychometric qualities studied were quite close and in agreement with the original study by Connor et al.. (2000), supporting the excellent adequacy of the SPIN for the evaluation of SP even in different languages, countries and cultures.

Another psychometric study with the SPIN is currently being conducted by our group. Osório et al. (2004) translated and adapted the SPIN to the population of Brazilian university students according to a rigorous process of transcultural validation. In this context, the psychometric qualities of the SPIN are being tested in the general population of university students (N = 2314) and of cases (N = 88) and non-cases of SP (N = 90). The results have indicated internal consistency ranging from 0.63 to 0.90, concurrent validity with the BAI

(0.10 to 0.63) and BSPS (0.24 to 0.82), and discriminative validity (sensitivity of 0.86, specificity of 0.84 to 0.87, positive predictive value of 0.84 to 0.86, negative predictive value of 0.85 to 0.86, and a 15% rate of incorrect classification for a cut-off score of 19 to 21). Factorial analysis indicated the presence of a varied number of factors in the different samples. Three factors were found for the general population sample, which in general explained 54.12% of data variance. Factor 1, denoted "fear and avoidance of situations of social evaluation and of authority figures and physiological symptoms", explained most of the variance of the results and comprised many of the situations feared and avoided by persons with SP, as well as all the physiological symptoms elicited by the situation. The other two factors together explained a lower percentage of the variance: Factor 2 "fear and avoidance of interaction with people, public speaking and being the center of attention", and Factor 3 "fear and avoidance of social events".

The number of factors found for SP cases was higher (N = 5), explaining, in general, 69.73% of the variance. Factor 1 consisted of items regarding the "fear and avoidance of situations of social evaluation and physiological symptoms". Compared to Factor 1 for the sample of the general population, the items related to fear and avoidance of authorities were not included here, demonstrating that for the cases these items have a lower discriminative power than for the general population compared to the fear and avoidance of situations of social evaluation. Factor 2 of the SP sample was denoted "fear and avoidance of figures of authority", being an independent factor compared to the study of the general population sample, since in the latter sample, as stated before, these items were grouped with Factor 1. Factor 3 refers to "fear and avoidance of social events" and is directly correlated with Factor 3 for the general population sample. Factor 4 ("fear and avoidance of interaction with strangers") and Factor 5 ("avoidance of public speaking and of being the center of attention") correspond to Factor 2 for the general population sample, showing interdependence. Comparison of these two analyses revealed that, for cases, some fears and avoidances are not directly correlated with others, as observed for the general population since they are not grouped together, demonstrating their specificity for the case sample.

Table 6. Psychometric studies conducted with the Social Phobia Inventory (SPIN) in different contexts and samples: main results

Study	Objective	Sample	Internal consistency	Concurrent validity	Discriminant validity	T/R Reliability
Vilete, 2002 (Brazil)	To investigate the psychometric properties - Brazilian version	N = 190 NSP adolescents	α = 0.88	----	Cut-off note 19/20 S = 0.75 Sp = 0.57	0.32 - 0.65 (2 weeks)
Johnson et al., 2006 (USA)	To investigate the psychometric properties – original version	N = 174 NSP adolescents	α = 0.69 - 0.92	SAS-A = 0.57- 0.82 SPAI-C = 0.71 - 0.91 CDI = 0.45-0.58	SP score > NSP score AUC = 0.81 Cut-off note 21: S = 0.68; Sp = 0.81	----

Antony et al., 2006 (Canada)	To investigate the psychometric properties – original version	N = 251 OAD Adults	α = 0.79 - 0.92	SPS = 0.61-0.71 SIAS = 0.23-0.68 DASS = ns ASI = ns	SP score > OCD/ agoraphobia pre-treatment score > post-treatment score	0.32 - 0.65 (1 - 3 weeks)
Radomsky et al., 2006 (Canada)	To investigate the psychometric properties – original and French versions	N = 202 NSP university students	α = 0.76 - 0.93	FSS-III = 0.56 – 0.76 BDI = 0.43 – 0.51	----	0.71 - 0.86 (25 days)
Ranta et al., 2007 (Finland)	To investigate the psycho-metric properties – Finnish version	N = 752 NSP adolescents	----	----	SP score > NSP score AUC = 0.92-0.82 Cut-off note19: S = 0.95; Sp = 0.70 PPV = 0.40	----

ASI = Anxiety Sensitivity Index; AUC = area under the ROC curve; BDI = Beck Depression Inventory; CDI = Children's Depression Inventory; DASS = Depression Anxiety Stress Scales; FSS-III = Fear Survey Schedule-III; N = number of subjects; NSP = subjects without social phobia; OAD = subjects with other anxiety disorders; OCD = Obsessive Compulsive Disorder; PPV = positive predictive value; S = sensitivity; SAS-A = Social Anxiety Scale for Adolescents; SIAS = Social Interaction Anxiety Scale; Sp = specificity; SP = subjects with social phobia; SPAI-C = Social Phobia and Anxiety Inventory for Children; SPS = Social Phobia Scale; T/R = test-retest; α = Cronbach alpha; ns = non significant correlation.

In general, the SPIN proved to have high validity for the assessment of different aspects of SP in different cultures. Because of its adequacy, its composition involving fear, avoidance and physiological symptoms and its practical and easy application, it seems to have reached an outstanding position among the other instruments available in the current research context. Since its proposal, the SPIN has been extensively used in empirical studies, especially in drug assays for the treatment of SP. Particularly important among these investigations are the studies of the efficacy of olanzapine (Barnett et al, 2002), mirtazapine (Mulhlbacher et al., 2005), slow-release venlafaxine (Rickels et al., 2004; Liebowitz et al., 2005), a botulinum toxin (Connor et al., 2006), quetiapine (Vaishnavi et al., 2007), and tiagabine (Dunlop et al. 2007).

Another line of SPIN studies deals with the development and psychometric evaluation of the reduced version of the instrument which was proposed by Connor et al. (2001) and was called MINI-SPIN. This reduced instrument consists of three items of the SPIN which were found to be indicative of SP in an empirical study. For the development of this instrument, on the basis of score analysis, the authors identified the items that best discriminated between subjects with SP and controls. A subgroup of three of the 17 items of the scale that reached the highest sensitivity and specificity for the diagnosis of SP were selected: item 6- *"Fear of embarrassment causes me to avoid doing things or speaking to people"*; item 9- *"I avoid activities in which I am the center of attention"*; and item 15- *"Being embarrassed or looking stupid is among my worst fears"*. The items are scored in the same way as done for the original version of the instrument, i.e., on a Likert scale from 0 to 4. This reduced instrument was tested initially in a sample of 7165 patients (managed care), showing 88.7% sensitivity, 90% specificity, 52.6% positive predictive value, 98.5% negative predictive value, and 89.9% diagnostic efficiency for a cut-off score of 6, suggested to be the most adequate for SP screening (Connor et al., 2001).

Another study of the discriminative validity of the MINI-SPIN was conducted by Wilson (2005) in Australia, where the instrument was applied to 666 college students. The results obtained differed considerably from those obtained in the study by Connor et al.. (2001), in which the cut-off score of 6 and 7 overestimated the prevalence of SP (30 and 18%, respectively), since the previous estimates indicated a 2.7% prevalence of the disorder in the Australian context. Analysis of this study shows that this finding may have been due to a faulty methodological design since the study did not use any diagnostic instrument as a parameter for comparison, possibly explaining this divergence.

Weeks et al.. (2007) also analyzed the psychometric properties of the MINI-SPIN in an initial sample of 291 adult subjects who had sought treatment at a clinic specializing in anxiety. Ninety-seven of these subjects fulfilled the diagnostic criteria of SP as determined by the ADIS. For this subsample the MINI-SPIN showed adequate internal consistency (α = 0.85) and concurrent validity with the LSAS (0.46), SIAS (0.57), SPS (0.34) and BFNE (0.44). Divergent validity was evaluated in relation to the following instruments: Generalized Anxiety Disorder Questionnaire for DSM-IV (GAD-Q-IV), Anxiety Sensitivity Index – revised (ASI-R), BDI and Penn State Worry Questionnaire (PSWQ). The correlations ranged from 0.05 to 0.19, demonstrating the adequacy of this psychometric quality of the MINI-SPIN. The sensitivity and specificity of the instrument, i.e., its discriminative validity, were also evaluated, showing that specificity was not very adequate for any of the cut-off scores between 4 and 9, varying from 0.45 and 0.77, with the cut-off score of 6 being the one that best balanced sensitivity (0.93), specificity (0.63) and diagnostic efficiency (0.88), being therefore recommended for use in the sample under study.

In Brazil, Osório et al. (2007) conducted a study evaluating the psychometric qualities of the MINI-SPIN, in which the discriminative validity of the instrument was analyzed in a sample of university students (N = 656). The total sample was submitted to ROC analysis. The area under the curve (AUC) for this ROC analysis was 0.81 and was significant versus chance or a random ROC line ($p<0.001$). Thus, it was observed that, for a cut-off score of 6, suggested in the original English version of the instrument, the sensitivity was 0.94, the specificity was 0.46, the positive predictive value was 0.58, and the negative predictive value was 0.92. For the cut-off score of 7, the authors observed an increase in the specificity and in the positive predictive value (0.68 and 0.65) while the sensitivity and negative predictive value (0.78 and 0.80) remained high. The conclusion was that the MINI-SPIN showed quite satisfactory psychometric qualities. The cut-off score of 6 seemed the most suitable to attest the tracking value of the tool. However, the cut-off score of 7 was most suitable as a minimum parameter in the studied group, with psychometric values more similar to those of the original study.

Later, the same authors demonstrated other psychometric aspects of the MINI-SPIN (Osório et al.. – manuscript submitted for publication) such as internal consistency and concurrent validity and investigated in depth the discriminating ability of the MINI-SPIN in samples of the general population and of university students (N = 2314), and of cases (N = 88) and non-cases of SP (N = 90). In that study the MINI-SPIN showed adequate internal consistency (Cronbach alpha = 0.49-0.73), concurrent validity with the SPIN (0.64-0.88), BSPS (0.40-0.67) and SSAS (0.22-0.54), and concurrent and divergent validity with the Beck Anxiety Inventory (BAI) (0.20-0.52). The discriminative validity of the MINI-SPIN in distinguishing SP cases from non-cases was also demonstrated (t = -8.921). The authors concluded that the psychometric properties observed were quite close to those of the original instrument, denoting the adequacy of the MINI-SPIN when applied to different samples and cultural contexts as a screening instrument and favoring its large-scale use, especially in contexts of primary health care.

Our research group is also involved in another line of research using the MINI-SPIN in Brazil. Our research is based on the study of the validity of the MINI-SPIN for samples of subjects with other disorders with a high rate of comorbidity with SP. One of our studies (Lemos et al., 2008) verified this validity in a sample of 87 subjects with Parkinson Syndrome aged 24 to 85 years (mean: 60.7 years). The cut-off note of 5 seems to be the most appropriate for the diagnosis of SP in this population sample, with 0.79 sensitivity, 0.71 specificity, 0.57 positive predictive value, 0.87 negative predictive value, and a 27% incorrect classification rate. Internal consistency was 0.83, with the MINI-SPIN being able to discriminate subjects with SP also in this context.

2.1.10. Social Phobia Spectrum Self-Report (SHY-SR)

The Social Phobia Spectrum Self-Report (SHY-SR) was proposed by Dell'Osso et al. (2002a). Italian and English versions of the instruments were developed in parallel, with the same level of comprehension being obtained in both languages. Its development was based on the SCDI-IV as a parameter. It is a self-administered instrument comprising 168 items that assess different domains of the SP spectrum such as: a) Childhood and Adolescence Anxiety Features domain (12 items) – explores fears and phobic avoidance during childhood and adolescence; b) Interpersonal Sensitivity domain (29 items) – assesses hypersensitivity to criticism, judgment and refusal, discomfort when the center of attention, low self-confidence, feeling of inferiority, poor assertiveness, and interpersonal difficulties; c) Behavioral Inhibition and Somatic Symptoms domain (23 items)– explores social behaviors and somatic symptoms associated with social anxiety; d) Specific Phobias domain (98 items) – assesses situations that may trigger anticipatory anxiety and avoidance behaviors. The questionnaire also includes an appendix on the use of psychoactive substances (6 items).

The items are scored on a dichotomous scale in the "yes or no" format according to the presence or absence of the manifestations described. The psychometric qualities of this instrument were studied in a sample of Italian subjects consisting of students, ophthalmology patients and patients with obsessive compulsive disorder, SP, and depression. The proposed self-applied version was compared to the hetero-applied version, with all items and domain showing a correlation of more than 0.74. However, comparative analysis of the areas composing the Specific Phobias domain, which involves a large number of items, indicated differences between data as a function of self- or hetero-evaluation. For some areas such as speaking and writing there was a highly significant agreement of more than 0.70, whereas for other areas such as driving, walking, meeting strangers, or going to a shopping mall the agreement was lower than 0.35, with the subjects tending to admit more difficulties with self-application than with hetero-application. The author concluded that the self-applied version was adequate and recommended it for use in both research and clinical contexts.

Dell'Osso and collaborators conducted other studies using the SHY-SR, especially in the epidemiological context. The SHY-SR was found to be able to discriminate groups as a function of sex and level of social anxiety (Dell'Osso et al., 2002b, 2003), and also subjects with different indicators of psychiatric disorders (Ducci et al., 2004).

Berrocal et al. (2006) performed the transcultural validation of the Spanish version of the SHY-SR using a careful methodological process. They also studied some psychometric qualities of this version in a sample of 62 clinical and non-clinical subjects, detecting adequate internal consistency (0.89-0.98), test-retest reliability (2 to 3 weeks: 0.95 to 0.99), concurrent validity with the LSAS (0.61 to 0.85) and discriminative validity (the score for subjects with SP was higher than the score for patients with depression and for non-phobic patients). The suggested cut-off score was 59, showing 100% sensitivity and specificity.

The above data reveal the wide amplitude of the aspects assessed with the SHY-SR, in agreement with its theoretical contribution, related to the assessment of the SP spectrum. It is a scale requiring a long time for application, about 35 to 40 minutes, a fact that may impair its use in some contexts. Its psychometric qualities seemed to be excellent for the Spanish version despite the limited sample size. The qualities of the English and Italian versions need to be further explored in large population samples.

No empirical study in which the SHY-SR was used as a measuring instrument is currently available.

2.1.11. Social Phobia Diagnostic Questionnaire (SPDQ)

The Social Phobia Diagnostic Questionnaire (SPDQ) was developed by Newman et al. (2003).In view of the limitations of the psychometric qualities of self-applied instruments available for the assessment of SP, with the SPDQ the authors intended to provide an instrument for the screening of this disorder based on the diagnostic criteria of the DM-IV, that would be psychometrically superior to all others.

The SPDQ consists of 15 items and includes two yes/no questions that assess excessive fearfulness in social, observational and evaluative situations, as well as fear of embarrassing oneself, and/or being viewed critically by others. In addition, it includes a question about whether the individual tries to avoid social situations. Next, it includes a list of 16 social situations for with fear and avoidance are rated on a Likert scale from 0 to 4 , with 0 equaling no fear or avoidance, and 4 equaling very severe fear or consistent avoidance. Following the ratings of individual social situations are two yes/no questions to determine whether the fear comes on as soon as the person encounters the feared social situation and every time that they are in such feared situations. An additional question assesses whether the person views the fear as unreasonable. Finally, it includes 4 point Likert scale ratings of level of severity, and overall impairment in functioning arising from social fears. Some of the items included in the questionnaire are: *"Saying no to unreasonable requests"; "Asking others to do something differently"; "Would you say that your social fear is excessive or unreasonable?"; "Has what you have been able to achieve in your job or in school been negatively effected by your social fear?"*

Some psychometric qualities of the SPDQ were assessed in the original study using clinical and non-clinical samples (N = 587). The results demonstrated good discriminative validity as evaluated by the ROC curve. For the cut-off score of 7.38, sensitivity was 82%, specificity 85%, false-positive rate 15%, false-negative rate 18%, and diagnostic efficacy 83%. The internal consistency of the SPDQ was 0.92, an extremely adequate value demonstrating coherence between the items. Concurrent and divergent validity was studied regarding measures of general anxiety (GADQ-IV = 0.28), measures of social anxiety (SIAS = 0.64; SADS = 0.61), and measures that assess worry (PSWQ = 0.32). Divergent validity was analyzed by comparing the SPDQ to other instruments that assess other specific diseases such as panic, depression, post-traumatic stress and, as expected, the significance of the correlations was low.

The data presented denoted the psychometric adequacy of the SPDQ. However, like the instruments most recently developed for the assessment of SP, such as the SSAS and SHY-SR, the SPDQ still is an instrument that has not been used in empirical studies, requiring psychometric studies that will assess its validity and reliability for different samples and contexts.

2.1.12. Social Interaction and Performance Anxiety and Avoidance Scale (SIPAAS)

The Social Interaction and Performance Anxiety and Avoidance Scale (SIPAAS), proposed by Pinto-Gouveia et al. (2003), is a self-report questionnaire to assess the level of distress and avoidance in a wide range of performance and social situations commonly feared by social phobics. The instrument, available in the Portuguese language, consists of 22 items of the LSAS and 22 additional items representative of different situations of social performance and interaction, for a total of 44 items. For each situation, respondents were asked to indicate both the degree of fear or anxiety the situation provokes or would provoke and how frequently they avoid or would avoid that situation. The items are scored on a 4 point Likert scale (1 = none; 4 = severe/usually). The scale was therefore formed by two subscales, the distress/anxiety subscale and avoidance subscale. Two blank lines permitted the respondent to add two social situations that provoked high levels of anxiety and were not represented on the scale. After having completed the scale, respondents were also asked to identify the five situations that would provoke the highest levels of anxiety, and write their number on a designated space. Examples of the items are: "working while being observed"; "Trying to convince someone to engage in a romantic/sexual relationship (courting)", "Resisting high pressure on the part of a salesman", "Talking to persons of a higher sociocultural condition."

The psychometric study of the SIPAAS was also conducted by Pinto-Gouveia et al. (2003) in a sample of 655 young adults from Portugal with and without a diagnosis of SP and with a diagnosis of other anxiety disorders. Internal consistency was 0.92 to 0.95 and test-retest reliability (4 weeks) was 0.83 to 0.86. The SIPAAS in its full format or in its subscales was also able to discriminate between subjects with SP and subjects with other anxiety disorders and non-phobic subjects. The cut-off score proposed to differentiate social phobics from non-social phobics was 115 for the distress subscale and 105 for the anxiety subscale. Concurrent validity was studied in relation to the SADS (0.60 to 0.67), FNE (0.51 to 0.61), SDS (0.34 to 0.50), and SPSBS (0.42 to 0.61) and found to be adequate.

The SIPAAS has also been studied in Brazil after being adapted to Brazilian Portuguese with the authorization of the authors using the transcultural validation process. The study of the psychometric properties of this instrument in Brazil using a sample of SP cases and non-cases (N =155) indicated an internal consistency of 0.97 to 0.98 and a test-retest reliability (2 weeks) of 0.50 to 0.97. Studies on the concurrent and discriminative validity of the SIPAAS are currently underway and the results will be published shortly.

In general, the SIPAAS seems to be an adequate instrument for the assessment of SP, involving a wide gamut of situations that may induce fear and avoidance on the part of individuals with SP. However, it differs little from other instruments already universally accepted for the assessment of these aspects, such as the SPIN and SPAI, among others. One of its limitations is the fact that it has not yet been translated into other languages, being available only in the Portuguese of Portugal and of Brazil. No other psychometric or empirical studies of the SIPAAS have been detected thus far. Such studies will be necessary to validate the aspects occurring in other samples and cultures.

2.2. Hetero-Assessment Scales

2.2.1. Liebowitz Social Anxiety Scale (LSAS)

The Liebowitz Social Anxiety Scale (LSAS), the first clinician-rating scale developed for assessment of SP, was designed to assess the range of social interaction and performance situations that individuals with SP may fear and/or avoid. Its 24 items are divided into two subscales that address social interaction (11 items) and performance (13 items) situations. The clinician asks the patient to rate fear and avoidance during the past week on 0-3 Likert type scales (0 = none/never; 3 = severe/usually); however, the clinician is given latitude to question the patient's responses and adjust the ratings accordingly. Thus, the LSAS provides six subscale scores: total fear, fear of social interaction, fear of performance, total avoidance, avoidance of social interaction and avoidance of performance. An overall total score is often calculated by summing the total fear and total avoidance scores. Two examples of the items composing the LSAS are: "*writing while being observed*"; "*meeting strangers*"; "*urinating in a public bathroom*".

Although the scale was developed by Liebowitz at al in 1987, the first psychometric study with the LSAS was conducted only in 1999 by Heimberg et al.. Several other studies were later conducted to assess the validity, factorial structure and use of the instrument in its self-applied version, as well as its transcultural validation. These studies are briefly summarized in Table 7.

Heimberg et al. (1999) studied the internal consistency and the concurrent and predictive validity of the LSAS, detecting highly acceptable values that demonstrated the adequacy of the scale. The study also revealed that the subscales proposed (social interaction and performance, fear and avoidance) were highly correlated with each other, a fact whose adequacy was questioned. In this respect, Safren et al. (1999) conducted a study of the factorial structure of the LSAS, demonstrating that the two-factor solution (fear and avoidance) was not the most adequate. Using exploratory factorial analysis, the authors found a four-factor model that explained 56.4% of the variance and that proved to be more appropriate. The factors are: Factor 1- social interaction; Factor 2- public speaking; Factor 3- observation by others; Factor 4- eating and drinking in public. These factors presented adequate indicators of internal consistency and convergent validity with measures of social anxiety.

The popularity of the LSAS as an index of SP has led some researchers to evaluate its utility as a self-report measure, to find a potential time saving alternative to the clinician version. Four studies exist to date that have explored the psychometric utility of a self-report version of the LSAS (LSAS-SR). Kobak et al. (1998) evaluated a computerized version of the LSAS-SR in comparison to the clinician-administered version. Their results indicated that the two versions were highly correlated, and demonstrated good internal consistency. However, these results should be interpreted with caution due to the brief time interval between completing the two versions. Cox et al. (1998) conducted another psychometric study using the LSAS-SR in which the proposed more care and methodological rigor regarding data collection. The results of their study indicated restrictions about the LSAS-SR, especially regarding its sensitivity to the changes obtained with treatment. In later studies, Fresco et al. (2001) and Backer et al. (2002) re-evaluated the psychometric qualities of the LSAS-SR. Fresco et al. (2001) compared the self and hetero versions in a sample of SP cases and non-cases, offering quite clear and detailed filling out instructions. They observed that the two versions did not differ in terms of reliability, internal consistency, mean score, convergent validity with measures of social anxiety, and divergent validity with measures of depression. Baker et al.. (2002) also reported good indicators of: a) reliability and internal consistency, b) convergent validity (especially in relation to the hetero version and the SPAI), c) divergent validity mainly when correlated with measures of depression, and d) predictive validity. These two more recent studies indicated equivalence of the two versions, confirming the adequacy of the self-administered version of the LSAS, also in terms of sensitivity.

In a study on the sensitivity of the LSAS, Mennin et al. (2002) determined the cut-off score for the total scale and the subscales for the diagnosis of SP and of the generalized subtype of SP. They pointed out that, for the total scale, a score of 30 favors a better balance between specificity and sensitivity. For the social interaction subscale, a score of 15 was the most adequate, correctly classifying 87.9% of subjects with SP. The score of 15 also proved to be more adequate for the performance subscale, classifying 94.5% of subjects with SP. For the identification of the generalized subtype, a score of 60 favored a better balance between sensitivity and specificity.

The factorial structure of the LSAS raised various questions and divergences. In addition to Safren et al. (1999), Backer et al. (2002) also performed a factorial study of the LSAS-SR and, using exploratory analysis (varimax rotation), detected five factors that explained 60.3% of the variance: social interaction (21.7%), non-verbal performance (10.3%), ingestion behavior (10.1%), public performance (9.5%), and confrontation (8.7%).

In another factorial study also using the self-applied version, Oakman et al.. (2003) tested several models and confirmed the inadequacy of the initial model proposed by Liebowitz. Similarly, they reported that the four-factor model (fear, avoidance, interaction and performance) was superior to the two-factor model, a fact indicating its utility in the clinical context. The authors concluded that the four-factor model proposed by Safren et al.. (1999) proved to be the most adequate when compared to the other models tested both for the self- and hetero-applied versions.

Heimberg & Holaway (2007) also demonstrated that the factorial model proposed by Safren et al. (1999) was the most adequate, with the Public Speaking and Social Interaction factors best discriminating between subjects with and without SP.

Regarding the studies for the validation of the LSAS in other languages, Yao et al. (1999) validated the French version, Bobes et al. (1999) the Spanish version, Levin et al. (2002) the Hebrew version, Asakura et al (2002) the Japanese version, Soykan et al. (2003) the Turkish version, and Terra et al (2006) and Crippa et al (unpublished results) the Brazilian one. All of these studies pointed out good indicators regarding convergent validity with measures of social anxiety and divergent validity with general measures of anxiety, depression, schizophrenia, shyness and overall functioning, in addition to adequate sensitivity especially to drug treatment and to cognitive-behavioral therapy. The Spanish, Turkish, Hebrew and Portuguese versions also showed good indicators of reliability and internal consistency. It should be emphasized that the study of the Hebrew version also analyzed the validity of the criterion of the scale and, in contrast to the other studies cited above, concluded that the three-factor model was the most adequate, while the study of the Brazilian version (Terra et al, 2006a) concluded that the five-factor model was the most adequate. Except for criterion validity, the remaining psychometric properties demonstrated in these studies of translations into other languages were found to be similar to those observed in studies of the original English version, indicating the adequacy and the possibility of using the scale in different cultural contexts.

In a study carried out by our group in Brazil to analyze the LSAS-SR in a sample of university students, SP cases and non-cases (N = 204 to 431), concurrent validity was found to be excellent in relation to specific measures of social anxiety (SPIN = 0.85; BSPS = 0.89) and general measures of anxiety (BAI = 0.59). Discriminative validity and test-retest reliability were also found to be excellent. The LSAS-SR discriminated between cases and non-cases of SP with a high level of significance ($p<0.0001$), and test-retest reliability in the interval of 2 weeks was 0.99.

In another group of studies of the LSAS, a version for the population of children and adolescents was proposed and developed by Masia et al (2003) and called Liebowitz_Social Anxiety Scale for Children and Adolescents (LSAS-CA). The LSAS-CA items were generated from two sources. First, items were formed from reports of the 10 most feared situations of a group of 33 adolescents with SP (Hofmann et al, 1999). Second, items on the adult version that were not generated by the first method were included with slight wording changes if they were considered developmentally appropriate. For example, the LSAS question, "*Participating in small groups*," was modified to "*Participating in work groups in the classroom.*" The majority of the LSAS-CA items (15 items) were consistent across both sources. The resulting measure consists of 24 items: 12 social interaction situations (e.g., "*looking at people you don't know well in the eye*") and 12 performance situations (e.g., "*asking questions in class*"). The administration procedure, rating scales, and scoring structure from the adult LSAS were retained. Clinician ratings of anxiety (0 = none, 1 = mild, 2 = moderate, 3 = severe) and avoidance (0 = never, 1 = occasionally, 2 = often, 3 = usually) are given for each of the 24 items for a total of 48 ratings. Thus, the LSAS-CA provides seven scores: anxiety related to social interaction; performance anxiety; total anxiety;

avoidance of social interaction; avoidance of performance situations; total avoidance; and a total LSAS-CA score.

Table 7. Psychometric studies conducted with the Liebowitz Social Anxiety Scale (LSAS) and psychometric qualities demonstrated

Study	Objective	Sample	Internal consi-tency	Concurrent/ divergent validity	Discrimin-ative validity	Factorial analysis Predictive validity	T/R Reliability
Heimberg et al., 1999 (USA)	Psychometric study: hetero-applied version	N = 382 SP x= 35.1 years	α = 0.81-0.96	SIAS = 0.52 – 0.76 SPS = 0.47 – 0.65	Fear and avoidance subscales = highly correlated	pre-treatment score >post-treatment score	
Safren et al., 1999 (USA)	Factorial analysis: hetero-applied version	N = 382 SP x= 35.1 years	----	FNE = 0.18 – 0.46 FQ = 0.38 – 0.53 SADS = 0.32 – 0.57 SIAS = 0.33 – 0.72 SPS = 0.37 – 0.47	----	4 factors: -social interaction - public speaking - observation by others - eating and drinking in public	----
Fresco et al., 2001 (USA)	Compar-ing hetero- and self-applied versions	N = 152 SP NSP adults	α = 0.71-0.95	Self = hetero SIAS = 0.58 – 0.77 SPS = 0.47 – 0.66 FQ = 0.47 – 0.64 BDI = 0.25 – 0.46 HRSD = 0.13 – 0.24	----	----	----
Levin et al., 2002 (Israel)	Study of factorial analysis	N = 207 SP OAD x =35.2 years	α = 0.91	CGI = 0.52 – 0.65 MMPI-SI = 0.51 – 0.64 SDS = 0.22 – 0.28 MADRS = 0.40 – 0.48	SP score> OAD score ♀ = ♂	3 factors: -group performance and group interaction - dyalic interaction - public activities pre-treatment score >post-treatment score	0.87 – 0.91 (6 weeks)

Table 7. (Continued)

Study	Objective	Sample	Internal consi-tency	Concurrent/ divergent validity	Discrimin-ative validity	Factorial analysis Predictive validity	T/R Reliability
Backer et al., 2002 (USA)	Psychometric study of the self-applied version	N = 175 SP x =32.2 years	α = 0.79 – 0.95	SPAI = 0.48 - 0.83 SPS = 0.08 - 0.44 Self x hetero = 0.78 -0.85 BDI = 0.44 – 0.48 ASI = 0.17 – 0.19	----	5 factors - social interaction - nonverbal performance - ingestion -public performance - assertiveness pre-treatment score >post-treatment score	0.53 - 0.85 (12 weeks)
Mennin et al., 2002 (USA)	Psychometric study of the hetero-applied version	N = 389 SP NSP 18- 65 years	----	----	Cut-off note30: DE = 93% (SP) Cut-off note 60: DE=72.5% (SPg)	----	----
Oakman et al., 2003 (Canada)	Factorial analysis of the self-applied version	N = 188 SP OAD x =34.3 years	α = 0.75 – 0.96	----	SP score > OAD score	4 factors: Proposed by Safren et al (1999)	----
Heimberg & Holaway 2007 (USA)	Psychometric study of the hetero-applied version	N = 107 SP NSP OAD x = 27 – 32.9 years	α = 0.84 – 0.97	----	SP score> NSP and OAD scores More discriminative factors: -public speaking -social interaction	----	----

Study	Objective	Sample	Internal consi-tency	Concurrent/ divergent validity	Discrimin-ative validity	Factorial analysis Predictive validity	T/R Reliability
Bobes et al., 1999 (Spain)	Psychometric study of the Spanish hetero-applied version	N = 57 SP NSP x =35.9 years	α = 0.61 – 0.93	HAM = 0.29 – 0.44 SEAG= -0.24 - - 0.29 EVA = -0.27 - - 0.40	SP score> NSP score Suggested cut-off note: between 19.6 and 26.1	----	0.82- 0.88 (2 weeks)
Yao et al., 1999 (France)	Psychometric study of the French self- and hetero-applied versions	N = 160 SP NSP x = 30 - 35.4 years	----	SISST = 0.48 – 0.52 BDI = ns	SP score> NSP (self and hetero)	pre-treatment score > post-treatment score	----
Soyakan et al., 2003 (Turkey)	Psychometric study of the Turkish hetero-applied version	N = 168 SP NSP OAD adults	α = 0.95 – 0.98	BAI = 0.21- 0.26	SP score> NSP and OAD score Cut-off note 50: DE = 95.5% (SP)	3 factors: - performance/ group interaction -dual interaction -individual activities in a group	0.97 (1 week)
Terra et al., 2006a (Brazil)	Psychometric study of the Brazilian hetero-applied version	N = 300 adult alcoholics	α = 0.95	----	----	5 factors: - speaking in groups -activity in public - social interaction/ unknown person -attitude disagreement or disapproval - social interaction in leisure activity 52.9% variance	----

Table 7. (Continued)

Study	Objective	Sample	Internal consistency	Concurrent/ divergent validity	Discriminative validity	Factorial analysis Predictive validity	T/R Reliability
Crippa et al (Brazil)	Psychometric study of the self-applied Brazilian version	N = 204 to 431 SP NSP X = 20.9 - 22.3 years university students	----	SPIN = 0.85 BSPS = 0.89 BAI = 0.59	SP score> NSP score	----	0.99

ASI = Anxiety Sensitivity Index; BAI = Beck Anxiety Inventory; BDI = Beck Depression Inventory; BSPS = Brief Social Phobia Scale; CGI = Clinical Global Impression; DE = diagnostic efficacy; EVA = Escala Visual Analógica del Cuestionario de Calidad de Vida SpuroQol; FNE = Fear Negative Evaluation; FQ = Fear Questionnaire; HAM = Hamilton Rating Scale for Anxiety; HRSD = Hamilton Rating Scale for Depression; MADRS = Montgomery and Asberg Depression Rating Scale; MMPI-SI = Minnesota Multiphasic Personality Inventory- subscale social introversion; N = number of subjects; NSP = subjects without social phobia; OAD = subjects com other anxiety disorders; SADS = Social Avoidance Distress Scale; SDS = Sheehan Disabilities Scales; SEAG = Subescala de Evaluación de la Actividad Global; SIAS = Social Interaction Anxiety Scale; SISST = Social Interaction Self-Statement Test; SP = subjects with social phobia; SPg = generalized social phobia; SPIN = Social Phobia Inventory; SPS = Social Phobia Scale; T/R = test-retest; α = Cronbach alpha; x = mean; ♀ = women; ♂ = men.

The psychometric study of the LSAS-CA was conducted on a sample of 154 US children and adolescents with a mean age of 13.4 years. The results revealed excellent internal consistency (α = 0.83 to 0.97) and test-retest reliability (0.89 to 0.94 – one week). Concurrent validity with the SPAI (0.69-0.82), SPAI-C (0.6-0.75), Clinical Global Impression (CGI = 0.61- 0.68) and Global Assessment of Functioning (GAF = -0.61 to 0.68) was also quite adequate. When discriminative validity was tested, subjects with SP presented higher scores than subjects without the disorder. For a cut-off score of 22.5, the diagnostic efficacy of the scale was 95.9%.

Later, Storch et al (2006) conducted another factorial study of the LSAS-CR in a sample of US children and adolescents aged on average 13.22 years. The children were healthy or had SP or other anxiety disorders. The results showed that the best factorial model was the two-factor one (Social Anxiety and School Performance Anxiety). The two factors showed adequate internal consistency (0.93 and 0.87, respectively) and concurrent validity with measures of social anxiety such as the SPAI (0.62 to 0.66) and with measures of functional impairment (GAF: 0.47 to 0.62).

Many studies have been conducted using the LSAS, with outstanding refinement compared to studies of previously validated instruments. All studies demonstrated good adequacy of the LSAS in its two versions, self- and hetero-applied, and in the version for children and adolescents, with good indicators of test-retest reliability, internal consistency, and convergent, divergent and discriminant validity, especially in the assessment of clinical populations. Regarding criterion validity, there was a consensus among studies about the fact that the initial two-factor model is poorly adequate and there are divergences about the most appropriate factorial model, with a tendency to a prevalent acceptance of the four-factor model described by Safren et al (1999). The good psychometric qualities of the scale have stimulated its use in different cultures, motivating the study of versions in other languages. This analysis shows that the LSAS tends to become the universally accepted as the main "gold standard" for studies on SP.

This tendency can be seen by examining the empirical studies conducted on SP, in which the LSAS was the instrument most extensively used. Exemples of these studies and their main objectives are: relationship between alexithymia and social anxiety in females with dermatological disorder presenting for psychiatric consultation (Evren & Evren, 2007); efficacy of SP treatment with fluvoxamine in Japan (Asakura et al, 2007); efficacy of cognitive behavioral therapy in Chinese subjects with SP (Wong & Sun, 2006); prevalence of SP among Brazilian alcoholics (Terra et al, 2006); efficacy of SP treatment with nefazodone (Van-Ameringen et al, 2007), escitalopram and paroxetine (Stein et al 2006); prevalence of SP in Saudi Arabia (Bassiony, 2005); efficacy of venlafaxine-ER for SP treatment (Rickels et al, 2004); efficacy of psychodynamic therapy for SP treatment in Brazil (Knijnik et al, 2004); efficacy of SP treatment with reboxetine (Atmaca et al, 2003), milnacipram (Nagata et al, 2003), and valproic acid (Kinrys et al, 2003), among others.

2.2.2. Brief Social Phobia Scale (BSPS)

The Brief Social Phobia Scale (BSPS) is a hetero-applicable instrument proposed by Davidson et al. (1991) in order to screen and quantitate the different symptoms characteristic of SP. It consists of 18 items divided into three subscales (fear, avoidance and physiological symptoms) which are scored on a five-point Likert scale (0 = none/ never; 4 = extremely incapacitating and/or very painfully distressing/always-100%), which, when summed, produce a total score of 0 to 76 points. Examples of its items are: "being embarrassed or humiliated"; and "trembling or shaking".

Davidson et al. (1997) studied the psychometric qualities of the instrument in a sample of SP cases (N = 275), which were found to be adequate. The internal consistency assessed by the Cronbach alpha ranged from 0.60 to 0.91 for the total scale and the subscales and the test-retest reliability was 0.91 with an interval of one week. Concurrent validity was studied in relation to the LSAS, FNE and Hamilton Anxiety Scale (HAM-A). High correlations (0.70 to 0.72) were detected with the LSAS, a scale for the hetero-assessment of social anxiety disorder (SAD), and with the FNE (0.43 to 0.51). In contrast, the correlations with the HAM-A, a general anxiety scale, ranged from 0.20 to 0.34.

The BSPS was found to be able to discriminate the effects associated with the pharmacological treatment of SP, a result demonstrating its predictive validity. Factorial analysis indicated the presence of the following six factors with self-values between 5.00 and 1.07: Factor 1 - general fears and avoidances (items 2M, 4M, 5M, 2E, 3E, 4E, 5E); Factor 2 - physiological symptoms (items 1SP, 2SP, 3SP, 4SP); Factor 3 - fear and avoidance of doing something while being observed (items 7M, 7E); Factor 4 - fear and avoidance of public speaking (1M, 1E); Factor 5- fear and avoidance of social events (items 6M, 6E); and Factor 6 – fear of talking to strangers (item 3M).

This instrument is being extensively used in pharmacological studies of SP (Stein et al, 1999; Allgulander, 1999; Walker et al, 2000; Emmanuel et al, 2000; Van-Amerigen et al, 2001; Barnett et al, 2002; Davidson et al, 2004; Zhang et al, 2005; Connor et al, 2006) but no other psychometric studies of BSPS have been detected in the literature, either in the American context or in different cultures or age ranges.

An exception is the studies conducted by our research group. Osório et al (2006) performed the transcultural validation of the BSPS for Brazilian Portuguese and also proposed a guide-question list in order to systematize the application of the instrument. This list consists of questions grouped into six categories of investigation: 1) Social Gatherings: part 1– item 6 (fear and avoidance); 2) Physiological Arousal: part 2– items 1, 2, 3 and 4; 3) Being Observed: part 1– item 7 (fear and avoidance); 4) Speaking/Talking: part 1– items 1, 2 and 3 (fear and avoidance); 5) Being Embarrassed: part 1– item 4 (fear and avoidance); 6) Feeling Criticized: part 1– item 5 (fear and avoidance).

The initial study of inter-rater reliability using the BSPS, assessed by the intraclass correlation coefficient, was quite adequate, with values from 0.76 to 0.88.

Other analyses regarding the validity and reliability of the BSPS are being performed by our group. In a study of a sample of cases (N = 88) and non-cases (N = 90) of SP, the internal consistency of the scale was found to be adequate, ranging from 0.48 to 0.88. Similarly, concurrent validity in relation to the BAI and SPIN was satisfactory, with correlations between 0.21 and 0.62 and 0.24 and 0.82, respectively. Discriminative validity proved to be escellent, with 0.84 to 0.88 sensitivity, 0.81 to 0.83 speficicity, 0.82 to 0.85 positive predictive value, 0.87 to 0.89 negative predictive value, and 85% diagnostic efficacy, for a cut-off note of 18 to 19. The BSPS was also sensitive in differentiating subjects as a function of gender.

In factorial analysis, the most adequate solutions consisted of six factors. In general, the factors explained 71.79% of data variance. Factor 1 consisted of items 3M, 3E, 4M, 4E, 5M and 5E and was called "fear and avoidance of interaction with strangers and of situations of social evaluation". This factor differed from Factor 1 of the original study ("general fears and avoidances") since items 2M and 2E of the original study were part of Factor 1, whereas in the later study the were part of Factor 6 exclusively ("fear and avoidance of figures of authority"), with an auto-value of 1.11. Factor 2, in agreement with the original study, consisted of four items of the physiological symptoms subscale. Factor 3 of the present study ("fear and avoidance of public speaking") was correlated with Factor 4 of the original study and consisted of the four items of the original study ("fear and avoidance of public speaking"), indicating that the aspects related to public speaking have a slightly more significant weight in the context of Brazilian university students. Factor 4 of the present study ("fear and avoidance of social events") was related to Factor 5 of the study by Davidson et al. (1997) ("fear and avoidance of social events"), again showing a more significant weight for this factor and for the aspects assessed by it within our context. In contrast, Factor 5 ("fear of being observed") was correlated with Factor 3 of the study by Davidson et al. (1997) ("fear and avoidance of doing something while being observed"), indicating a lower weight of this item in the Brazilian context.

Analysis of test-retest reliability confirmed the initial findings of excellent reliability of the BSPS applied with the aid of a guide question script, with correlations of 0.92 to 1.00.

In general, the Brazilian Portuguese version of the BSPS proved to have quite adequate psychometric qualities, with highly satisfactory validity and reliability rates, in agreement with the original study by Davidson et al (1997). Thus, the BSPS showed psychometric qualities compatible with those of the LSAS, although it has been less studied at this level, with the need for further exploration.

2.3. Scales for the assessment of non-generalized social phobia

2.3.1. Personal Report of Confidence as a Speaker Questionnaire (PRCS)

The Personal Report of Confidence as a Speaker Questionnaire (PRCS) originally proposed by Gilkinson (1942), was to assess the degree of confidence as a speaker. Paul (1966) later shortened this instrument to 30 items scored on a dichotomous scale (true or false), this being the version more frequently used. The PRCS shows adequate internal consistency and validity, but the test-retest reliability and its utility are limited by its scoring form.

No empirical studies using the PRCS were detected in the literature. However, a psychometric study was conducted using the Spanish version of the instrument (Mendez er al, 2004). The sample consisted of 788 adolescents aged 12 to 17 years and the results indicated adequate internal consistency (0.84) and test-retest- reliability (0.81). Convergent validity with the SPAI was 0.53, and factorial analysis indicated the presence of two factors: Security/Enjoyment of Public Speaking and Fear of Public Speaking. The study also revealed differences between sexes and ages regarding the aspects assessed by the scale, with women reporting less confidence in public speaking, which decreased with age.

2.3.2. Personal Report of Communication Apprehension (PRCA)

The Personal Report of Communication Apprehension (PRCA) was developed by McCroskey (1978) to assess apprehension during public speaking, public meetings and groups discussions. This is a 24 item scale that is rated on a 5 point Likert scale. Examples of items include the following: *"I dislike participating in group discussions"; " I am afraid to express myself at meetings"; " I feel relaxed while giving a speech*".

Many studies have been conducted using the PRCA since its publication, also involving the Japanese and Spanish versions of the instrument. Many of these studies involve a comparison of the level of communication apprehension in different cultures (Pryor et al 2005; Sarquisse et al, 2003; Yook & Ahn, 1999; Hansford & Hattie, 1982) and among students (Burk, 2001). The scale has also been used in studies of family communication patterns (Elwood & Schrader, 1998), stutter (Blood et al, 1994) and shyness (Manning & Ray, 1993), among others.

2.3.3. Self Statements During Public Speaking Scale (SSPS)

The Self-Statements During Public Speaking Scale (SSPS) is an instrument developed by Hofmann and DiBartolo (2000) based on the SISST for self-assessment in the public speaking situation, one of the most prevalent fears both in the general population and among subjects with SP. The instrument is based on cognitive theories that assume that social anxiety is the result of negative self-perception and a negative perception of others with respect to oneself. The instrument is self-applicable and consists of two subscales, i.e., positive self-assessment and negative self-assessment, each containing five items scored on a scale from 0 (not agree at all) to 5 (agree extremely), with a maximum total score of 50 points. Examples of its items are: *"What do I have to lose; it's worth a try"; "I feel awkward and dumb; they're bound to notice"*. The psychometric qualities of the scale were studied in a sample of the general population of healthy college students and non-students and in SP cases. The alpha value for SO non-cases was 0.75 to 0.86. Factorial analysis indicated the presence of two factors with self-values of 4.27 and 1.55, respectively, explaining 58.2% of the variance, i.e., positive self-assessment (Factor 1 - items 1, 3, 5, 6, 9) and negative self-assessment (Factor 2 – items 2, 4, 7, 8, 10).

Convergent validity in relation to the PRCS, FNE and SADS indicated significant correlations (-0.58 to 0.67, -0.29 to 0.49, and -0.30 to 0.37, respectively), confirming the adequacy of the SSPS. For cases, internal consistency ranged from 0.80 to 0.86 and test-retest reliability was 0.78 to 0.80 (three months). The SSPS was also able to discriminate between cases and non-cases of SP, with cases presenting higher scores on the negative subscales and lower scores on the positive subscale, and was also sensitive in pointing out changes due to behavioral treatment involving live exposure to the public speaking situation, with a significant reduction in score on the negative subscale after treatment.

The SSPS has also been studied by our research group in Brazil. After being translated into Portuguese, the scale was studied in terms of its psychometric adequacy in samples of the general population and of SP cases and non-cases. For the general population sample (N = 2314) the results revealed internal consistency of 0.78 to 0.90; concurrent validity with the BAI (0.18 to 0.53) and SPIN (0.22 to 0.65), discriminative validity regarding differences between sexes (a greater negative self-assessment among women than among men). Factorial analysis indicated the presence of two factors, positive self-assessment and negative self-assessment, explaining 52% of data variance. For the sample of cases and non-cases (N = 178), internal consistency was 0.64 to 0.94 and concurrent validity was 0.22 to 0.33 with the BAI and 0.22 to 0.33 with the SPIN. The SSPS was also sensitive in discriminating between subjects with SP and subjects without the disorder.

The above data demonstrate the adequacy of the SSPS for use in the Brazilian population, with psychometric qualities similar to those of the original study. The general scale was found to be quite adequate for use in different samples, with emphasis on the fact that, in contrast to the original study of the scale, the positive subscale seems to be more effective for the assessment of samples with identified or suspected SP and the negative subscale is characterized more by a screening quality for use in the general population.

The SSPS was also translated into German and its psychometric qualities were investigated in a sample of students with SP (Gerlach et al, 2007). The results indicated that the German version was adequate, with indicators close to those of the original study.

No empirical study using the SSPS was detected in the literature surveyed, although a "state" version (SSPS-E) has been used in the Simulated Public Speaking test, wich is a highly used model of anxiety.

2.3.4. Speech Anxiety Thoughts Inventory (SATI)

Proposed by Cho et al (2004), the Speech Anxiety Thoughts Inventory (SATI) was elaborated based on the 32 items of the original Korean version of the Speech Anxiety Automatic Thoughts Questionnaire (SAATQ – Cho, 2001) which were translated into English. Originally, the items were derived from dysfunctional thought records of 35 SP patients collected during cognitive behavioral treatment and thoughts reported by 140 undergraduate students while imagining a public speaking situation. The final version of the SATI was reached on the basis of factorial analysis and consisted of 23 items scored on a five-point Likert scale (1 = never; 5 = very often). Some of the items of the scale are: *"It would be terrible if my voice will tremble"; "It would be terrible if others think I'm not intelligent"; "My behavior will appear awkward to the audience"; " I must deliver a good speech in order to gain approval from the audience".*

The authors evaluated the factorial composition of the scale and detected two factors: Prediction of poor performance and Fear of negative evaluation by audience, which explained 51.3% of the data. The internal consistency of the SATI was 0.94 and its test-retest reliability was 0.64 to 0.71.Concurrent validity was analyzed in relation to the SSPS, PRCS and LSAS, with moderate and strong correlations being found with these instruments. The data of this study indicated adequacy of the SATI.

The SATI is a recently proposed instrument whose psychometric aspects have not been studied in depth after the original study. Also, its applicability to empirical studies has not yet been demonstrated.

2.4. Scales for the Assessment of Functional Disability Associated with Social Phobia

2.4.1. Liebowitz Self-Rated Disability Scale (LSRDS)

The Liebowitz Self-Rated Disability Scale (LSRDS) was proposed by Liebowitz (1987) with the objective of assessing functional disability due to SP. It consists of 11 items, with scores ranging from 0 (problem does not limit me at all) to 4 (problem limits me severely). It assesses current (past two weeks) and most severe lifetime impairment due to SP. Domains include school, work, family, marriage/ dating, friendship, other interests (e.g. hobbies and religious activities), activities of living, and suicidal behavior. It also includes items on alcohol, drug abuse, and mood regulation. Items may be totaled for current and lifetime disability assessments, or items may be reported separately for descriptive use. Examples of its items are: "*Having mostly comfortable interactions with the members of my family*"; "*Pursuing hobbies and other interests (e.g. religion, sports, etc)"; "Drinking alcohol in moderation (without overdoing it)*".

The first psychometric study of this instrument was carried out by Scheneir et al (1994) on a sample of 46 cases and non-cases of SP. The aspects studied were test-retest reliability (0.92), concurrent validity with the Sheehan Disability Scale (SDS: 0.56 – 0.73) and discriminative validity, with social phobics obtaining higher scores for disability compared to non-phobic subjects. Another psychometric study of the LSRDS was conducted by Hambrick et al (2004) on a sample of 153 social phobic subjects aged on average 32.8 years. The authors detected good psychometric indicators of the instrument, i.e., internal consistency of 0.75 to 0.82 concurrent validity with the disability profile (DP) (0.53 to 0.71), SDS (0.39 to

0.70), BFNE (0.40 to 0.43), SIAS (0.44 to 0.50), SPS (0.31 to 0.43), LSAS (0.42 to 0.51), BDI (0.39 to 0.60), and Quality of Life Inventory (QOLI: - 0.41 to -0.51), and discriminative validity, with the ability to discriminate between subjects with generalized and non-generalized SP.

In Brazil, our research group is also conducting a psychometric study of the LSRDS. The initial data obtained with a sample of 173 university students, cases and non-cases of SP, has revealed internal consistency of 0.83 to 0.93 and concurrent validity with the SPIN ranging from 0.21 to 0.50. Factorial analysis indicated the presence of three factors which, taken together, explain 64.4% of data variance: Activity and Performance, Relations and Interests, and Risk Indicators.

In an empirical study using the LSRDS, Wittchen et al (1999) assessed disability and quality of life in pure and comorbid SP and found that the scale was quite sensitive in detecting differences between the two groups.

In general, the LSRDS has proved to be a psychometrically adequate instrument for self-assessment of the impairment associated with SP. The scale is still little used in empirical investigations and needs more refined psychometric studies to expand its qualities at this level.

2.4.2. The Disability Profile (DP)

The Disability Profile (DP) is a interviewer-rated scale used to assess functional disability due to SP which was proposed by Liebowitz in 1987. It consists of eight items, the scores of which range from 0 to 4. An example of its items is: *Item 4 - Marriage/ Dating: 0- no impairment from this disorder; 1- distress but no impairment in dating or marriage; 2- moderate impairment (e.g. dating somewhat less frequently than desired, mildly impaired functioning on dates, or minor marital problems); 3- severe impairment (e.g. dating infrequently, markedly impaired functioning on dates, major marital problems, separation or divorce); 4- extreme (unable to date or marry).*

The first psychometric study of the DS was conducted by Schneier et al., only in 1994. These authors studied the instrument in a sample of 46 subjects with and without a diagnosis of SP and detected internal consistency of 0.87 (two weeks) and 0.90 (lifelong), and concurrent validity of 0.56 to 0.79 with the SDS. Hambrick et al (2004) also studied the qualities of the DP in a sample of 153 subjects with SP aged 19 to 65 years. Internal consistency was 0.71 to 0.79 and concurrent validity regarding different measures of social anxiety was 0.53 to 0.71 with the LSRDS, 0.47 to 0.50 with the BFNE, 0.60 to 0.61 with the SIAS, 0.38 to 0.48 with the SPS, and 0.63 to 0.72 with the LSAS. The correlation detected with the QOLI, a measure of quality of life, was -0.45 to -0.50. The discriminative validity of the DP was also demonstrated, with the instrument being able to discriminate between subjects with generalized SP and subjects with non-generalized SP.

Our group has also been studying this instrument. When applied to a sample of Brazilian university students with and without SP (N = 173), the DP showed 0.67 to 0.75 inter-rater reliability, 0.75 internal consistency, and 0.23 to 0.41 concurrent validity with the SPIN. Factorial analysis demonstrated the presence of two factors explaining 51.8% of the variance: Factor 1 – Performance and family relations, and Factor 2 – Self-care and self-maintenance activities, affective relations and suicidal behavior.

An important empirical study using the DP was conducted by Lochner et al (2006) to assess the efficacy of SP treatment with topiramate.

Although proposed long ago, the DP still needs psychometric studies that will dimension and attest to the good psychometric qualities demonstrated thus far only by the few studies cited above.

2.5. Scales for the evaluation of specific aspects of Social Phobia

2.5.1. Social Phobia Safety Behaviours Scale – SPSAS

The Social Phobia Safety Behaviours Scale (SPSAS) is a self-filled questionnaire designed to evaluate safety behaviors that social phobics use in the feared situations. Safety behaviors have been defined as a wide range of behaviors that social phobics carry out when in social situations and through which they try to reduce the risk of negative evaluation, trying to prevent feared outcomes from occurring. These behaviors have quite precise links with specific feared outcomes and can be overt or covert. Safety Behaviors function as important maintenance factors since they prevent disconfirmation from occurring, can increase their feared symptoms, and can contaminate the social situation.

The instrument was proposed by Pinto-Gouveia et al (2003). Based on clinical interviews with social phobics, a number of items representative of the safety behaviors most frequently used by these patients were selected. These items underwent a process of analysis in which the correlation of each with the total score of the scale was evaluated, and 15 were then used as components of the SPSBS. Using a 1 (never) to 4 (usually) scale, subjects were asked to evaluate how frequently they used each safety behavior once in the feared social situation. At the end of the scale, through the filling of two blank lines, subjects had the opportunity to add other safety behaviors they considered relevant and which had not been included in the scale.

Examples of its items are: *"Accelerating speech, talking rapidly and without pauses", "Walking while looking down at the ground", "Keeping one's hands in one's pockets", "Limiting oneself to being a passive spectator of the situation".*

The psychometric study of the SPSBS was performed by the creators of the scale (Pinto-Gouveia et al, 2003) using a sample of 655 subjects from the general population with a diagnosis of SP and of other anxiety disorders. The indicators studied were: internal consistency (0.82 to 0.87), test-retest reliability (4 weeks: 0.69), discriminative validity (the scores of subjects with SP are statistically higher than those of subjects with other anxiety disorders and subjects from the general population), and concurrent validity (SIPAAS = 0.42 to 0.61; SADS = 0.29 to 0.49; FNE =0.27 to 0.49; SDS = 0.24 to 0.42). The cut-off score proposed for the instrument was 36.

The studies conducted with this instrument in Brazil by our research group on samples of SP cases and non-cases (N =155) are still underway but have demonstrated internal consistency of 0.92, test-retest reliability of 0.41 to 0.90 (2 weeks), and convergent validity with the SPIN of 0.11 to 0.47. Factorial analysis of the SPSBS revealed the presence of a single factor explaining 54.1% of data variance. The instrument presented discriminative validity, with 0.96 sensitivity, and 1.00 specificity.

Although little studied, the SPSBS is important for its specific objective which is not considered in other instruments. The psychometric analyses within the context of the

Portuguese and Brazilian culture have proved to be adequate, but further studies assessing the instrument in other contexts would be relevant.

2.5.2. Social Thoughts and Beliefs Scale - STABS

The Social Thoughts and Beliefs Scale (STABS) was developed by Turner et al. (2003). It is a 21 item empirically derived self-report instrument that was developed to assess the presence of various pathologic cognitions in social phobia. The instrument asks the respondent to rate the degree to which a particular thought or belief is typical of his or her thinking when anticipating or participating in a social encounter. The items are scored on a four-point Likert scale (1 = not at all characteristic; 4 = extremely characteristic). The following items are examples of those composing the scale: *"I am a coward when it comes to interacting with other people"; "My mind is very likely to go blank when I am talking in a social situation"; "When other people laugh it feels as if they are laughing at me".*

The investigators who created the instrument performed the initial study of its psychometric qualities by applying the scale to a sample of 300 US subjects with a diagnosis of SP or with other anxiety disorders and normal controls aged on average 35.1 years. Factorial analysis pointed out the presence of two factors which, together, explain 62% of data variance. Factor 1 was denoted Social Comparison because it consisted of beliefs that others are more socially competent and capable. Factor 2 was denoted Social Ineptness because it consisted of beliefs that one will act awkwardly in social situations or appear anxious in front of others. The internal consistency of the STABS was 0.96 and the test-retest reliability over a period of 4 weeks was 0.94. The STABS as a whole and in terms of its factors was sensitive in discriminating between subjects with SP and those with other anxiety disorders and controls. The correct classification rate for subjects with SP was 91.7%. This study showed the psychometric potential of the scale, although further investigations are needed to assess its convergent validity and to study in depth the aspects regarding reliability and discriminability, especially in other cultural contexts. Studies with this objective have not been detected in the literature thus far. The STABS could be a significant step in fostering further understanding of how cognitions might be involved in the course and treatment outcome of SP, being of great value for the development of empirical studies.

FINAL CONSIDERATIONS

In general, all the instruments studied showed acceptable psychometric qualities within the patterns investigated. In most studies, these analyses were done using a wide variety of samples involving different age ranges, educational levels, and cultural contexts.

Regarding the diagnostic interviews, all four major scales (SCID-IV, CIDI, ADIS and MINI) proved to be adequate instruments for the systematic assessment of SP. Although they are seldom used, they may be of high values for the establishment of a diagnosis of both SP and of associated co-morbidities in clinical practice. In the research context, these instruments are particularly important and are used as the gold standard, with emphasis on the SCID-IV.

Most instruments are included in the category of self-evaluation and measurement of SP symptoms, assessing specific and general aspects of SP and aspects correlated with the disorder. The psychometric adequacy and empirical use of some instruments have been universally recognized. In general, these are the instruments developed long ago such as the FNE, SIAS, SPS and SPAI. Among the instruments proposed more recently, many differ little in their objectives compared to older instruments and therefore are little used in applied studies despite their good psychometric qualities. An exception is the SPIN, a scale that has gained great empirical applicability in more recent studies, with emphasis on the adequacy of its reduced version.

Current studies tend to be devoted to the development of reduced scales, favoring a rapid and practical application with a consequent large-scale use. Among the instruments presented, the reduced versions of the SPIN and FNE seem to be well established, while the reduced version of the SPAI still needs further studies for the validation of its applicability.

The SPAI-C stands out as the only self-applied scale specifically used for the evaluation of SP symptoms in children.

The number of hetero-evaluation scales available is much lower than the number of self-evaluation instruments even though SP is a disorder of difficult self-recognition. Among them is the LSAS, an instrument that has been studied in a large number of investigations with a high level of refinement. It is a fully recognized measure for the evaluation of SP and is currently available in different versions in addition to the original one, tending to be considered the gold standard in different studies. The BSPS, although less studied at the psychometric level, is also frequently used in important empirical studies, especially those related to clinical assays for the testing of medications.

The scales that assess aspects of non-generalized SP usually aim to evaluate aspects related to fear of public speaking. These instruments have been little studied regarding the remaining aspects pointed out earlier and will require further studies to demonstrate their adequacy. Among them, the PRCA and SSPS seem to have better recognition and applicability.

Regarding the scales that assess the losses associated with SP, the number of instruments available are small and of low applicability, and few psychometric studies of the proposed scales are available. Instruments of this nature are important for the planning of therapeutic interventions and for the assessment of their efficacy, with a need for further studies that will expand and validate their applicability in a more systematic manner.

The scales that evaluate specific aspects of SP have been proposed only recently but are of great importance because they expand the knowledge about the variables involved in the development of, and coping with, SP and should be further investigated in studies on more diversified samples.

Considering the instruments presented here as a whole, it can be seen that they form a vast and diversified arsenal covering different aspects of SP. We believe that the recognition and systematic evaluation of this disorder can be considerably facilitated by the use of these scales, favoring an early diagnosis and therefore preventing the development of co-morbidities that would lead to a more reserved prognosis for SP.

References

Allgulander, C. (1999). Paroxetina in social anxiety disorder: a randomized placebo controlled study. *Acta Psychiatrica Scandinavica, 100 (3)*,193-198.

American Psychiatric Association (APA). (1994). *Diagnostic and Statistical Manual of Mental Disorders (Fourth Edition).* Washingtonn, DC: American Psychiatric Association.

Amorin, P. (2000). Mini International Neuropsychiatric Interview (MINI): validation of a short structured diagnostic psychiatry interview. *Revista Brasileira de Psiquiatria, 22 (3)*, 106-115.

Andrews, P. & Peters, L. (1998). The psychometric properties of the Composite International Diagnostic Interview. *Social Psychiatry and Psichiatric Epidemiology, 33*, 80-88.

Antony, M.A.; Coons, M.J.; Mccabe, R.E.; Ashbaugh, A. & Swinson, R.P. (2006). Psychometric properties of the social phobia inventory: further evaluation. *Behaviour Research Therapy, 44*, 1177-1185.

Asakura, S.; Inoue, S.; Sasaki, F.; Sasaki, Y.; Kitagawa, N.; Inoue, T.; Denda, K.; Koyama, T.; Ito, M. & Matsubara, R. (2002). Reliability an validity of the Japanese version of the Liebowitz Social Anxiety Scale. *Seishin-Igaku, 44 (10)*, 1077-1084.

Asakura, S.; Tajima, O. & Koyama, T. (2007). Fluvoxamine treatment of generalized social anxiety disorder in Japan: a randomized double-blind, placebo-controlled study. *International Journal of Neuropsychopharmacology, 10 (2)*, 263-274.

Atmaca, M.; Tezcan, E. & Kuloglu, M. (2003). An open clinical trial of reboxetine in the treatment of social phobia. *Journal of Clinical Psychopharmacology, 23 (4)*, 417-419.

Backer, S.L.; Heinrichs, N.; Hyo-Jin, K. & Hofmann, S.G. (2002). The Liebowitz Social Anxiety Scale as a self-report instrument: a preliminary psychometric analysis. *Behaviour Research and Therapy, 40*, 701-715.

Baldwin, D.; Bobes, J.; Stein, D.J.; Scharwächter, I. & Faure, M. (1999). Paroxetine in social phobia/ social anxiety disorder. Randomised, double-blind placebo-controlled study. *British Journal of Psychiatry, 175*, 120-126.

Baños, R.M.; Botella, C.; Quero, S. & Medina, P. (2007). The social phobia and anxiety inventory: psychometric properties in a Spanish sample. *Psychological Reports, 100 (2)*, 441-450.

Barnett, S.D.; Kramer, M.L.; Casat, C.D.; Connor, K.M. & Davidson, J.R.T. (2002). Efficacy of olanzapine in social anxiety disorder: a pilot study. *Journal of Psychopharmacology, 16 (4)*, 365-368.

Bassiony, M.M. (2005). Social anxiety disorder and depression in Saudi Arabia. *Depression and Anxiety, 21 (2)*, 90-94.

Becker, C.B.; Namour, N.; Zayfert, C. & Hegel, M.T. (2001). Specifity on the Social Interaction Self-Statement Test in social phobia. *Cognitive Therapy and Research, 25 (2)*, 227-233.

Beidel, D.C.; Turner, S.M.; Stanley, M.A. & Dancu, C.V. (1989a). The Social Phobia and Anxiety Inventory: concurrent and external validity. *Behavior Therapy, 20 (3),* 417-427.

Beidel, D.C.; Borden, J.W.; Turner, S.M. & Jacob, R.G. (1989b). The Social Phobia and Anxiety Inventory: concurrent validity with a clinic sample. *Behaviour Research and Therapy, 27 (5)*, 573-576.

Beidel, D.C.; Turner, S.M. & Cooley, M.R. (1993). Assessing reliable and clinically significant change in social phobia: validity of the Social Phobia and Anxiety Inventory. *Behaviour Research and Therapy, 31*, 331-337.

Beidel, D.C.; Turner, S.M. & Morris, T.L. (1995). A new inventory to assess childhood social anxiety and phobia: The Social Phobia and Anxiety Inventory for Children. *Psychological Assessment, 7 (1)*, 73-79.

Beidel, D.C. (1996). Assessment of childhood social phobia: construct, convergent, and discriminative validity of the Social Phobia and Anxiety Inventory for Children (SPAI-C). *Psychological Assessment, 8 (3)*, 235-240.

Beidel, D.C.; Turner, S.M.; Hamlin, K. & Morris, T.L. (2000). The Social Phobia and anxiety Inventory for Children (SPAI-C): external and discriminative validity. *Behavior Therapy,* 31 (1), 75-87.

Benjamin, J.; Ben-zion, I.Z.; Karbofsky, E. & Dannon, P. (2000). Double-blind placebo controlled pilot study of paroxetine for specific phobia. *Psychopharmacology (Berl), 149 (2)*, 194-196.

Berrocal, C.; Moreno, M.A.R.; Montero, M.; Rando, M.A.; Rucci, P. & Cassano, G.B. (2006). Social anxiety and obsessive-compulsive spectra: validation of the SHY-SR and the OBS-SR among the Spanish population. *Psychiatry Research, 142*, 241-251.

Blood, G.W.; Blood, I.M.; Bennett, S. & Simpson, K.C. (1994). Subjetive anxiety measurements and cortisol responses in adults who stutter. *Journal of Speech and Hearing Research, 37 (4),* 760-768.

Bobes,J.; Badía, X.; Luque, A.; Garcia, M.; Gonzáles, M.P. & Dal-Rey, R. (1999). Validación de las versiones en español de los cuestionarios Liebowitz Social Anxiety Scale, Social Anxiety and Distress Scale y Sheehan Disability Inventory para la evaluación de la fobia social. *Medicina Clinica (Barcelona), 112*, 530-538.

Brown, E.S.; Turovsky, J.; Heimberg, R.G.; Juster, H.R.; Timothy, A. & Barlow, D.H. (1997). Validation of the Social Interaction Anxiety Scale and the Social Phobia Scale across the anxiety disorders. *Psychological Assessment, 9 (1)*, 21-27.

Brown, T.A.; White, K.S. & Barlow, D.H. (2005). A psychometric reanalysis of the Albany Panic and Phobia Questionnaire. *Behaviour Research and Therapy, 43 (3)*, 337-355.

Burk, J. (2001). Communication apprehension among Master's of Business Administration students: investigating a gap in communication education. *Communication Education, 50(1),* 51-58.

Carleton, R.N.; McCreary, D.R.; Norton, P.J. & Asmundson, G.J.G. (2006). Brief Fear of Negative Evaluation scale – revised. *Depression and Anxiety, 23*, 297-303.

Carleton, R.N.; Collimore, K.C. & Asmundson, G.J.G. (2007). Social anxiety and fear of negative evaluation: construct validity of the BNE-II. *Journal of Anxiety Disorders, 21*, 131-141.

Cho, Y.; Kim, E. & Won, H. (1997). Cognitive assessment of social anxiety (II): a study on the reliability and validity the Korean version of the Social Interaction Self-Statement Test. *Korean Journal of Clinical Psychology*, 16, 233-249.

Cho, Y. (2001). Cognitive assessment of speech anxiety: development and validation of an automatic thoughts questionnaire. *Korean Journal of Clinical Psychology, 19,* 831-851.

Cho, Y.; Smits, J.A.J. & Telch, M.J. (2004). The Speech Anxiety Thoughts Inventory: scale development and preliminary psychometric data. *Behaviour Research and Therapy, 42,* 13-25.

Chun-zi, P.; Xiao-ling, F. & Luo-chu, L. (2003). The validity and reliability of social avoidance and distress scale in Chinese students. *Chinese Journal of Clinical Psychology, 11 (4),* 279-281.

Clark, D.B.; Turner, S.M.; Beidel, D.C.; Donovan, J.E.; Kirisci, L. & Jacob, R.G. (1994). Reliability and validity of the Social Phobia and Anxiety Inventory for adolescents. *Psychological Assessment, 6(2),* 135-140.

Clark, D.B.; Feske, U.; Masia, C.L.; Spaulding, S.A.; Brown, C.; Mammen, O. & Shear, M.K.(1997). Systematic assessment of Social Phobia in clinical practice. *Depression and Anxiety, 6,* 47-61.

Collins, K.A.; Westra, H.A.; Dozois, D.J.A. & Stewart, S.H. (2005).The validity of the brief version of the Fear of Negative Evaluation Scale. *Anxiety Disorders, 19,* 345-359.

Compton, S.N.; Grant, P.J.; Chrisman, A.K.; Gammon, P.J.; Brown, V.L. & March, J.S. (2001). Sertraline in children and adolescents with social anxiety disorder: an open trial. *Journal of the American Academy of Child and Adolescent Psychiatry, 40 (5),* 564-571.

Connor, K.M.; Davidson, J.R.; Churchill, L.E.; Sherwood, A.; Foa, E. & Weisler, R.H. (2000). Psychometric properties of Social Phobia Inventory (SPIN). *British Journal of Psychiatry, 176,* 379-386.

Connor, K.M.; Kobak, K.A.; Churchill, L.E.; Katzelnick, D. & Davidson, J.R. (2001). Mini-Spin: A brief screening assessment for generalized social anxiety disorder. *Depression and Anxiety, 14,* 137-140.

Connor, K.M.; Cook, J.L. & Davidson, J.R.T. (2006). Botulinum toxin treatment of social anxiety disorder with hyperhidrosis: a placebo controlled double blind trial. *Journal of Clinical Psychiatry, 67 (1),* 30-36.

Cox, B.J.; Swinson, R.P. & Shaw, B.F. (1991). Value of the Fear Questionnaire in differentiating agoraphobia and social phobia. *British Journal of Psychiatric, 159,* 842-845.

Cox, B.J.; Parker, J.D.A.; Swinson, R.P. (1996). Confirmatory factor analysis of the Fear Questionnaire with social phobia patients. *British Journal of Psychiatry, 168 (4),* 497-499.

Cox, B.J.; Swinson, R.P. & Direnfeld, D.M. (1998). A comparison of social phobia outcome measures in cognitive-behavioral group therapy. *Behavior Modification, 22,* 285-297.

Crippa, J.A.; Osório, F.L.; Del-Ben, C.M.; Santos-Filho, A.; Baptista, C.A.; Freitas, M.C.S. & Loureiro, S.R. (2008). Comparability between telephone and face-to-face structured clinical interview for DSM-IV (SCID) in assessing social anxiety disorder. *Perspectives in Psychiatric Care.*

Davidson, J.R.; Potts, N.L.; Richichi, E.A.; Ford, S.M.; Krisnan, K.R.; Smith, R.D. & Wilson, W. (1991). The Brief Social Phobia Scale. *Journal of Clinical Psychiatry, 52(Suppl),* 48-51.

Davidson, J.R.; Miner, C.M.; De Veaygh-Guss, J.; Tupler, L.A.; Colket, J.T. & Potts, N.L.S. (1997). The Brief Social Phobia Scale: a psychometric evaluation. *Psychological Medicine, 27,* 161-167.

Davidson, J.R.; Foa, E.B.; Huppert, J.D.; Keefe, F.S.; Franklin, M.E.; Comptor, J.S.; Zhao, N.; Connor, K.M.; Lynch, T.R. & Gadde, K.M. (2004). Fluoxetine, comprrehensive cognitive behavioral therapy and placebo in generalized social phobia. *Archives of General Psychiatry, 61 (10),* 1005-1013.

Del-Ben, CM.; Vilela, J.A.A.; Crippa, J.A.S.; Halak, J.E.C.; Labate, C.M. & Zuardi, A.W. (2001). Test-retest reliability of the Structured Clinical Interview for DSM-IV – Clinical Version (SCID-CV) translated into portuguese. *Revista Brasileira de Psiquiatria, 23,*156-159.

Dell'Osso, L.; Rucci, P.; Cassano, G.B.; Maser, J.D.; Endicott, J; Shear, M.K.; Sarno, M.; Saettoni, M.; Grochocinski, V.J. & Frank, E. (2002a). Measuring social anxiety and obsessive-compulsive spectra: comparison of interviews and self-report instruments. *Comprehensive Psychiatry, 43 (2)*, 81-87.

Dell'Osso, L.; Saettoni, M.; Papasogli, A.; Rucci, P.; Ciapparelli, A.; Di-Poggio, A.B.; Ducci, F.; Hardoy, C. & Cassano, G.B. (2002b). Social Anxiety Spectrum: gender differences in Italian high school students. *Journal of Nervus and Menal Disiease, 190 (4)*, 225-232.

Dell'Osso, L.; Rucci, P.; Ducci, F.; Ciapparelli, A.; Vivarelli, L.; Carlini, M.; Ramacciotti, C. & Cassano, G.B. (2003). Social Anxiety Spectrum. *European Archives of Psychiatry and Clinical Neuroscience, 253 (6)*, 286-291.

Di Nardo, P.A.; O'Brien, G.T.; Barlow, D.H.; Waddell, M.T. & Blanchard, E. (1983). Reliability of DSM-III Anxiety Disorder Categories Using a New Structured Interview. *Archives of General Psychiatry, 40*, 1070-1074.

Di Nardo, P.A.; Moraes, K.; Barlow, D.H.; Rapee, R.M. & Brow, T.A. (1993). Reliability of DSM-III-R Anxiety Disorder Categories. *Archives of General Psychiatry, 50*, 251-256.

Dodge, C.S.; Hope, D.A.; Heimberg, R.G. & Becker, R.E. (1988). Evaluation of the Social Interaction Self-Statement Test with a social phobic population. *Cognitive Therapy and Research, 12 (2)*, 211-222.

Ducci, F.; Rucci, P.; Vivarelli, L.; Hardoy, M.C. & Dell'Osso, L. (2004). Social Anxiety Spectrum: correlation with other psychopatological dimensions. *Rivista di Psichiatria, 39 (2)*, 105-111.

Duke, D.; Krishnan M.; Faith M. & Storch, E.A. (2006). The psychometric properties of The Brief Fear of Negative Evaluation Scale. *Anxiety Disorders, 20*, 807-817.

Dunlop, B.W.; Papp, L.; Garlow, S.J.; Weiss, P.S.; Knight, B.T. & Ninan, P.T. (2007). Tiagabine for social anxiety disorder. *Human Psychopharmacology Clinical and Experimental, 22 (4),* 241-244.

Elwood, T.D. & Schrader, D.C. (1998). Family communication patterns and communication apprehension. *Journal of Social Behavior and Personality, 13 (3)*, 493-502.

Emmanuel, N.P.; Brawman-Mintzer, O.; Morton, W.A.; Book, S.W.; Johnson, M.R.; Lorberbaum, J.P.; Ballenger, J.C. & Lydiard, R.B. (2000). Buproprion-SR in treatment of social phobia. *Depression Anxiety, 12 (2),* 111-113.

Epkins, C.C. (2002). A comparison of two self-report measures of children's social anxiety in clinic and community samples. *Journal of Clinical Child and Adolescent Psychology, 31 (1)*, 69-79.

Evren, B. & Evren, C. (2007). Relationship between alexithymia and social anxiety in female outpatients with dermatological disorder presenting for psychiatric consultation. *Journal of Clinical Psychology in Medical Settings, 14 (3)*, 258-265.

Fernandez, F.; Jimenez, S.; Badia, A.; Jaurrieta, N.; Solano, R. & Vallejo, J. (2003). Ansiedad y fobia social en anorexia nerviosa: Un estudio de casos y controles. *Psicologia Conductual Revista Internacional de Psicologia Clínica de las Salud, 11 (3)*, 517-525.

First, M.B.; Spitzer, R.L.; Gibon, M. & Willians, J.B.W. (1997). *Structured Clinical Interview for DSM-IV Axis I Disorders – Clinican Version (SCID-CV).* Washington, DC: American Psychiatric Press.

Fresco, D.M.; Coles, M.E.; Heimberg, R.G.; Liebowitz, M.R.; Hami, S.; Stein, M.B. & Goetz, D. (2001). The Liebowitz Social Anxiety Scale: a comparison of the psychometric properties of self-report and clinician-administered formats. Psychological *Medicine, 31 (6)*, 1025-1035.

Garcia-Lopes, L.J.; Olivares, J.; Hidalgo, M.D.; Beidel, D.C. & Turner, S.M. (2001). Psychometric properties of the Social Phobia and Anxiety Inventory, the Social Anxiety Scale for Adolescents, the Fear of Negative Evaluation Scale, and the Social Avoidance and Distress Scale in a adolescent Spanish speaking sample. *Journal of Psychopathology and Behavioral Assessment, 23 (1)*, 51-59.

Gauer, G.J.; Picon, P.; Vasconcellos, S.J.; Turner, S.M. & Beidel, D.C. (2005). Validation of the Social Phobia and Anxiety Inventory for Children (SPAI-C) in a sample of Brazilian children. *Brazilian Journal of Medical and Bioloigal Research, 38 (5)*, 795-800.

Gelernter, C.S.; Uhde, T.W. & Cimbolic, P. (1992). Cognitive behavior and pharmacological treatment of social phobia: a controlled study. *Archives of General Psychiatry, 48*, 938-941.

Gerlach, A.L.; Heinrichs, N.; Bandl, C. & Zimmermann, T. (2007). SSPS- A German version of the questionnaire to assess the cognitive components of fear of public speaking. *Zeitschrift fur Klinische Psychologie und Psychotherapie: Forschung und Praxis, 36(2)*, 112-120.

Gilkinson, H. (1942). Social Fears as reported by students in college speech classes. *Speech Monography, 9*, 141-160.

Gillis, M.M.; Haaga, D.A. & Ford, G.T. (1995). Normative values for the Beck anxiety Inventory, Fear Questionnaire, Penn State Worry Questionnaire, and Social Phobia and Anxiety Inventory. *Psychological Assessment, 7 (4)*, 450-455.

Glass, C.R.; Merluzzi, T.; Biever, J. (1982). Cognitive assessment of social anxiety: development and validation of a self-statement questionnaire. *Cognitive Therapy Research, 6*, 37-55.

Gore, K.L; Crter, M.M. & Parker, S. (2002). Predicting anxious response to a social challenge: the predictive utility of the Social Interaction Anxiety Scale and the Social Phobia Scale in college population. *Behaviour Research and Therapy, 40* (6), 689-700.

Grabhorn, R.; Stenner, H.; Stangier, U. & Kaufhold, J. (2006). Social anxiety in anorexia and bulimia nervosa: the mediating role of shame. *Clinical Psychology and Psychotherapy, 13 (1)*, 12-19.

Habke, A.M.; Hewitt, P.L.; Norton, G.R. & Asmundson, G. (1997). The social phobia and social interaction anxiety scales: an exploration of the dimensions of social anxiety and sex differences in structure and relations with pathology. *Journal of Psychopathology and Behavioral Assessment, 19 (1)*, 21-39.

Hambrick, J.P.; Turk, C.L.; Heimberg, R.G.; Schneier, F.R. & Liebowitz, M.R. (2004) Psychometric properties of disability measures among patients with social anxiety disorder. *J. Anxiety Disord. 18,* 825-39.

Hansford, B.C. & Hattie, J.A. (1982). Communication apprehension: an assessment of Australian and United States data. *Applied Psychological Measurement, 6 (2)*, 225-233.

Hebert, J.D.; Bellack, A.S. & Hope, D.A. (1991). Concurrent validity of the Social Phobia and Anxiety Inventory. *Journal of Psychopathology and Behavioral Assessment, 13 (4)*, 357-368.

Heimberg, R.G.; Hope, D.A.; Rapee, R.M. & Bruch M.A. (1988). The validity of the Social Avoidance and Distress Scale and The Fear of Negative Evaluation Scale with social phobics patients. *Behaviour Research and Therapy , 26 (5)*, 407-413.

Heimberg, R.G; Dodge, C.S.; Hope, D.A.; Kennedy, C.R.; Zollo, L.J. & Becker, R.E. (1990). Cognitive behavioral group treatment for social phobia: comparison with a credible placebo. *Cognitive Therapy and Research, 14*, 1-23.

Heimberg, R.G.; Mueller, G.P.; Holt, C.S.; Hope, D.A. (1992). Assessment of anxiety in social interaction and being observed by others: The Social Interaction Anxiety Scale and the Social Phobia Scale. *Behavior Therapy, 23 (1)*, 53-73.

Heimberg, R.G.; Horner, K.J.; Juster, H.R. (1999). Psychometric properties of the Liebowitz Social Anxiety Scale. *Psychoogical Medicine, 29 (1)*, 199-212.

Heimberg, R.G. & Holaway, R.M. (2007). Examination of the known groups validity of the Liebowitz Social anxiety Scale. *Depression and Anxiety, 24 (7)*, 447-454.

Heinrichs, N.; Hahlweg, K.; Fiegenbaum, W.; Frank, M.; Schroeder, B. & Von-Witzeben, I. (2002). Validity and reliability of the Social Interaction Anxiety (SIAS) and Social Phobia Scale (SPS)

Higa, C.K.; Fernandez, S.N.; Nakamur, B.J.; Chorpita, B.F. & Daleiden, E.L. (2006). Parental assessment of childhood social phobia: psychometric properties of the social phoia and anxiety inventory for children parent report. *Journal of Clinical Child and Adolescent Psychology, 35 (4)*, 590-597.

Hofmann, S.G.; Albano, A.M.; Heimberg, R.G.; Tracey, S.; Chorpita, B.F. & Barlow, D.H. (1999). Subtypes of social phobia in adolescents. *Depression and Anxiety, 9,* 15-18.

Hofmann, S.G. & DiBartolo, P.M. (2000). An instrument to assess self-statements during public speaking: scale development and preliminary psycometric properties. *Behaviour Therapy, 31*, 499-515.

Hofmann, S.G.; DiBartolo, P.M.; Holaway, R.M. & Heimberg, R.G. (2004). Scoring error of social avoidance and distress scale and its psychometric implications. *Depression and Anxiety, 19*, 197-198.

Hong, S. & Cho, Y. (1999). Latent structure of the Social Interaction Self-Statement Test: an application of hierarchical confirmatory factor analysis. *Psychological Reports, 84*, 1303-1314.

Inderbitzen, N.H.; Avies, C.A. & McKeon, N.D. (2004). Investigating the construct validity of the SPAI-C: comparing the sensitivity and specificity of the SPAI-C and the SAS-A. *Journal of Anxiety Disorders, 18 (4)*, 547-560.

Ishiyama, F.I. (1999). Development and validation of a Situational Social Avoidance Scale. *Psychological Reports, 85*, 114-120.

Isolan, L.; Pheula, G.; Salum G.A.; Oswald, S.; Rohde, L.A. & Manfro, G.G. (2007). An open trial of escitalopram in children and adolescents with social anxiety disorder. *Journal of Child and Adolescent Psychopharmacology, 17 (6)*, 751-759.

Ito, L.M. & Ramos, R.T. (2000) Escalas de avaliação clínica do transtorno de pânico. In: Gorenstein, C.; Andrade, L.H.S.G.; Zuardi, A.W. *Escalas de avaliação clínica em psiquiatria e psicofarmacologia*. (145-156). São Paulo: Lemos Editorial.

Johnson, H.S.; Inderbitzen-Nolan, H.M. & Anderson, E.M. (2006). The social phobia inventory: validit and reliability in an adolescent community sample. *Psychological Assessment, 18 (3)*, 269-277.

Johnson, J.M. (2007). *A comparison of cognitive behavioral group therapy with and without an alcohol intervention to reduce socially anxious individual' alcohol consumption.* Dissertation Abstracts International: Section B: Sciences and Engineering, 68(5-B).

Kinrys, G.; Pollak, M.H.; Simon, N.M.; Worthington, J.; Nardi, A.E. & Versiani, M. (2003). Valproic acid for the treatment of social anxiety disorder. *International Clinical Psychopharmacology, 18 (3)*, 169-172.

Knijnik, D.Z.; Kapczinski, F.; Chachamovich, E.; Margis, R. & Eizirik, C.L. (2004). Psychodynamic group treatment for generalized social phobia. *Revista Brasileira de Psiquiatria, 26 (2)*, 77-81.

Kobak, K.A.; Schaettle, S.C.; Greist, J.H.; Jefferson, J.W.; Katzelnick, D.J. & Dottl, S.L. (1998). Computer-administered rating scales for social anxiety in a clinical drug trial. *Depression and Anxiety, 7*, 97-173.

Kolassa, I.T. & Miltner, W.H. (2006). Psychophysiological correlates of face processing in social phobia. *Brain Research, 1118 (1)*, 130-141.

Komiti, A.A.; Jackson, H.J.; Judd, F.K.; Cockram, A.M.; Kyrios, M.; Yeatman, R.; Murray, G.; Hordern, C.; Wainwright, K.; Allen, N. & Singh, B. (2001). A comparison of the Composite International Diagnostic Interview (CIDI-auto) with clinical assessment in diagnosing mood and anxiety disorders. *Australian and New Zeland Journal of Pychiatriy, 35 (2)*, 224-230.

Koydemir, S. & Demir, A. (2007). Psychometric properties of the brief version of the Fear of Negative Evaluation Scale in a turkish sample. *Psychological Reports, 100*: 883-893.

Leary, M.R. (1983). A brief version of the Fear of Negative Evaluation Scale. *Personality and Social Psychology Bulletin, 9*, 371-375.

Levin, J.B.; Marom,S.; Gur, S.; Wecheter, D. & Hermesh, H. (2002). Psychometric properties and three proposed subscales of a self-report version of the Liebowitz Social Anxiety Scale translated into Hebrew. *Depression and Anxiety, 16*, 143-151.

Liebowitz, M.R. (1987). Social Phobia. *Modern Problems in Pharmacopsychiatry, 22*, 141-173.

Liebowitz, M.R.; Mangano, R.M.; Bradwejn, J. & Asnis, G. (2005). A randomized controlled trial of venlafaxine extended release in generalized social anxiety disorder. *Journal of Clinical Psychiatry, 66 (2)*, 238-247.

Lochner, C.; Seedat, S.; Niehaus, D.J. & Stein, D.J. (2006). Topiramate in the treatment of trichotillomania: an open label pilot study. *International Clinical Psychopharmacology, 21 (5)*, 255-259.

Manning, P. & Ray, G. (1993). Shyness, self-confidence, and social interaction. *Social Psychology Quarterly, 56(3)*, 178-192.

Marks, I.M.; Mathews, A.M. (1979). Brief standard self-rating for phobic patients. *Behaviour Research and Therapy, 17,* 263-267.

Martín-Santos, R. & Crippa, J.A.S. (2003). Transtornos de ansiedad en atención primaria. In: Solá, V.P. (org**)**. *Abordaje de los problemas de salud mental en el ámbito extrahospitalario* (17-31). Barcelona: Profármaco.

Masia, W.C.; Storch, E.A.; Pincus, D.B.; Klein, R.G.; Heimberg, R.G.; Liebowitz, M.R. (2003). The Liebowitz Social Anxiety Scale for children and adolescents: n initial psychometric investigation. *Journal of the American Academy of Child and Adolescent Psychiatry, 42 (9)*, 1076-1084.

Mattick, R.P. & Clark, J.C. (1989). *Development and validation of measures of social phobia scruting fear and social interaction anxiety*. Unpublished manuscript, University of New South Wales, Australia.

Mattick, R.P. & Clark, J.C. (1998). Development and validation of measures of social phobia scrutiny fear and social interaction anxiety. *Behaviour Research and Therapy, 36 (4)*, 455-470.

Mavissakalian, M. (1986). The Fear Questionnaire: a validity study. *Behaviour Research and Therapy, 24*, 83-85.

Means-Christensen, A.; Sherbourne, C.D.; Roy-Byrne, P. Craske, M.G.; Bystrisky, A. & Stein, M.B. (2003). The Composite International Diagnostic Interview (CIDI-auto): problems and remedies for diagnosing panic disorder and social phobia. *Int J Methods Psychiatry Research, 12 (4)*, 167-181.

Melfsen, S.; Florin, I. & Walter, H.J. (1999). German version of the Social Phobia and Anxiety Inventory for Children (SPAI-C-D): its psychometric properties and norms. *Diagnostica, 45 (2)*, 95-103.

Melfsen, S.; lpers, G.W.; Walitza, S. & Warnke, A. (2006). Anxiety sensitivity in children with attention deficit hyperactivity disorder. *Verhaltenstherapie, 16 (1)*, 25-30.

Mendez, F.X.; Ingles, C.J. & Idalgo, M.D. (2004). The shortened Spanish version of the Personal Report of Confidence as Speaker: reliability and validity in adolescent population. *Psicologia Conductual Revista Internacional de Psicologia Clinica de las Salud, 12 (1)*, 25-42.

Mennin, D.S.; Fresco, D.M.; Heimberg, R.G.; Schneier, F.R.; Davies, S.O. & Liebowitz, M.R. (2002). Screening for social anxiety disorder in the clinical setting: using the Liebowitz Social Anxiety Scale. *Journal of Anxiety Disorder, 16*, 661-673.

Meningaud, J.P.; Benadiba, L.; Servant, J.M.; Herve, C.; Bertrand, J.C. & Pelicie, Y. (2001). Depression, anxiety and quality of life among scheduled cosmetic surgery patients: multicentre prospective study. *Journal of Craniomaxillofacial Surgery, 29 (3)*, 177-180.

McCroskey, J.C. (1997). Validity of the PRCA as an index of oral communication apprehension. *Communication Monographs, 45*, 192- 203.

McDougall, D.L. (2000). *The group treatment of social phobia with cognitive behavioural therapy and imagery.* Dissertion-Abstrats-International: Section-B: The /sciences and Engineering, 61(4-B).

Mizer, J.S. & Crawford, J. (1986). Normative values on the Marks and Mathews Fear Questionnaire: a comparison as a function of age and sex. *Journal of Psychopathoogy andl Behavioral Assessment, 8*, 253-262.

Morris, T.L. & Masia, C.L. (1998). Psychometric evaluation of the Social Phobia and Anxiety Inventory for Children: concurrent validity and normative data. *Journal of Clinical Child Psychology, 27 (4)*, 452-458.

Muehlbacher, M.; Nickel, M.K.; Nickel,C.; Kettler, C.; Lahmann, C.; Pedrosa-Gil, F.; Leiberich, P.K.; Rother, N.; Bachler, E.; Fartacek, R.; Kaplan, P.; Tritt, K.; Mitterlehner, F.; Anvar, J.; Rother, W.K.; Loew, T.H. & Egger, C. (2005). Mirtazapine treatment of social phobia in women: a randomized , double-blind, placebo-controlled study. *Journal of Clinical Psychopharmacology, 25 (6),* 580-583.

Musa, C.; Kostogianni, N. & Lépine, J.P. (2004). The Fear of Negative Evolution scale (FNE): psychometric properties of the French version. *Encephale, 30 (6)*, 517-524.

Nagata, T.; Oshima, J.; Wada, A.; Yamada, H.; Iketani, T. & Kiriike, N. (2003). Open trial of milnacipran for Taijin-Kyofusho in Japanese patients with social anxiety disorder. *International Journal of Psychiatry in Clinical Practice, 7 (2)*, 107-112.

Newman, M.G.; Kachin, K.E.; Zuellig, A.R.; Constantino, M.J. & Casman-Mcgrath, L. (2003). The social phobia diagnostic questionnaire: preliminary validation of a new self-report diagnostic measure of social phobia. *Psychological Medicine, 33,* 623-635.

Novy, D.M.; Stanley, M.A.; Averill, P. & Daza, P. (2001). Psychometric comparability of English and Spanish language measures of anxiety and related affective symptoms. *Psychological Assessments, 13 (3)*, 347-355.

Oakman, J.; Ameringen, M.V. & Mancini, C. (2003). A confirmatory factor analysis of a self-report version of the Liebowitz Social Anxiety Scale. *Journal of Clinical Psychology, 59 (1)*, 149-161.

Oei, T.P.S.; Gross, P.R. & Evans, L. (1989). Phobic disorders and anxiety states: how do they differ? *Australian and New Zealand Journal of Psychiatry, 23*, 81-88.

Oei, T.P.S.; Moyln, A. & Evans, L. (1991). Validity and clinical utility of the Fear Questionnaire for anxiety disorder patients. *Psychological Assessment, 3*, 258-297.

Olivares,J.; Garcia-Lopes, L.J.; Hidalgo, M.D.; Turner, S.M. & Beidel, D.C. (1999). The Social Phobia and Anxiety Inventory: reliability and validity in an adolescent Spanish population. *Journal of Psychopathology and Behavioral Assessment, 21 (1)*, 67-78.

Olivares, J.; Garcia-Lopes, L.J. & Hidalgo, M.D. (2001). The Social Phobia Scale and the Social Interaction Anxiety Scale: factor structure and reliability in a Spanish speaking population. *Journal of Psychoeducational Assessment, 19 (1)*, 69-80.

Osman, A.; Markway, K. & Osman, J.R. (1992). Psychometric properties of the Social Interaction Self-Statement Test in a college sample. *Psychological Reports, 71 (3 PT 2)*, 1171-1177.

Osman, A.; Barrios, F.X.; Aukes, D. & Osman, J.R. (1995). Psychometric evaluation of the Social Phobia and Anxiety Inventory in college students. *Journal of Clinical Psychology, 51 (2)*, 235-243.

Osman, A.; Barrios, F.X.; Haupt, D. & King, K. (1996). The Social Phobia and Anxiety Inventory: further validation in two nonclinical samples. *Journal of Psychopathology and Behavioral Assessment, 18 (1)*, 35-47.

Osman, A.; Gutierrez, P.M.; Barios, F.X.; Kopper, B.A. & Chiros, C.E. (1998). The Social Phobia and Social Interaction Anxiety Scales: evaluation of psychometric properties. *Journal of Psychopathology and Behavioral Assessment, 20 (3)*, 249-264.

Osório, F.L.; Crippa, J.A.S.; Zuardi, A.W.; Graeff, F.G.; Busatto, G.; Pinho, M.; Mazza, M.; Chaves, M.P.R. & Loureiro, S.R. (2004). Inventário de Fobia Social (SPIN): validação para o Brasil. *Revista Brasileira de Psiquiatria, 26 (Suppl II)*, S4.

Osório, F.L.; Crippa, J.A.C. & Loureiro, S.R. (2005). Instrumentos de avaliação do Transtorno de ansiedade social. *Revista de Psiquiatria Clínica, 32(2)*, 73-83.

Osório, F.L.; Crippa, J.A.S. & Loureiro. (2006) Cross-cultural validation of the Brief Social Phobia Scale for use in Portuguese and the development of a structured interview guide. *Revista Brasileira de Psiquiatria, 28 (3)*, 212-217.

Osório, F.L.; Crippa, J.A.S. & Loureiro, S.R. (2007). A study of the discriminative validity of a screening tool (Mini-Spin) for social anxiety disorder applied to brazilian university students. *European Psychiatry, 22*, 239-243.

Paul, G.I. (1966). *Insight and desensitization in psychotherapy: an experimental in anxiety reduction. Stanford*: Stanford University Press.

Peng, C.; Yan, L.; Ma, X. & Wu, W. (2003). Effect group therapy on social anxiety of college students. *Chinese Mental Health Journal, 17 (4)*, 229-231.

Peters, L. (2000). Discriminant validity of the social phobia and anxiety inventory (SPAI), the Social Phobia Scale (SPS) and the Social Interaction Anxiety Scale (SIAS). *Behaviour Research and Therapy, 38 (9)*, 943-950.

Picon, P.; Gauer, G.J.C.; Hirakata, V.N.; Haggstram, L.M.; Beidel, D.C.; Turner, S.M. & Manfro, G.G. (2005). Reliability of the Social Phobia and Anxiety Inventory (SPAI) Portuguese version in a heterogeneous sample of Brazilian university students. *Revista Brasileira de Psiquiatria, 27 (2)*, 124-130.

Picon, P.; Gauer, G.J.C.; Fachel, J.M.; Beidel, D.C.; Seganfredo, A.C. & Manfro, G.G. (2006). The Portuguese language version of Social Phobia and Anxiety Inventory: analysis of items and internal consistency in a Brazilian sample of 1014 undergraduate students. *Jornal Brasileiro de Psiquiatria, 55 (2)*, 114-119.

Pinto, A. & Phillips K.A. Social anxiety in body dysmorphic disorder. (2005). *Body Image, 2 (4)*, 401-405.

Pinto-Gouveia, J.; Cunha, M.I. & Salvador, M.C. (2003). Assessment of Social Phobia by self-report questionnaires: the Social Interaction and Performance Anxiety and Avoidance Scale and the Social Phobia Safety Behaviours Scale. *Behavioural and Cognitive Psychoterapy, 31*, 291-311.

Pollack, M.H. (2001). Comorbidity, neurobilogy, and pharmacotherapy of social anxiety disorder. *Journal of Clinical Psychiatry, 62(suppl 12),* p.24-29.

Popali-Lehane, L. (2007). *Predicting alcohol problem use in college students with social phobia*. Dissertation Abstracts International: Section B: Sciences and Engineering, 67(8-B).

Pryor, B.; Butler, J. & Boehringer, K. (2005). Communication Apprehension and Cultural Context: A Comparison of Communication Apprehension in Japonese and American Students. *North American Journal of Psychology, 7 (2)*, 247-252.

Quintana, M.I.; Gastal, F.L.; Jorge, M.R.; Miranda, C.T. & Andreolli, S.B. (2007). Validity and limitations of the Brazilian version of the Composite International Diagnostic Interview (CIDI 2.1). Revista Brasileira de Psiquiatria, 29 (1), 18-22.

Rabung, S.; Jaeger, U.; Streek, U. & Leichsering, F. (2006). Psychometric analysis of the Social Phobia Scale (SPS) and the Social Interaction Anxiety Scale (SIAS) in an inpatient sample, *Diagnostica*, 52(3), 143-153.

Radomsky, A.S.; Ashbaugh, A.R.; Saxe, M.L.; Ouimet, A.J.; Golden, E.R.; Lavoie, S.L. & O'Connor, K.P. (2006). Psychometric properties of the French and English versions of the Social Phobia Inventory. *Canadian Journal of Behavioural Science, 38 (4)*, 354-360.

Ranta, K.; Kaltiala-Heino, R.; Rantanen, P.; Tuomisto, M.T. & Marttunen, M. (2007). Screening social phobia in adolescents from general population: the validity of the Social Phobia Inventory (SPIN) against a clinical interview. *European Psychiatry, 22 (4),* 244-251.

Rickels, K.; Mangano, R. & Khan, A. (2004). A double-blind, placebo-controlled study of a flexible dose of venlafaxine ER in adult outpatients with generalized social anxiety disorder. *Journal of Clinical Psychopharmacology, 24 (5)*, 488-496.

Ries, B.J.; McNeil, D.W.; Boone, M.L.; Turk, C.L.; Carter, L.E. & Heinmberg, R.C. (1998). Assessment of contemporary social phobia verbal report instruments. *Behaviour Research and Therapy, 36*, 983-994.

Roberson-Nay, R.; Strong, D.R.; Nay, W.T.; Beidel, D.C. & Turner, S.M. (2007). Development of an abbreviated Social Phobia and Anxiety Inventory (SPAI) using item response theory: the SPAI-23. *Psychological Assessment, 19 (1)*, 133-145.

Rodebaugh, T.L.; Chambless, D.L.; Terrill, D.R.; Floyd, M. & Uhde, T. (2000). Convergent, discriminant, and criterion related validity of the Social Phobia and Anxiety Inventory. *Depression and Anxiety, 11 (1)*, 10-14.

Rodebaugh, T.L.; Woods, C.M.; Thisen, D.M.; Heimberg, R.G.; Chambles, D.L. & Rapee, R.M. (2004). More information from fewer questions: the factor structure and item properties of the original and Brief Fear of Negative Evaluation Scale. *Psychological Assessment, 2*, 169- 181.

Rodebaugh, T.L.; Woods, C.M.; Heimberg, R.G.; Liebowitz, M.R. & Scheneier, F.R. (2006). The factor structure abd screening utility of the Social Interaction Anxiety Scale. *Psychological Assessment, 18 (2)*; 231-237.

Rodebaugh, T.L.; Woods, C.M. & Heimberg, R.G. (2007). The reverse of social anxiety is not always the opposite: The reverse-scored items of the social interaction anxiety scale do not belong. *Behavior Therapy, 38 (2)*, 192-206.

Safren, S.A.; Turk, C.L. & Heimberg, R.G. (1998). Factor structure of the Social Interaction anxiety Scale and the Social Phobia Scale. *Behaviour Research and Therapy, 36 (4)*, 443-453.

Safren, S.A.; Heimberg, R.G.; Horner, K.J.; Juster, H.R.; Schneier, F.R. & Liebowitz, M.R. (1999). Factor Structure of Social Fears: Liebowitz Social Anxiety Scale. *Journal of Anxiety Disorders, 13 (3)*, 253-270.

Sakurai, A.; Nagat, T.; Harai, H.; Yamada, H.; Mohri, I.; Ibuki, M.; Nakano, Y. Noda, Y.; Ogawa, S.; Lee, K.; Kiyoe, L. & Furukawa, T.A. (2005). Is relationship fear unique to Japan? Symptom factors and patient clusters of the social anxiety disorder among the Japanese clinical population. *Journal Affective Disorders, 87 (1)*, 131-137

Sarquisse,V.; Butler, J. & Pryor, B. (2003). A comparison of communication apprehension scores between Americans and Argentineans. *North American Journal of Psychology, 5 (2)*, 223-227.

Schelver, S.R. & Gutsch, K.U. (1983). The effects of self-administered cognitive therapy on social evaluative anxiety. *Journal of Clinical Psychology, 39 (5)*, 658-666.

Scheneir, F.R.; Heckelman, L. R.; Garfinkel, R.; Campeas, R.; Fallon, B.A.; Gitow, A.; Sreeet, L.; Del Bene, D.; Liebowitz, M. R. (1994). Functional impairment in social phobia. *Journal of Clinical Psychiatry, 55 (8)*, 322-331.

Sica,C.; Musoni, I.; Chiri, L.R.; Bisi, B.; Lolli, V. & Sighinolfi, C. (2007). Social Phobia Scale (SPS) and Social Interaction Anxiety Scale (SIAS): Italian translation and adaptation. *Bollettino di Psicologia Applicata, 252*, 59-71.

Smari,J.; Petursdottir, G. & Porsteinsdottir, V. (2001). Social anxiety and depression in adolescents in relation to perceived competence and situational appraisal. *Journal of Adolescence, 24 (2)*, 199-207.

Smith, R.J. (2003). *Adolescent social anxiety and co-occurring alcohol use: the moderating role of discrete coping styles*. Dissertation Abstracts International: Section B – The Sciences and Engineering, 64 (5-B).

Soykan, Ç.; Özgüven, H.D. & Gençoz, T. (2003). Liebowitz Social Anxiety Scale: the Turkish version. *Psychological Reports, 93*, 1059-1069.

Stangier, U.; Heidenreich, T.; Berardi, A.; Golbs, U. & Hoyer, J. (1999). Assessment of social phobia by the Social Interaction Anxiety Scale (SIAS) and the Social Phobia Scale (SPS). *Zeitschrift fur Klinische Psychologie, 28 (1)*, 28-36.

Stein, M.B.; Fyer, A.J.; Davidson, J.R.; Pollak, M.H. & Wiita, B. (1999). Fluvoxamine treatment of social phobia: a double- blind, placebo-controlled study. *American Journal Psychiatry, 156 (5)*, 756-760.

Stein, D.J.; Andersen, E.W. & Lader, M. (2006). Escitalopram versus paroxetine for social anxiety disorder: an analysis of efficacy for different symptom dimensions. *European Neuropsychopharmacology, 16 (1)*, 33-38.

Storch, E.A. (2003). *The relationship of peer victimization to social anxiety and distress in adolescence*. Dissertation Abstracts International: Section B – The Sciences and Engineering, 64 (6-B).

Storch, E.A.; Masia-Warner, C.; Dent, H.C.; Roberti, J.W. & Fisher, P.H. (2004). Psychometric evaluation of the Social and Anxiety Scale for Adolescents and the Social

Phobia and Anxiety Inventory for Children: construct validity and normative data. *Journal of Anxiety Disorders, 18 (5)*, 665-679.

Storch, E.A.; Masia, W.C.; Heidgerken, A.D.; Fisher, P.H.; Pincus, D.B. & Liebowitz, M.R. (2006). Factor structure of the Liebowitz Social Anxiety Scale for Children and Adolescents. *Child Psychiatry and Human Development, 37 (1)*, 25-37.

Taylor, S. (1993). The structure of fundamental fears. *Journal of Behavior Therapy and Experimental Psychiatry, 24*, 289-299.

Terra, M.B.; Barros, H.M.; Stein, A.T.; Figueira, I.; Athayde, L.D.; Gonçalves, M.S.; Tergolina, L.P.; Rovani, J.S. & da Silveira, D.X. (2006a). Internal consistency and factor structure of the Portuguese version of the Liebowitz Social anxiety Scale among alcoholic patients. *Revista Brasileira de Psiquiatria, 28 (4)*, 265-269.

Terra, M.B.; Barros, H.M.; Stein, A.T.; Figueira, I.; Jorge, M.R.; Palermo, L.H.; Athayde, L.D.; Gonçalves, M.S.; Spanemberg, L.; Possa, M.A.; Filho-Ledo, D. & da Silveira, D.X. (2006b). Social anxiety disorder in 300 patients hospitalized for alcoholism in Brazil: high prevalence and undertreatment. *Comprehensive Psychiatry, 47 (6)*, 463-467.

Tharwani, H.M. & Davidson, R.T. (2001). Symptomatic and functional assessment of social anxiety disorder in adults. *Psychiatric Clinics of North American, 24(4)*, 643-659.

Toth, C.G. (2007). *Shyness as a mediating factor in theft of embarrassing items.* Dissertation Abstracts International: Section B: Sciences and Engineering, 68(6-B).

Turner, S.M.; McCanna, M. & Beidel, D.C. (1987). Validity of the Social Avoidance and Distress And Fear of Negative Evaluation. *Behaviour Research Therapy, 25 (2)*, 113-115.

Turner, S.M.; Beidel, D.C.; Dancu, C.V. & Stanley, M.A. (1989a). An empirically derived inventory to measure social fears and anxiety: The Social Phobia and Anxiety Inventory. *Psychological Assessment, 1 (1)*, 35-40.

Turner, S.M.; Stanley, M.A.; Beidel, D.C. & Bond, L. (1989b). The Social Phobia and Anxiety Inventory: construct validity. *Journal of Psychopathology and Behavioral Assessment, 11 (3)*, 221-234.

Turner, S.M.; Johnson, M.R.; Beidel, D.C.; Heiser, N.A. & Lydiard, R.B. (2003) The Social Thoughts and Beliefs scale: a new inventory for assessing cognitions in social phobia. *Psychological Assessment, 15 (3)*, 384-391.

Upadhyaya, H.P.; Brady, K.T.; Wharton, M. & Liao, J. (2003). Psychiatric disorders and cigarette smoking among child and adolescent psychiatry inpatients. *The American Journal on Addictions, 12 (2)*, 144-152.

Vaishnavi, S.; Alamy, S.; Zhang,W.; Connor, K.M. & Davidson, J.R.T. (2007). Quetiapine as monotherapy for social anxiety disorder: a placebo controlled study. *Progress in Neuro Psychopharmacology and Biological Psychiatry, 31 (7)*, 1464-1469.

Van-Amerigen, M.; Mancini, C. & Oakman, J.M. (1999). Nefazodone in social phobia. *Journal of Clinical Psychiatry, 60 (2)*, 96-100.

Van-Amerigen, M.A.; Lane, R.M.; Walker, J.R.; Bowen, R.C.; Chokka, P.R.; Goldner, E.M.; Johnston, D.G.; Lavallee, Y.J.; Nandy, S.; Pecknold, J.C.; Hadrava, V. & Swinson, R.P. (2001). Sertraline treatment of generalized social phobia: a 20 week, double-blind, placebo-controlled study. *American Journal Psychiatry, 158 (2)*, 275-281.

Van-Ameringen, M.; Mancini, C.; Oakman, J.; Walker, J.; Kjernisted, K.; Chokka, P.; Johnston, D.; Bennett, M. & Patterson, B. (2007). Nefazodone in treatment of generalized social phobia: a randomized, placebo-controlled trial. *Journal of Clinical Psychiatry, 68 (2)*, 288-295.

Van-Zurren, F.J. (1988). The Fear Questionnaire: some data on validity, reliability and layout. *British Journal of Psychiatry, 153*, 659-662.

Vilela, J.A.A.(2000). *Estudo da confiabilidade e validade da escala de avaliação de mania-versão modificada da Young Mania Rating Scale.* Dissertação de Mestrado. Faculdade de Medicina de Ribeirão Preto da Universidade de São Paulo.

Vilete, L.M.P. (2002). *Tradução, adaptação para o português e estudo da qualidade de uma escala para a identificação da fobia social em uma população de adolescentes.* Dissertação de Mestrado. Escola Nacional de Saúde Pública.

Voges, M. & Addington, J. (2005). The association between social anxiety and social functioning in first episode psychosis. *Schizophrenia Research, 76 (2-3)*, 287-292.

Walker, J.R.; Van Amerigen, M.A.; Swinson, R.; Bowen, R.C.; Chokka, P.R.; Goldner, E.; Johnston, D.C.; Lavallie, Y.J.; Nandy, S.; Pecknold, J.C.; Hadrava, V. & Lane, R.M. (2000). Prevention of relapse in generalized social phobia: results of a 24-week stydy in responders to 20 weeks of sertraline treatment. *Journal of Clinical Psychopharmacology, 20 (6)*, 636-644.

Watson, D. & Friend, R. (1969). Mesurement of social evaluative anxiety. *Journal of Consulting and Clinical Psychology, 33,* 448-457.

Weeks, J.W.; Heimberg, R.G.; Fresco, D.M.; Hart, T.; Turk, C.L.; Schneier, F.R. & Liebowitz, M.R. (2005). Empirical validation and psychometric evaluation of the Brief Fear of Negative Evaluation scale in patients with social anxiety disorder. *Psychological Assesment, 17 (2)*, 179-190.

Weeks, J.W.; Spokas, M.E.; Heimberg, R.G. (2007). Psychometric evaluation of the Mini-Socal Phobia Inventory (Mini-Spin) in a treatment-seeking sample. *Depression and Anxiety, 24*, 382-391.

Wilson, I. (2005). Screening for social anxiety disorder in first year university study – a pilot study. *Australian Family Physician, 34 (11)*, 983- 984.

Wong, D.F.K. & Sun, S.Y.K. (2006). A preliminary study of the efficacy of group cognitive behavioural therapy for people with social anxiety in Hong-Kong. *Hong-Kong Journal of Psychiatry, 16 (2)*, 50-56.

World Health Organization (WHO). (1997). *The Composite International Diagnostic Interview (CIDI).* Genova, Switzerland: World Health Organization.

Yao, S.N.; Cottraux, J.; Mollard, E.; Albuisson, E.; Note, I.; Jalencques, I.; Fanget, F.; Robbe-Grillet, P.; Dechassey, M.; Ektmedjian, N. & Bouvard, M. (1998). The French version of the Social Interactional Self-Statement Test (SISST): a validation and sensitivity study in social phobics. *Behavioral and Cognitive Psychotherapy, 26 (3),* 247-259.

Yao, S.N.; Note, I.; Fanget, F.; Albuisson, E.; Bouvard, M.; Jalenques, I. & Cottraux, J. (1999). Social Anxiety in patients with social phobia: validation of the Liebowitz Social Anxiety: the French version. *L'Encéphale, 25 (5)*, 617-641,

Yao, S.N.; Cottraux, J.; Note, I.; De Mey-Guillard, C.; Mollard, E. & Ventureyra, V. (2003). Evaluation of post-traumatic stress disorder: validation of a measure, the PCLS. *Encephale, 29 (3 Pt 1)*, 232-238.

Ye, D.M.; Qian, M.Y.; Liu, X.H. & Chen, X. (2007). Revision of Social Interaction Anxiety Scale and Social Phobia Scale. *Chinese Journal of Clinical Psychology, 15 (2)*, 115-117.

Yook, E.L. & Ahn, B.L. (1999). Comparison of apprehension about communication between Koreans and Americans. *Perceptual and Motor Skills, 89 (1)*, 161-164.

Zhang, W.; Connor, K.M. & Davidson, J.R. (2005). Leviteracetam in social phobia: a placebo controlled pilot study. *Journal of Psychopharmacology, 19(5)*, 551-553.

Zweig, D. & Brown, S.D. (1985). Psychometric evaluation of a written stimulus presentation format for the Social Interaction Self-Statment Test. *Cognitive Therapy and Research, 9 (3)*, 285-295.

Zubeidat, I.; Salinas, J.M.; Sierra, J.A.; Fernandez-Parra, A. (2007). Psychometric properties of the Social Interaction Scale and separation criterion between Spanish youths with and without subtypes of social anxiety. *Journal of Anxiety Disorders, 21 (5)*, 603-624.

In: Social Phobia: Etiology, Diagnosis and Treatment
Editor: Clayton P. Axelby
ISBN 978-1-60692-159-3
© 2009 Nova Science Publishers, Inc.

Chapter II

ANIMAL MODELS AND THE BIOLOGICAL BASES OF SHYNESS: CONTRIBUTIONS TO THE UNDERSTANDING OF SOCIAL PHOBIA

Carla M. Yuede[1,2] *and George T. Taylor*[1,*]
[1]Behavioral Neuroscience, University of Missouri, St. Louis, MO 63121 USA
[2]Department of Psychiatry, Washington University School of Medicine, St. Louis, MO 63010 USA

ABSTRACT

Behavioral biologists and psychologists of various stripes have an interest in identifying the relation of social phobia to factors such as genetic contributions, early experiences, and neurological functions. The phenotypic expression of social phobia bears some relation to extreme shyness. Whether the conditions exist on the same plane is debatable among clinicians, however support exists for the notion that the two are related. Exploring the biological factors underlying extreme shyness may therefore help in understanding aspects of social phobia. An initial discovery in a literature review is that neuroscientists using animals in their research seldom use the DSM term of social phobia. On the other hand, there are scores of published papers with animal models on behavioral traits that we will make the case are closely linked to the human condition. Terms used by behavioral neuroscientists include behavioral inhibition, neophobia, social fear, timidity, social anxiety, and our preference, shyness. Many of these empirical reports are not specific to social interactions but our literature review will focus on shyness in social settings. In addition, field biologists have identified shy individuals in animal species ranging from rainbow trout to bighorn sheep. One outcome of these data

* Correspondence concerning this article should be addressed to: George T. Taylor, Ph.D. Professor of Psychology, Behavioral Neuroscience, University of Missouri - St. Louis, 8001 Natural Bridge Rd. St. Louis, MO 63121 U.S.A. Tel/ FAX: (314) 516-5475/ (314) 516-5392; e-mail:geot@UMSL.edu.

and subsequent discussions is a renewed interest in biology for individual differences in "personality" of conspecifics. Another outcome has been to posit the existence of a shyness-boldness behavioral axis in the same mold as the five axes of personality traits (extraversion - introversion, neuroticism etc) suggested for humans. Implications for evolution of behavior are notable. The goals of this chapter will be to review the existing literature using animals models relevant to social phobia and discuss how the results compare to findings in human studies, and to point future research in directions that appear to be fruitful for a better understanding of the condition and for developing new treatment possibilities.

INTRODUCTION

In most social groups there is a subset of individuals who tend to be reticent to approach unfamiliar conspecifics or objects. These individuals are often termed as being shy, with varying degrees in the expression of behavioral inhibition or timidity (Kagan et al., 1988; Schwartz et al., 2003). Field biologists have identified shy members of a feral species, suggesting that shyness is a ubiquitous temperament in vertebrates (Wilson et al., 1994). This has given hope to behavioral neuroscientists interested in developing animal models to understand the biological bases of the debilitating forms of social phobia in humans (Taylor & Yuede, 2005).

An inhibited temperament in humans can be manifested as simple shyness or as social anxiety of varying degrees of daily impairment. The trait is perhaps related to the extreme social dysfunction often accompanying schizophrenia and autism (Truitt et al., 2007). Although there is disagreement on the relation of shyness to clearly organic disorders, a spectrum model has been proposed that relates shyness to neuropsychiatric disorders involving disrupted social behaviors, most notably avoidant personality disorders, social anxiety and social phobia. Henderson and Zimbardo (Henderson & Zimbardo, 1998) describe shyness as varying along a continuum from mild social awkwardness to totally debilitating social phobia. Other researchers, however, disagree with the concept that social phobia belongs on the same plane as shyness, even extreme shyness. Beidel and Turner (Beidel et al., 1999) concluded that there are overlapping behavioral features of shyness and social phobia and support for the notion that the two may be related. However, the suggestion is that shyness may predispose, but not predict, later development of social phobia (Stemberger et al., 1995). In general, most clinical investigators agree that there is a practical difference between transient shyness and total social impairment, but the boundary between normal and abnormal facets of the behaviors is blurred. Moreover, there is disagreement among clinicians if social phobics suffer from a deficit in the ability to form attachments or a reduced desire or capacity for social affiliation, such as that seen in autistic or schizophrenic individuals. Some social phobics seem to crave social affiliation and social approval, but their fear of rejection inhibits them from seeking out and sustaining relationships (Stein, 1995).

On the other hand, there are sound reasons to accept the continuum model (Bienvenu et al., 2007; Reznick et al., 1992). Social phobia and shyness share many of the same symptoms (Henderson & Zimbardo, 1998), and social phobia is certainly more prevalent among shy than outgoing individuals (Chavira et al., 2002; Heiser et al., 2003).

In this chapter we have adopted the continuum model with acceptable shyness at one end and debilitating shyness at the other end highlighted by the DSM-IV-TR diagnostic categories of the two forms of social anxiety disorder. One form is specific social phobia that is limited to situations in which the individual shows varying levels of activation of the sympathetic nervous system accompanying being specifically observed, e.g., public speaking. The broader, and usually more debilitating, form is generalized social phobia. Here the person experiences sympathetic activation and full-blown fear of being observed in varied situations from dining in a restaurant to sitting among people in a full theater (Hofmann et al., 2004).

We will include studies involving anxiety-related social deficits and those involving abnormal social motivation or interest, all with an emphasis on animal models. The abundance of research linking shyness to social phobia (Chavira et al., 2002; Turner et al., 1990), social anxiety disorder (Rosenbaum et al., 1988; Rosenbaum et al., 1991), aspects of autism (Crawley, 2007), and asocial negative symptomology of schizophrenia (Goldberg & Schmidt, 2001; Jetha et al., 2007) recommend the study of shy behaviors in animals for elucidating the biological mechanisms involved in normal and aberrant social behaviors.

We also will refer to non-human animals as possessing a shy temperament or trait. Biologists and neuroscientists are now comfortable referring to non-human animals as having distinct "personalities" of which temperament is a key component (Ray et al., 2006; Wolf et al., 2007). The definition of temperament as stable affective styles that bias how the individual responds to stimuli (Clarke & Boinski, 1995) would surely apply to non-human animals as well as humans.

Basic assumptions in the study of temperament are that individuals differ in the features of their nervous systems that underlie general personality dispositions and variations in neuropsychological functions (Hollandsworth, 1990). Also, traits or temperaments are presumed to be heritable and under genetic control. Indeed, the data suggest social phobia has particularly strong associations with personality traits of both neuroticism and introversion that appears to concentrate in certain families (Rosenbaum et al., 1991; Stein, 1998). A particularly interesting example is a report of elevated incidences of social phobia among first-degree relatives of autistic children (Smalley et al., 1995).

Temperament is likely to exert an important influence on many aspects of animal ecology and evolution, and individual variation in temperament seems to be pervasive among animal species (Wilson et al., 1994). The importance of studying temperament in animals within the framework of ecology and evolution is becoming increasingly recognized. One drawback is lack of coherence in terminology – a similar problem may occur within the medical research setting in relating social phobia in humans to similar phenomena in animal studies. Reale and associates (Reale et al., 2007) proposed a terminology involving 5 categories of temperamental traits that exist on a continuum. These traits include shyness-boldness, exploration-avoidance, activity, sociability, and aggressiveness. There are some parallels between these categories of animal temperament and the features of the Big Five factors of personality traits used in psychiatry: extroversion-introversion, neuroticism, agreeableness, conscientiousness, and openness (Lamiell, 2000). Still, there are major differences in how each factor is operationally defined based on the difference in modes of communication among animals and humans, especially in the social domain.

FINDINGS WITH FERAL ANIMALS

Field and laboratory studies of feral animals have made it increasingly evident that behavior varies non-randomly among individuals along particular axes across a range of taxa including primates, birds, fish and even insects (Gosling, 2001). Comparative psychologists and behavioral biologists document that individual animals show stable differences in their aggressiveness, activity, exploration, risk-taking, fearfulness, and reactivity (Sih et al., 2004a; Sih et al., 2004b), most of which show correspondence in non-social and social situations.

Individual variation in temperament in feral and farm animals has been observed and discussed in an anecdotal manner for some time (Armitage, 1986; Barnett & Cowan, 1976; Boissy & Bouissou, 1994). More recently, studies have been designed to confirm the existence of stable behavioral temperaments in feral animals. One behavioral trait that has received some attention is the bold/ shy continuum, although the interest has been for shyness in non-social investigation as well as in social interactions. These reports establish validity of the concept of temperaments in a wide range of feral animals in naturalistic settings or captured and brought into the lab (Gosling, 1998).

Evidence for shy members of a group being less active is found in a report on rainbow trout (*Oncorhynchus mykiss*) (Sneddon, 2003). Dingemanse and colleagues (Dingemanse et al., 2002) reported consistent individual differences in investigatory behaviors among a flock of great tits (*Parus major*) and determined shy and bold phenotypes to be heritable. That this evaluation was conducted in feral birds is noteworthy because heritability estimates are typically much smaller in the field than in the environmentally controlled laboratory setting. Indeed, an intra-strain, bidirectional selective breeding program of the common lab strain of rats, the Wistar strain, was successful in developing lines of animals showing high or low investigation tendencies (Landgraf, 2003). It is notable that the bold and shy behaviors in the two lines were consistent in both non-social and social interaction tests.

In a series of experiments, Brown and colleagues (Brown et al., 1996) conducted studies of populations of a fish species (*Brachyraphis episcopi*) found in the streams emptying into the Panama Canal. Their primary interest was confirming the heritability of shy-bold temperaments. In a recent report (Brown et al., 2007), fish collected from regions of high- and low-predation pressure were found to be shy and bold, respectively. The animals were bred and their offspring reared in the laboratory under varying conditions and tested for non-social shyness in an open-field paradigm. First-generation laboratory-reared fish showed similar behaviour to their wild parents suggesting that shyness has a heritable component. Further evidence of heritability was the finding of stable differences between males and females in of the offspring. A similar study of wild-caught pumpkin-seed sunfish (*Lepomis gibbosus*) reached a comparable conclusion (Wilson et al., 1994).

Most pet owners of dogs and cats would agree with the idea that domesticated animals possess unique "personalities" that are stable over the lifetime and across non-social and social situations. A study of privately owned dogs (Svartberg et al., 2005) confirmed the pet owners' observations. The dogs, of varied breeds and both genders, were rated on personality dimensions across test sessions over months. The authors concluded that trait scores of playfulness, chase-proneness, sociability and shy/ boldness were stable over sessions, pointing to the behaviors being based on genetic and biological factors. Curiosity, fearlessness and aggressiveness were influenced by repeated exposures, suggesting that these behavior clusters were heavily influenced by different experiences or ongoing internal factors.

A hypothesis has been proposed that more extreme individuals should be more consistent in their behavior than intermediate individuals (Bem & Allen, 1974; Wilson et al., 1994). This would suggest that more extremes of a trait are more resistant to change. Individuals that possess these extremes may have trouble adapting to a situation, which may lead to anxiety or avoidance of the situation. In the case of individuals exhibiting a shy temperament, an extreme of this trait may have important correlations with the experiences of humans with social phobia.

Regardless, further studies of individual differences in social behaviors within feral species may lead to designing carefully controlled pre-clinical medical research. The goal will be to develop animal models or paradigms that more closely represent dysfunctional social interactions in humans. The ultimate goal will be identifying structural, physiological, biochemical, genetic and environmental factors that are responsible for individuals displaying shy behaviors and drive some to social phobia. Below, we provide an overview of our current knowledge on each of these goals.

Laboratory Animal Models

Mathew (Mathew et al., 2001) reviewed the nonhuman primate animal models of social anxiety that could be organized as one of three types. Social subordination is based on the observation that submissive members of the group spent more time alone, variable foraging stress is designed to reduce the predictability of mother – infant contacts and the social attachment model is based on the fear and anxiety of some animals during social interactions. Mathew concluded, however, that all three of the animal models were inadequate.

Behavioral neuroscientists have developed varied paradigms to measure social behaviors in a variety of animal species typically used in experimental research from rats and mice to voles and primates (Ray & Hansen, 2004). A common paradigm is the social interaction test developed 30 years ago by File and her colleagues (File, 1980). This paradigm was designed as a measure of anxiety in which environmental conditions can be altered to either suppress or facilitate social interaction depending on current anxiety levels of the animal. The amount of time the test animal spends interacting with a stimulus animal is measured over several encounters. A great virtue of the paradigm is that it can also be used to evaluate general levels of shyness in social interactions in different strains of animals, including knock-out and transgenic mice, as well as well-established experimental interventions on social behavior.

Concerns about the potential confounds of direct interactions have led other researchers to minimize direct physical contact between the subject animals. The so-called stimulus animal, or target, is placed behind a mesh screen or other enclosure that allows for visual, auditory and olfactory contact but prevents the confounds of aggression between same-sex animals and of sexual contacts between males and females (Taylor et al., 1984).

Another method is to remove the stimulus animal entirely and use investigation of bedding containing the odors of a stimulus animal (Halpin, 1986; Sawyer et al., 1984). Clean bedding and soiled bedding from conspecifics are placed in separate containers and the time the animal spends investigating the containers are measured. Investigation times of soiled bedding have been used markers of social interest, social motivation and social recognition. Confirmation that the paradigm is a legitimate measure of social behavior comes from (unpublished) data from our lab. Rats displaying low investigation times of soiled bedding often show decreased social interaction in a standard social interaction test.

Decreased interaction with direct or indirect social paradigms relative to other members of the species can be used to identify a shy temperament. Their face validity as animal models includes findings of reduced social contact often being reported in human studies (Kagan et al., 1988; Van Ameringen et al., 1998).

Neuroanatomy of Shyness

Structural anomalies that impair function are candidates for symptomology of social anxiety. Neuroanatomical sites have been implicated in the pathophysiology of dysfunctional social behaviors, including parts of the limbic system, cerebral cortex and cerebellum (Adolphs et al., 2002; Prather et al., 2001). In addition, a large body of work put forth by Kagan and colleagues has shown that the amygdala plays a clear role in shyness in children and adults (Kagan, 1992; Kagan et al., 1988; Schwartz et al., 2003). These classic studies show differential activation of the amygdala in children behaviorally characterized as having either inhibited or uninhibited temperaments. A subgroup of these inhibited children experience social phobia as adults with continued overactivation of the amygdala (Schwartz et al., 2003).

Indeed, the amygdala has been the focus of the bulk of the anatomical studies of fear and anxiety and their relation to behavioral inhibition in humans (Birbaumer et al., 1998; Schmidt et al., 1997; Thomas et al., 2002). As but one example, adults with social phobia exposed to mildly hostile facial expressions experienced an exaggerated amygdalar activation (Morris et al., 1996). Moreover, discovery of functional connections of the amygdala to other brain regions has suggested a fear circuit that is likely to play a role in social anxiety (Kim & Gorman, 2005; LeDoux, 2003). The circuit involves the prefrontal cortex and the limbic "bridge" to the amygdala, the anterior cingulate gyrus, as well as structures adjacent to the amygdala such as the bed nucleus of the stria terminalis. Lesion studies and pharmacological manipulation in animal models have confirmed the involvement of these brain regions in responses to social stimuli (Myers et al., 1973; Rangel et al., 2003; Rudebeck et al., 2006).

Imaging studies of social phobics indicate increased medial temporal lobe activity, specifically in the hippocampus, in recognition of facial stimuli (Kim & Gorman, 2005). Also, Tillfors and her associates (Tillfors et al., 2001; 2002) reported increases in cerebral blood flow to the amygdala, prefrontal cortex and caudate in individuals diagnosed with social phobia in anticipation of public speaking. Results from an fMRI suggested a similar pattern of activation in social phobics to the presentation of facial stimuli (Birbaumer et al., 1998). These patterns indicate brain activation that is similar to the other anxiety disorders. The conclusion is that social phobia has a neuroanatomical basis in an "alarm system" in the brain centered in the amygdaloid-hippocampal region (LeDoux, 2000; Tillfors, 2004).

Recently there has been a surge of interest in the basolateral nucleus of the amygdala (BLA). Specifically, the interest centers on BLA function to provide cues about the emotional salience of a stimulus and the emotional state of the partner in a social interaction (Truitt et al., 2007). This is thought to occur through projections from the BLA to the orbito-frontal cortex and the prefrontal cortex. The result is a self-monitoring circuit that regulates the animal's social interactions and allows for dynamic, adaptive changes while the interaction is taking place (Rosenkranz et al., 2003).

The BLA consists of glutamatergic projection neurons regulated by four separate populations of inhibitory GABAergic interneurons (McDonald & Mascagni, 2002). It is proposed that disruption of this inhibitory tone in the BLA could result in improper assignment of salience to a social stimulus leading to a social anxiety-like response, whereas dysfunctional connections between the BLA and prefrontal cortex could result in faulty emotional assessment and ability to modulate appropriate responses producing deficits in social behavior resembling social deficits relevant to schizophrenia and autism (Bachevalier & Malkova, 2006).

A study by Truitt and colleagues (Truitt et al., 2007) modeled dysfunction in the BLA of rats by disrupting BLA inhibitory tone through priming or lesioning GABAergic interneurons to impair connectivity with the PFC/OFC. Rats with overactive BLA displayed persistent social inhibition which could be overcome with habituation while rats with selective lesions of GABAergic interneurons also exhibited persistent social inhibition that was not reversed with habituation to a stimulus animal. Results of this study again highlight the importance of the amygdala in social behaviors. Moreover, the suggestion is that the common progressive increases of social anxiety during a person's lifetime may reflect the progressive disruptions in amygdalar functioning over time.

Electrophysiological correlates of limbic system function confirm the importance of the amygdala in social phobia. The N400 event related potential (ERP) reflects a temporal correlate of a cortico-amygdala pathway of emotional processing (LeDoux, 2003; Williams et al., 2004). In adult patients with social phobia, there was a decrease in cortical activity in association with increased amygdala activation during simulated public speaking (Tillfors et al., 2001; Van Ameringen et al., 2000).

Battaglia and colleagues (Battaglia et al., 2005) analyzed the N400 ERP responses of children to different emotional facial expressions and the genetic variability at the locus of the serotonin transporter promoter gene, known as 5-HTTLPR. The S allele of the 5-HTTLPR in shy children predicted smaller N400 amplitudes in response to hostile or neutral facial expressions. This response is indicative of decreased cortical activity co-occurring with increased subcortical activity. Their data suggest that a biased pattern of processing emotional information of social relevance can be recognized and characterized with psychophysiological measures early in life in children with heightened indexes of shyness or with 1 or 2 copies of the 5-HTTLPR S allele.

Indeed, much of the interest in both genetics and neurotransmitter involvement in social phobia has focused on serotonin. Many anxiety-related disorders are responsive to serotonin specific re-uptake inhibitors (SSRIs) (Bouwer & Stein, 1998; Katzelnick et al., 1995) and there are reports suggesting that SSRIs can increase sociability in non-socially impaired volunteers (Knutson et al., 1998). The serotonergic system is one of several neurochemicals that have been related to normal and dysfunctional social behaviors.

Neuroendocrine Contributions to Shyness

Extensive work by Sapolsky has shown that social status and degree of social affiliation are associated with altered hypothalamic – pituitary – adrenal (HPA) axis functioning (Sapolsky, 1982; Sapolsky, 2004). Submissive members of a social group can be described as behaviorally inhibited in both social and non-social settings. Experiments performed on feral baboons revealed that subordinate animals have higher baseline corticosteroid (CORT) levels, a sluggish negative feedback and prolonged CORT response to unfamiliar stimuli.

Other results from field studies of great tits indicate that the shy birds show higher body temperatures and breathing rates in response to acute stress than their bold counterparts (Carere et al., 2005; Carere & van Oers, 2004). The shy birds also experience greater CORT release in response to social stress compared to bold animals.

Circulating CORT was a primary measure in the famous studies by Kagan and associates of the biological bases for shyness in children. Beginning in the mid-1980s (Kagan et al., 1984), the researchers tested young, sometimes very young, children in a variety of novel non-social and social settings. The latter included meeting an unfamiliar experimenter, interacting with a stranger and brief separation from the mother. Kagan's research group was particularly interested in the children showing extremes on a continuum of behaviorally inhibited or uninhibited. The most remarkable outcomes were: 1) the high probability that inhibited, shy children remained shy into later childhood and even into young adulthood (Gest, 1997; Schwartz et al., 2003) and 2) the stability of a host of peripheral physiological measures (Kagan et al., 1988). Extremely shy children and adults experienced clear evidence of sympathetic nervous system activation with higher heart and breathing rates, laryngeal muscle tension, pupillary dilation, and elevated titers of norepinephrine and CORT. The relevance of these findings for social phobia is indicated by findings of behavioral inhibition being a predictor of adult social anxiety (Rosenbaum et al., 1991)

Findings with a laboratory animal model by Cavigelli and colleagues (Cavigelli & McClintock, 2003; Cavigelli et al., 2007) offer additional support for the involvement of the HPA axis in behavioral inhibition. The initial experiment found that fear of non-social novelty in infant rats correlated with higher corticosterone levels in response in adulthood to an unfamiliar environment and increased early mortality (Cavigelli & McClintock, 2003). Subsequently, they reported that inhibited behavior towards a social stimulus was a better predictor than non-social inhibition of adult CORT baseline levels and endocrine reactivity to an unfamiliar stimulus (Cavigelli et al., 2007). The implication is that even in domesticated animals, social interactions have a more profound influence on the endocrine stress response than non-social situations in individuals with a shy temperament.

It may be that HPA axis abnormalities are not the cause, but the consequence of being socially phobic. The negative feedback of the axis could perpetuate or exacerbate the propensity for social anxiety. For example, a study of behaviorally inhibited young children in a daycare center confirmed that shyness is associated with elevated CORT levels.

However, both shy and bold children experienced a pulse of CORT upon encountering a stranger, but only the shy children used poorer emotional regulation strategies that led to more frequent activation of the HPA axis (Zimmermann & Stansbury, 2004).

Today, interest in endocrine influences on social function and dysfunction has turned to pituitary peptides and hypothalamic neuropeptides. Work by Insel (Insel & Young, 2000), Carter (Carter, 1998) and others (Bielsky et al., 2004; Young & Wang, 2004) has revealed the important link between social behaviors and the hormones oxytocin and vasopressin released from the posterior pituitary. Much of this research is directed at understanding the relation of the hormones to social attachment in adults using prairie voles, *Microtus orchragaster*, and social memory in various laboratory species. Nonetheless, both affiliation and social recognition are key components of social anxiety because, for example, they are involved in the recognition and response to individuals of varying degrees of familiarity and attachment.

Oxytocin (OT) regulates social attachment and behaviors in voles (Insel, 1997; Bartz & McInnes, 2007). Research on the OT receptors in the brain suggests that it is not the overall expression of receptors but differences in the distribution of OT receptors that underlie social behavior differences (Young et al., 1997). High levels of OT receptors in the prelimbic cortex and nucleus accumbens (areas involved in reinforcement and conditioning) are associated with strong social bonding. Oxytocin also facilitates social recognition in rodents while OT antagonists disrupt social memory (Englemann et al., 1998).

More specific evidence for OT involvement in shy animals is that microinjection of the hormone into the central amygdala alleviates the social deficits induced by prenatal stress in rats (Lee et al., 2007). The OT knock-out mouse experiences social deficits that appear to be the result of specific impairments in social recognition (Winslow & Insel, 2002). The mice show normal cognitive function on tests of spatial and olfactory memory (Ferguson et al., 2002), suggesting that the memory deficit is specific to the social domain. Oxytocin is regulated partly by the serotonergic neurotransmitter system and the observed differences in behavioral response may be reflective of distinct disruption of this component of the biological systems involved in regulating social behaviors. In fact, Crawley and colleagues (Crawley et al., 2007) recently demonstrated that social approach behavior is not disrupted in two separate lines of OT knockouts at two separate facilities. It has also been reported that OT knockout mice display more anxiety-like behaviors and release more CORT in response to stress (Amico et al., 2001). It is possible that impairments in social memory in humans may indirectly lead to shy behavior, however, developing an animal model based on this possibility is difficult. Social animals tend to investigate a novel conspecific more than a familiar one.

Arginine vasopressin (AVP) is a direct regulator of the HPA axis (Aguilera & Rabadan-Diehl, 2000) and has been shown to be elevated in individuals with stress-related disorders (Purba et al., 1996; van Londen et al., 1997). Egashira and associates (Egashira et al., 2007) reported impaired social interaction in a knockout mouse model in which the vasopressin V1a receptor subtype was deleted. This reduced amount of social interaction was accompanied with a decrease in anxiety-related behavior as well; however anxiety was measured in the open-field and not in direct relation to the social interaction test. One could speculate that if the decrease in social interaction is not due to anxiety towards the social situation, which may be the condition in shyness or social phobia, it may be resultant of a decreased motivation towards social activity. If this is the case, these findings may reflect a fundamental difference between certain aspects of neuropsychiatric disorders involving social behavior such as autism or schizophrenia and anxiety disorders including social phobia.

An antagonist of the vasopressin V1B receptor subtype promoted increases in social interaction in rats. That hypophysectomized rats were not responsive to the AVP antagonist suggested the enhanced social responsiveness was mediated by the pituitary (Shimazaki et al., 2006). In addition, the AVP receptor gene has been found to be different in social and asocial voles (Young et al., 1999).

Finally, several studies have identified posterior pituitary hormones as an important mediator of human social behavior as well (Fries et al., 2005; Kosfeld et al., 2005; Zak et al., 2005). For example, OT administered to human subjects improved recognition memory for faces (Savaskan et al., 2008).

Neurotransmitter Pathways and Shyness

Only recently has attention turned to neurotransmitters and shyness. SSRIs have shown some efficacy in relieving social phobia in humans suggesting involvement of the serotonergic system in the disorder (Bouwer & Stein, 1998). The involvement of specific neurotransmitters in the regulation of social behavior has been elucidated through several studies using animal models. Greatest interest has been in the serotonergic system (Manuck et al., 2003).

Wistar rats have been shown to display increased serotonergic activity in response to anxiety-like behaviors (Rex et al., 2004). The fawn-hooded rat is characterized as having impairments of uptake and vesicular storage of serotonin and other abnormalities in serotonergic function (Arora et al., 1983, Aulakh et al., 1992). In addition, the FH strain also shows hypersensitivity in the noradrenergic system paralleling findings from human studies of individuals with anxiety and panic disorders (Dajas et al., 1986). These findings lend support to hypothesis of defective serotonergic or hypersensitive noradrenergic systems in the etiology of social phobia and anxiety disorders.

In an exhaustive study of shy lab rats, we examined the influence of manipulations of the dopamine and serotonin neurotransmitter systems (Taylor & Yuede, 2005). We developed a methodology for selecting shy females and testing changes in social attraction in an animal model of behavioral timidity. In the first experiment, randomly selected female rats were chronically administered either more or less specific antagonists of dopamine and serotonin and tested over 3 weeks for changes in attraction to a social stimulus. Findings revealed a statistically significant decrease in social investigation in the animals treated with the non-specific dopamine antagonists compared to controls but no significant differences among the other groups. In the second experiment, however, we employed pretests to select behaviorally timid animals. Only female rats having little initial attraction to unfamiliar non-social and social stimuli were chosen to serve as subjects for the experiment using the same drug exposure regiments and behavioral measures used in the first experiment. Results with pre-selected timid animals indicated that only the animals administered the serotonin antagonist significantly increased social investigation. Indeed, the non-specific dopamine antagonist, haloperidol, appears to have magnified avoidance of social contact. Conclusions are that timidity may involve aspects of the serotonergic system, and the animal model of the second experiment may prove useful for studies of the biological underpinnings of shyness.

A large body of research links disruptions in serotonergic transmission to decreased social interaction (File et al., 1993; 1999). Rats with selective impairments in serotonin storage, reuptake, and receptor function have been reported to show more anxiety resulting in decreased social interaction (Gonzalez et al., 1998; Kantor et al., 2000).

The atypical antipsychotic clozapine, which has serotonin antagonistic properties, has been shown to reverse social interaction deficits produced by phencyclidine (PCP) (Lee et al., 2005; Qiao et al., 2001). Clozapine improved sociality in both PCP-treated and NR1 knockdown animals, while haloperidol was ineffective (Sams-Dodd, 1999; Mohn et al., 1999). Clozapine also is more effective than typical antipsychotics in improving the asociality symptoms of schizophrenics (Azorin et al., 2001; Buchanan et al., 1998). Our studies also found that clozapine, but not dopamine antagonists, were effective in increasing social behavior in inherently timid rats (Taylor & Yuede, 2005). The findings with clozapine provide more support for the involvement of the serotonergic system in social behaviors. Our results suggest that clozapine provides some correction of an already observable deficit or interacts with certain genetic variations as we did not find increases in social interactions in animals that did not originally display an inhibited temperament.

That disturbances in the excitatory amino acid neurotransmitter system, glutamate, may underlie the negative symptom of social avoidance in schizophrenia (Javitt & Zukin, 1991) has focused attention on the glutamate NMDA receptor as playing a role in behavioral inhibition. Decreased activity of the glutamatergic NMDA receptor system results in deficits in social behavior resembling the negative symptoms of schizophrenia (Farber, 2003; Mouri et al., 2007). Knockdown mice targeting NMDA receptor 1 (NR1) subtype have low numbers of NMDA receptors and also show social abnormalities (Mohn et al., 1999).

PCP, a noncompetitive NMDA antagonist, produced reliable deficits in social interaction in a variety of species (Qiao et al., 2001; Sams-Dodd, 1995). In addition to altering glutamatergic neurotransmission, subchronic administration of PCP resulted in impaired social interaction in combination with reduced V1a receptor density in several brain regions (Tanaka et al., 2003). PCP-induced models of social deficits are most often used to mimic the social deficits observed in schizophrenia but they also may have some similarities to underlying features of social phobia.

These data suggest a more focused assessment of brain structures and neuroendocrine and neurotransmitter functions related to reward and low anxiety. One attractive perspective is that pathways from the rostral hypothalamus to the ventral tegmental area may be critical for integrating social information with reward pathways, especially in highly affiliative species that respond to social stimuli as reinforcers (Insel, 1997). Stein (Stein, 1998) speculated that this represents a model of social phobia as a disorder characterized by dysfunction within the systems that evaluate the risks and benefits of social affiliation. These brain systems appear to be concentrated in the amygdala, serotonergic and glutamatergic pathways and neuroendocrine functions of vasopressin and oxytocin. Social phobia may then be characterized by exaggerated appraisal of the risks involved in social contacts. At the same time, there is dysfunction in systems that register the reward of social interactions.

GENETIC CONTRIBUTIONS TO A SHY PHENOTYPE

As with many neuropsychiatric conditions, social phobia likely involves some degree of genetic susceptibility. Support comes from studies of both human and non-human animals (Andrews et al., 1990; Flint, 2002; Reichborn-Kjennerud et al., 2007). Animal studies have focused mainly on differences in social behaviors among inbred mouse and rat strains, and various knock-out and transgenic mice displaying abnormal social behaviors. The general picture emerging is one of social behavior involving the interaction of many genes of small influence rather than one specific gene. Genes related to vasopressin, oxytocin and serotonin appear to show the most robust effects on social behavior.

Strain differences among inbred mice and rats offer a starting point for developing genetic animal models of sociality. Knowing normal level of sociality in an animal model is particularly critical when conducting studies on the biology of behavioral inhibition. This is of special importance in choosing and comparing the many inbred strains of mice. For example, BALB/cJ mice show more social avoidance towards a novel conspecific, while mice of the C57BL/6J and FBN strains are more social (Brodkin et al., 2004).

A widely used experimental procedure in these studies is cross-fostering, a method used to dissociate relative influences of genetic versus early environmental factors on various neurobiological phenotypes. The procedure uses timed pregnancies of two females and, upon parturition, exchanges the litters. Females of most lab animals are quite tolerant of the switch and care for the litter as they do their own.

Inbred strains of mice offer valuable translational tools to study the interplay of genetic and environmental factors in neurodevelopmental disorders. The BTBR strain, for example, was developed as an animal model of autism. These mice display a phenotype that includes aberrant reciprocal social interactions. Cross-fostering BTBR mice to B6 dams and vice versa did not change social dynamics of strains. The shy phenotypes common in BTBR mice are stable, genetically based traits that are not malleable to different maternal environments (Yang et al., 2007). Interestingly, in an open field both BTBR and B6 mice show similar levels of activity while in the social interaction test the BTBR mice were much less active. The suggestion is that decreased investigation was specific to social interactions.

Similar effects of strain have also been reported in the rat social interaction test. Sprague-Dawley rats are more social than Wistar rats and the increased level of sociality in Sprague-Dawley animals is unchanged by pharmacological or environmental manipulations such as treatment with low-doses of diazepam or altering the light-dark cycle. In contrast, the amount of social interaction shown by the "more anxious" Wistar rats was susceptible to both pharmacological and environmental changes (Rex et al., 2004).

The Fawn-hooded rat strain (FH) is a putative genetic model for neuropsychiatric disorders with possible abnormalities in serotonergic function. These rats show more freezing behavior in response to stress (Overstreet et al., 1992), increased expression of fearful behaviors (Satinder & Woolridge, 1986), and increased preference for alcohol (Drewek & Broudhurst, 1979). Fawn-hooded rats show decreased social interaction time compared to Wistar and Sprague-Dawley rats in the social interaction test under both stressful and non-stressful situations (Kantor et al., 2000). The authors' interpreted the results as pointing to FH rats experiencing discomfort in social situations whereas rats from the common Sprague-Dawley and Wistar strains appear to be more comfortable.

Genetic background of the animal clearly has an influence on the level of social interaction displayed and receptiveness to experimental manipulations. In addition, QTL analysis or other large genetic screening studies may be able to use information on strain differences to pinpoint areas of the genome that may be related to social phobia.

While strain differences can provide broad pictures of which genetic backgrounds are more likely to be shy and socially avoidant, gene knock-out models can lend insight into the influence of specific genes on social behaviors. Most often these studies are focused on social avoidance or shyness related to autism or schizophrenia. However, it is possible that these same genes may be defective or altered in social phobia as well.

Genes related to AVP and OT, the neurohypophyseal peptides discussed above, have been characterized as having significant involvement in impaired social interaction. Studies with social and asocial strains of voles have shown that an expanded microsatellite, or simple sequence repeat, area upstream of the transcription start site for the AVP receptor gene was directly related to increase in affiliative behavior (Young et al., 1999). The suggestion is that variability in AVP receptor microsatellite length could help account for differences in normal personality traits, such as shyness, and possibly influence disorders of sociability.

Genetic predisposition for development of social phobia has also been reported in the human literature. Children of social phobics are at an increased risk for the development of social phobia and other anxiety disorders (Mancini et al., 1996). Stein and associates (Stein, 1998) refined this conclusion by demonstrating that only the generalized type of social phobia is elevated among first-degree relatives of generalized social phobic probands, and the morbid risk was approximately ten times that of relatives of non-affected individuals. It is likely that what is inherited is a temperament that predisposes the individual to the development of anxiety disorders in general and social phobia in particular.

Finally, there is evidence for a genetic contribution to the involvement of amygdaloid circuitry in the predisposition to excessive shyness (Rowe & Plomin, 1977). The suggestion is that shyness is part of a broader tendency toward fearfulness that has high heritability.

Environmental Influences on Shyness

The prenatal environment and subsequent environmental or parental effects are also thought to contribute to the variation in the expression of social behavior. A key aspect of the vulnerability-stress model of psychiatric disease is that an individual may have the potential to develop a disorder but it does not manifest itself without an environmental trigger (Schmidt & Fox, 1999). Research into environmental effects has identified possible triggers in susceptible populations.

For example, mice reared in a communal nesting situation where three dams and their pups were housed together and shared care-giving roles, showed greater social interaction in adulthood compared to mice reared in a single nest environment. Interestingly, communal nesting also resulted in increased anxiety-like behavior in non-social measures such as open-field and elevated plus maze (Branchi & Alleva, 2006; Branchi et al., 2006; D'Andrea et al., 2007).

Altering lighting conditions in the early postnatal period in rats also has significant effects on social interactions of the animals in adolescence and adulthood. Prolonged dark periods decreased social interaction while prolonged light periods increased social interaction later in life (Toki et al., 2007). Social stress during adolescence in rats has been shown to reduce social interaction when tested in adulthood. Rats who experienced social defeat through several encounters with an unfamiliar aggressive rat displayed long-lasting suppression of social interest in another unfamiliar rat compared to adolescent who did not experience social stress (Vidal et al., 2007). In addition, maternal separation during the postnatal period and noisy housing conditions resulted in decreased social interaction (Maciag et al., 2002).

Prenatal environments may also contribute to shyness. Repeated stress exposure during the later stages of pregnancy in rats produces a robust decrease in social interaction in the offspring as measured in adolescence and adulthood (Cabrera et al., 1999; Lee et al., 2007). These results again point to specificity of the effects. The stressful experiences were not related to a generalized state of anxiety because the rats did not show anxiogenic effects on behaviors in non-social settings (Gurtman et al., 2002; Prut & Belzung, 2003).

Similar to the effects observed in animals, daylength during pregnancy may affect the development of shyness in children. Decreased hours of daylight during the midpoint of gestation resulted in increased incidence of shyness in children from both northern and southern hemispheres (Gortmaker et al., 1996). This effect could be related to changes in certain hormone levels, such as melatonin, that are directly affected by exposure to daylight. Adverse social experiences such as bullying in childhood and adolescence may affect social behavior functioning and may also increase the vulnerability to develop social phobia in adulthood (Gladstone et al., 2006; Grossman et al., 2003; Wals & Verhulst, 2005).

EVOLUTION OF SHY PHENOTYPES

A central issue in evolutionary biology is to understand the factors contributing to variability in a species. Natural selection and the rarity of genetic mutation suggest little variability in the genotype of conspecific animals. Yet, genomic characterizations indicate considerable genetic variability within a species, albeit often equal numbers of pseudogenes and functional genes (Ache & Young, 2005). Although environment-gene interactions could explain some of the phenotypic variation, it remains puzzling that behavioral extremes such as a bold or shy temperament remains in the populations over evolutionary time (Dingemanse et al., 2002).

The key to the puzzle is the recognition that the temperament is consistent over time and perhaps across generations. Individual animals will certainly adjust their behaviors to adapt the current conditions (Dall et al., 2004). Sometimes it is clearly adaptive to be bold and other times to be shy. Yet, animals expressing a shy temperament appear to be behaviorally inhibited in many situations.

One answer to the question of animal personalities being fixtures in a species is that there is selective advantage to behavioral extremes. It is easy to imagine reproductive advantages conferred on a socially bold individual. In most vertebrate animals, sociability is an important part of survival, for example, group protection from predators. Although the levels of social interaction may be markedly different across species, social contact is critical for the ultimate force of evolution, sexual reproduction.

Earlier in this chapter, we cited a number of empirical studies that would appear to confer reproductive advantages on bold animals. They include findings of bold individuals being more active (Sneddon, 2003), investigating the environment and other animals more thoroughly (Dingemanse et al., 2002). Higher aggression in bolder members of a species likely directly benefits reproductive success.

It may be that bold animals have characteristics that convey a more subtle reproductive advantage. Shy members of a group of rainbow trout (*Oncorhynchus mykiss*) learned a simple conditioning task more slowly than did the bold fish (Sneddon, 2003). Selectively breeding lab rats for high and low anxiety lines yielded unexpected results. The high anxiety lines produced sperm of greater motility, and presumably higher fertility, compared to the low anxiety lines (Sato et al., 2002).

The direct and indirect advantages for boldness suggest, by extension, the same factors are disadvantageous to socially shy individuals. Behaviorally timid animals experience more social stress and often an excess of physical stressors. They may have to work harder for their food and have less fat reserves. They may be the target of unprovoked displacement aggression and be exposed more often to predators by being forced into more dangerous feeding areas (Sapolsky, 2004). The physiological and endocrine anomalies cited earlier in this chapter also point to potential health problems in the shy animals, for example, disturbances in the serotonergic pathways are associated with sexual dysfunction (Hull et al., 2004)

There is evidence in non-human animals that behavioral inhibition is adaptive. Examples include settings in which there is a high risk of predation where reticence confers a selective advantage. Avoiding social interactions may have the benefits of safety from attack by aggressive members of the group (Hofmann et al., 2004). Indeed, evolutionary models of social phobia (Gilbert, 2001) view submissive social displays as defensive behaviors. Submissive signals, diverting one's eyes to prevent direct eye contact for instance, may serve as cues that the individual is not a serious threat to another animal. Even cues revealed by an unconsciously activated sympathetic nervous system, in humans this is blushing, sweating and such, may serve a similar function. And, future research may yield surprising advantages, some directly reproductive in nature.

A recent example is a particularly fascinating study of twins. A registry of 1,101 people tracked over decades was used to correlate personality variables earlier in adult life with reproductive success. People identified as introverted, or shy, had higher numbers of biological children than extraverted, bold individuals. This was only the case, however, if the shy individuals were also high in neuroticism (Eaves et al., 1990).

Regardless, that shyness persists over evolutionary time in vertebrate populations is confirmation that behavioral timidity is not an evolutionary handicap. This is an important observation because selection does not typically optimize adaptive traits as much as it gradually eliminates unfit traits (McGuire & Troisi, 1998). In the case of timidity, it is either that a shy temperament has proven adaptive, or that shyness does not have significant reproductive disadvantages. The implication is that from a Darwinian psychiatric perspective, shyness in humans, at least in its non-debilitating expression, is not a behavioral disorder.

CONCLUSION

Individual differences in core behaviors are observed in many vertebrate species. When the behavior is expressed across situations and is a relatively permanent feature of the animal, it is said to constitute temperaments that contribute to the animal's "personality." Extremes of the continuum that identifies shy and bold animals in social settings is a prominent temperament. It is the one in which we are most interested.

Our goal in this chapter has been to explore possible biological factors underlying shyness that may help us better understand social phobia. The approach has been to review paradigms and findings of human and animal studies that provide an insight into the biological underpinnings of shyness and, perhaps, social phobia.

Unfortunately, we have been unable to use animal models to provide a definitive answer to the relation of shyness to disruptive social anxieties. The literature we reviewed fails to clearly identify the features of shyness that distinguish between normal reticence in the presence of unfamiliar conspecifics and psychopathology.

Generating useful assays and animal models for social phobia will continue to be a challenge for the behavioral neuroscience community. There is the recurrent circular problem in modeling symptoms without knowing causes, which is a common phenomenon in experimental research at the early stages of understanding human disease (Crawley, 2007). Animal models of social phobia will be refined as mechanisms emerge from the current models investigating proposed genetic, biochemical, neuroanatomical and environmental factors involved in the disorder.

The picture that emerges is an intricate system involving neurotransmitters such as serotonin and glutamate, their interactions and involvements with other neurochemicals such as vasopressin and oxytocin especially in regions involved in reward, fear or emotional processing, and subsequent activation of the HPA axis. Impairment in any of these components may lead to an exacerbation of the shy response to the point where it becomes extreme or dysfunctional. Individual differences in the susceptibility to develop this type of response are likely mediated by genetic factors involving these processes. That there are so many possible factors in the biology of social behaviors and their connections with anxiety will likely conclude the obvious; social anxieties result from a complex interaction among biological factors.

Still, we can offer conclusions in which we are moderately confident. One is that a shy temperament is likely related to the development of social phobia in genetically susceptible individuals. Also, we believe it is important to acknowledge that shyness is not unnatural, our evolutionary assessment would argue the opposite, and should not be reflexively treated as a behavioral disorder. On the other hand, extreme forms of shyness, expressed as debilitating social phobia, are worthy of continued study for underlying mechanisms and for biologically based treatments.

Future studies should continue to focus on these issues to identify biological correlates for specific subtypes in the symptomology of disorders involving social dysfunction. In addition, more research into the link between shyness and neuropsychiatric disorders should uncover at what point this type of behavior becomes problematic for the individual and leads to the debilitating human condition known as social phobia.

REFERENCES

Ache, B. W., & Young, J. M. (2005). Olfaction: diverse species, conserved principles. *Neuron, 48*, 417-430.

Adolphs, R., Baron-Cohen, S., & Tranel, D. (2002). Impaired recognition of social emotions following amygdala damage. *Journal of Cognitive Neuroscience, 14*, 1264-1274.

Aguilera, G., & Rabadan-Diehl, C. (2000). Vasopressinergic regulation of the hypothalamic-pituitary-adrenal axis: implications for stress adaptation. *Regulatory Peptides, 22*, 23-29.

Amico, J. A., Morris, M., & Vollmer, R. R. (2001). Mice deficient in oxytocin manifest increased saline consumption following overnight fluid deprivation. *American Journal of Physiology, 281*, R1368-R1373.

Andrews, G., Stewart, G., Allen, R., & Henderson, A. S. (1990). The genetics of six neurotic disorders: a twin study. *Journal of Affective Disorders, 19*, 23-29.

Armitage, K. B. (1986). Individuality, social behavior, and reproductive success in yellow-bellied marmots. *Ecology, 67*, 1186-1193.

Arora, R. C., Tong, C., Jackman, H. L., Stoff, D., & Meltzer, H. Y. (1983). Serotonin uptake and imipramine binding in blood platelets and brain of Fawn-Hooded and Sprague Dawley rats. *Life Sciences, 33*, 437-442.

Azorin, J. M., Spiegel, R., Remington, G., Vanelle, J. M., Pere, J. J., & Giguere, M. (2001). A double-blind comparative study of clozapine and risperidone in the management of severe chronic schizophrenia. *American Journal of Psychiatry, 158*, 1305-1313.

Bachevalier, J., & Malkova, L. (2006). The amygdala and development of social cognition: theoretical comment on Bauman, Toscano, Mason, Lavanex, and Amaral (2006). *Behavioural Neuroscience, 120*, 989-991.

Barnett, S. A., & Cowan, P. E. (1976). Activity, exploration, curiosity and fear: an ethological study. *Interdisciplinary Science Reviews, 1*, 43-62.

Bartz, J. A., & McInnes, L. A. (2007). CD38 regulates oxytocin secretion and complex social behavior. *BioEssays, 29*, 837-841.

Battaglia, M., Ogliari, A., Zanoni, A., & Others, X. (2005). Influence of the serotonin transporter promoter gene and shyness on children's cerebral responses to facial expressions. *Archives of General Psychiatry, 62*, 85-94.

Beidel, D. C., Turner, S. M., & Morris, T. I. (1999). Psychopathology of childhood social phobia. *Journal of the American Academy of Child & Adolescent Psychiatry, 38*, 643-650.

Bem, D. J., & Allen, A. (1974). On predicting some of the people some of the time: the search for cross-cultural consistencies in behavior. *Psychological Review, 81*, 506-520.

Bielsky, I. F., Young, L. J., & Altstein, M. (2004). Oxytocin, vasopressin, and social recognition in mammals. *Peptides, 25*, 1565-1574.

Bienvenu, O. J., Hettema, J. M., Neale, M. C., Prescott, C. A., & Kendler, K. S. (2007). Low extraversion and high neuroticism as indices of genetic and environmental risk for social phobia, agoraphobia, and animal phobia. *American Journal of Psychiatry, 164*, 1714-1721.

Birbaumer, N., Grodd, W., Diedrich, O., Klose, U., Erb, M., Lotze, M., Schneider, F., Weiss, U., & Flor, H. (1998). fMRI reveals amygdala activation to human faces in social phobics. *NeuroReport, 9*, 1223-1226.

Boissy, A., & Bouissou, M. (1994). Effects of androgen treatment on behavioral and physiological responses of heifers to fear-eliciting situations. *Hormones & Behavior, 28*, 66-83.

Bouwer, C., & Stein, D. J. (1998). Use of the selective serotonin reuptake inhibitor citalopram in the treatment of generalized social phobia. *Journal of Affective Disorders, 49*, 79-82.

Branchi, I., & Alleva, E. (2006). Communal nesting, an early social enrichment, increases the adult anxiety-like response and shapes the role of social context in modulating the emotional behavior. *Behavioural Brain Research, 172*, 299-306.

Branchi, I., D'Andrea, I., Sietzema, J., Fiore, M., Di Fausto, M., Aloe, L., & Alleva, E. (2006). Early social enrichment augments adult hippocampal BDNF levels and survival of BrdU-positive cells while increasing anxiety- and "depression-like" behavior. *Journal of Neuroscience Research, 83*, 965-973.

Brodkin, E. S., Hagemann, A., Nemetski, S. M., & Silver, L. M. (2004). Social approach-avoidance behavior of inbred mouse strains towards DBA/2 mice. *Brain Research, 1002*, 151-157.

Brown, C., Burgess, F., & Braithwaite, V. (2007). Heritable and experiential effects on boldness in a tropical poeciliid. *Behavioral Ecology & Sociobiology, 62*, 237-243.

Brown, C., Jones, F., & Braithwaite, V. (2005). In situ examination of boldness-shyness traits in the tropical poeciliid, Brachyraphis episcopi. *Animal Behaviour, 70*, 1003-1009.

Brown, L. L., Tomarken, A. J., Orth, D. N., Loosen, P. T., Kalin, N. H., & Davidson, R. J. (1996). Individual differences in repressive-defensiveness predict basal salivary cortisol levels. *Journal of Personality & Social Psychology, 70*, 362-371.

Buchanan, R. W., Breier, A., Kirkpatrick, B., Ball, P., & Carpenter Jr, W. T. (1998). Positive and negative symptom response to clozapine in schizophrenic patients with and without the deficit syndrome. *American Journal of Psychiatry, 155*, 751-760.

Cabrera, R. J., Rodriguez-Echandia, E. L., Jatuff, A. S., & Foscolo, M. (1999). Effects of prenatal exposure to a mild chronic variable stress on body weight, preweaning mortality and rat behavior. *Brazilian Journal of Medical and Biological Research, 32*, 1229-1237.

Carere, C., Drent, P. J., Privitera, L., Koolhaas, J. M., & Groothuis, T. G. (2005). Personalities in great tits, Parus major: stability and consistency. *Animal Behaviour, 70*, 795-805.

Carere, C., & vanOers, K. (2004). Shy and bold great tits (Parus major): body temperature and breath rate in response to handling stress *Physiology & Behavior, 82*, 905-912.

Carter, C. S. (1998). Neuroendocrine perspectives on social attachment and love. *Psychoneuroendocrinology, 23*, 779-818.

Cavigelli, S., & McClintock, M. (2003). Fear of novelty in infant rats predicts adult corticosterone dynamics and an early death. *Proceedings of the National Academy of Sciences, 100*, 16131-16136.

Cavigelli, S. A., Stine, M. M., Kovacsics, C., Jefferson, A., Diep, M. N., & Barrett, C. E. (2007). Behavioral inhibition and glucocorticoid dynamics in a rodent model. *Physiology & Behavior, 92*, 897-905.

Chavira, D. A., Stein, M. B., & Malcarne, V. L. (2002). Scrutinizing the relationship between shyness and social phobia. *Journal of Anxiety Disorders, 16*, 585-598.

Clarke, A. S., & Boinski, S. (1995). Temperament in nonhuman primates. *American Journal of Primatology, 37*, 103-114.

Crawley, J. N. (2007). Testing hypotheses about autism. *Science, 318*, 56-57.

Crawley, J.N., Chen, T., Puri, A., Washburn, R., Sullivan, T.L., Hill, J.M., Young, N.B., Nadler, J.J., Moy, S.S., Young, L.J., Caldwell, H.K., Young, W.S. (2007). Social approach behaviors in oxytocin knockout mice: comparison of two independent lines tested in different laboratory environment. *Neuropeptides, 41,* 145-163.

Dajas, F., Nin, A., & Barbeito, L. (1986). Urinary norepinephrine excretion in panic and phobic disorders. *Journal of Neural Transmission, 65*, 75-81.

Dall, S. R. X., Houston, A. I., & McNamara, J. M. (2004). The behavioural ecology of personality: consistent individual differences from an adaptive perspective. *Ecology Letters, 7*, 734-739.

DAndrea, L., Alleva, E., & Branchi, I. (2007). Communal nesting, an early social enrichment, affects social competences but not learning and memory abilities at adulthood. *Behavioural Brain Research, 183*, 60-66.

Dingemanse, N. J., Both, C., Drent, P. J., vanOers, K., & vanNoordwijk, A. J. (2002). Repeatibility and heritability of exploratory behaviour in great tits from the wild. *Animal Behaviour, 64*, 929-938.

Drewek, K., & Broudhurst, P. (1979). Alcohol selection by strains of rats selectively bred for behavior. *J Stud Alcohol, 5*, 99-102.

Eaves, L. J., Martin, N. G., Heath, A. C., & Hewitt, J. K. (1990). Personality and reproductive fitness. *Behavioral Genetics, 20*, 563-568.

Egashira, N., Tanoue, A., Matsuda, T., Koushi, E., Harada, S., Takano, Y., Tsujimoto, G., Mishima, K., Iwasaki, K., & Fujiwara, M. (2007). Impaired social interaction and reduced anxiety-related behavior in vasopressin V1A receptor knockout mice. *Behavioural Brain Research, 178*, 123-127.

Englemann, M., Ebner, K., Wotjak, C. T., & Landgraf, R. (1998). Endogenous oxytocin is involved in short-term olfactory memory in female rats. *Behavioural Brain Research, 90*, 89-94.

Farber, N. B. (2003). The NMDA receptor hypofunction model of psychosis. *Annals New York Academy of Science, 1003*, 119-130.

Ferguson, J. N., Young, L. J., & Insel, T. R. (2002). The neuroendocrine basis of social recognition. *Frontiers in Neuroendocrinology, 23*, 200-224.

File, S. E. (1980). The use of social interaction as a method for detecting anxiolytic activity of chlordiazepoxide-like drugs. *Journal of Neuroscience Methods, 2*, 219-238.

File, S. E., Ouagazzal, A. M., Gonzalez, L. E., & Overstreet, D. H. (1999). Chronic fluoxetine in tests of anxiety in rat lines selectively bred for differential 5-HT1A receptor function. *Pharmacology, Biochemistry and Behavior, 62*, 695-701.

File, S. E., Zangrossi, H., & Andrews, N. (1993). Social interaction and elevated plus-maze tests: Changes in release and uptake of 5-HT and GABA. *Neuropharmacol., 32*, 217-221.

Flint, J. (2002). Animal models of personality. In J. Benjamin, R. P. Ebstein & R. H. Belmaker (Eds.), *Molecular genetics and the human personality* (pp. 63-90). Washington, D.C.: American Psychiatric Press.

Fries, A. B., Ziegler, T. E., Kurian, J. R., Jacoris, S., & Pollak, S. D. (2005). Early experience in humans is associated with changes in neuropeptides critical for regulating social behavior. *Proceedings of the National Academy of Science U.S.A, 102*, 17237-17240.

Gest, S. D. (1997). Behavioral inhibition: Stability and associations with adaptation from childhood to early adulthood. *Journal of Personality & Social Psychology, 72*, 467-475.

Gilbert, P. (2001). Evolution and social anxiety. The role of attraction, social competition, and social hierarchies. *Psychiatric Clinics of North America, 24*, 723-751.

Gladstone, G. L., Parker, G. B., & Malhi, G. S. (2006). Do bullied children become anxious and depressed adults? A cross-sectional investigation of the correlates of bullying and anxious depression. *Journal of Nervous and Mental Disorders, 194*, 201-208.

Goldberg, J. O., & Schmidt, L. A. (2001). Shyness, sociability, and social dysfunction in schizophrenia. *Schizophrenia Research, 48*, 343-349.

Gonzalez, L. E., File, S. E., & Overstreet, D. H. (1998). Selectively bred lines of rats differ in social interaction and hippocampal 5-HT1A receptor function: a link between anxiety and depression? *Pharmacology, Biochemistry and Behavior, 59*, 787-792.

Gortmaker, S. L., Kagan, J., Caspi, A., & Silva, P. A. (1996). Daylength during pregnancy and shyness in children: results from northern and southern hemispheres. *Developmental Psychobiology, 31*, 107-114.

Gosling, S. D. (1998). Personality dimensions in spotted hyenas (Crocuta crocuta). *Journal of Comparative Psychology, 112*, 107-118.

Gosling, S. D. (2001). From mice to men: what can we learn about personality from animal research? *Psychological Bulletin, 127*, 45-86.

Grossman, A. W., Churchill, J. D., McKinney, B. C., Kodish, I. M., Otte, S. L., & Greenough, W. T. (2003). Experience effects on brain development: possible contributions to psychopathology. *Journal of Child Psychology and Psychiatry, 44*, 33-63.

Gurtman, C. G., Morley, K. C., Li, K. M., Hunt, G. E., & McGregor, I. S. (2002). Increased anxiety in rats after 3,4-methylenedioxymethamphetamine: association with serotonin depletion. *European Journal of Pharmacology, 446*, 89-96.

Halpin, Z. T. (1986). Individual odors among mammals: origins and functions. *Adv.Study Behav., 16*, 39-70.

Heiser, N. A., Turner, S. M., & Beidel, D. C. (2003). Shyness: relationship to social phobia and other psychiatric disorders. *Behavioral Research Therapy, 41*, 209-221.

Henderson, L., & Zimbardo, P. (1998). Shyness. In R. C. Silver (Ed.), *Encyclopedia of Mental Health* (pp. 497-510). San Diego, CA: Academic Press.

Hofmann, S. G., Heinrichs, N., & Moscovitcha, D. A. (2004). The nature and expression of social phobia: Toward a new classification. *Clinical Psychology Review, 24*, 769-797.

Hollandsworth, J. G. (1990). *The Physiology of Psychological Disorders: Schizophrenia, depression, anxiety, and substance abuse*. New York: Plenum Press.

Hull, E. M., Muschamp, J. W., & Sato, S. (2004). Dopamine and serotonin: influences on male sexual behavior *Physiology & Behavior, 83*, 291-307.

Insel, T. R. (1997). A neurobiological basis of social attachment. *American Journal of Psychiatry, 154*, 726-735.

Insel, T. R., & L.J., Y. (2000). Neuropeptides and the evolution of social behavior. *Current Opinion in Neurobiology, 10*, 784-789.

Javitt, D. C., & Zukin, S. R. (1991). Recent advances in the phencyclidine model of schizophrenia. *American Journal of Psychiatry, 148*, 1301-1308.

Jetha, M. K., Schmidt, L. A., & Goldberg, J. O. (2007). Stability of shyness, sociability, and social dysfunction in schizophrenia: A preliminary investigation of the influence of social skills training in a community-based stable outpatient sample. *European Journal of Psychiatry, 21*, 189-198.

Kagan, J. (1992). Behavior, biology, and the meanings of temperatmental constructs. *Pediatrics, 20 (Suppl)*, 510-513.

Kagan, J., Reznick, J. S., Clarke, C., Snidman, N., & Garcia-Coll, C. (1984). Behavioral inhibition to the unfamiliar. *Child Development, 55*, 2212-2225.

Kagan, J., Reznick, J. S., & Snidman, N. (1988). Biological bases of childhood shyness. *Science, 240*, 167-171.

Kantor, S., Anheuer, Z. E., & Bagdy, G. (2000). High social anxiety and low aggression in Fawn-hooded rats. *Physiology and Behavior, 71*, 551-557.

Katzelnick, D. J., Kobak, K. A., Greist, J. H., Jefferson, J. W., Mantle, J. M., & Serlin, R. C. (1995). Sertraline for social phobia: a double-blind, placebo-controlled crossover study. *American Journal of Psychiatry, 152*, 1368-1371.

Kim, J., & Gorman, J. (2005). The psychobiology of anxiety. *Clinical Neuroscience Research, 4*, 335-347.

Knutson, B., Wolkowitz, O., Cole, S., Reus, V., Chan, T., & Moore, E. (1998). Selective alteration of personality and social behavior by serotonergic intervention. *American Journal of Psychiatry, 155*.

Kosfeld, M., Heinrichs, M., Zak, P. J., Fischbacher, U., & Fehr, E. (2005). Oxytocin increases trust in humans. *Nature, 435*, 673-676.

Lamiell, J. T. (2000). A periodic table of personality elements? The "big five" and trait "psychology" in critical perspective. *Journal of Theoretical & Philosophical Psychology, 20*, 1-23.

Landgraf, R. (2003). HAB/LAB rats: an animal model of extremes in trait anxiety and depression. *Clinical Neuroscience Research, 3*, 239-244.

LeDoux, J. (2003). The emotional brain, fear, and the amygdala. *Cellular and Molecular Neurobiology, 23*, 727-738.

LeDoux, J. E. (2000). Emotion circuits in the brain. *Annual Reviews of Neuroscience, 23*, 155–184.

Lee, P. R., Brady, D., Shapiro, R. A., Dorsa, D. M., & Koenig, J. I. (2005). Social interaction deficits caused by chronic phencyclidine administration are reversed by oxytocin. *Neuropsychopharmacology, 30*, 1883-1894.

Lee, P. R., Brady, D. L., Shapiro, R. A., Dorsa, D. M., & Koenig, J. I. (2007). Prenatal stress generates deficits in rat social behavior: reversal by oxytocin. *Brain Research, 1156*, 152-167.

Maciag, C. M., Dent, G., Gilligan, P., He, L., Dowling, K., Ko, T., Levine, S., & Smith, M. A. (2002). Effects of a non-peptide CRF antagonist (DMP696) on the behavioral and endocrine sequelae of maternal separation. *Neuropsychopharmacology, 26*, 574-582.

Mancini, C., Van Ameringen, M., Szatmari, M., Fugere, P., & Boyle, M. (1996). A high-risk pilot study of the children of adults with social phobia. *Journal of the American Academy of Child and Adolescent Psychiatry, 35*, 1511-1517.

Manuck, S. B., Kaplan, J. R., Rymeski, B. A., Fairbanks, L. A., & Wilson, M. E. (2003). Approach to a social stranger is associated with low central nervous system serotonergic responsivity in female cynomolgus monkeys (*Macaca fascicularis*). *American Journal of Primatology, 61*, 187-194.

Mathew, S. J., Coplan, J. D., & Gorman, J. M. (2001). Neurobiological mechanisms of social anxiety disorder. *American Journal of Psychiatry, 158*, 1558-1567.

McDonald, A. J., & Mascagni, F. (2002). Immunohistochemical characterization of somatostatin containing interneurons in the rat basolateral amygdala. *Brain Research, 943*, 237-244.

McGuire, M., & Troisi, A. (1998). *Darwinian Psychiatry*. New York: Oxford University Press.

Mohn, A. R., Gainetdinov, R. R., Caron, M. G., & Koller, B. H. (1999). Mice with reduced NMDA receptor expression display behaviors related to schizophrenia. *Cell, 98*, 427-436.

Morris, J. S., Frith, C. D., Perrett, D. I., Rowland, D., Young, A. W., Calder, A. J., & Dolan, R. J. (1996). A differential neural response in the human amygdala to fearful and happy facial expressions. *Nature, 383*, 812-815.

Mouri, A., Noda, Y., Enomoto, T., & Nabeshima, T. (2007). Phencyclidine animal models of schizophrenia: approaches from abnormality of glutamatergic neurotransmission and neurodevelopment. *Neurochemistry International, 51*, 173-184.

Myers, R. E., & Others, X. (1973). Loss of social group affinity following prefrontal lesions in free-ranging macaques. *Brain Research, 64*, 257-269.

Overstreet, D. H., Rezvani, A. H., & Janowsky, D. S. (1992). Genetic animal models of depression and ethanol preference provide support for cholinergic and serotonergic involvement in depression and alcoholism. *Biological Psychiatry, 31*, 919-936.

Prather, M. D., Lavenex, P., Mauldin-Jourdain, M. L., Mason, W. A., Capitanio, J. P., Mendoza, S. P., & Amaral, D. G. (2001). Increased social fear and decreased fear of objects in monkeys with neonatal amygdala lesions. *Neuroscience, 106*, 653-658.

Prut, L., & Belzung, C. (2003). The open field as a paradigm to measure the effects of drugs on anxiety-like behaviors: a review. *European Journal of Pharmacology, 463*, 3-33.

Purba, J. S., Hoogendijk, W. J., Hofman, M. A., & Swaab, D. F. (1996). Increased number of vasopressin and oxytocin-expressing neurons in the paraventricular nucleus of the hypothalamus in depression. *Archives General Psychiatry, 53*, 137-143.

Qiao, H., Noda, Y., Kamei, H., Nagai, T., Furukawa, H., Miura, H., Kayukawa, Y., Ohta, T., & Nabeshima, T. (2001). Clozapine, but not haloperidol, reverses social behavior deficit in mice during withdrawal from chronic phencyclidine treatment. *NeuroReport, 12*, 11-15.

Rangel, A., Gonzalez, L. E., Villarroel, V., & Hernandez, L. (2003). Anxiolysis followed by anxiogenesis relates to coping and corticosterone after medial prefrontal cortical damage in rats. *Brain Research, 992*, 96–103.

Ray, J., & Hansen, S. (2004). Temperament in the rat: sex differences and hormonal influences on harm avoidance and novelty seeking. *Behavioral Neuroscience, 118*, 488-495.

Ray, J., Hansen, S., & Waters, N. (2006). Links between temperamental dimensions and brain monoamines in the rat. *Behavioral Neuroscience, 120*, 85-92.

Reale, D., Reader, S. M., Sol, D., McDougall, P. T., & Dingemanse, N. J. (2007). Integrating animal temperament within ecology and evolution. *Biological Reviews, 82*, 291-318.

Reichborn-Kjennerud, T., Czajkowski, N., Torgersen, S., Neale, M. C., Orstavik, R. E., Tambs, K., & Kendler, K. S. (2007). The relationship between avoidant personality disorder and social phobia: a population-based twin study. *American Journal of Psychiatry, 164*, 1722-1728.

Rex, A., Voigt, J. P., Gustedt, C., Beckett, S., & Fink, H. (2004). Anxiolytic-like profile in Wistar, but not Sprague-Dawley rats in the social interaction test. *Psychopharmacology, 177*, 23-34.

Reznick, J. S., Hegeman, I. N., Kaufman, E. R., Woods, S. W., & Jacobs, M. (1992). Retrospective and concurrent self-report of behavioral inhibition and their relation to adult mental health. *Development and Psychopathology, 4*, 301-321.

Rosenbaum, J. F., Biederman, J., Gersten, M., Hirshfeld, D. R., Meminger, S. R., Herman, J. B., Kagan, J., Reznick, J. S., & Snidman, N. (1988). Behavioral inhibition in children of parents with panic disorder and agoraphobia: a controlled study. *Archives General Psychiatry, 45*, 463-470.

Rosenbaum, J. F., Biederman, J., Hirshfeld, D. R., Bolduc, E. A., & Cahloff, J. (1991). Behavioral inhibition in children: A possible precursor to panic disorder or social phobia. *Journal of Clinical Psychiatry, 52 (Suppl)*, 5-9.

Rosenbaum, J. F., Biederman, J., Hirshfeld, D. R., Bolduc, E. A., Faraone, S. V., Kagan, J., Snidman, N., & Reznick, J. S. (1991). Further evidence of an association between behavioral inhibition and anxiety disorders: results from a family study of children from a non-clinical sample. *Journal of Psychiatry Research, 25*, 49-65.

Rosenkranz, J. A., Moore, H., & Grace, A. A. (2003). The prefrontal cortex regulates lateral amygdala neuronal plasticity and responses to previously conditioned stimuli. *Journal of Neuroscience, 23*, 11054-11064.

Rowe, D. C., & Plomin, R. (1977). Temperament in early childhood. *Journal of Personality Assessment, 41*, 150-156.

Rudebeck, P. H., Buckley, M. J., Walton, M. E., & Rushworth, M. F. S. (2006). A role for the macaque anterior cingulate gyrus in social valuation. *Science, 313*, 1310-1312.

Sams-Dodd, F. (1995). Distinct effects of D-amphetamine and phencyclidine on the social behaviour of rats. *Behavioural Pharmacology, 6*, 55-65.

Sams-Dodd, F. (1999). Phencyclidine in the social interaction test: an animal model of schizophrenia with face and predictive validity. *Reviews in the Neurosciences, 10*, 59-90.

Sapolsky, R. M. (1982). The endocrine stress response and social status in the wild baboon. *Hormones & Behavior, 16*, 279-292.

Sapolsky, R. M. (2004). Social status and health in humans and other animals. *Annual Review of Anthropology, 33*, 393-418.

Satinder, K., & Woolridge, G. (1986). Emotional reactivity and alcohol-preference among genetic crosses of the Moudsley and Roman rats. *Pharmacology, Biochemistry and Behavior, 24*, 879-881.

Sato, M., Ohta, R., Kojima, K., & Shirota, M. (2002). Differences in sperm motion between high- and low- shuttlebox avoidance rats (Hatano Strains). *Journal of Andrology, 23*, 250-258.

Savaskan, E., Ehrhardt, R., Schulz, A., Walter, M., & Schachinger, H. (2008). Post-learning intranasal oxytocin modulates human memory for facial identity. *Psychoneuroendocrinology, 33*, 368-374.

Sawyer, T. K., Hengehold, A. K., & Perez, W. A. (1984). Chemosensory and hormonal mediation of social memory in male rats. *Behavioral Neuroscience, 98*, 908-913.

Schmidt, L. A., & Fox, N. A. (1999). Conceptual biological and behavioral distinctions among different types of shy children. . In L. A. Schmidt & J. Schulkin (Eds.), *Extreme Fear, Shyness, and Social Phobia: Origins, biological mechanisms, and clinical outcomes* (pp. 47-66). New York: Oxford University Press.

Schmidt, L. A., Fox, N. A., & Others, X. (1997). Behavioral and neuroendocrine responses in shy children. *Developmental Psychobiology, 30*, 127-140.

Schwartz, C. E., Wright, C. I., Shin, L. M., Kagan, J., & Rauch, S. L. (2003). Inhibited and uninhibited infants "grown up": Adult amygdalar response to novelty. *Science, 300*, 1952-1953.

Schwartz, C. E., Wright, C. I., Shin, L. M., Kagan, J., Whalen, P. J., McMullin, K. G., & Rauch, S. L. (2003). Differential amygdalar response to novel versus newly familiar neutral faces: A functional MRI probe developed for studying inhibited temperament. *Biological Psychiatry, 53*, 854-862.

Shimazaki, T., Iijima, M., & Chaki, S. (2006). The pituitary mediates the anxiolytic-like effects of the vasopressin V1B receptor antagonist, SSR149415, in a social interaction test in rats. *European Journal of Pharmacology, 543*, 63-67.

Sih, A., Bell, A., & Johnson, J. C. (2004). Behavioral syndromes: an ecological and evolutionary overview. *Trends in Ecology and Evolution, 19*, 372-378.

Sih, A., Bell, A. M., Johnson, J. C., & Ziemba, R. E. (2004). Behavioral syndromes: an integrative overview. *Quarterly Review of Biology, 79*, 2410-2477.

Smalley, S. L., McCracken, J., & Tanguay, P. (1995). Autism, affective disorders, and social phobia. *American Journal of Medical Genetics, 60*, 19-26.

Sneddon, L. U. (2003). The bold and the shy: Individual differences in rainbow trout. *Journal of Fish Biology, 62*, 971-975.

Stein, M. B. (1995). *Social Phobia: Clinical and Research Perspectives*. Washington D.C.: American Psychiatric Press.

Stein, M. B. (1998). Neurobiological perspectives on social phobia: from affiliation to zoology. *Biological Psychiatry, 44*, 1277-1285.

Stemberger, R. T., Turner, S. M., Beidel, D. C., & Calhoun, K. S. (1995). Social phobia: an analysis of possible developmental factors. *Journal of Abnormal Psychology, 104*, 526-531.

Svartberg, K., Tapper, I., Temrin, H., Radesäter, T., & Thorman, S. (2005). Consistency of personality traits in dogs. *Animal Behaviour, 69*, 283-291.

Tanaka, K., Suzuki, M., Sumiyoshi, T., Murata, M., Tsunoda, M., & Kurachi, M. (2003). Subchronic phencyclidine administration alters central vasopressin receptor binding and social interaction in the rat. *Brain Research, 992*, 239-245.

Taylor, G. T., Haller, J., Rupich, R., & Weiss, J. (1984). Testicular hormones and intermale aggressive behaviour in the presence of a female rat. *Journal of Endocrinology, 100*, 315-321.

Taylor, G. T., & Yuede, C. (2005). Behaviorally timid rats respond differentially to conventional and atypical neuroleptics. *Pharmacology, Biochemistry & Behavior, 81*, 478-484.

Thomas, K. M., Drevets, W. C., & Others, X. (2002). Amygdala response to fearful faces in anxious and depressed children. *Archives of General Psychiatry, 59*, 1057-1063.

Tillfors, M. (2004). Why do some individuals develop social phobia? A review with emphasis on the neurobiological influences. *Nordic Journal of Psychiatry, 58*, 267-s276.

Tillfors, M., Furmark, T., Marteinsdottir, I., Fischer, H., Pissiota, A., Langstrom, B., & Fredrikson, M. (2001). Cerebral blood flow in subjects with social phobia during stressful speaking tasks: a PET study. *American Journal of Psychiatry, 158*, 1220-1226.

Tillfors, M., Furmark, T., Marteinsdottir, I., & Fredrikson, M. (2002). Cerebral blood flow during anticipation of public speaking in social phobia: a PET study. *Biological Psychiatry, 52*, 1113-1119.

Toki, S., Morinobu, S., Imanaka, A., Yamaoto, S., Yamawaki, S., & Honma, K. (2007). Importance of early lighting conditions in maternal care by dam as well as anxiety and memory later in life of offspring. *European Journal of Neuroscience, 25*, 815-829.

Truitt, W. A., Sajdyk, T. J., Dietrich, A. D., Oberlin, B., McDougle, C. J., & Shekhar, A. (2007). From anxiety to autism: spectrum of abnormal social behaviors modeled by progressive disruption of inhibitory neuronal function in the basolateral amygdala in Wistar rats *Psychopharmacology, 191*, 107–118.

Turner, S. M., Beidel, D. C., & Townsley, R. M. (1990). Social phobia: relationship to shyness. *Behaviour Research and Therapy, 28*, 497-505.

van Ameringen, M., Mancini, C., Farvolden, P., & Oakman, J. (2000). The neurobiology of social phobia: from pharmacotherapy to brain imaging. *Current Psychiatry Reports, 2*, 358-366.

Van Ameringen, M., Mancini, C., & Oakman, J. M. (1998). The relationship of behavioral inhibition and shyness to anxiety disorder. *Journal of nervous and mental disease, 186*, 425-431.

van Londen, L., Goekoop, J. G., van Kempen, G. M., Frankhuijzen-Sierevogel, A. C., Weigant, V. M., van der Velde, E. A., & De Wied, D. (1997). Plasma levels of arginine vasopressin elevated in patients with major depression. *Neuropsychopharmacology, 17*, 284-292.

Vidal, J., de Bie, J., Granneman, R. A., Wallinga, A. E., Koolhaas, J. M., & Buwalda, B. (2007). Social stress during adolescence in Wistar rats induces social anxiety in adulthood without affecting brain monoaminergic content and activity. *Physiology & Behavior, 92*, 824-830.

Wals, M., & Verhulst, F. (2005). Child and Adolescent antecedents of adult mood disorders. *Current Opinion Psychiatry, 18*, 15-19.

Williams, L. M., Liddell, B. J., Rathjen, J., Brown, K. J., Gray, J., Phillips, M., Young, A., & Gordon, E. (2004). Mapping the time course of non-conscious and conscious perception of fear: an integration of central and peripheral measures. *Human Brain Mapping, 21*, 64-74.

Wilson, D. S., Clark, A. B., Coleman, K., & Dearstyne, T. (1994). Shyness and boldness in humans and other animals. *Trends in Ecology and Evolution, 9*, 442-445.

Winslow, J. T., & Insel, T. R. (2002). The social deficits of the oxytocin knockout mouse. *Neuropeptides, 36*, 221-229.

Wolf, M., van Doorn, G. S., Leimar, O., & Weissing, F. J. (2007). Life-history trade-offs favour the evolution of animal personalities. *Nature, 447*, 581-584.

Yang, M., Zhodzishsky, V., & Crawley, J. N. (2007). Social deficits in BTBR T + tf/J mice are unchanged by cross-fostering with C57BL/6J mothers. *International Journal of Developmental Neuroscience, 25*, 515-521.

Young, L. J., Nilsen, R., Waymire, K. G., MacGregor, G. R., & Insel, T. R. (1999). Increased affiliative response to vasopressin in mice expressing the V1a receptor from a monogamous vole. *Nature, 400*, 766-768.

Young, L. J., & Wang, X. (2004). The neurobiology of pair bonding. *Nature Neuroscience, 7*, 1048-1054.

Young, L. J., Winslow, J. T., Wang, Z., Gingrich, B., Guo, Q., Matzuk, M. M., & Insel, T. R. (1997). Gene targeting approaches to neuroendocrinology: oxytocin, maternal behavior, and affiliation. *Hormones and Behavior, 31*, 221-231.

Zak, P. J., Kurzban, R., & Matzner, W. T. (2005). Oxytocin is associated with human trustworthiness. *Hormones and Behavior, 48*, 522-527.

Zimmermann, L. K., & Stansbury, K. (2004). The influence of emotion regulation, level of shyness, and habituation on the neuroendocrine response of three-year-old children. *Psychoneuroendocrinology, 29*, 973-982.

In: Social Phobia: Etiology, Diagnosis and Treatment
Editor: Clayton P. Axelby
ISBN 978-1-60692-159-3
© 2009 Nova Science Publishers, Inc.

Chapter III

BRAIN ACTIVATION TO PHOBIA-RELATED STIMULI IN SOCIAL PHOBIA

Thomas Straube*
Department of Biological and Clinical Psychology, Friedrich-Schiller-University, D-07743 Jena, Germany.

ABSTRACT

Individuals suffering from social phobia are excessively concerned about being negatively evaluated by others. Etiological models suggest that information processing biases and hypersensitivity to signals of social threat play a central role for the development and maintenance of the disorder. Indeed, it has been shown that individuals with SP display an increased sensitivity towards social cues of disapproval by others. Consistent with this notion, functional imaging studies have repeatedly revealed enhanced neural activity to negative facial expressions. Furthermore, new studies extended these findings to the domain of verbal stimuli and of emotional prosody expressed by the human voice. For these classes of social stimuli, socially phobic subjects show also remarkably altered brain activation, as compared to healthy subjects. In this chapter, recent findings concerning neural correlates of the processing of phobia-related stimuli in patients suffering from social phobia are reviewed and the implications for the understanding of altered information processing in social phobia are discussed.

1. INTRODUCTION

Social phobia is characterized by intensive self-monitoring and rumination in social situations (Clark and Wells, 1995). Furthermore, several models as well as an extensive body

* Correspondence concerning this article should be addressed to: Thomas Straube, Department of Biological and Clinical Psychology, Friedrich-Schiller-University, Am Steiger 3 // 1; D-07743 Jena, Germany. Fax: +49 / 3641 / 9-45 142; Phone: +49 / 3641 / 9-45 154; Email: straube@biopsy.uni-jena.de.

of research suggest that the etiology and maintenance of social phobia might be due to cognitive biases in the processing of social information (e.g., Beck et al., 1985; Clark and Wells, 1995). In particular, social anxiety has been associated with an increased sensitivity towards clear or ambiguous signals of negative evaluation by others (for review see Heinrichs and Hofmann, 2001; Bögels and Mansell, 2004). Hypersensitivity to negative social signals in social phobia has been demonstrated across studies of attention, memory, interpretation and/or judgment (for review see Heinrichs and Hofmann, 2001; Bögels and Mansell, 2004) and partly by means of changed explicit emotional evaluation of stimuli (Schmidt et al., submitted; Straube et al., 2004; Straube et al., 2005).

There are increasing efforts to reveal the neural mechanisms underlying abnormal information processing in social phobia. During the last years, this research has resulted in several new findings, which are mainly based on the use of functional imaging method, such as functional magnetic resonance imaging (fMRI). On the one hand, the investigation of neural activation during exposure to phobia-related stimuli can help to reveal the neural basis of altered processing of social information in individuals with social phobia. On the other hand, neuroscientific research offers the possibility to investigate hypersensitivity to specific stimuli in social phobia even in the absence of distorted behaviour (in terms of reaction times, explicit judgements, memory performance, etc.). From this perspective, measures of brain activation can be regarded as an additional method, besides conventional paradigms in experimental psychology, to generally answer the question whether and, if so, under what conditions persons with social phobia show an abnormal processing of social information.

In the following paragraphs, findings from studies on cognitive (with a focus on "attentional bias") and emotional biases (explicit emotional judgements) in individuals with social phobia are briefly summarized. Then, in chapter 3, actual findings from functional imaging studies and their relevance for altered information processing in social phobia will be discussed in detail.

2. Processing of Social Stimuli in Individuals with Social Phobia: Behavioural Studies

The strongest research interest in the context of biased processing of external information in social phobia has been spend to the question whether individuals with social phobia/ social anxiety show increased vigilance to phobia-related stimuli. This question has been investigated with different experimental tasks, such as modified stroop tasks, the dot-probe task, or visual search tasks (for review see Heinrichs and Hofmann, 2001; Bögels and Mansell, 2004). Findings from studies investigating attentional biases suggest that the abnormal processing of (potentially) threatening stimuli in social phobia might be best explained in terms of a hypervigilance-avoidance model (e.g., Mogg and Bradley, 2002; Mogg et al., 2004; Vassilopoulos, 2005). According to this view, subjects with social phobia show an initial, more or less automatic and rapid hypervigilant processing of social threat cues, while during sustained or controlled processing of these stimuli rather avoidance behaviour can be observed. Remarkably, while there is growing evidence for a hypersensitivity of social phobic subjects to specific kinds of social stimuli, there is only limited evidence that these effects are accompanied by changed explicit evaluation or identification of these stimuli (see below). In the following, findings from studies investigating altered information processing in social phobia/ social anxiety are described for three different kinds of social stimuli: faces, voices, and words.

2.1. Processing of Facial Stimuli

The emotional information displayed by the facial expression of others has been of specific relevance for the research on social phobia. Accurate interpretation of such signals, which are more or less overt signs of social approval and disapproval, is of paramount importance for successful social interaction. Angry faces, for example, provide a clear signal of social threat and disapproval. A hypersensitivity to angry facial expressions in social phobia has been repeatedly shown (e.g. for review see Heinrichs and Hofmann 2001; Bögels and Mansell, 2004). Individuals with social phobia, but also subjects with high scores in trait social anxiety, show biased performance in response to threatening faces during cognitive tasks such as visual search tasks or the dot probe task (e.g., Lundh and Öst 1996; Gilboa-Schechtmann et al. 1999; Mogg and Bradley 2002; Mogg et al., 2004; Pishyar et al., 2004). Furthermore, subjects with social phobia display hyperscanning (increased scanpath length) and avoidance (reduced foveal fixations) of the eyes, particularly evident for angry faces (Horley et al., 2004). Garner et al. (2005) reported that subjects with high social anxiety were relatively quicker to look at emotional faces than neutral faces but looked at emotional faces for less time, compared with low social anxiety individuals, consistent with a vigilant-avoidant pattern of bias. However, there are also contradictory results, showing rather a general avoidance of angry faces in social phobia (Chen et al., 1999). As pointed out in the introduction, these findings might be associated with a hypervigilance-avoidance pattern of threat processing in social phobia. This pattern depends, for example, on the exposure duration of the threat stimuli and specific experimental tasks (e.g., Mogg and Bradley, 2002; Mogg et al., 2004). Attention of social phobics tends to be more or less automatically captured by threat cues (at least under conditions where attention has to be paid to the external environment), but then attention is directed away from such cues.

Regarding explicit judgements of facial expressions, no altered recognition or intensity judgements concerning negative facial expressions have been observed in subjects with social phobia compared to healthy controls (Philippot and Douilliez, 2005). However, Joorman and Gotlib (2006) reported that individuals with social phobia, as compared to healthy controls, needed less intensity in facial expression to identify angry faces. Most studies have failed to find any evidence that individuals with social phobia differ from normal controls in the explicit evaluation of negative emotional facial expression on dimensions such as valence or arousal (e.g., Stein et al., 2002; Straube et al., 2004; Amir et al., 2005; but see Straube et al., 2004, Straube et al., 2005).

For happy facial expressions, there is evidence that individuals with social phobia rate these stimuli as pleasant and arousing (Philippot and Douilliez, 2005; Straube et al., 2005), but they seem to lack a so-called positivity bias towards happy faces as shown by healthy individuals (Coles and Heimberg, 2005, for memory bias; Eastwood et al., 2005 and Pishyar et al., 2004, for attentional bias).

2.2. Processing of Voice Stimuli

Studies investigating the processing of auditory stimuli in social phobia are seriously lacking. Thus, only two behavioural studies concerned with auditory processing in individuals with social phobia have been published so far (Bruder et al., 2004; Quadflieg et al., 2007). The study of Bruder et al. did not relate to the processing of emotional or socially threatening information. Rather, it was aimed at the investigation of changed hemispheric asymmetry in social phobia. The study showed that the normally occurring left hemisphere advantage for the processing of words and syllables is reduced in social phobics compared to subjects without social phobia. In contrast, the processing of complex tones was similar across individuals with or without social phobia.

The study of Quadflieg et al. (2007) investigated whether biased processing of emotional signals in social phobia is also displayed in response to prosodic components of human speech. Whenever listeners perceive human voices they simultaneously process variations in duration, amplitude, pitch contour, tempo, and loudness of an utterance. These prosodic features are powerful signals during interpersonal contact since they enable the reliable discrimination and identification of a speaker's emotional state (Frick, 1985; Banse and Scherer, 1996). Angry voices, in particular, signal rejection and threat similar to angry faces (Frick, 1985; Banse and Scherer, 1996). In the study of Quadflieg et al. (2007), individuals with generalized social phobia and healthy controls completed a recognition test consisting of meaningless utterances spoken in a neutral, angry, sad, fearful, disgusted or happy tone of voice. Participants also evaluated the stimuli with regard to valence and arousal. These ratings did not differ significantly between groups. This finding corresponds to a lack of difference in explicit evaluation of emotional facial expressions (see above).

Analysis of the recognition test revealed enhanced identification of sad and fearful voices and decreased identification of happy voices in individuals with social phobia compared to healthy controls. The finding that individuals with social phobia made more errors than healthy controls in recognizing happy prosody supports the idea that social phobia might be characterized by a bias not only with regard to negative but also to positive emotional cues (Pishyar et al., 2004; Coles and Heimberg, 2005; Eastwood et al., 2005). A misidentification of positive emotional signals might be associated with decreased experience of social approval by emotional prosody in everyday interactions in social phobia.

The study of Quadflieg et al. is a first step in the investigation of altered processing of emotional prosody in social phobia. Future behavioural studies are strongly needed. These studies should investigate not only the recognition and evaluation of emotional prosody in social phobia, but should also examine whether evidence for attentional or mnemonic biases in response to prosodic cues can be found. Especially concerning angry voices, direct comparisons with findings from studies that utilized angry faces should be of great relevance for a general understanding of biases in the processing of social stimuli.

2.3. Processing of Verbal Stimuli

Support for heightened attention towards socially threatening information comes also from studies with linguistic stimuli. Using emotional (modified) stroop tasks, several studies reported longer color-naming latencies for words with a socially threatening connotation than for neutral words (e.g., for review see Heinrichs and Hofmann, 2001; Bögels and Mansell, 2004). The emotional stroop task, however, has been criticised because the basis of the interference effect, operationalized by increased response times to threat-related distractors, is widely unclear (for review see Bögels and Mansell, 2004). Thus, other tasks, such as the visual search or the dot probe task, might be a more suited to investigate selective attention to threat words. Using a modified visual search task, Rinck et al. (2003) did not find any effects of disorder-related words on behavioural performance in patients with social phobia. For the dot-probe task, results are inconsistent. Several studies failed to find an attentional bias in social phobia (e.g., Horenstein und Segui, 1997; Pishyar et al., 2004). Pishyar et al., (2004), for example, found an attentional bias for negative faces but not for negative words in social phobia. Findings of Amir et al. (2003) suggest that social phobia might be associated with a problem to disengage from threat words. Vassilopoulos (2005) reported that processing of threat words in social phobia, as assessed with the dot probe task, follows an hypervigilant-avoidance pattern. Moreover, Musa et al. (2004) reported an attentional bias with the dot probe task in social phobia, when controlling for comorbid depression, suggesting the need for careful further research.

Concerning explicit evaluation of verbal stimuli, there is evidence that phobia-related words - in contrast to angry faces and voices - are rated as more unpleasantly and arousing than phobia-unrelated, neutral words by subjects with social phobia, as compared to healthy subjects (Schmidt et al., submitted).

3. Brain Activation in Social Phobia during the Processing of Social Stimuli

Consistent with the notion that individuals with social phobia display an increased sensitivity towards social cues of disapproval by others, functional imaging studies have repeatedly revealed enhanced neural activity to negative but also to ambiguous facial expressions, as described in detail below. Furthermore, recent studies extended these findings to the domain of verbal stimuli (Schmidt et al., submitted) and of emotional prosody expressed by the human voice (Quadflieg et al., 2008). For these classes of social stimuli, socially phobic subjects show also significantly altered brain activation, as compared to healthy subjects.

Functional imaging not only allows detecting the magnitude of brain activation but also the anatomical location of brain activation with high spatial resolution. A relatively consistent finding from functional imaging studies concerned with altered information processing in social phobia is a hyperactivation of the amygdala to negative or ambiguous facial expressions (Birbaumer et al 1998; Veit et al 2002; Stein et al., 2002; Straube et al., 2004a; Straube et al., 2005; Phan et al., 2006; Cooney et al., 2006; Yoon et al., 2007).

Increased activation of the amygdala was also shown in response to phobia-related words (Schmidt et al., submitted). The amygdala, a subcortical structure in the anterior medial temporal lobe, has been suggested to be relevant for the detection and processing of aversive and especially of threat-relevant information and to initiate rapid physiological and behavioural responses to perceived threat (LeDoux, 2000). Beside this function, there is increasing evidence for a more general involvement of the amygdala in the processing of emotionally salient stimuli regardless of stimulus valence (e.g., Hamann and Mao, 2002; Straube et al., 2005). However, the amygdala seems to respond preferentially to negative stimuli under conditions of restricted attentional resources or awareness (Williams et al., 2004; Straube et al., 2007, Straube et al., 2008). Stronger initial responses of the amygdala to negative vs. positive stimuli supports the assumption of a negativity bias, which leads to preferred processing of threat-related information to enable rapid adaptive responses.

Other areas that have been found being activated by phobia-related stimuli in social phobia across different studies and different classes of social stimuli are the insula (Straube et al., 2004; Straube et al., 2005; Schmidt et al., submitted) and the orbitofrontal cortex (Veit et al., 2002; Quadflieg et al., 2008; Schmidt et al., submitted). The results for the insula suggest a crucial role of this brain area in the processing of socially threatening signals in social phobics. The insular cortex has been shown to be generally involved in the recognition and experience of aversive states such as disgust, fear or pain (e.g. Phillips et al., 1997; Peyron et al., 2002; Straube et al., 2006). The insular cortex represents arousal states of the organism and seems to integrate interoceptive information (Craig, 2002). This area might assist the assessment of danger and provide a warning centre, due to the perception of arousal states (Craig 2002; Paulus and Stein, 2006). Thus, a relation between insular hyperactivity, increased awareness of bodily states and anxiety proneness has been suggested (Craig, 2002; Critchley et al., 2004; Paulus and Stein, 2006; Straube et al., 2006). Furthermore, insula activation during anxiety-provoking paradigms has been repeatedly shown (e.g., Critchley et al., 2004; Straube et al. 2006). Thus, increased activation of the insula in social phobia might be related to self-monitoring concerning bodily responses when confronted with social threat.

The orbitofrontal cortex has previously been proposed to evaluate sensory signals to enable appropriate affective and behavioral responses (Damasio et al., 1994; Rolls, 2000). More specifically, its role in the representation of rewards and punishments guiding learning and behavioral adjustments has repeatedly been pointed out (e.g., Damasio et al., 1994; Rolls et al., 1994; Rolls, 2000). A lack of orbitofrontal modulation due to brain damage results in severely disturbed social behavior and inappropriate impulsiveness (Damasio, 1994; Rolls et al., 1994; Hornak et al., 2003). Thus, in social phobia, the functional role of orbitofrontal activation might be found in supporting avoidance behavior or in the inhibition of actual behaviour in the case of perceived social threat.

Besides the activation in areas related to emotion processing and behavioural control there is also evidence that activation in individual with social phobia is increased in the visual cortex in response to task-irrelevant angry faces (Straube et al., 2004). This finding supports the hypotheses of an automatic hypervigilance to social threat cues in social phobia, which is expressed as hyperactivation in those brain areas that are involved in sensory processing of the threatening stimuli.

Notably, there is only one study yet, which explicitly tried to associate the individual behavioural performance of individuals with social phobia with brain activation. Schmidt et al. (submitted) correlated explicit ratings of stimuli with brain activation and found effects in the amygdala, insula, and the OFC (see below). Until now, there are no studies which adopted experimental designs from cognitive psychology in order to investigate, for example, the neural mechanisms that might underlie attentional biases as described in the previous paragraphs. In the following paragraphs, results of functional imaging studies for different classes of social stimuli are described in more detail and implications are discussed.

3.1. Processing of Facial Stimuli

Several lines of neuroscientific research have provided evidence that faces are processed in domain-specific neural networks of the cerebral cortex (Bruce and Young, 1986; Haxby and Gobbini, 2002). The perception and recognition of a person's identity by face identification was shown being based on rather invariant aspects of the face (Haxby and Gobbini, 2002). In contrast, the identification of emotional facial expressions and speech-related movements of the mouth were demonstrated to depend on the ability to process dynamic aspects of the face. Based on lesion and functional imaging studies Haxby and colleagues (Haxby and Gobbini, 2002) suggested a core and an extended system involved in face processing. In the core system, the inferior occipital sulcus processes features of the face. From here, information is then passed to two subunits, of which one is localized in the superior temporal sulcus (STS) and the other in the lateral fusiform gyrus. The fusiform gyrus projects information to anterior temporal structures in order to further process the identity of the face. These structures are relevant for the association of the subject's name and different biographical information with the face. In contrast, facial aspects related to non-static features of the face activate areas in the STS and this brain region plays a critical role for encoding facial expressions. The STS is further linked to the intraparietal sulcus where spatial attention is organized and to the auditory cortex where prelexial components of speech are activated. Furthemore, both the STS and the fusiform gyrus project to limbic and para-limbic areas, such as the insula, the amygdala, or the orbitofrontal cortex where the emotional meaning of facial expressions become tagged and adaptive emotional responses are initiated. For the rapid attention to and recognition of facial expressions research has emphasized a significant role of the amygdala (Adolphs et al., 1999; Haxby and Gobbini, 2002).

Using functional brain imaging methods, increased activation of the amygdala was found in social phobics in response to pictures depicting angry (Phan et al., 2006; Stein et al., 2002; Straube et al., 2004a; Straube et al., 2005; Yoon et al., 2007), contemptuous (Stein et al 2002) or neutral facial expressions (Birbaumer et al 1998; Veit et al 2002; Cooney et al., 2006). These results support the widely recognized role of the amygdala in the processing of threat-relevant stimuli (LeDoux, 2000; Öhman and Mineka 2001). Phan et al. (2006) showed that symptom severity of social phobia correlated positively with amygdala activation to negative faces. Notably, amygdala activation in social phobia has been also found in response to happy faces during unrestricted passive viewing of faces (e.g., Straube et al., 2005); an effect, which is not seen during attentional distraction (Stein et al., 2002). Furthermore, Veit et al., (2002) described increased activation of the OFC to neutral faces in social phobia, suggesting strong behavioural control in response to faces in social phobia.

The only study that varied attentional conditions while subjects with social phobia were presented with facial expressions is the study of Straube et al. (2004a). In this study, individuals with SP had either to attend to facial expression of angry and neutral faces or to facial features that were unrelated to facial expression. Individuals with social phobia showed, relative to healthy controls, greater responses to angry vs. neutral faces in the insula regardless of task, while the amygdala, parahippocampal gyrus, fusiform gyrus, and STS showed increased activation only during the implicit task. Furthermore, under both task conditions, phobics exhibited similarly strong brain responses, suggesting that angry facial expressions were intensively processed even when this was not required.

The finding for the insula is in line with studies with healthy subjects that demonstrated enhanced insula activation to threatening faces when subjects were explicitly instructed to process the facial expressions (e.g., Gorno-Tempini et al 2001; Winston et al 2003). In the study of Straube et al., the same phenomenon was observed for control subjects, while phobics seemed intensively to evaluate the threat relevance of angry faces and/or the own emotional reactions regardless of task condition. However, some studies failed to find any insula activation to negative faces in social phobia (e.g., Stein et al., 2002; Phan et al., 2006), which indicates that experimental conditions for the occurrence of this effect are not clear yet.

Results of the study of Straube et al. (2004a) suggest that especially during the indirect task individuals with social phobia show increased processing of threatening faces in extrastriate visual areas. Studies with healthy subjects have also shown a strong influence of the emotional valence of visual stimuli, such as facial expressions, on activation of extrastriate visual cortex. Most consistently, enhanced responses to unpleasant vs. neutral faces were described in the fusiform gyrus (e.g., Vuilleumier et al., 2001; Winston et al., 2003) and STS (e.g., Narumoto et al., 2001; Winston et al., 2003). As described above, the posterior fusiform gyrus is strongly involved in face detection and recognition and the posterior STS is implicated in the evaluation of the social relevance of stimuli. The finding that hyperresponsitivity of visual areas to facial threat in social phobia was specific for the implicit task supports hypervigilance-avoidance models of information processing in this disorder.

3.2. Processing of Voice Stimuli

Although angry facial expressions are a prominent social cue to reveal a person's disapproval of others, corresponding inferences can also be drawn based on other, non-facial social cues, such as human voices, as described above. Surprisingly though, altered neural processing of prosodic cues in social phobia has yet been investigated only by one study (Quadflieg et al., 2008).

The neural network underlying the processing of emotional prosody has been studied intensively in studies with healthy subjects. Growing evidence indicates that a network spatially distributed across both hemispheres contributes to the appropriate comprehension of emotional prosody (e.g., Adolphs, et al., 2002; Kotz et al., 2003; Wildgruber et al., 2005; Schirmer and Kotz, 2006). Above all, a bilateral fronto-temporal pattern of brain activation has been shown to be associated with processing emotional prosody from normal speech (Kotz et al., 2003). While it is assumed that the superior temporal region serves as an input region mainly involved in the fast analysis of acoustic features, subsequent processes which are more complex and integrative in nature such as labelling the affective tone and/or retrieving its reward value, are thought to be accomplished by bilateral frontal brain regions, for example by the OFC (Hornak et al., 1996; Wildgruber et al., 2005; Kotz et al., 2003). Additionally, lesion studies suggest that not only damage to the temporal (Adolphs et al., 2002) and the OFC (Hornak et al., 2003) is likely to impair the discrimination of emotional prosody, but also lesions of the basal ganglia (Cancelliere and Kertesz, 1990; Peper and Irle, 1997), and the amygdala (Scott et al., 1997; but see Anderson and Phelps, 1998; Adolphs and Tranel, 1999).

In line with these findings from lesion studies, the comprehension of anger prosody has been shown to rely on a neural network including the striatum (Calder et al., 2004), the rolandic operculum/insula region (Kotz et al., 2003), the amygdala (Scott et al., 1997; Sander et al., 2005), the STS (Grandjean et al., 2005) and the OFC (Sander et al., 2005). Initial evidence suggests that some areas such as the STS and the amygdala respond to anger prosody even when voices have to be ignored while the OFC seems to show increased activation when attention is focused to the utterances (Sander et al., 2005). There is evidence that the OFC response to anger prosody is correlated with inter-individual differences in proneness to anxiety reactions in general (Sander et al., 2005).

The study of Quadflieg et al. investigated the role of task-relevance of prosodic information and social phobia on brain activation to angry compared to neutral utterances. During scanning, participants performed two tasks: an emotion identification task and a gender identification task. For the emotion task, participants were instructed to identify the emotion conveyed by the utterance (emotional prosody is task-relevant). For the gender task, subjects were instructed to identify the gender of the speaker (emotional prosody is task-irrelevant). The imaging results showed that, regardless of task, both phobic and non-phobic participants recruited a network comprising frontotemporal regions, the amygdala, the insula, and the striatum, when listening to angry compared to neutral prosody. Across participants, increased activation in orbitofrontal cortex during task-relevant as compared to task-irrelevant emotional prosody processing was found. Compared to healthy controls, individuals with social phobia displayed significantly stronger orbitofrontal activation in response to angry vs. neutral voices under both conditions. These results suggest a disorder-associated increased involvement of the orbitofrontal cortex in reponse to threatening voices in social phobia.

This finding occurred in the absence of differential behavioural effects in socially phobic and healthy subjects (explicit ratings, reaction times, error rates). Previous investigations using facial emotional expressions as stimulus material have shown a similar dissociation between behavioral and neural effects (e.g., Stein et al., 2002; Straube et al., 2004; Straube et al., 2005).

The fMRI findings indicate that increased neural activation towards interpersonal threat cues in social phobia goes beyond angry facial expressions, suggesting biased processing of cues of social disapproval both in vision and hearing. Importantly, the increased OFC activation in individuals with SP occurred regardless of whether processing of emotional prosody was required or not, suggesting some automaticity of neural and potentially specific behavioral reactions. For individuals with SP, who are highly concerned about social disapproval, it can most likely be assumed that angry voices are experienced as intense kind of punishment or disapproval during social interactions. The enhanced orbitofrontal activation might reflect this strong negative evaluation of the incoming auditory information and might be related in priming avoidance behaviors or in the inhibition of actual behavior in the case of perceived anger in others.

In contrast to the expectations based on investigations using angry facial expressions (see above) the study of Quadflieg et al. failed to reveal any activation differences in the insula or the amygdala between socially phobic and non-phobic individuals. This suggests that potential differences in the processing of anger prosody in these two groups might be not comparable with findings for faces. It seems that, in the case of auditory signals, differences between phobic subjects and controls occur relatively late in the stream of prosodic information processing. However, these conclusions have to be considered with caution given that only a single study on neural correlates of prosody processing in social phobia has been conducted yet.

3.3. Processing of Verbal Stimuli

While word stimuli have been used frequently in behavioural studies, only one study has explored the neural correlates of the processing of threat-related words in social phobia yet (Schmidt et al., submitted). In healthy subjects, processing of negative vs. neutral words elicits increased amygdala activation (Isenberg et al., 1999; Hamann and Mao, 2001; Maddock et al., 2003). In patients with obsessive compulsive disorder or panic disorder, the amygdala also shows hyperactivity during the presentation of anxiety-related words (e.g., van den Heuvel et al., 2005), while in specific phobia no amygdala activation in response to phobia-related words has been found (Straube et al., 2004b).

The fMRI study of Schmidt et al. investigated brain activation during the processing of phobia-relevant and neutral words in twenty patients with generalized social phobia and twenty healthy controls. The words were presented under two different task conditions. During the implicit task, subjects categorized the grammatical type of the word. During the explicit task, subjects had to decide whether words related to social interaction situations or not. Analysis of postscanning rating data showed that phobia-related words were evaluated as more arousing, negative, and frightening by patients with social phobia as compared to controls. There were no group effects in response times or error rates.

The fMRI-data did not reveal between-group differences during the explicit task. However, during the implicit task, social phobic subjects, as compared to controls, showed increased activation in the right orbitofrontal cortex and in the left amygdala. Activation in both regions correlated significantly with phobics' valence ratings of words. The results suggest a specific role of the OFC and the amygdala during processing of phobia-relevant distracting information. The fact that findings for these areas were specific for the implicit task supports the hypothesis that increased vigilance to threat words might be especially pronounced under conditions, which reduce the possibility for strategic avoidance or control of stimuli. The study revealed that the role of the amygdala is not restricted to processing of phylogenetically-relevant threat cues like angry facial expressions in social phobia. Furthermore, the finding that activation in the amygdala and OFC was correlated with valence ratings of linguistic stimuli within the group of phobic subjects suggests that the personal relevance of threat words was an important basis for these neural effects. This relation might be a difference to the processing of faces. Brain activation in the amygdala during processing of negative facial expression correlates with symptom severity (Phan et al., 2002) or state anxiety (Cooney et al., 2006), but not with valence ratings, since angry faces are not rated as more negative by social phobic subjects as compared to healthy subjects.

Furthermore, the study of Schmidt et al. showed that the activation of the insula correlates with symptom severity of social phobia especially under the explicit task. This supports the hypothesis that the insula is associated with monitoring a person's emotional state in social phobia, which might occur more strongly under explicit emotional conditions. Notably, also in the study of Straube et al. (2004; see above), which used faces as stimulus material, only an activation of the insula was detected during the explicit emotional condition.

4. Conclusion

In this chapter, I first reviewed the behavioural evidence for altered processing of different classes of social stimuli in social phobia in terms of reaction times, eye movements, and explicit stimuli ratings. There is some evidence that socially phobic individuals show an initial hypervigilance to social threat stimuli, at least for angry faces, while threat words might be more strongly related to a general distraction effect leading to slowing of reaction times. Taken together, hypervigilance-avoidance models are, at the current stage of research, the best explanation for the pattern of behavioural results. While attentional biases have been repeatedly described in social phobia, there is no clear association between social phobia and altered explicit identification/ ratings of faces. However, there is initial evidence for altered identification of emotional prosody. Generally, there is a lack of research on cognitive and emotional biases in response to emotional prosody in social phobia. In contrast to negative faces and prosody, negative words are clearly rated as more unpleasant and arousing by individual with social phobia, as compared to healthy subjects.

Second, I have described the current evidence for changed patterns of brain activation in social phobia, as measured with functional neuroimaging methods. Actual findings confirm the hypothesis that subjects with social phobia show altered information processing at the neural level, such as neural hyperactivation to threat stimuli (even in the absence of distorted behaviour). However, there is only limited transfer from research in cognitive experimental psychology to neuroscientific research on stimuli processing in social phobia. Thus, experimental designs that allow investigating in detail attentional and other biases were not used in functional neuroimaging studies with individuals with social phobia. Furthermore, only three studies have varied attentional conditions in order to examine the role of attentional focus on brain activation in response to threat stimuli in social phobia. These studies showed that differences between patients with social phobia and healthy controls during the processing of threat stimuli seem to be more pronounced during attentional distraction from the emotional meaning of these stimuli.

Concerning the processing of negative and ambiguous faces, there is a relative consistent picture that individuals with social phobia show increased amygdala activation as compared to healthy controls. Furthermore, increased amygdala activation in social phobia has been also shown in response to threat words. The amygdala was suggested to be relevant for the rapid detection of threat stimuli and for the initiation of automatic responses to these stimuli. Other brain areas that have been found being activated by phobia-related stimuli in social phobia across different studies and different classes of social stimuli are the insula and the orbitofrontal cortex. While the insula activation in social phobia might be related to increased awareness of it's own bodily responses when confronted with social threat, the role of the OFC might be related to inhibited behaviour in phobia-related contexts, for example in response to negative/ ambiguous social cues such as angry or neutral faces, angry prosody or negative verbal information during social interactions.

The investigation of the neural correlates of the processing of social signals in social phobia is a relatively new research area. Future studies should relate experimental designs more strongly to methods developed in experimental psychology. Most importantly, brain activation should be associated with behavioural performance. Furthermore, future studies should allow us to separate different stages or components of information processing. For example, parametric variation of attentional resources or awareness can help to answer the question whether there is an automatic hyperresponsitivity of specific brain areas, such as the amygdala, in response to specific social cues. Another question, besides the neural basis of the initial hypervigilance, concerns the neural correlates of the avoidance responses and of the increased self-focus in socially phobic subjects when confronted with social threat.

Finally, the investigation of changed information processing in social phobia (at the behavioural and neural level) should be based on a variety of different social stimuli. Altered processing of facial expressions, emotional prosody, gestures, and/or verbal cues might amplify the development of pathological fears towards embarassment and rejection by others. Therefore, increasing our understanding of biased processing of social cues in social phobia across a wide range of ecologically valid stimuli poses a major challenge.

References

Adolphs, R., Damasio, H., & Tranel, D. (2002). Neural systems for recognition of emotional prosody: A 3-D lesion study. *Emotion, 2 (1)*: 23-51

Adolphs, R., & Tranel, D. (1999). Intact recognition of emotional prosody following amygdala damage. *Neuropsychologia, 37 (11)*: 1285-1292

Adolphs, R., Tranel, D., Hamann, S., Young, A. W., Calder, A. J., Phelps, E. A., Anderson, A., Lee, G. P., & Damasio, A. R. (1999). Recognition of facial emotion in nine individuals with bilateral amygdala damage. *Neuropsychologia, 37 (10)*: 1111-1117

Allison, T., Puce, A., & McCarthy, G. (2000). Social perception from visual cues: role of the STS region. *Trends in Cognitive Sciences, 4 (7)*: 267-278

Amir, N., Elias, J., Klumpp, H., Przeworski, A. (2003). Attentional bias to threat in social phobia: facilitated processing of threat or difficulty disengaging attention from threat? *Behav Res Ther, 41(11)*:1325-35.

Amir, N., Klumpp, H., Elias, J., Bedwell, J.S., Yanasak, N., Miller, L.S. (2005). Increased activation of the anterior cingulate cortex during processing of disgust faces in individuals with social phobia. *Biological Psychiatry, 57*: 975–981.

Anderson, A. K., Phelps, E. A. (1998). Intact recognition of vocal expressions of fear following bilateral lesions of the human amygdala. *Neuroreport, 9 (16)*: 3607-3613

Bamiou, D.-E., Musiek, F. E., Luxon, L. M. (2003). The insula (Island of Reil) and its role in auditory processing – Literature review. *Brain Research Reviews, 42 (2)*: 143-154

Banse, R., & Scherer, K. R. (1996). Acoustic profiles in vocal emotion expression. *Journal of Personality and Social Psychology, 70 (3)*: 614-636

Baum, S. R., & Pell, M. D. (1999). The neural bases of prosody: Insights from lesion studies and neuroimaging. *Aphasiology, 13 (8)*: 581-608

Beck, A. T., Emery, G., & Greenberg, R. L. (1985). *Anxiety disorders and phobias: a cognitive perspective*. New York: Basic Books

Birbaumer, N., Grodd, W., Diedrich, O., Klose, U., Erb, M., Lotze, M., Schneider, F., Weiss, U., Flor, H. (1998). fMRI reveals amygdala activation to human faces in social phobics. *Neuroreport, 9 (6)*: 1223-1226

Blair, R. J. R., Mitchell, D. G. V., Richell, R. A., Kelly, S., Leonard, A., Newmann, C., Scott, S. K. (2002). Turning a deaf ear to fear: impaired recognition of vocal affect in psychopathic individuals. *Journal of Abnormal Psychology, 11 (4)*: 682-686

Bögels SM, Mansell W. (2204). Attention processes in the maintenance and treatment of social phobia: hypervigilance, avoidance and self-focused attention. *Clin Psychol Rev. 24 (7)*:827-56.

Bruder, G. E., Schneier, F. R., Stewart, J. W., McGrath, P. J., Quitkin, F. (2004). Left hemispheric dysfunction during verbal dichotic listening tests in patients who have social phobia with or without comorbid depressive disorder. *The American Journal of Psychiatry, 161 (1)*: 72-78

Bruce, V., & Young, A. (1986). Understanding face recognition. *British Journal of Psychology, 77*, 305 – 327.

Buchanan, T. W., Lutz, K., Mirzazade, S., Specht, K., Shah, N. J., Zilles, K., Jäncke, L. (2000). Recognition of emotional prosody and verbal components of spoken language: An fMRI study. *Cognitive Brain Research, 9 (3)*: 227-238

Calder, A. J., Keane, J., Lawrence, A. D., Manes, F. (2004). Impaired recognition of anger following damage to the ventral striatum. *Brain, 127 (9)*: 1985-1969

Calder, A. J., Young, A. W., Rowland, D., Perrett, D. I., Hodges, J. R., & Etcoff, N. L: (1996). Facial emotion recognition after bilateral amygdala damage: differentially severe impairment of fear. *Cognitive Neuropsychology, 13 (5)*: 699-745

Cancelliere, A.E.B., & Kertesz, A. (1990). Lesion localization in acquired deficits of emotional expression and comprehension. *Brain and Cognition, 13 (2)*: 133-147

Chen, Y.P., Ehlers, A., Clark, D.M., Mansell, W. (2002). Patients with generalized social phobia direct their attention away from faces. *Behaviour Research and Therapy, 40(6)*:677-87.

Clark, D. M., & Wells, A. (1995). A cognitive model of social phobia. In: R. G. Heimberg, M. R. Liebowitz, D. A. Hope, F. R. Schneier (Eds.), *Social phobia: diagnosis, assessment, and treatment* (pp. 69-93), New York, NY: Guilford Press.

Coles, M.E., Heimberg, R.G. (2005). Recognition bias for critical faces in social phobia: a replication and extension. *Behaviour Research and Therapy, 43(1)*:109-20.

Cooney, R.E., Atlas, L.Y., Joormann, J., Eugène, F., Gotlib, I.H. (2006) Amygdala activation in the processing of neutral faces in social anxiety disorder: is neutral really neutral? *Psychiatry Research, 148(1)*:55-9.

Craig, A. D. (2002). How do you feel? Interoception: the sense of the physiological condition of the body. *Nat Rev Neurosci, 3*: 655-666.

Critchley, H. D., Wiens, S., Rotshtein, P., Öhman, A., Dolan, R. J. (2004). Neural systems supporting interoceptive awareness. *Nat Neurosci. 7*, 189-195

Critchley, H., Daly, E., Phillips, M., Brammer, M., Bullmore, E., Williams, S., Van Amelsvoort, T., Robertson, D., David, A., Murphy, D. (2000). Explicit and implicit neural mechanisms for processing of social information from facial expressions: A functional magnetic resonance imaging study. *Human Brain Mapping, 9 (2)*: 228-234

Damasio, A.R. (1998). The somatic marker hypothesis and the possible functions of the prefrontal cortex. In A. C. Roberts, T. W. Robbins, & L. Weiskrantz (Eds.), *The prefrontal cortex: Executive and cognitive function* (pp. 103-116). Oxford: Oxford University Press.

Damasio, H., Grabowski, T., Frank, R., Galaburda, A. M., Damasio, A. R. (1994). The return of Phineas Gage: clues about the brain from the skull of a famous patient. *Science, 264 (5162)*: 1102-1105

Das, P., Kemp, A. H., Liddell, B. J., Brown, K. J., Olivieri, G., Peduto, A., Gordon, E., & Williams, L. M. (2005). Pathways for fear perception: Modulation of amygdala activity by thalamo-cortical systems. *Neuroimage, 26*: 141-148

Eastwood, J., Smile, D., Oakman, J., Farvolder, P., van Ameringen, M., Mancini, C., Merikle, P. (2005). Individuals with social phobia are biased to become aware of negative faces. *Visual Cognition, 12 (1)*: 159-179

Frick, R. W. (1985). Communicating emotion: The role of prosodic features. *Psychological Bulletin, 97 (3)*: 412-429

Garner, M., Mogg, K., Bradley, B.P. (2006). Orienting and maintenance of gaze to facial expressions in social anxiety. *Journal of Abnormal Psychology, 115(4)*:760-70.

Gilboa-Schechtman, E., Foa, E. B., & Amir, N. (1999). Attentional bias for facial expressions in social phobia: The face-in-the-crowd paradigm. *Cognition and Emotion, 13 (3)*: 305-318

Gorno-Tempini, M. L., Pradelli, S., Serafini, M., Pagnoni, G. Baraldi, P., Porro, C., Nicoletti, R., Umita, C., Nichelli, P. (2001). Explicit and incidental facial expression processing: an fMRI study. *Neuroimage, 14 (2)*: 465-473

Grandjean, D., Sander, D., Pourtois, G., Schwartz, S., Seghier, M. L., Scherer, K. R., Vuilleumier, P. (2005). *The voices of wrath: brain responses to prosody in meaningless speech, 8(2)*:145-6

Hamann, S., & Mao, H. (2002). Positive and negative emotional verbal stimuli elicit activity in the left amygdala. *Neuroreport, 13 (1)*: 15-19

Haxby, J. V., & Gobbini, M. I. (2002). Human neural systems for face perception and social communication. *International Journal of Psychophysiology, 45(1-2)*, 56-57.

Heinrichs, N., & Hofman, S. G. (2001). Information processing in social phobia: a critical review. *Clinical Psychology Review, 21 (5)*: 751-770

Horenstein M, Segui J. (1997). Chronometrics of attentional processes in anxiety disorders. *Psychopathology, 30(1)*:25-35.

Horley K, Williams LM, Gonsalvez C, Gordon E. (2004). Face to face: visual scanpath evidence for abnormal processing of facial expressions in social phobia. *Psychiatry Research, 127(1-2)*:43-53

Hornak, J., Bramham, E. T., Morris, R. G., O'Doherty, J., Bullock, P. R., Polkey, C. E. (2003). Changes in emotion after circumscribed surgical lesions of the orbitofrontal and cingulate cortices. *Brain, 126 (7)*: 1691-1712

Hornak, J., Rolls, E. T., & Wade, D. (1996). Face and voice expression identification in patients with emotional and behavioral changes following ventral frontal lobe damage. *Neuropsychologia, 34 (4)*: 247-261

Joormann, J., Gotlib, I.H. (2006). Is this happiness I see? Biases in the identification of emotional facial expressions in depression and social phobia. *Journal of Abnormal Psychology, 115(4)*:705-14.

Kotz, S., Meyer, M., Alter, K., Besson, M., von Cramon, Y., Friederici, A. (2003). Perception of emotions from faces and voices following unilateral brain damage. *Neuropsychologia, 41 (8)*: 1082-1090

Lange, K., Williams, L. M., Young, A. W., Bullmore, E.T., Brammer, M. J., Williams, S. C. R., Gray, J. A., Phillips, M. L. (2003). Task instructions modulate neural responses to fearful facial expressions. *Biological Psychiatry, 53 (3)*: 226-232

LeDoux, J. E., 2000. Emotion circuits in the brain. *Annu Rev Neurosci. 23*, 155-184.

Lorberbaum, J. P., Kose, S., Johnson, M. R., Arana, G. W., Sullivan, L. K., Hamner, M. B., Ballenger, J. C., Lydiard, R. B., Brodrick, P. S., Bohning, D. E. und George, M. S., 2004. Neural correlates of speech anticipatory anxiety in generalized social phobia. *Neuroreport. 15*, 2701-2705.

Lundh, L. G., & Öst, L. G. (1996). Recognition bias for critical faces in social phobia. *Behaviour Research and Therapy, 34 (10)*: 787-794

Mogg, K., Philippot, P., Bradley, B.P. (2004). Selective attention to angry faces in clinical social phobia. *Journal of Abnormal Psychology, 113(1)*:160-5.

Mogg, K., Bradley, B.P. (2002). Selective orienting of attention to masked threat faces in social anxiety. *Behaviour Research and Therapy, 40(12)*:1403-14.

Musa, C. Z., Lépine, J. P., Clark, D. M., Mansell, W., Ehlers, A. (2003). Selective attention in social phobia and the moderating effect of a concurrent depressive disorder. *Behaviour Research & Therapy, 41 (9)*: 1043-1054

Narumoto, J., Okada, T., Sadato, N., Fukui, K., Yonekura, Y. (2001). Attention to emotion modulates fMRI activity in human right superior temporal sulcus. *Cognitive Brain Research, 12 (2)*: 225-231

Öhman, A. und Mineka, S., 2001. Fears, phobias, and preparedness: toward an evolved module of fear and fear learning. *Psychol Rev. 108*, 483-522.

Paulus, M.P., and Stein, M.B. (2006). An insular view of anxiety. *Biol Psychiatry 60*, 383-387.

Peper, M., & Irle, E. (1997). Categorical and dimensional decoding of emotional intonations in patients with focal brain lesions. *Brain and Language, 58 (2)*: 233-264

Phan, K. L., Wager, T., Taylor, S. F., Liberzon, I. (2002). Functional neuroanatomy of emotion: A meta-analysis of emotion activation studies in PET and fMRI. *Neuroimage, 16 (2)*: 331-348

Philippot, P., & Douilliez, C. (2005). Social phobics do not misinterpret facial expression of emotion. *Behaviour Research and Therapy, 43*: 639–652.

Pishyar, R., Harris, L. M., & Menzies, R. G. (2004). Attentional bias for words and faces in social anxiety. *Anxiety, Stress, and Coping, 17 (1)*: 23-36

Puce, A., Syngeniotis, A., Thompson, J. C., Abbott, D. F., Wheaton, K. J., Castiello, U. (2003). The human temporal lobe integrates facial form and motion: evidence rom fMRI and ERP studies. *Neuroimage, 19 (3)*: 861-869

Quadflieg, S., Mohr, A., Mentzel, H.J., Miltner, W.H., Straube, T. (2008) Modulation of the neural network involved in the processing of anger prosody: The role of task-relevance and social phobia. *Biological Psychology, 78(2)*:129-37.

Quadflieg, S., Wendt, B., Mohr, A., Miltner, W.H., Straube, T. (2007). Recognition and evaluation of emotional prosody in individuals with generalized social phobia: a pilot study. *Behaviour Research and Therapy, 45(12)*:3096-103.

Rauch, S. L., Savage, C. R., Alpert, N. M., Fischman, A. J., Jenike, M. A. (1997). The functional neuroanatomy of anxiety: a study of three disorders using positron emission tomography and symptom provocation. *Biological Psychiatry, 42 (6)*: 446-452

Reiman, E.M. (1997). The application of positron emission tomography to the study of normal and pathologic emotions. *Journal of Clinical Psychiatry, 58 (16)*: 4-12

Rolls, E. T. (2002). The functions of the orbitofrontal cortex. In D. T. Stuss, & B. T. Knight (Eds.), *Principles of Frontal Lobe Function* (pp. 354-376). New York: Oxford University Press.

Rolls, E. T., Hornak, J., Wade, D., McGrath, J. (1994). Emotion-related learning in patients with social and emotional changes associated with frontal lobe damage. *Journal of Neurology, Neurosurgery, & Psychiatry, 57 (12)*: 1518-1524

Sander, D., Grandjean, D., Pourtois, G., Schwartz, S., Seghier, M. L., Scherer, K. R., Vuilleumier, P. (2005). Selective attention modulates orbitofrontal response to emotional prosody. *Neuroimage, 28 (4)*: 848-858

Scherer, K. R., Banse, R., Wallbott, H. G. (2001). Emotion inferences from vocal expression correlate across languages and cultures. *Journal of Cross-Cultural Psychology, 32 (1)*: 76-92

Schirmer, A., & Kotz, S.A. (2003). ERP Evidence for a sex-specific stroop effect in emotional speech. *Journal of Cognitive Neuroscience, 15 (8)*: 1135-1148

Schmidt, S., Mohr, A., Mentzel, H.J., Miltner, W.H., & Straube, T. (submitted for publication). *Neural correlates of explicit and implicit processing of phobia-related verbal stimuli in generalized social phobia.*

Scott, S. K., Young, A. W., Calder, A. J., Hellawell, D. J., Aggleton, J. P., Johnson, M. (1997). Impaired auditory recognition of fear and anger following bilateral amygdala lesions. *Nature, 385 (6613)*: 254-257

Stein, M. B., Goldin, P. R., Sareen, J., Zorrilla, L. T., Brown, G. G. (2002). Increased amygdalar activation to angry and contemptuous faces in generalized social phobia. *Archives of General Psychiatry, 59 (11)*: 1027-1034

Straube, T., Kolassa, I.-T., Mentzel, H.-J., Miltner, W. H. R. (2004). Effect of task conditions on brain responses to threatening faces in social phobics: An event-related functional magnetic resonance imaging study. *Biological Psychiatry, 56 (12)*: 921-930

Straube, T., Mentzel, H.-J., & Miltner, W. H. R. (2005a) Common and distinct brain activation to threat and safety signals in social phobia. *Neuropsychobiology, 52 (3)*: 163-168

Straube, T., Mentzel, H.-J., & Miltner, W. H. R. (2006). Neural mechanisms of automatic and direct processing of phobogenic stimuli in specific phobia. *Biological Psychiatry, 59*:162–70. 330

Straube, .T., Weiss, T., Mentzel, H.J., Miltner, W.H. (2007). Time course of amygdala activation during aversive conditioning depends on attention. *Neuroimage, 34(1)*:462–9.

Straube, .T., Pohlack, S., Mentzel, H.J., Miltner, W.H. (2008). Differential amygdala activation to negative and positive emotional pictures during an indirect task. *Behavioural Brain Research, 191(2):285-8.*

Vassilopoulos, S. (2005). Social anxiety and vigilance-avoidance pattern of attentional processing. *Behavioural & Cognitive Psychotherapy, 33 (1)*:13-24

Veit, R., Flor, H., Erb, M., Hermann, C., Lotze, M., Grodd, W., Birbaumer, N. (2002). Brain circuits involved in emotional learning in antisocial behaviour and social phobia in humans. *Neuroscience letters, 328 (3)*: 233-236

Vuilleumier, P., Armony, J. L., Driver, J. und Dolan, R. J., 2001. Effects of attention and emotion on face processing in the human brain: an event-related fMRI study. *Neuron. 30,* 829-841.

Wildgruber, D., Riecker, A., Hertrich, I., Erb, M., Grodd, W., Ethofer, T., Ackermann, H. (2005). Identification of emotional intonation evaluated by fMRI. *Neuroimage, 24 (4)*: 1233-1241

Williams, M. A., McGlone, F., Abbott, D. F., Mattingley, J. B. (2005). Differential amygdala responses to happy and fearful facial expressions depend on selective attention. *Neuroimage, 24 (2)*: 417-425

Winston, J. S., O'Doherty, J., & Dolan, R. J. (2003). Common and distinct neural responses during direct and incidental processing of multiple facial emotions. *Neuroimage, 20 (1)*: 84-97

Zald, D. H. (2003). The human amygdala and the emotional evaluation of sensory stimuli. *Brain Research Reviews, 41 (1)*: 88-123.

In: Social Phobia: Etiology, Diagnosis and Treatment
Editor: Clayton P. Axelby
ISBN 978-1-60692-159-3
© 2009 Nova Science Publishers, Inc.

Chapter IV

LIFE EVENTS AND THE DEVELOPMENT OF SOCIAL PHOBIA

Iulian Iancu *** and Jennie Goldstein***
Rehovot Mental Health Center, and the Sackler School of Medicine, Tel Aviv University, Tel Aviv, Israel.

ABSTRACT

Inherited temperamental variables such as behavioral inhibition are important in the pathogenesis of social anxiety disorder (SAD) (Schwartz et al, 1999). However, research suggests that early interpersonal experiences influence temperamental variables and interact with them in later development of social avoidance and shyness (Neal & Edelmann, 2003). In this chapter, we will describe the research on the role of stressful life events (SLE) in the pathogenesis of SAD.

The studies in the field show that individuals with SAD report parental conflicts (Magee et al, 1999) and also frequent history of physical and sexual abuse (Chartier et al, 2001; Stein et al, 1996). Individuals with SAD also describe experiences of peer neglect and rejection, as well as harassment, teasing and bullying (Beidel et al. 1999; La Greca et al, 1998; Storch et al, 2004).

It is not clear whether these experiences have a causal effect on SAD or are either non-disorder specific or a result of behavioral inhibition and excessive submission. However, a vicious cycle has been described by Rubin & Burgess (2001) and by Gazelle & Ladd (2003), in which youngsters with a biological vulnerability to overreact in social situations, perhaps also influenced by parental overprotection, withdraw from peers. This withdrawal leads to a lack of sufficient peer interactions, which precludes development of appropriate social skills and positive relationships. This in turn leads to increased social anxiety and feelings of inferiority.

* Correspondence concerning this article should be addressed to: Dr. Iulian Iancu, Director, Rehovot Mental Health Center, Remez 80 str., Rehovot 76449, Israel. Tel: 972-8-9461893; Fax: 972-8-9468962; e-mail: iulian1@bezeqint.net.

At present, our knowledge about SAD's etiology is far from conclusive. Clearly, further research about SLE and their role in the development of SAD is important and should use prospective studies that assess both temperament and SLE. The elucidation of these important factors might allow us to develop more targeted interventions in the prevention and treatment of SAD.

INTRODUCTION

SAD, also known as social phobia, is a disabling, lifelong disorder characterized by fear of humiliation in social performance and/or interactional situations (Stein & Stein, 2008). Epidemiological studies show that SAD is a common disorder with prevalence rates up to 16% (see Iancu et al, 2006). As with other psychiatric conditions, the etiology of SAD is not known. Over the past two decades, however, there has been an explosion of research publications devoted to delineating the pathophysiology of SAD (Stein & Hollander, 2002). Unfortunately, few replication studies have been done and data are insufficient for integrating the available literature. In this chapter, we will focus on the possible role of SLE in the pathogenesis of SAD, and review studies that have assessed the rate of SLE in SAD patients and controls. We will conclude with a proposal for further study.

Multiple pathways probably lead to the clinical manifestation of SAD in any given patient, and it is unlikely that a single gene, experience, or environmental condition will explain all cases (Stein & Hollander, 2002). More likely, SAD is the result of complex interactions between genetic vulnerability, home environment, temperament, and personal experiences. Trauma exposure interacts with genetic vulnerability and other factors, leading to the emergence of the disorder. For example, Kendler et al (1992) reported findings from a large twin study that 30-40% of the development of SAD is genetic, and the remainder is caused by nonspecific environmental experiences.

Having said that it is possible that diagnostic and psychometric issues, as well as differences between SAD samples (students scoring above a median split, non-treatment seeking and treatment seeking SAD patients), could complicate the possibility of elucidating the pathogenesis of this condition (Stein & Hollander, 2002).

Several psychological and developmental models have been proposed for the development of SAD (Stein & Hollander, 2002). Models based on conditioning, ethological, personality, behavioral inhibition, and cognitive theories have been proposed. However, these models are quite difficult to test empirically, especially with regard to the development or onset of the disorder. For example, once the anxiety has developed, it is easy to see how conditioning, cognitive, or learning theories could explain the maintenance of the anxiety; what is not clear from these models is how the problem initially developed.

From the perspective of SLE, the conditioning model states that a conditioned aversive situation can lead to the development of phobias. The available empirical data are not consistent; some reports support such a model (Townsley Stemberger et al, 1995) but others do not (Hoffmann et al, 1995). Nevertheless, Ost & Hugdahl (1981) reported that 58% of SAD patients traced the origin of their fears to an aversive conditioning incident, whereas 13% traced the origin to vicarious experiences, 3% to informational learning and 26% had no recall. Others pointed out, however, that this study failed to take into account the responses of a nonphobic control group (Mulkens & Bogels, 1999). It is important to note that in general there is often a delay of greater than 10 years between the onset of symptoms (David et al, 1995) and seeking help for the symptoms, and many traumatic events may have been forgotten.

Bandelow et al. (2004) provide the following example: a father is an alcoholic, beats his child, is frequently away from home, and has marital discord. When his son develops SAD, is that mainly due to the alcoholism of his father, familial violence, frequent separation from the father, parental marital discord, or simply because the child has inherited SAD from his father, whose SAD symptoms originally led him to drink? David et al. (1995) also add that being a shy or anxious child increases the risk of becoming an abuse victim, which then enhances the chances of developing SAD. Thus, it becomes clear that risk factors should not be examined independently, but rather in an integrative model.

In the following section we will review studies of the rate of adverse life events in SAD patients. Notwithstanding, it is important to note that it is yet unclear whether these experiences cause SAD, are a result of SAD or are coincidental co-occurrences.

Review of the Literature

The literature on the role of environmental factors in the development of SAD has rapidly grown in the last two decades. However, studies were retrospective, used small samples and relied on recall creating a significant bias. Also, they had various methodological limitations as regards tools used, samples' characteristics and diagnostic procedures. Finally, the majority of studies did not distinguish between SLE that occurred prior or after the onset of the disorder. Research has focused on two main issues: parental rearing style and the occurrence of SLE, as the two main contributing environmental factors.

1) Parental Characteristics

Retrospective reports of adults with SAD describe common aversive parenting experiences. SAD patients describe parents as controlling, overprotective, rejecting, and critical (Arrindel et al., 1989; Rapee & Melville, 1997; Wittchen et al., 2003). Whereas parental psycho-pathology, particularly SAD (O.R. =4.7) and depression (OR=3.6), were found to predict SAD among offspring, **parental style** was also modestly predictive (Lieb et al., 2000). Parental overprotection (OR= 1.4) and rejection (O.R.= 1.4) were found to be associated with SAD, and are considered to be additional family-environment risk factors for SAD, independent of parental psychopathology (Lieb et al., 2000).

Rapee & Melville (1997) compared patients with DSM-III-R SAD (N=38), panic disorder (PD) (N=26) and a control group (N=25) on two measures of perceived parental overprotection. The first measure examined the broad presence of overprotection, and the second examined specifically the presence of control over socializing. The same questionnaires were given to a subgroup of the subjects' mothers to examine the degree of agreement between the mothers and their children. The questionnaires also included questions about other potentially influential variables, such as early introverted behaviors, parental socialization, childhood illness, and family size and position.

In examining the data provided by the mothers, though questions about general over-protectiveness did not yield clearly statistically significant differences between the groups, the more specific measure of control over socialization did show a significant difference, in that the mothers of social phobics reported greater control than the mothers of the other two groups. Two widely discussed early SLE such as family death and childhood illness were however not associated with either PD or SAD.

Thus, mothers of adults with anxiety disorders are perceived as being more controlling than the mothers of the controls, with the findings being stronger for the SAD group. In addition, both mothers and children agreed that the parents of anxiety patients engaged in fewer social activities than did the parents of non-clinical subjects. The authors suggested that this minimal socialization indicated to impressionable children that social situations are threatening. Mothers and children were also in agreement about the greater degree of introverted or anxious behaviors in the childhood years of SAD and PD patients. This may indicate temperamental factors found in these subjects even at a young age.

2) SLE in SAD

Brown et al. (1998) studied 45 treatment seeking SAD patients. The patients were diagnosed with a structured interview, whereas the controls (N=15) were recruited through announcements requesting for individuals who were neither anxious nor depressed. Subjects completed various questionnaires, including the Life Experiences Survey. The SAD subjects experienced more negative (mean 18.6 events) and fewer positive (5.3) life events than did the normal controls (9.6 and 10.1 respectively). It is plausible that the patients had more negative life events or viewed the events occurring to them as more negative due to their bias. Also, it is possible that due to their fears, SAD patients actively refrain from attending positive events (such as a social gathering or a wedding). In the patients' sample, the frequency of negative life events was associated with depression, hopelessness, and general anxiety.

David et al (1995) attempted to replicate studies linking developmental trauma (such as early parental loss or incest) with later emergence of SAD. Fifty one patients with a DSM-III-R diagnosis of PD with agoraphobia and/or SAD were recruited at an anxiety clinic and were assessed for developmental trauma by the Life Experience Questionnaire (LEQ). A control group of 51 demographically similar non-clinical subjects (45% mental health professionals) completed a questionnaire that included the LEQ and screening questions for lifetime psychopathology. The research findings included a statistically significant association between patients with SAD and a past history of sexual or physical abuse. Specifically, 50% of 24 patients with SAD had a history of abuse, as compared to 22.2% of the 27 patients without SAD, and 5 (9.8%) of the controls (considered to be a statistically significant difference). There was a trend for less separation and loss among the patients with SAD as compared with the patients with PDAG.

In a study of adult incest victims (Pribor & Dinwiddie, 1992), an increased lifetime prevalence rate for several anxiety disorders (PD, agoraphobia, SAD and simple phobia) was found, as well as increased affective and substance use disorders in comparison with control subjects recruited from self-help groups.

DeWit et al (2005) used a random probability sample of Canadian residents aged 15-64 (n=8116) diagnosed with structured diagnostic interviews. The authors noted gender differences in the effects of family adversity on the risk of SAD. They reported that childhood risk factors were the absence of a parent or other adult or close confidant during childhood among males and physical abuse by a father figure, maternal mania and parental conflict during childhood, among females. Based on the same sample, Chartier et al (2001) described a positive relationship between SAD and lack of close relationships with an adult, marital conflict in the family of origin, parental history of mental disorder, moving more than 3 times as a child, juvenile justice and child welfare involvement, running away from home, childhood physical and sexual abuse, failing a grade, requirement of special education before age 9 and dropping out of high school.

Gibb et al. (2007) examined the specificity of childhood emotional, physical, and sexual abuse to the later emergence of depressive versus anxiety disorders. Their study comprised 857 psychiatric outpatients. The subjects were diagnosed with the SCID-I and the Childhood Trauma Questionnaire was used as a measure of abuse. 252 patients had SP (29.4%). The authors found that reports of childhood emotional abuse were more strongly related to the presence of SAD than were reports of childhood physical or sexual abuse. The same pattern was found for the diagnosis of major depressive disorder (MDD). These findings contrasted with those seen in patients with posttraumatic stress disorder (PTSD), who reported higher rates of all three forms of childhood abuse as compared to patients without PTSD. In addition, patients with comorbid MDD and SAD reported higher levels of emotional abuse than did patients with MDD with no comorbid SAD.

The researchers concluded that whereas PTSD appears to be related to a history of all forms of childhood abuse, MDD and SAD are related specifically to a history of emotional abuse. They additionally pointed out that given evidence that SAD may contribute vulnerability to the development of depression, further longitudinal studies should focus on the sequential relationship between the development of these two disorders in children with a history of emotional abuse.

Marteinsdottir et al (2007) examined the role of SLE throughout the life cycle of individuals with SAD. This study is the first to report specifically on SLE, such as conflicts with a partner, in the year prior to the debut of symptoms in adult life. Thirty subjects with a DSM-IV diagnosis of SAD diagnosed with the SCID and 75 controls matched for age and gender from the local population registry (although not screened for psychopathology) participated in the study.

SAD subjects reported more SLE during childhood (i.e. having a close relative who was medically ill, endured a trauma or was addicted to drugs or alcohol) than did a group of controls, and more SLE during the SAD debuting year. No increased rate of sexual assault was found.

The writers conclude from their data that the life events that occurred within the SAD group during the year in which their symptoms first began, more often involved conflicted relationships with close relatives. Thus, they argue that problems with close relationships play a special role in the development of SAD. However, the authors themselves point out that this causal effect is difficult to prove, as one might argue that the interpersonal struggles experienced by these patients are a result of their already developing SAD.

Additionally, the data showed fewer life events in overall adult life for SAD subjects as compared to controls. This is attributed to the avoiding, socially reserve style typical of SAD. Though there was no gender differences noted in the frequency of SLE in SAD patients, the data did reflect that more SAD women than men had experienced death among close relatives during the year prior to the emergence of symptoms and more SLE in the women's adult life. In contrast, men with SAD had experienced more mobbing and other insulting events, both in childhood and during the year prior to the emergence SAD.

Safren et al (2002) surveyed the literature pertaining to whether specific anxiety diagnoses are associated with childhood abuse. The authors examined the prevalence of self-reported childhood physical or sexual abuse in a sample of 75 PD patients, 46 SAD patients and 28 Generalized Anxiety Disorder patients. The patients were recruited from a population seeking treatment. Diagnoses were made using a structured interview and subjects were also given a semistructured interview about childhood history (e.g., divorce, parental death or abuse). The authors reported that patients with PD had significantly higher rates of past childhood physical or sexual abuse than patients with SAD.

Tiet et al (2001) examined whether SAD is associated with adverse life events and hypothesized that parental separation, divorce or remarriage would be associated with anxiety disorders, including SAD, as well as with depressive and disruptive disorders. A probability sample of youth aged 9-17 (N=1285) at 4 sites was used (MECA study). The authors evaluated relationships between 25 adverse life events and 9 common child and adolescent psychiatric disorders. The subjects underwent a structured interview and filled out a life events questionnaire. SAD (N=194) and agoraphobia were associated with fewer life events than other illnesses. They found a strong association in boys between school change and several psychiatric disorders, including a three-fold increase in SAD. This relationship was absent in girls. In spite of their hypothesis, their data showed that SAD was directly related to only one SLE: family member with a drug or alcohol problem.

Bandelow et al. (2004) attempted to examine the influence of a wide range of childhood traumatic experiences in patients with "pure" SAD (N-50) diagnosed with the SCID as compared to healthy controls (n=120). These traumas included separation from parents, parental marital problems, childhood illness, violence in the family, and sexual abuse. Only 6 (12%) of the SAD patients, but 63 (52%) of the controls did not report any severe traumatic event at all. Compared to controls, SAD patients described their parents' rearing style as significantly more unfavorable. The results revealed higher rates of separations from parents, marital problems, violence, and sexual abuse in the families of those diagnosed with SAD. Within the age range of 0 -15 years, there was no evidence in this study that trauma at a specific age was more likely to lead to the development of symptoms.

When analyzed by logistic regression, the data indicated that familial anxiety disorders were the most relevant risk factor for the presence of SAD. Separation from parents also had a significant, but smaller influence. There was only a trend towards a significant contribution of childhood sexual abuse. The authors of this study caution that for statistical reasons, the results of this study can only be viewed descriptively and as hypothesis-generating, but not as providing confirmative results.

Townsley Stemberger et al. (1995) evaluated possible etiological factors for SAD. These factors included the presence of SAD symptoms in first-degree relatives, the presence of other anxiety disorders in first-degree relatives, childhood shyness, extraversion and neuroticism, and a history of traumatic experiences considered to be conditioning episodes. The study involved a group of 68 patients with a primary diagnosis of SAD from a treatment seeking population and 25 controls. Fifty two patients had the generalized subtype of SAD and 16 had the specific subtype.

The findings of the study confirm that traumatic social conditioning experiences are associated with SAD (44%). Though both groups of social phobics reported the presence of traumatic conditioning experiences, only the specific SAD subtype percentage (56%) was actually statistically significant as compared to the controls (20%) and the SAD generalized subtype (40%). Similarly, only the generalized subtype had a significantly greater history of childhood shyness as compared to the controls (76% vs 52%).

Patients with the generalized subtype were found to be more introverted and exhibited more neuroticism than controls, while the specific subtype also exhibited more neuroticism but were no more introverted than the controls. The authors speculated that this neurotic and introverted tendency in the generalized subtype makes then shyer, more vulnerable to the negative impact of aversive social experiences, and more likely to develop SAD.

Finally, Erwin et al. (2006) examined the frequency of symptoms most often associated with PTSD, including re-experiencing, avoidance, and hyperarousal, among patients with SAD and a group of controls, in response to an extremely stressful social event. This event did not meet requirements to satisfy DSM –IV's PTSD Criterion A. The sample included 45 patients with SAD and 30 non-anxious controls. More than one third of patients with SAD had PTSD-like symptoms in connection with a stressful social event. Patients who reported both socially stressful and Criterion A events reported greater number of hyperarousal symptoms for their worst socially stressful event. The authors concluded that patients with SAD demonstrated PTSD-like symptoms associated with a socially stressful event at intensities sufficient to complicate the processing of such events.

Treatment Implications

The occurrence of SLE patients might hold some therapeutic implications. It is obvious that the psychotherapist should obtain information on various SLE experienced by the patient and then discuss with the patient his or her feelings as regards the SLE experienced (David et al., 1995). In addition, Erwin et al. (2006) suggested that treatments found to be effective for treating PTSD patients may be useful in treating SAD patients as well. Specifically, they suggest that in order to improve the treatment response of SAD, clinicians should work with SAD patients to access all aspects of their "fear memory" and help in the emotional processing of memories associated with the SLE.

Patients should relive stressful memories in order to access distorted meanings and transforming them into memories with less distorted and over-generalized meanings

(Hackmann et al., 2000). Interestingly, in an interventional study, patients with a high rate of SLE improved more on SAD measures in CBT group therapy (Brown et al., 1998). The reprocessing of SLE in weekly CBT role-plays in a more adapta-ative cognitive framework might have helped (Brown et al., 1998).

CONCLUSION

SAD subjects usually report more SLE (bullying, negative parental rearing practices and various types of abuse) as compared to normal controls. However, as compared to other psychiatric groups, they have similar rates of SLE, although sometimes qualitatively different (Gibb et al.. 2007). In addition, SLE is possibly more associated with the specific subtype of SAD, although shy individuals with the generalized subtype might also be prone to the aversive effects of SLE. Last, but not least, whether SAD subjects have less SLE after the development of the disorder is yet unclear.

Environmental factors, specifically those related to stress, have been identified as playing a significant role in the development of psychiatric disorders. The role of SLE has been explained in three ways (Gothelf et al., 2004). First, the general quantitative theory states that it is the amount and weight of the SLE which is significant. Second, the general qualitative theory states that it is the threatening quality of the SLE which is significant. Third, the specific qualitative theory states that specific SLE are important for specific pathologies. In this chapter, we provided a concise summary of the SLE research as it pertains to SAD, a field in its beginning stages (thus we did not elaborate on each of these hypotheses due to the paucity of studies).

An interesting point was raised by Bandelow et al. (2004). Whereas SAD was seen as a disorders caused by traumatization very early in life, Bandelow et al. (2004) found no evidence of a particular abundance of SLE at a certain age within the age range of 0-15 years.

The relation between genetics, personality, life events and anxiety disorders in general has been suggested to be as follows (Gothelf et al., 2004): genetic factors (which may be related to allelic variations of genes of the serotonergic system) induce a harm avoidance tendency in children. When these children encounter a life stressor, they tend to perceive it more negatively such that pathological anxious mechanisms are activated, which leads to the onset of an anxiety disorder. In addition, overprotection may restrict the offspring' development of autonomy and social competence; the combination of rejection and overprotection may lead to a dysfunctional parent-child bond, which may result in difficulties and anxieties in social situations; in addition, overprotection may prevent the offspring from engaging in social situations, thereby restricting the opportunities to learn social skills (Lieb et al., 2000). Moreover, the occurrence of SLE might convince the individual that the world is indeed dangerous and that he/she is unfit for it, resulting in the construction of a negative cognitive schema. Socially anxious subjects report more frequent intrusive thoughts and images about a past anxiety-provoking social event, which interferes with their concentration (Rachmann et al.., 2000; Hackman et al., 2000). It is further plausible that the symptoms of anxiety (e.g. palpitations) can in turn become further sources of perceived danger. The events lead to negative images of their social selves that are repeatedly activated in subsequent social situations and not updated in the light of subsequent favorable experiences. Finally from a biological perspective, childhood trauma is associated with chronic increased pituitary-adrenal and autonomic responses to stress (Heim et al., 2008). Also, SLE could change levels of BDNF (Trajkovska et al., 2008). Overall, the development of SAD after SLE has several biological and psychological underpinnings.

Finally, although the etiology of SAD is unclear, most researchers believe that it is multifactorial and includes temperament, familial mental disorders, separation experiences, and SLE. Shyness is a predisposing factor, but other variables, such as traumatic conditioning experiences, may trigger the development of the disorder (Townsley Stemberger et al., 1995). This interaction is far from clear and certainly deserves further scrutiny. Future studies are needed to understand the process or mechanism by which negative childhood experiences contribute to the development of psychopathology.

Using regression analyses, one might identify the 'true' contribution of a certain risk factor to a certain outcome by partializing out mediator variables (Bandelow et al., 2004). However it seems that only prospective, longitudinal evaluation of large samples of youths at risk for SAD will help address the role, if any, of conditioning by SLE in the development of SAD.

REFERENCES

Arrindell, W.A., Kwee, M.G., Methorst, G.J., van der Ende, J., Pol, E., Moritz, B.J. (1989). Perceived parental rearing styles of agoraphobic and socially phobic in-patients. *Br J Psychiat 155*:526-535.

Bandelow, B., Torrente, A.C., Wedekind, C., Brooks, A., Hajak, G., Ruther, E. (2004). Early traumatic life events, parental rearing styles, family history of mental disorders, and birth risk factors in patients with social anxiety disorder. *Eur Arch Psych Clin Neurosci 254*:397-405.

Beidel, D.C., Turner, S.M., Morris, T.L. (1999). Psychopathology of childhood social phobia. *J Am Acad Child Adolesc Psychiat 38*:643-650.

Brown, E.J., Juster, H.R., Heimberg, R.G. & Winning, CD. (1998). Stressful life events and personality styles: relation to impairment and treatment outcome in patients with social phobia. *J Anx Disord 12*:233-251.

Chartier, M.J., Walker, J.R., Stein, M.B. (2001). Social phobia and potential childhood risk factors in a community sample. *Psychol Med 31*:307-15.

David, D., Giron, A., Mellman, T.A. (1995). Panic-Phobic Patients and Developmental Trauma. *J Clin Psychiat 56*: 113-117.

DeWit, D.J., Chandler-Coutts, M., Offord, D.R., King, G., McDougall, J., Specht, J., Stewart, S. (2005). Gender differences in the effects of family adversity on the risk of onset of DSM-III-R social phobia. *Anx Disord 19*:479-502.

Erwin, B.A., Heimberg, R.G., Marx, B.P., Franklin, M.E. (2006). Traumatic and Socially Stressful Life Events among persons with Social Anxiety Disorder. *Anx Disord 20*: 896-914.

Gazelle, H. & Ladd, G.W. (2003). Anxious solitude and peer exclusion: a diathesis-stress model of internalizing trajectories in childhood. *Child Dev 74*:257-278.

Gibb, B.E., Chelminski, I., Zimmerman, M. (2007). Childhood Emotional, Physical, and Sexual Abuse, and Diagnoses of Depressive and Anxiety Disorders in Adult Psychiatric Outpatients. *Dep Anx 24*:256-263.

Gothelf, D., Aharonovsky, O., Horesh, N., Carty, T. & Apter, A. (2004). Life events and personality factors in children and adolescents with obsessive-compulsive disorder and other anxiety disorders. *Compr Psychiat 45*: 192-198.

Hackmann, A., Clark, D.M., McManus, F. (2000). Recurrent images and early memories in social phobia. *Behav Res Ther 38*:601-610.

Heim, C., Mletzko, T., Purselle, D., Musselman, D.L., Nemeroff, C.B. (2008). The dexamethasone/corticotropin-releasing factor test in men with major depression: role of childhood trauma. *Biol Psychiat 63*:398-405.

Hofmann, S.G., Ehlers, A., Roth, R.T. (1995). Conditioning theory: a model for the etiology of public speaking anxiety? *Behav Res Ther 33*: 567-571.

Iancu, I., Levin, J., Hermesh, H., Dannon, P., Ben-Yehuda, Y., Kaplan, Z., Marom, S. & Kotler, M. (2006). Prevalence of Social Phobia Symptoms and Socio-demographic correlates in an Israeli sample of young conscripts. *Compr Psychiat 47*:399-405.

Kendler, K.S., Neale, M.C., Kessler, R.C., Heath, A.C., Eaves, L.J. (1992). The genetic epidemiology of phobias in women. The interrelationship of agoraphobia, social phobia, situational phobia, and simple phobia. *Arch Gen Psychiat 49*:273-81.

LaGreca, A.M. & Lopez, N, (1998). Social anxiety among adolescents: linkages with peer relations and friendships. *J Abnorm Child Psychol 26*:83-94.

Lieb, R., Wittchen, H.U., Hofler, M., Fuetsch, M., Stein, M.B., Merikangas, K.R. (2000). Parental psychopathology, parenting styles, and the risk of social phobia in offspring. *Arch Gen Psychiat 57*:859-866.

Marteinsdottir, I., Svensson, A., Svedburg, M., Anderberg, U.M., Knorring, L.V. (2007). The Role of Life Events In Social Phobia. *Nord J Psychiat 61*:207-212.

Mulkens, S. & Bogels, S.M. (1999). Learning history in fear of blushing. *Behav Res Ther 37*:1159-1167.

Neal, J.A. & Edelmann, R.J. (2003). The etiology of social phobia: toward a developmental profile. *Clin Psychol Rev 23*:761-786.

Ost, L.G. & Hugdahl, K. (1981). Acquisition of phobias and anxiety response patterns in clinical patients. *Behav Res Ther 19*:439-447.

Pribor, E.F., Dinwiddie, S.H. (1992). Psychiatric correlates of incest in childhood. *Am J Psychiat 149*:52-6.

Rachman, S., Gruter-Andrew, J., Shafran, R. (2000). Post-event processing in social anxiety. *Behav Res Ther 38*:611-617.

Rapee, R.M., Melville, L.F. (1997). Recall of Family Factors in Social Phobia and Panic Disorder: Comparison of Mother and Offspring Reports. *Dep Anx 5*:7-11.

Rubin, K.H. & Burgess, K.B. (2001). Social withdrawal and anxiety. In MW Vasey & MR Dadds (Eds). *The developmental psychopathology of anxiety*. pp 407-434, NY: Oxford University Press.

Safren, S.A., Gershuny, B.S., Marzol, P., Otto, M.W., Pollack, M.H. (2002). History of Childhood Abuse in Panic Disorder, Social Phobia, and Generalized Anxiety Disorder. *J Nerv Ment Dis 190*:453-6.

Schwartz, C.E., Snidman, N., Kagan, J. (1999). Adolescent social anxiety as an outcome of inhibited temperament in childhood. *J Am Acad Child Adolesc Psychiat 38*:1008-1015.

Stein, M.B., Walker, J.R., Anderson, G., Hazen, A.L., Ross, C.A., Eldridge, G., Forde, D,R. (1996). Childhood physical and sexual abuse in patients with anxiety disorders and in a community sample. *Am J Psychiat 153*:275-7.

Stein, D.J. & Hollander, E. (2002). *Textbook of Anxiety Disorders*. APPI.

Stein, M.B., Stein, D.J. (2008). Social anxiety disorder. *Lancet 371*(9618):1115-25.

Storch, E.A., Roth, D.A., Coles, M.E., Heimberg, R.G., Bravata, E.A., Moser, J. (2004). The measurement and impact of childhood teasing in a sample of young adults. *J Anx Disord 18*:681-694.

Tiet, Q.Q., Bird, H.R., Hoven, C.W., Moore, R., Wu, P., Wicks, J., Jensen, P.S., Goodman, S., Cohen, P. (2001). Relationship Between Specific Adverse Life Events and Psychiatric Disorders. *J Abnorm Child Psychopathol 29*:153-164.

Townsley Stemberger, R., Turner, S.M., Beidel, D.C., Calhoun, K.S. (1995). Social Phobia: An analysis of possible developmental factors. *J Abnorm Psychol 104*:526-531.

Trajkovska, V., Vinberg, M., Aznar, S., Knudsen, G.M., Kessing, L.V. (2008). Whole blood BDNF levels in healthy twins discordant for affective disorder: association to life events and neuroticism. *J Affect Disord 108*:165-9.

Wittchen, H.U. & Fehm, L. (2003). Epidemiology and natural course of social fears and social phobia. *Acta Psychiatr Scand 417*:s4-s18.

In: Social Phobia: Etiology, Diagnosis and Treatment
Editor: Clayton P. Axelby
ISBN 978-1-60692-159-3
© 2009 Nova Science Publishers, Inc.

Chapter V

Social Phobia and Alcohol or Other Psychoactive Substance Abuse: A Co-morbidity Review

Mauro Barbosa Terra[1], Helena Maria Tannhauser Barros[2], Airton Tetelbom Stein[3], Ivan Figueira[4], Luciana Dias Athayde[1] and Dartiu Xavier da Silveira[5]

[1]Department of Psychiatry and Forensic Medicine, Federal University of Health Sciences of Porto Alegre, Brazil
[2]Division of Basic and Clinical Pharmacology, Federal University of Health Sciences of Porto Alegre, Brazil
[3]Department of Preventive Medicine, Federal University of Health Sciences of Porto Alegre, Brazil
[4]Department of Psychiatry of the Federal University of Rio de Janeiro, Brazil
[5]Department of Psychiatry of the Federal University of São Paulo, Brazil

Abstract

Introduction: The chapter was designed to describe the association between social phobia and alcohol or other psychoactive substance abuse. It aims to determine the frequency of social phobia among drug addicts and to describe the influence of this anxiety disorder on the occurrence of relapses and on adherence to treatment for substance use disorders, such as Alcoholic Anonymous (AA) and psychotherapy.

Methods: A literature review will be carried out of articles published for the last 20 years using the following databases: Medline, Cochrane, Lilacs and Scielo. The keywords chosen were: "social phobia", "drug abuse", "drug dependence", "alcohol abuse", "alcohol dependence", "co-morbidity", " drug use treatment", "alcoholics anonymous", and "narcotics anonymous'. The text is focused on topics related to prevalence of drug use, chronological and causal relationship between social phobia and alcohol or other drug use, diagnosis of the co-morbidity and impact of co-morbidity on drug abstinence and treatments adherence.

Results: Social phobia is highly frequent among drug addicts, being observed at a higher frequency than in the general population. Nevertheless, it is underdiagnosed and, hence, undertreated. The adherence to such groups as Alcoholics Anonymous and Narcotic Anonymous tends to be weaker among social phobic drug users. Not all studies indicate that social phobia increases the relapse rates.

Discussion: Although social phobia is a frequent co-morbidity, it is underdiagnosed among alcohol or other psychoactive substance dependents, which can lead to nonadherence to drug use treatment and may potentially increase relapses, and a worse clinical progress. Only if both disorders are properly evaluated and treated the cycle of social phobia and drug abuse can be broken. Early identification of social phobia and appropriate interventions are needed to improve treatment response and the quality of life of the alcohol or other psychoactive substance-dependent patients.

1) Introduction

Social phobia increases the risk of disorders related to alcohol and other drugs abuse. The social-phobic alcohol addicts quite often use such drug as a self-medication, that means, they drink to decrease their social anxiety (Naftolowitz et al., 1994). Data suggest that phobic disorders may be a contributing factor to the development of alcohol and other drugs dependence (Kushner et al., 1999). Thus, one must consider the possibility of co-morbidity in patients that present both alcohol addiction and social phobia. In such case, when both disorders are properly identified and treated, there will be a change in the patient's phobic condition, which enables a better adherence to the treatment of alcohol abuse (Lépine, Pélissolo, 1998)

The identification of patients with anxiety disorders, like social phobia, is the first step in the individual treatment of an alcohol or other drug-dependent patient. Recognizing the anxiety disorders leads to the improvement of such patients' life quality, which may interfere in the alcohol addiction course, provided that there are specific pharmacological and behavioral treatments for such disorders. However, in patients with phobic anxiety prone to an addictive behavior, the drug-abuse problem quite often becomes the focus of attention and the basic anxiety condition is neglected (Wesner, 1990)

This chapter aims at studying the prevalence of social phobia among psychoactive substance addicts, raising hypotheses about the causal and chronological relation among co-morbidity disorders and also assessing the clinical impact of co-morbidity as well as its influence in the adherence and abstinence of such drug-addict patients.

2) Prevalence of Co-morbidity

Among the anxiety disorders, social phobia acquires a special relevance for being frequent, disabling and able to be treated. Variations in the prevalence of the social phobia and alcoholism co-morbidity have been reported in clinical and epidemiological studies. It can be imputed to different definitions of social phobia, alcohol dependence or abuse and, mainly, to methodological differences, like the use of diverse instruments and the variations in the study designs (prospective or retrospective) (Lépine, Pélissolo, 1998).

The prevalence of social phobia estimated along the life in general population is 3 to 13% (Schneier et al., 1992; Kessler et al., 1994; Grant et al., 2005). In an alcohol-addicts population, however, the prevalence is much higher, ranging, in most of times, between 16 and 30% (Kushner et al., 1990; Lydiard et al., 1992). Besides, the prevalence along the alcohol dependence or abuse among individuals with social phobia is estimated between 15 and 28% (Regier et al, 1990; Himle, Hill, 1991; Van Ameringen et al., 1991; Davidson et al., 1993; Degonda, Angst, 1993; Page, Andrews, 1996; Magee et al., 1996), which may be twice as bigger as the prevalence in the general population, about 14%, according to the results of the National Co-morbidity Survey (NCS)(Kessler et al., 1994).

Thus, in regard to the prevalence of social phobia in alcohol-addicts population, Terra et al. (2006a), when evaluating 300 interned alcohol addicts, they found social phobia in 24.7% of the sample. Lydiard et al (1992), when studying 49 alcohol-dependents, also found 24.4% of social phobic individuals. Among community epidemiological studies, the NCS found that the prevalence of lifetime social phobia to be 10.8% in males and 24.1% in females with a history of alcohol abuse. Among those with alcohol dependence, the percentage was 19.8% in males and 30.3% in females (Kessler et al., 1997).

Yet regarding the prevalence of alcohol addiction among social phobic people, Schneier et al (1989) reported that 16.3% of a sample of patients with social phobia presented alcohol abuse according to the DSM-III-R criteria. Himle and Hill (1991), in the ECA study, observed that among social phobic individuals, 27.6% were alcohol dependents. Davidson et al. (1993), in this same study, found a prevalence of 17% for alcohol dependence, and Degonda and Angst (1993) found a prevalence of 15%. At the NCS, it was reported a lifetime prevalence of 23.9% for alcohol dependence and 10.9% for alcohol abuse (Magee et al., 1996).

Thus, while patients with social phobia develop problems related to alcohol, with a risk twice higher to develop alcohol abuse or dependence than those who are not social phobic, individuals with disorders caused by the use of alcohol are nine-fold more likely to present social phobia than the general population, what results in one of the most frequent co-morbid conditions in the clinic (Kushner et al., 1990, Lépine, Pélissolo,1998).

An interesting finding is that the alcohol addiction or alcohol abuse co-morbidity is stronger in social phobia with an early beginning than in that starting after 15 years (Lecrubier, 1997). In relation to the type of social phobia, the patients with generalized social phobia present a significantly more frequent form of alcohol abuse than the patients with circumscribed phobia (Mannuzza et al., 1995)

The high rates of alcohol addiction co-morbidity with social phobia show that individuals with this double diagnosis comprehend a substantial stratum of the alcohol addicts population, although few studies have compared alcohol addicts with and without social phobia (Thomas et al., 1999). In this study, the phobic alcohol addicts reported a more severe alcohol dependence than the non-phobic alcohol addicts. Their dependence may be based partly on the fact that the social phobic individuals needed more alcohol to improve their social skills and their functioning.

According to the study that analyzed the results of two epidemiological researches carried out in the United States and Canada, social phobia is also significantly associated with the amphetamine, cocaine, hallucinogens and heroin use (Sareen et al., 2006). Another study also pointed that the social phobia is more commonly associated with the use of sedatives, tranquilizers and opioids (Agrawal et al., 2007). In relation to cannabis, findings from the National Co-morbidity Study (NCS) indicate that there is a 4.2% lifetime prevalence rate for cannabis dependence in the general population, whereas among individuals with social anxiety disorder (SAD), the prevalence rate of cannabis dependence is elevated to 29.0% (Agosti et al., 2002).

3) Temporal and Causal Relation among Co-morbid Disorders

Patients with social phobia have significantly more co-morbid disorders than patients with other psychiatric disorders, provided that social phobia usually precedes the other related disorder (Lépine, Pelissolo, 1998; Dingemans et al., 2001; Lang, 2001). The substance abuse was described as a complication of the phobic-anxious syndrome. In a study with social-phobic individuals, the beginning of social phobia preceded the beginning of alcohol addiction in 15 of 16 double-diagnosed patients. The average age for the beginning of social phobia was much more precocious (10.4 years old) than the beginning of alcohol addiction (20.7 years old) (Schneier et al., 1989). In the ECA study, it was verified in a sample of 361 social phobic individuals that social phobic preceded the alcohol abuse in 85% of the cases (Schneier et al., 1992). In Brazil, Maciel and Gentil Filho (1998) noted that 70% of the social phobic individuals studied by them reported that their phobic condition started before alcohol addiction, where 60% drank deliberately to bear the phobia. In a study carried out in Porto Alegre, Brazil, in a sample of 41 alcohol-addicted patients, 39% presented social phobia, provided that, in all cases, the phobic condition started before the alcohol addiction (Terra et al., 2004). In another study with 300 alcohol-addicted patients, where 74 presented social phobia, the social anxiety disorder preceded the alcohol dependence in 90,2% of the patients. Concerning the chronic alcohol effects on phobic symptoms, there was worsening of social phobia symptoms during alcohol abstinence, at the same time as the phobic patients reported improvement of symptoms during alcohol intoxication. (Terra et al., 2006a). Thus, the disorders due to the use of alcohol are liable to start after the social phobia manifestation (Falk et al., 2008). Such anxiety disorder seems to have an early beginning in adolescence, with potentially severe consequences, providing to the affected individuals a bigger vulnerability to major depression and addictive disorder (Regier et al., 1990).

The evaluation of the chronological order of the manifestation of social phobia and alcohol or other psychoactive substances abuse may assist in the investigation of the self-medication hypothesis. According to such hypothesis, social phobia would precede the problems with drug abuse, which would be used to reduce anxiety (Kushner et al., 1990; Swendsen et al., 1998). A study pointed that those that experienced a reduction in anxiety during the treatment reported a smaller use of alcohol compared to those that reported an increase in anxiety (Sloan et al., 2003). There are evidences that a significant rate of drug-addicted individuals with social phobia use psychoactive substances as a self-medication to treat their anxiety (Sareen, Stein, 2000).

It is certain that alcohol reduces anxiety, especially social anxiety what, as a belief, it could by itself influence anxiety, as observed through psycho-social experiments. On the other hand, anxiety symptoms are common during the deintoxication and excessive consumption period. The alcohol effects in the anxiety conditions seem to be limited to the reduction of the physical symptoms of anxiety. Small doses don't seem to have a consistent effect on anxiety, but moderate and large amounts can substantially reduce anxiety. High doses of alcohol reduce the observable and objective signs of anxiety, without reducing the subjective anxiety experience. This effect can be beneficial for anxious patients because the reduction of heart frequency or tremors can enable the patient to support the pathologic anxiety in a more easily manner. Another conclusion is that the phobic men seem to use alcohol as a self-medication more often than women do. All in all, the alcohol effect on anxiety seems to be unconscious and depends on several variables, including dose, cultural beliefs and sex (Wesner,1990).

The idea that alcohol can reduce the anxiety severity proceeds from Antiquity. We can mention a Hypocrates' prescription that says: "drinking wine in equal proportion to water keeps anxiety and terrors away" (Kushner, 1990). Likewise, Westphal perspicaciously stated, in the late XIX century, that the "use of beer or wine enables the agoraphobic patient to pass through feared places at ease". Such considerations lead to the hypothesis, which is the most studied, of the alcohol anxiolytic use, as a self-medication method, promoting the abusive use of the substance (Westphal, 1871; Kushner, 1990).

Another study concluded that the individuals with social phobia use alcohol to reduce anxiety, but raises a doubt whether alcohol can really reduce social anxiety (Carrigan, Randall, 2003). Abrams et al (2001) also assessed the effect of alcohol in the intensity of the anxiety response in social phobic individuals. In this study, 61 individuals with social phobia were divided into three groups and participated in two challenges of talking in public prior to and after consuming: alcohol, where they were told that they were consuming alcohol; or a non-alcoholic beverage, where they were told that they were consuming alcohol (placebo group); or even a non-alcoholic beverage, where they were told that they were not consuming alcohol (control group). Both the group that drank alcohol and the placebo group showed a better reduction of anxiety from the first to the second lecture than the control group. It was observed a reduction in the social anxiety due to the pharmacological effects of alcohol and also due to the belief that the consumption of alcohol would reduce anxiety. Thus, the purpose to reduce the phobic symptoms can be the stimulation to alcohol consumption among social-phobic individuals.

On the other hand, the idea that alcohol-related disorders induce anxiety disorders was the subject matter of several studies. The alcohol may increase the response to stress to aggravate anxiety states, suggesting that an anxiolytic effect in the short run can combine with anxiogenic effects in the long run, producing an upward-spiraling vicious circle of alcohol use and anxiety symptoms (Kushner, 1990).

Naftolowitz et al (1994) say that the alcohol may be effective to attenuate the symptoms of social phobia and that the alcohol addicts use it as a self-medication. Such authors even present other assumptions: the alcohol could exert a placebo effect; the alcohol addicts could have anxiety disorders due to abstinence or to social difficulties caused by their dependence; anxiety could be used as an excuse to drink. Nunes et al (1995) emphasize the following assertions as myths: "Every alcohol addiction is a self-treatment for anxiety" and "Every anxiety in alcohol-addicted patients is caused by alcohol".

Thus, there are several possibilities of relationship between social phobia and alcohol abuse/dependence: a) social phobia may "cause" the alcohol abuse by self-medication; b) social phobia may "cause" the alcohol abuse through another mechanism, besides self-medication; in these two first cases, social phobia can be just one among several causes that contribute to alcohol abuse; c) both social phobia and alcohol abuse may be caused by a third underlying factor and not have any direct causal relation between each other; d) social phobia may increase the alcohol abuse severity and, therefore, lead to an increased seek for treatment, without having any role in the alcohol abuse etiology; e) social phobia and alcohol abuse may coexist by coincidence, without having any relation between them; f) social phobia may be a toxic result of the alcohol use or abstinence, what may be rapidly solved by ending abstinence. Among such assumptions, the self-medication is the one with the biggest clinical relevance, being often formulated to elucidate the alcohol abuse in social phobia (Figueira et al., 1993).

The self-medication theory proposes that the victims of anxiety find out, by their own experience, that the alcohol is able to suppress or reduce the symptoms that disturb them. This solution, which is efficient at first, becomes ill-adaptive as the person develops tolerance and the symptoms of abstinence syndrome arise. At last, the alcohol dependence aggravates and intensifies the social phobia. This theory is empirically based by three types of findings: the fact that the appearance of social phobia quite often precedes the alcohol dependence; the patients' report saying that they started drinking with the purpose of consciously suppress the social phobia symptoms; and, finally, the corroboration that the effective treatment of social phobia leads to the cure of compulsive drinking. Another aspect to be mentioned is that the reported cases of association between social phobia and drug abuse/dependence involve central nervous system activity depressants like alcohol or sedatives, which correspond, by analogy, to the medical treatment with benzodiazepinics (Terra et al., 2004).

According to Kushner et al (1999), cross-section studies point an important association between anxiety disorders and disorders related to alcohol abuse; however, this methodology does not allow testing causal models. These authors, in the attempt to overcome this limitation, noted this relation prospectively. They examined 454 student men and women, when freshmen (year 1), and then, once more in the years 4 and 7 for anxiety disorders (generalized anxiety disorders, agoraphobia, social phobia or panic), diagnosed according to the DIS (*Diagnostic Interview Schedule)* and DSM-III and for disorders related to alcohol abuse (alcohol dependence or abuse). They found that the probability to suffer from an anxiety disorder or an alcohol-abuse disorder was two to five-fold bigger when the other condition was present. Prospectively, the probability to develop a new diagnosis of alcohol dependence in the year 7 increased 3.5 to 5-fold for those individuals diagnosed with an anxiety disorder in the years 1 and 4. Inversely, the probability to develop a new anxiety disorder in the year 7 increased about 4 times for those individuals diagnosed with alcohol dependence in the years 1 or 4. Thus, they concluded that the disorders related to alcohol abuse (specially alcohol dependence) and the anxiety disorders presented a mutual causal relationship with the anxiety disorders, leading to alcohol dependence or vice-versa. Another cohort study estimated a relative risk of 2.30 for individuals with subclinical social phobia to develop alcohol abuse or dependence compared with those without social phobia (Crum, Pratt, 2001).

4) Clinical Impact of Co-morbidity

Patients with mental disorder and concomitant psychoactive substance dependence present more severe and more persistent states, being more resistant to treatments than patients with a single isolated disorder (Brady et al., 2004). The treatment for alcohol addiction reaches worse outcomes when there is the presence of co-morbid anxiety disorders (Driessen et al., 2001). Thus, the presence of a psychiatric disorder is among the main factors that compromise the treatment efficacy with pharmacodependents (Da Silveira, Jorge, 1999). Inversely, the drug abuse may cause the reemergence or aggravate the severity of the mental disorders. The use of drugs can also disguise or mask other mental disorders (Terra et al., 2004).

For treating patients with double diagnosis, having knowledge of the facts that make the adaptation of certain groups of patients difficult is essential in order to be able to take measures that attenuate such difficulties (Kelly et al., 2003). There is a growing evidence that patients with double diagnosis of alcohol addiction or other drugs abuse and a mental disorder present different needs of treatment, contrary to those with a simple diagnosis (Attia, 1988).

More recently, the biggest importance given to the different diagnostic categories of anxiety disorders, assisted by the DSM-III and later by the DSM-III-R and DSM-IV, allowed to study in a more accurate and specific manner the relations among the different anxiety disorders on one side and the addictive behaviors on the other side (Chignon, Lepine, 1993). Several authors have tried to distinguish subgroups of patients with anxiety disorders and concomitant alcohol addiction. When their studies refer to clinical subgroups, the response to the treatment and prognosis, the relevance of such differences is increased (Lotufo Neto, Gentil, 1994).

In regard to social phobia, few investigators have dedicated to the study of the co-morbidity, whether in epidemiological researches (Schneier et al., 1992; Davidson et al., 1993), or in clinical researches (Figueira et al., 1993).

4.1) Impact of the Co-morbidity on Diagnosis and Treatment

The presence of co-morbid disorders may change the case prognosis and treatment. Social phobia worsens significantly the morbidity of a co-morbid substance-abuse disorder and is frequently associated with reduced responses to treatment (Zimmermann et al., 2004). If individuals with social phobia rarely seek help for their anxiety disorder, alcohol addicts with social phobia are less likely to seek treatment for problems with alcohol than alcohol addicts with no social phobia (Thomas et al., 1999).

When defining treatment strategies for social-phobic alcohol addicts, it is necessary to take into account the social phobia in order to avoid a possible increase of alcohol abuse relapses due to the possibility to use it as a self-medication for anxiety symptoms. Only when both disorders are properly assessed and treated, the social phobia and the alcohol abuse cycle can be broken (Lépine, Pélissolo,1998). The relapse rates among drug-addicts with anxiety disorders can be reduced if the agoraphobia and social phobia symptoms are better evaluated during the treatment (LaBounty et al.,1992). The early diagnosis of social phobia and adequate interventions for those patients are necessary to improve the response to treatment in relation to life quality and prevention of relapses (Zimmermman et al., 2004).

Sometimes it is difficult to include social phobia in the differential diagnosis when assessing an alcohol or other psychoactive substance-dependent patient. In daily clinic, the use of semi-structured anamneses that comprise the psychopathological spectrum in a systematic manner can protect us from our natural and negligence tendencies regarding atypical clinical manifestations (Marques et al., 1994). If an untreated or undertreated phobia predisposes to alcohol addiction, the adequate treatment of the phobia may prevent alcohol addiction in a subgroup of patients. For the prevention, it is important to make an accurate diagnosis of the social phobia (Terra et al., 2004).

It is necessary to stimulate researchers engaged in the treatment of substance-addicted individuals so that they become interested in the recognition and treatment of anxiety disorders in their patients. The identification of patients with anxiety disorders is of fundamental importance for the most accurate treatment of an alcohol-addicted patient (Wesner, 1990).

Among alcohol-addicted patients diagnosed with social phobia, Terra et al., (2006a) verified that only one-fifth received a medication that could be useful in the disorder treatment. Not even the phobia intensity showed to build a significant factor to determine the treatment. This finding reaffirms previous studies on the underdiagnosis of social phobia, although it is highly disabling and treatable (Liebowitz et al., 1985; Dingemans et al., 2001). As a result of this little recognition, only about 25% of the patients with social phobia receive a specific treatment, where most of them is improperly treated (Dingemans et al., 2001).

Such findings may result from the fact that, in the treatment initial phase, the focus was on alcohol addiction or other drugs dependence, while social phobia tends to be seen as a secondary problem. Another study showed that the prevalence of social phobia in a clinical sample is nine-fold higher with the use of structured interviews, like the SCID-I, and that the identification of social phobia only occurs when it is the main reason to see a doctor, but that it would not be detected when it was a secondary problem. Nevertheless, only 1% of the patients presented social phobia as the main reason to see a doctor, but similarly, they would like to receive a treatment for the problem, regardless of whether it was or not the main reason to see a doctor (Sheeran, Zimmerman, 2002).

The reasons for the underdiagnosis comprise: the failure of the generalist doctors to recognize the social phobia; the disguise of this condition by other co-morbidities; the embarrassment to express the condition inherent to the patients with social phobia; and even the lack of knowledge by them that it is a psychiatric disorder. At last, social phobia is almost always underestimated both by doctors and patients (Dingemans et al., 2001; Lydiard, 2001).

The low rates of efficacy found in the treatment of drug-dependent individuals could be, at least in part, imputed to the little attention given to the psychiatric co-morbidity in those patients (Ross et cols., 1988). Quite often the treatment of both alcohol-addicted and anxious individuals is directed either to one or another aspect, without taking into account the interaction between the two conditions. Thus, if the alcohol or other psychoactive substances dependence is the focus of the treatment, the anxiety condition is quite often disregarded and the need of medication is not evaluated. On the other hand, if the anxiety disorder is seen as the focus of the treatment, the alcohol addition is frequently disregarded (George et al., 1990).

Taking into account that most of the phobias occur prior to the beginning of the disorders related to alcohol and other drugs, it is important to make the early diagnosis and treatments of social phobia to reduce the risk of alcohol and other psychoactive substances abuse and dependence. Thus, one should perform a more careful investigation in search of phobic disorders in alcohol-dependent and other drug-dependent patients with phobic disorders in order to allow a better prognosis. (Lépine, Pelissolo, 1998; Sareen et al., 2001; Thase et al., 2001). Another reason to make a more careful diagnosis in this co-morbidity is the fact that we know that the social-phobic alcohol addicts present a more severe social phobia when compared to non-alcoholists (Schneier et al., 1989).

4.2) Impact of Co-morbidity on Abstinence

In a study with an initial sample of 300 alcohol-addicted patients, where 24% are social phobics, the social phobia could not be defined as a risk factor for relapse. Three and six months after hospital discharge, no significant differences were found regarding the relapse rates. At 6 months follow-up, 21.3% of patients with social phobia remained in abstinence, 14.7% drank on 1 to 10 occasions, and 63.9% drank on more than 10 occasions. Among patients without social phobia, the rates for drinking were very similar: 25%, 11.8%, 63.3%, respectively (Terra et al., 2006b).

This study didn't identify, therefore, any significant difference among the phobic and non-phobic alcohol addicts regarding the relapse rate after the discharge from hospital, provided that it is not possible from this observation to justify the need of an individualized treatment directed to social phobia for this subgroup of alcohol addicts. Taking into account that the phobic alcohol addicts adhered more to the psychotherapy treatment than the non-phobic alcoholists, after six months of follow up, although this difference is not statistically significant, the biggest adherence could be imputed to the absence of difference in the relapse rates in both groups of alcoholists (Terra et al., 2006b).

This result was similar to that observed in a meta-analysis on the theme, which could not determine which co-morbid anxiety disorders in alcohol-dependent patients pointed to the need of a specific treatment to prevent relapses among social-phobic alcoholists (Schadé et al., 2003). However, a previous study had shown that co-morbid anxiety disorders predicted a worse result in the treatment of alcohol-dependence after six months (Driessen et al., 2001). This difference in the results could be partly explained by different types of anxiety disorders identified in the studies.

Another study compared the effects of a concomitant treatment for social phobia and alcohol addiction with an isolate treatment for alcohol addiction in individuals with a double diagnosis of social anxiety disorder and alcohol dependence. The analysis of intention to treat showed that both groups had improvements in the alcohol addiction and social phobia after treatment. Contrary to the initial assumption, the group treated for both problems had worse results in 3 of 4 rates of alcohol consumption gauging, that means, they drank more often, had a higher total number of doses and had frequently more days of heavy alcohol consumption compared to those that received treatment only for alcohol. No additional effect of the concomitant treatment was observed in the rates of social anxiety (Randall et al., 2001). On the other hand, in another study it was observed that even severely alcohol-dependent patients with an anxiety disorder could benefit from psychotherapy for their anxiety disorder like social phobia (Schadé et al., 2007).

A more recent study also pointed that anxiety treatment for alcohol-dependent patients with a co-morbid anxiety disorder can alleviate anxiety symptoms but has no significant effect on the outcome of alcohol treatment programs (Schadé et al., 2008). In substance use disorder treatment settings, patients with coexisting social phobia do not represent a distinctly high-needs or at-risk group in the broader context of patient populations, for which coexisting psychiatric diagnoses are the norm rather than the exception (Adamson et al., 2008). For Kushner et al. (2005), screening for co-morbid anxiety disorder in alcoholism treatment patients is warranted and, where found, should be considered a marker of high relapse risk relative to that of non-co-morbid patients. The capacity of specific anxiety treatment to mitigate relapse risk among co-morbid patients remains an open question.

4.3) Impact of Co-morbidity on the Adherence to Treatment

In a study previously mentioned, social phobia was not identified either as a risk factor for non-adherence to the psychotherapy treatment or the alcoholics anonymous group after a 6-month follow up after an internment period. In relation to the adherence to AA, although no statistically significant difference was found, it could be noted that phobic individuals tended to adhere less both with a three-month follow up (adherence of 15.7% for phobic and 20.8% for non-phobic individuals), and six-month follow up (adherence of 14.8% for phobic and 20.4% for non-phobic individuals). According to this latter observation, there is the evidence that lower scores at the Liebowitz' Social Anxiety Scale, found in the sample, are related to the bigger adherence to AA. It is possible to assume that the absence of difference with statistical significance regarding the adherence to AA among phobic and non-phobic individuals may be due to the lack of statistical power for the study and that, in a larger sample, such difference may appear (Terra et al., 2006b).

In this same study, the adherence to AA appeared to be low (19%), having been surpassed by the adherence to the psychotherapy treatment both for social phobic and non-phobic individuals. Such findings are in agreement with a 6-month follow up study after an interment period, which pointed that 21% of the patients had not had any relapse and that those that adhered to AA had better outcomes than those who didn't (Gossop et al., 2003). However, this treatment was limited to a small rate of patients, once the adherence found was of 40%, being even higher than that found in the study previously mentioned (Terra et al., 2006b).

In the Terra et al.'s study, (2006b), among those individuals who adhered to AA, both in the three-month and the six-month follow up period, compared to non-phobic individuals, the social-phobic alcoholists took less the upper end of the table at AA and thought that their attendance to the groups was not enough. In relation to the feeling to participate in the AA, the phobic individuals felt less integrated to the group, where this was a statistically significant difference for the six-month follow-up. Besides, the phobic individuals also reported more frequently to be embarrassed to attend AA after three months. There was not a sufficient number of patients to make such comparison after six months of follow up. The social-phobic alcoholists, due to their psychopathology, are likely to attend AA less often than they would like to do, because they feel less integrated to the group. When they go, they take the end of the table much less often than the non-phobic individuals, for fear of social exposure. An assumption to be raised is that, due to a high self-criticism, the phobic individuals more frequently consider their attendance as inadequate, provided that no significant difference in the adherence was found when compared to the non-phobic individuals. Another study also raises the matter that the social-phobic alcoholists have more difficulty to adhere or benefit from a treatment that requires an active participation in groups, like that quite often used in the approach to drug-dependent patients (Myrick, Brady, 1997).

Specific personalities may be predictive of abstinence or engagement in self-help meetings in the case of alcoholists recently deintoxicated, and it may have both a therapeutic and prognostic meaning. Introverted people attend group self-help meeting less frequently (Janowsky et al., 1999). Actually, social phobia, even in the slightest forms, may prevent the drug-dependent patient from benefiting from the treatment, specially if activities like group therapy and AA and NA (Narcotics Anonymous) meetings are involved, reducing the adherence and putting the patient in risk of relapse (Zimmermann et al., 2004).

Thus, social-phobic alcoholist patients could have more difficulties to engage in a group treatment of a drug-addiction recovery program that involves the participation in alcoholics anonymous meetings, in which there would be a bigger social exposure. For Morris et al. (2005), treatment can be very problematic for an individual with social phobia and alcohol dependence, as the group settings (e.g., 12-step program) likely cause significant social anxiety that could lead to avoidance of the setting or difficulty actively participating and attending to the group content. For these authors, further understanding is also needed in determining whether individual or group cognitive-behavioral therapy is best for co-morbid individuals, as some may find the group atmosphere highly intimidating (possibly contributing to drop out) while others may find that group treatment really gives them the support they need to conquer their alcohol addiction as well as an ideal setting for practicing social exposure.

5) Conclusion

Social phobia is quite frequent among psychoactive substance addicts, provided that it tends to precede the use of alcohol, what emphasizes the hypothesis of this drug use as a self-medication. However, the use of medication for social phobia in interned social-phobic alcoholists is less frequent. It can also be noted that the alcoholists seem to improve the social-phobic symptoms during the alcohol intoxication and become worse during abstinence.

Social phobia cannot be considered as a risk factor for relapse in most of the studies, since the frequency of relapse tends to be high both for phobic and non-phobic alcoholists. Social phobia may significantly interfere in the adherence to AA, but not to the psychotherapy treatment. The phobic alcoholists' adherence to AA tends to be smaller than the non-phobic individuals'. Among the alcoholists who adhere to the AA group, comparatively to the non-phobic individuals, the social-phobic ones feel less integrated to the group, sought to expose themselves less and more commonly thought that their attendance to AA was insufficient.

Thus, due to this frequent association, every social-phobic patient should be carefully evaluated regarding the alcohol or other psychoactive substances consumption level, as well as regarding the family background for alcohol addiction, just like every patient with alcohol or other drugs abuse or dependence may benefit from a complete assessment regarding the presence of this anxiety disorder, provided that the co-morbidity non-identification could lead to the treatment failure and the symptomatology persistence.

REFERENCES

Abrams K, Kushner M, Medina KL, Voigh A. The pharmacologic and expectancy effects of alcohol on social anxiety in individuals with social phobia. *Drug Alcohol Dependent* 2001; 64: 219-31.

Adamson SJ, Sellman JD, Robertson PJ. Social phobia in an outpatient alcohol and drug treatment sample. *Aust N Z J Psychiatry* 2008, 42(2): 134-40.

Agosti V, Nunes E, Levin F. Rates of psychiatric comorbidity among U.S. Residents with lifetime cannabis dependence, *Am J Drug Alcohol Abuse* 2002; 28:643–52.

Agrawal A, Lynsky MT, Maden PA, Bucholz KK, Heath AC. A latent class analysis of illicit drug abuse/dependence: results from the National Epidemiological Survey on Alcohol and Related Conditions. *Addiction* 2007; 102(1): 94-104.

Attia PR. Dual diagnosis: definition and treatment. *Alcohol Treat Q* 1988; 5: 53-63.

Brady TM, Krebs CP, Laird G. Psychiatric comorbidity and not completing jail-based substance abuse treatment. *Am J Addict* 2004; 13: 83-101.

Carrigan MH, Randal CL. Self-medication in social phobia. A review of the alcohol literature. *Addict Behav* 2003; 28(2): 269-84.

Chignon JM, Lépine JP. Trouble panique et alcoolisme: influence de la comorbidité. *Rev Can Psychiatr* 1993; 38(7): 485-93.

Crum RM, Pratt LA. Risk of heavy drinking and alcohol use disorders in social phobia: a prospective analysis. *Am J Psychiatry* 2001; 158: 1693-700.

Da Silveira DX, Jorge MR. Co-morbidade psiquiátrica em pacientes dependentes de substâncias psicoativas: resultados preliminares. *Rev Bras Psiquiatr* 1999; 21(3): 145-51.

Davidson JRT, Hughes DL, George LK, Blazer DG. The epidemiology of social phobia: findings from the Duke Epidemiological Catchment Area Study. *Psychol Med* 1993; 23: 709-18.

Degonda M, Angst J. The Zurich study. XX. Social phobia and agoraphobia. *Eur Arch Psychiatry Clin Neurosci* 1993; 243: 95-102.

Dingemans AE, Van Vliet IM, Couveé J, Westenberg HG. Characteristics of patients with social phobia and their treatment in specialized clinics for anxiety disorders in the Netherlands. *J Affect Disord* 2001; 65: 123-9.

Driessen M, Meier S, Hill A, Wetterling T, Lange W, Junghanns K. The course of anxiety, depression and drinking behaviours after completed detoxification in alcoholics with and without comorbid anxiety and depressive disorders. *Alcohol Alcohol* 2001; 36(3), 249-55.

Falk DE, Yi HY, Hilton ME. Age of onset and temporal sequencing of lifetime DSM-IV alcohol use disorders relative to comorbid mood and anxiety disorders. *Drug Alcohol Depend* 2008; 94(1-3): 234-45.

Figueira I, Nardi AE, Marques C, Mendlowicz M, Ventura P, Saboya E, et al. Abuso de álcool e fobia social - Revisão da literatura e relato de seis casos de comorbidade. Programa de Ansiedade e Depressão - UFRJ. Série Psicofarmacologia -12. *J Bras Psiquiatr* 1993; 42(2): 63-8.

George DT, Nutt DJ, Dwyer BA, Linnoila M. Alcoholism and panic disorder: is comorbidity more than coincidence? *Acta Psychiatr Scand* 1990; 81: 97-107.

Gossop M, Harris J, Best B, Lan-Ho M, Manning V, Marshall J et al. Is attendance at alcoholics anonymous meetings after inpatient treatment related to improved outcomes? A 6-month follow-up study. *Alcohol Alcohol* 2003; 38(5): 421-26.

Grant BF, Hasin DS, Blanco C, Stinson FS, Chou SP, Goldstein RB, Dawson DA, Smith S, Saha TD, Huang B. The epidemiology of social anxiety disorder in the United States: results from the National Epidemiologic Survey on Alcohol and Related Conditions. *J Clin Psychiatry* 2005; 66(11):1351-61

Himle JA, Hill EM. Alcohol abuse and the anxiety disorders: Evidence from the Epidemiologic Catchment Area Survey. *J Anxiety Disord* 1991; 51: 237-45.

Janowsky DS, Boone A, Morter S, Howe L. Personality and alcohol/substance-use disorder patient relapse and attendance at self-help group meetings. *Alcohol Alcohol* 1999; 34(3): 359-69.

Kelly JF, McKellar JD, Moos R. Major depression in patients with substance use disorders: relationship to 12-step self-help involvement and substance use outcomes. *Addiction* 2003; 98: 499-508.

Kessler RC, Crum RM, Warner LA, Nelson CB, Schulenberg J, Anthony JC. Lifetime co-occurrence of DSM-III-R alcohol abuse and dependence with other psychiatric disorders in the National Comorbidity Survey. *Arch Gen Psychiatry* 1997; 54: 313-21.

Kessler RC, McGonagle KA, Zhao S, Nelson CB, Hughes M, Eshleman S, et al. Lifetime and 12-month prevalence of DSM-III-R psychiatric disorders in the United States: results from the National Comorbidity Survey. *Arch Gen Psychiatry* 1994; 51: 8-19.

Kushner MG, Abrams K, Thuras P, Hanson KL, Brekke M, Sletten S. Follow-up study of anxiety disorder and alcohol dependence in comorbid alcoholism treatment patients. *Alcohol Clin Exp Res* 2005; 29(8):1432-43.

Kushner MG, Sher KJ, Beitman BD. The relation between alcohol problems and the anxiety disorders. *Am J Psychiatry* 1990; 147: 685-95.

Kushner MG. Kenneth JS, Erickson DJ. Prospective analysis of the relation beetween DSM-III anxiety disorders and alcohol use disorders. *Am J Psychiatry* 1999; 156: 723-32.

LaBounty LP, Hatsukami D, Morgan SF, Nelson L. Relapse among alcoholics with phobic and panic symptoms. *Addict Behav* 1992; 17: 9-15.

Lang AJ, Stein MB. Social phobia: prevalence and diagnostic threshold. *J Clin Psychiatry* 2001; 62(Suppl 1): 5-10.

Lecrubier Y. Implications of early onset social phobia on outcome. *Eur Neuropsychopharmacol* 1997; 7(Suppl 2): 85.

Lépine J, Pélissolo A. Social Phobia and alcoholism: a complex relationship. *J Affect Disord* 1998; 50(Suppl 1): 23-8.

Liebowitz MR, Gorman JM, Fryer AJ, Klein DF. Social phobia: review of neglected anxiety disorder. *Arch Gen Psychiatry* 1985; 42: 729-36.

Lotufo Neto F e Gentil V. Alcoholism and phobic anxiety - a clinical-demographic comparison. *Addiction* 1994; 89: 447-53.

Lydiard RB, Brady K, Ballenger JC. Anxiety and mood disorders in hospitalized alcoholic individuals. *Am J Addict* 1992; 1: 325-31.

Lydiard RB. Social anxiety disorder: comorbidity and its implications. *J Clin Psychiatry* 2001; 58(Suppl 1): 17-23.

Maciel LMA, Gentil Filho V. Transtorno de pânico e alcoolismo - um estudo retrospectivo. *Rev ABP-APAL* 1998; 10(1): 8-11.

Magee WJ, Eaton WW, Wittchen HU, McGonagle KA, Kessler RC. Agoraphobia, simple phobia and social phobia in the National Comorbidity Survey. *Arch Gen Psychiatry* 1996; 53: 159-68.

Manuzza S, Schneier FR, Chapman TF, Liebowitz MR, Klein DF, Fyer AJ. Generalized social phobia: reliability and validity. *Arch Gen Psychiatry* 1995; 52: 230-7.

Marques C, Figueira I, Mendlowicz M, Nardi AE, Andrade Y, Versiani M, et al. Comorbidade: fobia social generalizada, anorexia nervosa e abuso de psicoestimulantes. Série Psicofarmacologia - 21. *J Bras Psiquiatr* 1994; 43(1): 3-9

Myrick H, Brady KT. Social phobia in cocaine-dependent individuals. *Am J Addict* 1997; 6: 99-104.

Morris EP, Stewart SH, Ham LS. The relationship between social anxiety disorder and alcohol use disorders: a critical review. *Clin Psychol Rev* 2005; 25(6):734-60

Naftolowitz DF, Vaughn BV, Rane J, Tancer ME. Response to alcohol in social phobia. *Anxiety* 1994; 1: 96-9.

Nunes EV, McGrath PJ, Quitkin FM. Treating anxiety in patients with alcoholism. *J Clin Psychiatry* 1995; 56(Suppl 2): 3-9.

Page AC, Andrews G. Do specific anxiety disorders shown specific drug problems? *Aust N Z J Psychiatry* 1996; 30(3): 803-6.

Randall CL, Thomas S, Thevos AK. Concurrent alcoholism and social anxiety disorder: a first step toward developing effective treatments. *Alcohol Clin Exp Res* 2001; 25: 210-20.

Regier DA, Farmer ME, Rae DS, Locke BZ, Keith SJ, Judd LL et al. Comorbidity of mental disorders with alcohol and other drug abuse. *JAMA* 1990; 264: 2511-18.

Ross HE, Glaser FB, Germanson T. The prevalence of psychiatric disorders in patients with alcohol and other drug problems. *Arch Gen Psychiatry* 1988; 45: 1023-31.

Sareen J, Chartier M, Kjernisted KD, Stein MB. Comorbidity of phobic disorders with alcoholism in a canadian community sample. *Can J Psychiatry* 2001; 46: 733-40.

Sareen J, Chartier M, Paulus MP, Stein MB. Illicit drug use and anxiety disorders: findings from two community surveys. *Psychiatry Res* 2006; 142(1): 11-17.

Saaren J, Stein M. A review of the epidemiology and approaches to the treatment of social anxiety disorder. *Drugs* 2000; 59(3): 497-509.

Schadé A, Marquenie LA, Van Balkon EB, Koeter MW, De Beurs E, Van Dyck R, Van den Brink W. Anxiety disorders: treatable regardless of the severity of comorbid alcohol dependence. *Eur Addict Res* 2007; 13(2): 109-15.

Schadé A, Marquenie LA, Van Balkon EB, Koeter MW Van den Brink W, Van Dyck R. The effectiveness of anxiety treatment on alcohol-dependent patients with a comorbid phobic disorder: a randomised controlled trial. *Tijdschr Psychiatr* 2008; 50(3): 137-48.

Schadé A, Marquenie LA, Van Balkon EB, Van Dyck R, Van den Brink W. Do comorbidity anxiety disorders in alcohol-dependent patients need specific treatment to prevent relapse? *Alcohol Alcohol* 2003; 38: 255-62.

Schneier FR, Johnson J, Hornig CD, Liebowitz MR, Weissmann MM. Social phobia: comorbidity and morbidity in na epidemiologic sample. *Arch Gen Psychiatry* 1992; 49: 282-8.

Schneier FR, Martin LY, Liebowitz MR. Alcohol abuse in social phobia. *J Anxiety Disord* 1989; 3: 15-23.

Sheeran T, Zimmerman M. Social phobia: still a negleted anxiety disorder? *J Nerv Ment Dis* 2002; 190(1): 786-8.

Sloan TB, Roache JD, Johnson BA. The role of anxiety in predicting drinking behaviour. *Alcohol Alcohol* 2003; 38(4): 360-3.

Swendsen JD, Merikangas KR, Canino GJ, Kessler RC, Rubio-Stipec M, Angst J. The comorbidity of alcoholism with anxiety depressive disorders in four geographic communities. *Compr Psychiatry* 1998; 39(4), 176-84.

Terra MB, Barros HMT, Stein A, Figueira I, Jorge MR; Palermo LH, Athayde LD, Gonçalves MS, Spanemberg L, Possa MA, Daruy Filho L, Da Silveira DX. Social anxiety disorder in 300 patients hospitalized for alcoholism in Brazil: high prevalence and undertreatment. *Compr Psychiatry*, 2006a; 47:463-7.

Terra MB, Barros HMT, Stein A, Figueira I, Athayde LD, Spanemberg L, Possa MA, Daruy Filho L, Da Silveira DX. Does co-occurring social phobia interfere with alcoholism treatment adherence and relapse?. *J Subst Abuse Treat*; 2006b; 31(4): 403-9.

Terra MB, Figueira I, Barros HMT. Impact of alcohol intoxication and withdrawal syndrome on social phobia and panic disorder in alcoholic inpatients. *Rev Hosp Clin Fac Med S Paulo* 2004; 59(4): 187-92.

Thase ME, Salloum IM, Cornelius JD. Comorbid alcoholism and depression: treatment issues. *J Clin Psychiatry* 2001; 62(Suppl 20), 32-41.

Thomas SE, Thevos AK, Randall CL. Alcoholics with and without social phobia: a comparison of substance use and psychiatric variables. *J Stud Alcohol* 1999; 60: 472-9.

Van Ameringen M, Mancini C, Styan G, Donison D. Relationship of social phobia with other psychiatric illness. *J Affect Disord* 1991; 21: 93-9.

Wesner RB. Alcohol use and abuse secondary to anxiety. *Psychiatr Clin North Am* 1990; 13(4): 699-713.

Westphal C. Die agoraphobie: eine neuropathische erscheinung. *Arch Psychiatr Nervenker* 1871; 3: 138-171.

Zimmerman G, Pin MA, Krenz S, Bouchat A, Favrat B, Zullino DF, et al. Prevalence of social phobia in a clinical sample of drug dependent patients. *J Affect Dis* 2004; 83(1): 83-7.

In: Social Phobia: Etiology, Diagnosis and Treatment
Editor: Clayton P. Axelby
ISBN 978-1-60692-159-3
© 2009 Nova Science Publishers, Inc.

Chapter VI

Cognitive Behavioral Therapy for Childhood Anxiety Disorders: Social Anxiety Predicts Treatment Response

Katharina Manassis*[*] *and Janis L. Wolfe
University of Toronto, Canada

Abstract

Objectives: To determine if social anxiety and other specific child characteristics predict cognitive behavioral therapy (CBT) outcomes in anxious children, and if these characteristics improve with CBT. High social anxiety was hypothesized to have an adverse effect on outcome.

Method: Children with anxiety disorders (n=110) ages 8 to 12 years and their mothers completed measures of children's general level of anxiety, social anxiety, depression, negative self-statements, self-esteem, locus of control, coping style and social skills pre- and post-CBT. Outcome measures were clinician-rated child functioning and child- and parent-rated child anxiety.

Results: Low initial social anxiety predicted child- and mother-rated improvement in anxiety. Initial use of active coping predicted clinician-rated improvement in functioning. Several child characteristics including social anxiety improved with CBT though they were not targeted directly.

Conclusion: In anxious children specific child characteristics, particularly social anxiety, predict less favorable response to CBT. Tailored treatments for children with these characteristics merit investigation.

[*] Correspondence concerning this article should be addressed to: Dr. Katharina Manassis, Department of Psychiatry, Hospital for Sick Children, 555 University Avenue, Toronto, Ontario, M5G 1X8, Canada. Tel: 416-813-7464 (direct); 416-813-7531 (secretary); FAX: 415-813-5326; E-mail: katharina.manassis@sickkids.ca.

Cognitive Behavioral Therapy for Childhood Anxiety Disorders: Social Anxiety Predicts Treatment Response

Anxiety disorders affect up to ten percent of school-aged children, resulting in substantial distress and impaired functioning (Bernstein & Borchardt, 1991). Moreover, they tend to have a chronic course, often functioning as precursors of anxiety problems and other psychopathologies in adulthood (Keller et al., 1992; Last, 1988). Given the prevalence and sequelae of childhood anxiety, effective treatment is essential. Multiple randomized controlled trials have shown that cognitive behavioral therapy (CBT) can reduce children's anxiety and improve their functioning (James et al., 2005).

Nevertheless, some anxious children respond more favorably to CBT than others. Research examining factors related to children's treatment response or non-response is sparse (Crawford & Manassis, 2001). Although the relationship between parental, family, and demographic characteristics and treatment outcome for anxious children has been explored (Crawford & Manassis, 2001; Victor et al., 2007), few specific child characteristics have been examined in relation to outcome.

The presence of high levels of social anxiety may particularly affect response to standard CBT interventions for childhood anxiety. Social anxiety may affect the child's ability to engage with the therapist or therapy group, make it difficult to apply CBT strategies in social situations, and affect social competence resulting in negative peer interactions that maintain or exacerbate anxiety. While there are efficacious treatments specifically focused on social phobia in youth (Garcia-Lopez et al., 2006; Hayward et al., 2000), most child anxiety programs target a variety of symptoms including worries, different types of phobic avoidance, and physiological signs of anxiety and are thus not specific to social anxiety (Kendall, 1994; Kendall et al., 1997). The child with high social anxiety may therefore be at a disadvantage relative to her more socially comfortable peers in such a treatment program.

The present investigation examines social anxiety and several other aspects of internalizing psychopathology in children with anxiety disorders that may moderate CBT response, and also potentially improve with CBT. Increased understanding and attention to such factors may enhance treatment outcomes. Examining these factors together is consistent with a cognitive-behavioral understanding of anxiety, which postulates bidirectional influences between anxious affects, cognitions, and behaviors (Beck & Emery, 1985).

One might argue that these factors overlap with each other and with anxiety, together representing a more general vulnerability to internalizing distress (Watson & Clark, 1984). The constructs, however, are both clinically and psychometrically distinct. For example, in measuring overall anxiety versus social anxiety (MASC and SASC-R respectively), only 13% of MASC items overlap with 23% of SASC-R items, leaving the remainder of items evaluating distinct aspects of children's anxiety. Similarly, anxiety and depression, despite being highly correlated, maintain unique clinical features (e.g., relative absence of positive mood in depression, and physiological hyperarousal in anxiety; Akiskal, 1985; Watson & Clark, 1984).

To begin, evidence relating anxiety to these factors is briefly reviewed. They include: social anxiety and social competence, depression, negative self-statements, locus of control, self-esteem, and coping style.

Social Anxiety and Childhood Anxiety Disorders

Chansky and Kendall (1997) found that children with anxiety disorders self-report higher levels of social anxiety, more negative social expectancies, and lower self-competence than control children. These findings illustrate the relationship between clinically anxious children's socially anxious affect, cognitive expectations of threat and rejection, and compromised behavioral social competence. Interestingly, high levels of social anxiety were the best predictor of negative social expectancies with respect to joining a peer game in this population, suggesting that social anxiety may predict and perpetuate social avoidance.

Exposure to anxiety-provoking situations is a crucial element of successful CBT for child anxiety (Bouchard et al., 2004). By promoting avoidance, social anxiety may interfere with this treatment element. Similarly, anxiety about being evaluated by the therapist or by peers (in the case of group-based CBT) may reduce involvement in therapy, and child involvement has also been found to relate to treatment success (Chu and Kendall, 2004).

Ginsburg and colleagues (1998) found that children's high social anxiety was significantly associated with low levels of social acceptance and more negative peer interactions, such as being teased or having enemies. Girls with high self-reported social anxiety were also rated by their parents as having poor social skills, especially low assertion and responsible social behavior (Ginsburg et al., 1998) suggesting impairment in social competence. Some caution is warranted in interpreting this finding though, as parental ratings may be biased given limited opportunities to observe their child's social interactions (Mesman and Koot, 2000) and possible anxiety about their child.

There may be a bidirectional effect between social anxiety and social competence: that is, social anxiety may occur in response to low social competence, and social competence may deteriorate through prolonged avoidance of social situations due to anxiety (Ginsburg et al., 1998). Similarly, negative peer interactions may be both a marker for low social competence and a contributing factor to social anxiety and social difficulties. It is therefore important to examine both social anxiety and social competence in relation to CBT outcome, recognizing that one or both factors may interfere with treatment success.

Other Characteristics Linked to Childhood Anxiety Disorders

Comorbidity estimates for anxiety and depression in children range from 15.9% to 61.9% (Bernstein, 1991; Brady & Kendall, 1992; Kovacs et al., 1989), varying with different samples and methodologies. Youth who present with both disorders tend to be older at presentation than children with anxiety disorders alone (Strauss et al., 1998). Comorbid depression in anxious children has been linked longitudinally to poorer adjustment in young adulthood than anxiety alone (Last et al., 1997).

Anxious children have a high frequency of negative self-statements and cognitions (i.e., focusing on worry and danger), especially when exposed to perceived threatening stimuli (Chansky & Kendall, 1997; Treadwell & Kendall, 1996). Threat-related biases in anxious children's attention, memory, as well as dichotic listening and interpretation of ambiguous stimuli, have also been discovered (reviewed in Manassis et al., 1996). These biases may interfere with performance of cognitive activities and adaptive behaviors (Kindt et al., 1997).

Locus of control refers to the perception of events being under either personal control (internal locus of control) or non-personal control (external locus of control) (Nowicki & Strickland, 1973). Anxious children maintain an external locus of control regarding their successes, and an internal locus of control with respect to their failures (Bell-Dolan & Wessler, 1994). Such cognitions tend to lead to increased worry and sadness, and problem-solving deficits (Bell-Dolan & Wessler, 1994; Stark et al., 1990).

Children with anxiety disorders are reported to have lower self-esteem levels, and lower self-perceptions of social acceptance and global self-worth, relative to non-anxious children (Ginsburg et al., 1998; Messer & Beidel, 1994). High levels of self-esteem often, but not always, reflect high self-efficacy (Muris, 2002). This is relevant to anxiety disorders, in that children with high self-efficacy are more likely to exhibit confidence in their judgments and believe that they can manage challenging situations through their own efforts. Facing challenging situations, particularly those that are anxiety-provoking is a key component of successful CBT.

Anxious children tend to avoid activities they perceive as threatening, thus failing to overcome their anxiety and remaining distressed (Kendall et al., 1997). In some anxious children, this behavior appears to reflect a lower threshold of response to unfamiliar situations (Kagan et al., 1987). Unfortunately, consistent withdrawal from novelty often becomes routine, decreasing anxious children's opportunity to learn effective coping strategies (Kagan et al., 1987), and supporting their distorted cognitions. Fortunately, coping strategies have been found to change with CBT, decreasing avoidant behaviors and increasing active management of negative emotional arousal (Mendlowitz et al., 1999).

Predictors of CBT Outcome

CBT is a brief, structured, directive therapy that targets cognitions and behaviors likely to maintain anxious children's exaggerated perceptions of threat. Little research has examined predictors of treatment response (Victor et al., 2007). This area is critical to examine, given that 30-50% of children who receive CBT interventions continue to meet diagnostic criteria for anxiety disorders post-treatment (Barrett, 1998; Kendall, 1994; Kendall et al., 1997).

Crawford and Manassis (2001) examined whether family factors predicted outcome following a CBT intervention for 8-12 year old anxious children using the Coping Bear Workbook, a group adaptation of Kendall's Coping Cat (Scapillato & Mendlowitz, unpublished, available from authors). Children's lower ratings of family dysfunction and children's lower frustration with their families predicted greater clinician-rated child improvement following CBT. Parental reports of less family dysfunction and mothers' lower parenting stress levels predicted greater mother-rated child improvement (i.e., decreased anxiety), and lower father-rated somatization and child-rated family dysfunction and frustration ratings also predicted more improvement in child-rated anxiety outcome. In a similar study, Victor and colleagues (2007) examined group CBT outcomes for anxious children ages 7 to 11 years in relation to family functioning, parenting stress, and parental psychopathology. Higher family cohesion pre-treatment predicted significantly greater decreases in child anxiety for participants who received CBT than lower family cohesion. No other significant predictors were found.

In one of the few studies to examine child characteristics in relation to CBT, Treadwell and Kendall (1996) found that anxious children's pre-treatment negative self-statements not only related to their pre-treatment anxiety, but predicted the severity of their anxiety symptoms after treatment. Other child characteristics have not been examined in relation to treatment outcome.

Hypotheses

A cognitive behavioral understanding of anxiety postulates bidirectional influences between cognitive distortions, anxious affect, and maladaptive behavior. Based on this understanding, measures of the affective, cognitive, and behavioral systems should be highly correlated. A particular disturbance in any one area (for example, high social anxiety) should adversely affect how children respond to CBT treatment generally, but on the other hand several areas should improve with treatment even if they are not targeted directly. Therefore, we hypothesized that high social anxiety would be a predictor of decreased improvement in overall anxiety with CBT, but also that children would show reduced social anxiety with treatment. Other child characteristics discussed above were also examined as potential outcome predictors and as potentially responsive to CBT. Age and gender effects are also examined, but with no a priori hypotheses.

METHOD

Participants

This study was approved by the Research Ethics Board of our hospital. Participants were 110 children (57 males, 53 females) aged eight to twelve years (M = 9.9, SD = 1.3) and their mothers. All children participating met criteria for at least one *DSM-IV* (American Psychiatric Association, 1994) anxiety disorder based on semi-structured diagnostic interviews (derived from the Diagnostic Inventory for Children and Adolescents-Revised, revised to meet *DSM-IV* criteria; Reich & Welner, 1988), administered by trained psychiatrists and corroborated by maternal completion of a computerized version of the instrument (Reich et al., 1997). Primary diagnoses included: generalized anxiety disorder (66%), separation anxiety disorder (20%), simple phobia (5%), social phobia (4%), and other (such as panic disorder, depression, OCD, and oppositional defiant disorder; 5%). Forty-two percent of children had a secondary anxiety disorder diagnosis, 2% of children had a comorbid depression diagnosis, and 34% of children had a comorbid non-anxiety, non-depressive diagnosis (i.e., ADHD, ODD).

Children having psychotic disorders, a medical condition which would interfere with treatment, an IQ of less than 80 (based on two subtests of the WISC-III; Wechsler, 1991), or who were not proficient in the English language, were excluded from participation in the study. Children receiving psychoactive medication (n=8; all on serotonin reuptake inhibitors) were included but medication was kept at constant dosage throughout treatment, with final dosage adjustment at least one month prior to starting CBT.

The majority of the sample was Caucasian (85%); the rest were of African American or Asian descent (15%). Ninety-two percent of the mothers had some post-secondary education, suggesting a bias towards more educated or affluent families relative to the general population. The families were consecutively referred by physicians and mental health professionals for assessment at a tertiary care Anxiety Disorders Clinic at a large children's hospital.

Procedure

After obtaining informed consent from parents and assent from children, psychologists and supervised psychology interns administered questionnaires assessing a variety of internalizing symptoms. The order of the presentation of the questionnaires was counterbalanced. Clinicians completed a measure of children's functioning level (Children's Global Assessment Scale, CGAS; Shaffer et al., 1983).

After the initial assessment, children were randomly assigned to either individual or group manual-based treatment conditions[1]. Detailed methodology and main therapeutic outcomes for this randomized trial have been reported (Manassis et al., 2002), but child characteristics were not addressed. Fifty-three percent (n=58) of the children received group treatment, and 47% (n=52) received individual treatment. Children in both conditions received 12 weekly sessions of CBT treatment, and parents received a similarly structured 12 week program that taught problem-solving in relation to child anxiety. Therapist contact time and therapist experience were comparable for the two treatment modalities, and acceptable treatment adherence was confirmed for both (see Manassis et al., 2002) using coding of a randomly selected subset of session audiotapes (10%). As outcomes were comparable for the two treatment modalities (Manassis et al., 2002), and are not the focus of the present study, results are pooled across modalities except for cases where modality-specific main or interaction effects were found.

Following the treatment program, children, parents, and clinicians completed the same questionnaires as those given prior to treatment. Treatment attendance was excellent for children and parents attending both group and individual treatment, with an average of 10.5

[1] There was no comparison waitlist control group used in this study. This is because significant treatment effects for this particular intervention, for several of the measures used in the current study (as detailed below), have been demonstrated in previous studies as compared to a waitlist period (Barrett, 1998; Kendall, 1994; Kendall et al., 1997; Mendlowitz et al., 1999).

out of 12 sessions attended (range 8 to 12), and no correlations between attendance and measures in the present study. The group and individual conditions had 10% and 7% treatment attrition, respectively. There were no significant differences between those children who dropped out of the study and those who remained in the study in age, gender, or symptom severity.

Treatment Manuals

The *Coping Bear Workbook* (Scapillato & Mendlowitz, 1993) used in this research study was an adaptation of the *Coping Cat Workbook*, developed by Kendall (1990), for CBT for anxious children. Children are educated as to how to: identify their physical reactions to anxiety, relax, modify maladaptive cognitions, and use and self-reinforce adaptive coping responses.

Therapy for parents was modeled after the book *Keys to Parenting Your Anxious Child* (Manassis, 1996). The parent group emphasized psychoeducation and problem-solving around children's anxiety-related behaviors. Parents learned strategies to understand and manage their children's anxiety and help their children cope with anxiety-provoking situations. The content of the parent portion roughly paralleled the content of the children's program. Both treatment conditions included homework assignments and problem-solving to reinforce strategies introduced in the manuals.

Measures

The following measures were completed before and after the CBT treatment.

Outcome Measures

The *Multidimensional Anxiety Scale for Children (MASC; March, 1997)* is a 39-item, Likert style self-report measure designed to assess a broad range of anxiety symptoms (four subscales: physical symptoms, social anxiety, harm avoidance, and separation/panic) in 8 to 19 year old youth. It is a well-validated measure with high internal and test-retest reliability, and established factorial, discriminant, and convergent validities (March, 1997).

The *Children's Global Assessment Scale (CGAS; Shaffer et al., 1983)* provides clinician ratings of 4 to 16 year old children's adaptive functioning during the previous month. It is rated on a 100 point scale, with 1 representing the most functionally impaired child and 100 representing the healthiest (Shaffer et al., 1983), with descriptors provided for each 10-point interval. To obtain more objective ratings, three clinicians (all psychiatrists and psychologists) who were not involved in the study and blind to treatment and to pre- and post-treatment status estimated child participants' global functioning using detailed clinical assessment notes. For all cases, the three initial clinician ratings fell within the same 10-point interval; the exact rating was discussed until a consensus was reached, and the agreed-upon consensus rating is reported.

Child- and Parent-rated Measure of Child Characteristics

The Social Anxiety Scale for Children-Revised (SASC-R; La Greca & Stone, 1993) is a 22-item measure of children's anxiety in relation to peers and social situations with established reliability and concurrent validity (LaGreca and Stone, 1993). It also has high construct validity, successfully discriminating socially anxious from non-socially anxious children (Ginsburg et al., 1998). Three subscales include fear of negative evaluation (eight items reflecting fears, concerns, or worries regarding negative evaluation from peers), specific social anxiety (six items reflecting social avoidance and distress with new social situations or unfamiliar peers), and general social anxiety (four items reflecting more generalized or pervasive social distress, discomfort, and inhibition).

Parent-rated Measure of Child Characteristics

The Social Skills Rating System - Parent Form Elementary Level (SSRS; Gresham & Elliott, 1990) assesses parents' perceptions of the frequency of a wide range of social behaviors for children in kindergarten through sixth grade. Social Skills (cooperation, assertion, responsibility, and self-control subscales; 38 items) and Problem Behaviors (internalizing, externalizing, and hyperactive; 17 items) were measured in the present study, as these two subscales have the best psychometric properties and correlate well with other parent-report measures of these constructs (for example, corresponding Child Behavior Checklist scales; Achenbach & Edelbrock, 1983).

Child-rated Measures of Child Characteristics

All measures were selected for their psychometric properties, availability of norms, and previous reported use in this population.

The *Children's Depression Inventory (CDI; Kovacs, 1982)* is a 27-item self-report survey designed to measure 7 to 17 year old children's overt symptoms associated with a state of depression. It has high internal consistency, and established test-retest reliability and discriminant validity (Kovacs, 1992).

The *Negative Affect Self-Statement Questionnaire for 7-10 year olds (NASSQ: 7-10; Ronan, Kendall, & Rowe, 1994)* assesses anxious and depressive self-statements in children. Fourteen negative self-statements comprise the NASSQ: 7-10, with eleven anxiety-specific cognitions (e.g., "I thought I would fail") and three depression-specific self-statements (e.g., "Life is terrible").

The *Nowicki-Strickland Locus of Control Scale (NSLOC; Nowicki & Strickland, 1973)* consists of forty reinforcement situations across interpersonal and motivational realms (e.g. achievement, dependency) with responses that indicate internal or external control orientation. Scores range from 0 (high internal locus of control) to 40 (high external locus of control). The cut-off score between an externally- and internally-oriented locus of control for anxious children in this study was 16. It has good test-retest reliability and established construct validity (Nowicki & Strickland, 1973).

The Self-Perception Profile for Children (SPPC; Harter, 1985) assesses third through sixth grade children's self-reported judgments of self-adequacy and competence across scholastic, athletic, physical, behavioral, social, and global self-worth domains. There is evidence of good construct validity and internal consistency for this measure (Harter, 1985).

The Children's Coping Strategies Checklist-Revised (CCSC-R; Sandler & Ayers, 1990) assesses coping strategies used by children when they experience a problem. The 57-item checklist yields four relevant coping factors: active (direct problem-solving, positive cognitive restructuring), avoidant (avoidant actions, cognitive avoidance), distraction (distracting actions, physical release of emotions), and support (problem-focused, and emotion-focused, support). The measure shows good internal consistency and good construct validity (Sandler & Ayers, 1990).

RESULTS

Prior to testing the main hypotheses, data were examined for accuracy, missing values, outliers, distributions and other assumptions of multivariate analysis. If a single item was missing for a subscale, it was replaced with the mean score for the other items of the subscale; if more than one item was missing the subscale was not included for that subject. Several variables were transformed to reduce skewness and kurtosis, and transformed variables are used in subsequent analyses.

As predicted, various child characteristics were highly intercorrelated prior to treatment. Significant correlations included: self-reported anxiety with self-reported social anxiety, depressive feelings, negative self-statements, external locus of control, avoidant coping, support-focused coping, and lower self-esteem; mother-reported anxiety with maternal ratings of child social anxiety and maternal reports of child behavior problems; clinician ratings of child functioning with child self-esteem and maternal reports of child behavior problems. Older children were rated as lower functioning than younger children by clinicians, but older children reported less anxiety.

To test the hypothesized association between higher levels of social anxiety and other child characteristics and less optimal treatment outcomes, a series of multiple linear regressions was done. Pearson product-moment correlations were determined for all pre-treatment child predictor measures and post-treatment outcome measures (child- and mother-rated MASC, clinician-rated CGAS). For clarity, only significant correlations are shown in Table 1.

Because of the high degree of intercorrelation among predictor variables, significant correlates of outcome were entered in regression analyses as follows: To isolate the contribution of each full-scale predictor variable, a three-step enter/remove procedure was used as described in Crawford & Manassis (2001). First, all significant correlates were entered into a regression equation for the relevant outcome. Second, pre-treatment reports for that outcome were removed from the equation. The resulting equation provided an estimate of the proportion of the variance accounted for by the predictor variables, *without* the influence of pre-treatment ratings. Third, the contribution of each predictor variable (adjusted partial R square) was calculated by removing the variance due to all predictors but the predictor of interest. This procedure avoided obscuring the individual contributions of intercorrelated predictors. A <.05 type I error rate was applied to all regressions. When the number of predictor variables exceeded the number of participants appropriate for sample size (<10 participants per predictor; applied only to CGAS analyses), various sets of predictor variables were entered to determine the equation that accounted for the greatest amount of outcome variance.

Table 1. Significant Correlations Between Post-treatment Outcome Variables and Pre-treatment Predictor Variables (Determination of Regression Variables)

Pre-treatment Predictor Measure		Post-treatment Outcome Measure
	MASC - Child	
1.	CDI	.217**
2.	CCSC-R Avoidant Coping	.315**
3.	LOC	.340**
4.	SPPC	.377**
5.	NASSQ	.433**
6.	SASC-R	.531**
	MASC-Mother	
1.	Child gender	-.214*
2.	SSRS-HOT-Mother	-.219*
3.	SSRS-HOT-Father	-.230*
4.	Child treatment assignment	-.238**
5.	SSRS-PI-Mother	.379*
6.	SASC-R-Mother	.505**
	CGAS-Clinician	
1.	CCSC-R Active Coping	.188*
2.	SSRS-PE-Mother	-.188*
3.	LOC	-.206*
4.	SSRS-HOT-Mother	.222*
5.	Child age	-.250**
6.	SSRS-HOT-Father	.251*
7.	SSRS-PI-Mother	-.260**
8.	Child treatment assignment	.303**

* p <.05 (1-tailed)'; **p<.01 (1-tailed)

MASC = Multidimensional Anxiety Scale for Children; CGAS = Children's Global Assessment scale; *CDI* = Children's Depression Inventory; *NASSQ* = Negative Affect Self-Statements Questionnaire; *LOC* = Locus of Control Scale; *SPPC* = Self Perception Profile for Children; *CCSC-R* = Children's Coping Strategies Checklist (Revised); *SASC-R* = Social Anxiety Scale for Children (Revised); *SSRS* = Social Skills Rating Scale (*HOT*=how often total social skills observed; *PI* = internalizing problems observed; *PE* = externalizing problems observed).

Table 2 shows the results of the regression analyses for each outcome measured, after removing the contribution of pre-treatment reports. For the post-treatment child MASC, the predictors together accounted for 29% of the variance, with child pre-treatment social anxiety, negative self-statements, and self-esteem each making significant contributions. Note that due to intercorrelations among predictor variables and overlapping variance being extracted from various predictors, the sum of the adjusted partial R square values is greater than the R square for the model.

Table 2. Results of Regression of Each Outcome Variable

	t	Adjusted Partial R^2
MASC – Child [a]		
SASC-R-Child	5.37**	.276
NASSQ	3. 82**	.157
SPPC	3.40**	.126
CCSC-R: Avoidant Coping	2.63†	.075
CDI	1.88†	.033
LOC	1.74†	.027
MASC – Mother [b]		
SASC-R-Mother	5.16**	.257
SSRS-PI-Mother	3.92**	.163
SSRS-HOT-Mother	-3.26**	.115
Child gender	-2.77**	.083
Child treatment assignment	-2.41*	.061
CGAS – Clinician [c]		
Child treatment assignment	2.99**	.090
SSRS-PI-Mother	-2.57*	.068
Child age	-2.53*	.066
SSRS-HOT-Mother	2.18*	.050
LOC	-2.00*	.042
CCSC-R-Active Coping	1.88†	.038

*p <.05; **p<.01; †p<.10

Note: MASC = Multidimensional Anxiety Scale for Children; *CGAS* = Children's Global Assessment Scale; *SASC – R* = Social Anxiety Scale for Children (Revised); *CDI* = Children's Depression Inventory; *NASSQ* =Negative Affect Self-Statements Questionnaire; *LOC* = Locus of Control Scale; *SPPC* = Self Perception Profile for Children; *CCSC - R* = Children's Coping Strategies Checklist; SSRS = Social Skills Rating Scale (*HOT* = how often total social skills observed; *PI* = internalizing problems observed).

[a] Total sample (n) = 74; *df*=7, 66; Adjusted R^2 for model = .29;

[b] Total sample (n) = 75; *df*=6, 68; Adjusted R^2 for model =.35;

[c] Total sample (n) = 93; *df*=7, 85; Adjusted R^2 for model = .14.

For the post-treatment MASC as rated by mothers, the predictors together accounted for 35% of the variance, with pre-treatment maternal ratings of social anxiety, maternal ratings of internalizing problems, maternal ratings of social skills, child gender, and treatment condition each making significant contributions. Mothers rated boys and children assigned to group treatment as more anxious post-treatment than girls or children assigned to individual treatment.

For the post-treatment clinician ratings of child functioning on CGAS, the predictors together accounted for 14% of the variance, with maternal reports of children's internalizing behavior problems and social skill use before treatment, child age, child treatment assignment (better functioning after individual treatment), and locus of control making significant contributions.

Additional analyses were done to determine if removing the contribution of any one predictor in addition to removing the pre-treatment value for the dependent measure eliminated the significance of other predictors (ie. if one predictor in each set was most salient). For child self-reported anxiety, pre-treatment self-reported social anxiety was most salient, and for mother-rated anxiety, pre-treatment mother-rated social anxiety was most salient. Children's active coping style was the most salient predictor of clinician-rated treatment outcome.

To test the hypothesis that CBT would affect not only the main outcomes of interest (as reported in Manassis et al., 2002) but also social anxiety and other child characteristics, a multivariate analysis (MANOVA) was done for all child-rated measures. Time was entered as a within-subjects factor and treatment condition as a between subjects factor. Results of evaluation of assumptions of normality, homogeneity of variance and covariance matrices, and multicollinearity were acceptable (Tabachnik & Fidell, 2001).

Table 3. Effects of Treatment on Child-rated Full-scale Variables: MANOVA Pre- and Post—Treatment Means and Standard Deviations

Measure	Pre-treatment		Post-treatment		Univariate F
	M	SD	M	SD	(1,70)
MASC-Child	3.96	.21	3.90	.25	6.08*
SASC-R-Child	6.35	1.23	5.98	1.27	10.42**
CDI	3.88	.17	3.75	.23	27.80**
NASSQ	3.04	.27	2.94	.34	6.99**
LOC	16.57	4.56	14.49	5.24	10.59**
SPCC	4.84	.03	4.83	.02	$3.52^{\dagger}$
CCSC-R-Avoidant	5.05	1.13	4.83	1.26	1.40
CCSC-R-Distracting	3.73	1.32	3.97	1.20	4.14*
CCRC-R-Active	4.33	1.01	4.78	1.13	10.43**
CCSC-R-Support	3.69	.97	3.85	1.04	1.62

*p <.05; **p<.01; †p<.10

Note: MASC = Multidimensional Anxiety Scale for Children; *SASC – R* = Social Anxiety Scale for Children (Revised); *CDI* = Children's Depression Inventory; *NASSQ* =Negative Affect Self-Statements Questionnaire; *LOC* = Locus of Control Scale; *SPPC* = Self Perception Profile for Children; *CCSC - R* = Children's Coping Strategies Checklist; (Revised).

With the use of the Pillai's trace criterion in the MANOVA, the combined variables were significantly affected by time/treatment, F (10, 59) =6.15, p<.001, but not by treatment modality or the time by treatment modality interaction. Therefore, only pre-post treatment differences are addressed further. Univariate F test results (ANOVAs) from the MANOVA are displayed in Table 3. A Bonferroni adjustment was made to maintain the type I error rate at p<.05. Child self-reports of anxiety, social anxiety, depression, negative self-talk, and external locus of control all decreased, and use of distracting and active coping strategies increased.

Possible age and gender effects were also examined by repeating the MANOVA with each as an additional between-subjects factor. No significant main or interaction effects were determined for gender. There was a main effect for age on the children's locus of control ratings, F (4, 64) =2.66, p<.05, indicating that younger children maintained a more external locus of control both before and after treatment relative to older children.

Discussion

As predicted, several aspects of children's internalizing distress were intercorrelated, were predictive of suboptimal CBT response, and improved with CBT. These findings are consistent with the cognitive behavioral model of anxiety, which postulates that influences between cognitive distortions, anxious and sad affect, and maladaptive behavior are bidirectional, allowing a change in one to effect a change in the others even when these are not directly targeted in therapy (Beck & Emery, 1985). Most outcome predictors were informant-specific, consistent with previous work showing that correspondence between informants is only fair for internalizing symptoms (Bernstein et al., 1996).

Also consistent with initial hypotheses, social anxiety was endorsed as an important outcome predictor by both mothers and children. As suggested by previous studies reviewed above, social anxiety may limit CBT participation, interfere with exposure in social contexts, and contribute to negative social interactions that perpetuate anxiety, all potentially limiting gains. Interestingly, clinician ratings did not relate social anxiety to impaired functioning. It may be that socially anxious children achieve functional gains with treatment comparable to other anxious children, but retain a higher level of distress. If ongoing, this distress could contribute to difficulties in the long term for socially anxious youth. For example, the risk of alcohol or cannabis abuse has been linked specifically to social anxiety, versus other anxiety disorders (Buckner et al., 2008).

Alternatively, socially anxious children and their mothers may report more limited gains, regardless of actual improvement, for several reasons. First, CBT interventions target dysfunctional thoughts more than social or interpersonal problems. Persistence of interpersonal problems may be discouraging to socially anxious children, reducing their self-reported treatment gains. Second, children are highly dependent on their social contexts, so may perceive even limited remaining social anxiety as more pervasive or debilitating than other forms of anxiety, also causing them to report limited gains. Lastly, the fact that social anxiety and its precursors (for example, behavioral inhibition) are noticeable at a very early age and throughout development may reduce maternal beliefs in the child's capacity for improvement, causing mothers to report limited gains.

Low self-esteem and low social skills (often related to social anxiety) were also related to adverse outcomes in this study. While both improved with CBT, this finding suggests that additional interventions to enhance self-esteem and social skills may be helpful either before or during cognitive-behavioral intervention. This may be particularly relevant in social phobia, where social skills training is sometimes a prerequisite for successful exposure to social situations (Eisen & Kearney, 1995). Similarly, focusing on positive relationships and aptitudes that children have independent of their anxiety may be helpful in bolstering self-esteem, and thus enhance response to CBT. Self-efficacy, a construct closely linked to self-esteem, has previously been found to relate (inversely) to anxiety symptom levels (Muris, 2002).

Clinicians' perception that functioning improved most in children with an internal locus of control and high use of active coping skills is interesting, in light of the external locus of control reported by younger children. It may be that, from an adult point of view, the high degree of self-direction implied by these characteristics is considered adaptive resulting in high ratings of functioning. For a young child, who has limited control over his or her circumstances, however, reliance on others (for example, coping by seeking adult support) may be equally adaptive. It is also possible, however, that those children who develop an internal locus of control and active coping style early are more active therapy participants, and therefore show genuinely greater improvements in functioning.

Our results also replicate Treadwell and Kendall's (1996) finding that negative self-statements are predictive of reduced CBT response in this population, at least by self-report. Such self-statements may impact therapeutic optimism and engagement in therapy, potentially affecting outcome, although they also appear to improve with CBT. It is also possible, of course, that high initial negative self-statements reflect a generally negative reporting bias in the child that continues to some extent, and this bias may exert a negative influence on all of the child's post-treatment reports.

Age and gender influences, while modest, deserve some comment. The parental perception that boys improved less with CBT than girls may have been accurate and related to biological, cognitive, or environmental factors that limited treatment-related gains in boys. Alternatively, these perceptions may have been influenced by parental gender or parent-child communication. In other words, mothers may have more difficulty seeing improvements in their sons than in their daughters, or boys may be more reticent about communicating positive changes to their mothers than are girls. Similarly, the clinicians' perception that older children improved less than younger children may be accurate (perhaps reflecting less entrenched symptom patterns in younger children), or may be reflective of decreased therapeutic optimism as patients approach adolescence.

Limitations

The present study is limited by sample size constraints, implementation in a hospital setting, lack of an untreated control group, and limited cultural and economic diversity of the sample. These factors may limit the generalizability of the findings and suggest that replication is warranted. Further, although the inclusion of multiple informants was advantageous, several constructs were only rated by one informant, making it challenging to integrate some findings. Future research should utilize multiple informants for all constructs where this is possible, and better address methods of interpreting or combining information from different raters.

Clinical and Research Implications

Future studies should consider the inclusion of qualitative data to provide a richer understanding of the inter-related constructs examined in this study, and possibly reduce social desirability biases that are sometimes present to a greater degree with quantitative measures. Observational measures, particularly of social skills, would help reduce reporter biases and address the situational specificity of social behavior (Gresham & Elliott, 1990). These measures would also help elucidate the nature of the relationship between social anxiety, social competence, and CBT response. Longitudinal studies are also indicated to better understand the direction of various effects (for example, whether social anxiety resutls from poor social competence or more often contributes to it by promoting social avoidance), as are studies of mediator effects to better understand what aspects of child CBT are crucial to therapeutic change (Prins & Ollendick, 2003).

Child characteristics predictive of poorer outcomes, especially social anxiety, may merit greater attention in implementing CBT with anxious children, either prior to or during therapy. Highly socially anxious children may benefit from pre-treatment social skills training, or pre-treatment sessions to accustom them to the treatment situation and reduce fears of negative evaluation there (Eisen & Kearney, 1995). The possibility of bullying or other negative peer interactions that could perpetuate social anxiety should be explored, as the child may not volunteer this information. Similarly, children with low self-esteem may benefit from restructuring their erroneous cognitions regarding low self-efficacy, to improve motivation and effort in CBT. Finally, treatment adaptations for anxious children that may have been screened out of the present sample (for example, children with significant cognitive limitations) require further development and study.

References

Achenbach, T., & Edelbrock, C. (1983). *Manual for the child behavior checklist and revised child behavior profile.* Burlington, VT: University of Vermont.

Akiskal, H. S. (1985). Anxiety: Definition, relationship to depression, and proposal for an integrative model. In A. H. Tuma & J. D. Maser (Eds.), *Anxiety and the anxiety disorders* (pp. 787-797). Hillsdale, NJ: Erlbaum.

American Psychiatric Association. (1994). *Diagnostic and statistical manual of mental disorders* (4th ed.). Washington, DV: Author.

Barrett, P. M. (1998). Evaluation of cognitive-behavioral group treatments for childhood anxiety disorders. *Journal of Clinical Child Psychology, 27(4),* 459-468.

Beck, A. T., & Emery, G. (1985). *Anxiety disorders and phobias: A cognitive perspective.* New York: Basic Books.

Bell-Dolan, D., & Wessler, A. E. (1994). Attributional style of anxious children: Extensions from cognitive theory and research on adult anxiety. *Journal of Anxiety Disorders, 8(1),* 79-96.

Bernstein, G. A. (1991). Comorbidity and severity of anxiety and depressive disorders in a clinic sample. *Journal of the American Academy of Child and Adolescent Psychiatry, 30(1),* 43-50.

Bernstein, G. A., & Borchardt, C. M. (1991). Anxiety disorders of childhood and adolescence: A critical review. *Journal of the American Academy of Child and Adolescent Psychiatry, 30(4),* 519-532.

Bernstein, G. A., Borchardt, C. M., & Perwien, A. R. (1996). Anxiety disorders in children and adolescents: A review of the past 10 years. *Journal of the American Academy of Child and Adolescent Psychiatry, 35(9),* 1110-1119.

Bouchard S., Mendlowitz S.L., Coles M.E., & Franklin M. (2004). Considerations in the use of exposure with children. *Cog Beh Practice, 11*, 56-65.

Brady, E. U., & Kendall, P.C. (1992). Comorbidity of anxiety and depression in children and adolescents. *Psychological Bulletin, 111(2),* 244-255.

Buckner J.D., Schmidt N.B., Lang A.R., Small J.W., Schlauch R.C., & Lewinsohn P.M. (2008). Specificity of social anxiety disorder as a risk factor for alcohol and cannabis dependence. *J Psychiatr Res, 42*, 230-239.

Chansky, T. E., & Kendall, P. C. (1997). Social expectancies and self-perceptions in anxiety-disordered children. *Journal of Anxiety Disorders, 11,* 347-363.

Chu B.C., & Kendall P.C. (2004). Positive association of child involvement and treatment outcome within a manual-based cognitive-behavioral treatment for children with anxiety. *J Consult Clin Psychol, 72*, 821-829.

Crawford, A. M., & Manassis, K. (2001). Familial predictors of treatment outcome in childhood anxiety disorders. *Journal of the American Academy of Child and Adolescent Psychiatry, 40(10),* 1182-1189.

Eisen, A. R., & Kearney, C. A. (1995). *Practitioner's guide to treating fear and anxiety in children and adolescents: A cognitive-behavioral approach.* Northvale, NJ: Jason Aronson.

Garcia-Lopez L.J., Olivares J., Beidel D., Albano A.M., Turner S., & Rosa A.I. (2006). Efficacy of three treatment protocols for adolescents with social anxiety disorder: A 5-year follow-up assessment. *J Anxiety Disord, 20,* 175-191.

Ginsburg, G. S., La Greca, A. M., & Silverman, W. K. (1998). Social anxiety in children with anxiety disorders: Relation with social and emotional functioning. *Journal of Abnormal Child Psychology, 26(3),* 175-185.

Gresham, F. M., & Elliott, S. N. (1990). *Social Skills Rating System Manual.* Circle Pines, MN: American Guidance Service.

Harter, S. (1985). *Manual for the self-perception profile for children.* Denver, CO: University of Denver.

Hayward C., Varady S., Albano A.M., Thienemann M., Henderson L., & Schatzberg A.F. (2000). Cognitive-behavioral group therapy for social phobia in female adolescents: Results of a pilot study. *J Am Acad Child Adolesc Psychiatry, 39,* 721-726.

James, A., Soler, A., & Weatherall, R. (2005). Cognitive behavioural therapy for anxiety disorders in children and adolescents. *Cochrane Database Syst Rev, (4),* CD004690.

Kagan, J., Reznick, J. S., & Snidman, N. (1987). The physiology and psychology of behavioral inhibition in children. *Child Development, 58,* 1459-1473.

Keller, M., Lavori, P., Wunder, J., Beardslee, W., Schwartz, C., & Roth, J. (1992). Chronic course of anxiety disorders in children and adolescents. *Journal of the American Academy of Child and Adolescent Psychiatry, 31,* 595-599.

Kendall, P. C. (1990). *The Coping Cat Workbook.* Merion Station, PA: Temple University.

Kendall, P. C. (1994). Treating anxiety disorders in children: Results of a randomized clinical trial. *Journal of Clinical Child Psychology, 63,* 100-110.

Kendall, P. C., & Flannery-Schroeder, E. (1998). Methodological issues in treatment research for anxiety disorders in youth. Journal *of Abnormal Child Psychology, 26(1),* 27-38. K1 30.

Kendall, P. C., Flannery-Schroeder, E., Panichelli-Mindel, S. M., Southam-Gerow, M., Henin, A., & Warman, M. (1997). Therapy for youths with anxiety disorders: A second randomized clinical trial. *Journal of Consulting and Clinical Psychology, 65,* 366-380.

Kindt, M., Brosschot, J. F., & Everaerd, W. (1997). Cognitive processing bias of children in a real life stress situation and a neutral situation. *Journal of Experimental Child Psychology, 64,* 79-97.

Kovacs, M. (1982). *The Children's Depression Inventory: A self-rated depression scale for school-aged youngsters.* Unpublished manuscript, University of Pittsburgh, Pittsburgh, PA.

Kovacs, M. (1992). *Manual of the Children's Depression Inventory.* Toronto: Multi-health Systems.

Kovacs, M., Gatsonis, C., Paulauskas, S. L., & Richards, C. (1989). Depressive disorders in childhood: IV. A longitudinal study of comorbidity with and risk for anxiety disorders. *Archives of General Psychiatry, 46,* 776-782.

La Greca, A. M., & Stone, W. (1993). Social anxiety scale for children – Revised: Factor structure and concurrent validity. *Journal of Clinical Child Psychology, 22,* 17-27.

Last, C. (1988). Anxiety disorders in childhood and adolescence. In C. Last & M. Hersen (Eds.) *Handbook of anxiety disorders* (pp. 531-540). New York: Plenum.

Last, C. G., Hansen, C., & Franco, N. (1997). Anxious children in adulthood: a prospective study of adjustment. *Journal of the American Academy of Child and Adolescent Psychiatry, 36(5*), 645-652.

Manassis, K. (1996). *Keys to parenting your anxious child.* New York: Barrons Educational Series.

Manassis, K., Mendlowitz, S., Scapillato, D., Avery, D., Fiksenbaum, L., Freire, M., Monga, S., & Owens, M. (2002). Group and individual cognitive-behavioral therapy for childhood anxiety disorders: A randomized trial. *Journal of the American Academy of Child and Adolescent Psychiatry, 41(12),* 1423-1430.

Manassis, K., Tannock, R., & Masellis, M. (1996). Cognitive differences between anxious, normal, and ADHD children on a dichotic listening task. *Anxiety, 2,* 279-285.

March, J. S. (1997). *Manual for the multidimensional anxiety scale for children.* Toronto: Multi-Health Systems.

Mendlowitz, S. L., Manassis, K., Bradley, S., Scapillato, D., Miezitis, S., & Shaw, B. F. (1999). Cognitive-behavioral group treatments in childhood anxiety disorders: The role of parental involvement. *Journal of the American Academy of Child and Adolescent Psychiatry, 38,* 1223-1229.

Mesman J., & Koot H.M. (2000). Child-reported depression and anxiety in preadolescence: I. Associations with parent- and teacher-reported problems. *J Am Acad Child Adolesc Psychiatry, 39,* 1371-1378.

Messer, S. C., & Beidel, D. C. (1994). Psychosocial correlates of childhood anxiety disorders. *Journal of the American Academy of Child and Adolescent Psychiatry, 33(7),* 975-983.

Muris, P. (2002). Relationships between self-efficacy and symptoms of anxiety disorders and depression in a normal adolescent sample. *Personality and Individual Differences, 32,* 337-348.

Nowicki, S., & Strickland, B. R. (1973). A locus of control scale for children. *Journal of Consulting and Clinical Psychology, 40,* 148-154.

Prins, P.J., & Ollendick, T.H. (2003). Cognitive change and enhanced coping: missing mediational links in cognitive behavior therapy with anxiety-disordered children. *Clin Child Fam Psychol Rev, 6,* 87-105.

Reich, W. & Welner, Z. (1988). *Diagnostic Interview for Children and Adolescents-Parent version, revised.* St. Louis, MO: Washington University.

Reich, W., Welner, Z., Herjanic, B. (1997), *Computerized Diagnostic Interview for Children and Adolescents-IV (Windows Version).* Toronto: Multi-Health Systems.

Ronan, L., Kendall, P. C., & Rowe, C. (1994). Negative affectivity in children: Development and validation of a self-statement questionnaire. *Cognitive Therapy and Research, 18(6),* 509-528.

Sandler, L., & Ayers, T. (1990). *The children's coping strategies checklist.* Symposium presented at the meeting of the American Psychological Association, Boston, MA.

Shaffer, D., Gould, M. A. Brasic, J., Ambrosini, P., Fisher, P., Bird, H., & Aluwahlia, S. (1983). A children's global assessment scale (CGAS). *Archives of General Psychiatry, 40,* 1228-1231.

Stark, K. D., Humphrey, L. L., Crook, K., & Lewis, K. (1990). Perceived family environments of depressed and anxious children: Child's and maternal figure's perspectives. *Journal of Abnormal Child Psychology, 18(5),* 527-547.

Strauss, C. C., Lease, C. A., Last, C.G., & Francis, G. (1998). Overanxious disorder: An examination of developmental differences. *Journal of Abnormal Child Psychology, 16(4),* 433-443.

Tabachnik, B. G., & Fidell, L. S. (2001). *Using multivariate statistics* (4th ed). Boston, MA: Allyn & Bacon.

Treadwell, K. R. H., & Kendall, P. C. (1996). Self-talk in youth with anxiety disorders: States of mind, content specificity, and treatment outcome. *Journal of Consulting and Clinical Psychology, 64(5),* 941-950.

Victor, A. M., Bernat, D. H., Bernstein, G. A., & Layne, A. E. (2007). Effects of parent and family characteristics on treatment outcome of anxious children. *Journal of Anxiety Disorders, 21,* 835-848.

Watson, D., & Clark, L. A. (1984). Negative affectivity: The disposition to experience aversive emotional states. *Psychological Bulletin, 96,* 465-490.

Wechsler, D. (1991). *Wechsler Intelligence Scale for Children – Third Edition (WISC-III).* San Antonio, TX: Psychological Corporation.

In: Social Phobia: Etiology, Diagnosis and Treatment
Editor: Clayton P. Axelby
ISBN 978-1-60692-159-3
© 2009 Nova Science Publishers, Inc.

Chapter VII

SOCIAL PHOBIA IN CHILDREN AND ADOLESCENTS

Xenia Anastassiou-Hadjicharalambous
Department of Psychology, University of Nicosia, 1700 Nicosia, Cyprus.

ABSTRACT

The purpose of this chapter is to review the current state of literature on *social phobia* in children and adolescents as well as identify areas for future research on this understudied disorder. The chapter begins with a brief overview of the clinical characteristics of the disorder. The next section covers the up to date empirical literature on the epidemiology and comorbidity followed by risk factors and correlates of *social phobia* in children and adolescents. The developmental course of the disorder is described next. The final section reports on the evidence-based status of the treatment approaches for social phobia in the child and the youth.

INTRODUCTION

"Manos is a quiet 14 year old boy. He is socially withdrawn from his peers and described as worrisome and interpersonally awkward by his teachers. His classmates often laugh at him about how odd it is that he can blush for no apparent reason. Jokes about how shy Manos is always get a few laughs. For everyone except Manos. Some people think that Manos chose to be socially isolated and he is happy in his own world. Manos is not happy in his own world. But, why doesn't he join in and contribute to the world around him? The reason is that social interaction makes Manos intensely anxious. So anxious that he can't think straight. Often he can't even talk properly because his heart is pounding so hard he can't hear his own voice. Manos will most likely live his life avoiding the situations that will provoke his anxiety and thus he will be able to conceal

his suffering from the individuals around him. Few people will realize that he is suffering; most will just think that he is awkward. Underneath the facade, however, Manos will be locked in his fears distressed and angry for not being able to join in and enjoy social life."

A basic expectation that parents have from their children as they grow up is to enjoy social interaction and gradually as they become older to initiate and maintain healthy social relationships which will be valuable for their healthy socioemotional development. While for most children social experiences are enjoyable, for children like *Manos* social interaction is particularly troublesome, worrying and often extremely painful. These children historically have been described in various ways, in our days are thought to be suffering from *social phobia*.

Social phobia is considered to be a serious mental health problem characterised by marked and persistent fear of acting in an embarrassing or humiliating way in social or performance situations (APA, 2000). *Social phobia* first appeared as a psychiatric disorder in the 4th edition of the *Diagnostic and Statistical Manual of Mental Disorders* (*DSM-IV*, American Psychiatric Association, 1994). Prior to the 4th edition of the *DSM* fears leading to avoidance of social situations were diagnosed in two categories based on age: *Social phobia* for adults and *avoidant disorder* for children. The *DSM-IV* combined the two differential diagnoses for children and adults into one, but yet acknowledged age related features associated with the disorder. Consequently, children, previously diagnosed with *avoidant disorder*, are now considered for a diagnosis of *social phobia*.

Although once an ignored disorder, *social phobia* in the child and the youth has in the past two and a half decades received increased attention by investigators (Albano, 1995; Albano, Chorpita & Barlow, 1996; Francis, Last, & Strauss, 1992; Last, Perrin, Hersen, & Kazdin, 1992; Strauss & Last, 1993). This increased research activity that childhood *social phobia* received likely resulted from two factors. First, the *DSM-III* (1980) and *DSM III-R* (1987) provided a separate category for "*anxiety disorders of childhood*". Specific categories were provided for *separation anxiety disorder*, *avoidant disorder* and *overanxious disorder*. This classification highlighted the fact that child and adolescent anxiety disorders are important in their own right. Following this categorization, the *DSM-IV* went further to provide even more refined criteria for *social phobia* in the child and the adolescent. These refinements provided researchers with a way of operationalising the diagnosis of childhood *social phobia* and thereby facilitated research efforts.

Clinical Features

Children and adolescents with *social phobia* display phobic responses to social activities such as speaking, reading, writing or performing in public, speaking to adult authority figures, initiating or maintaining conversations (Beidel, Turner & Morris, 1999) or even performing every day activities such as eating, or drinking in front of others (Albano, Chorpita, & Barlow, 2003).

The *DSM* criteria (APA, 2000) acknowledge that *social phobia* may be expressed differently by children relative to adults. *In young children*, the anxiety may be expressed by crying, tantrums, or becoming clinging to familiar others mainly the parents. If *social phobia* is severe the child may become mute. Although *selective mutism* is a separate *DSM* disorder some evidence suggests that it can be conceptualised as an extreme form of social phobia (Standart & Le Couteur, 2003). *In older children,* social phobia may be expressed relatively less vividly in trembling hands, a shaky voice or other obvious signs of anxiety.

A notable differentiate feature of *social phobia* in children relative to adults is that while in adults there is some kind of recognition that the fear is unrealistic, in children and especially the younger ones this feature may not be present (APA, 2000).

A critical feature that distinguishes *social phobia* from other differential diagnoses is that in children with *social phobia* there must be some evidence that they can display age appropriate social relationships with familiar people and also to experience the symptoms of *social phobia* when they are with their peers as well and not just when they are with unfamiliar adults (APA, 2000).

A diagnosis of *social phobia* mandates the presence of somatic manifestations of anxiety such as muscle tension, heart palpitations, tremors, chills, sweating, and gastrointestinal discomfort (APA, 2000, Beidel & Morris, 1995, Essau, Conradt & Petermann, 1999). The degree of distress and confusion which occurs in such situations can reach the level of a panic attack.

Children with *social phobia* not only become anxious when they are actually confronted with socially phobic situations. They are typically characterised by *anticipatory anxiety* often before actually confronting the phobic situation. This *anticipatory anxiety* can hinder the child's ability to function in a wide range of areas including the development of age-appropriate social activities.

Attempts to avoid the phobic social situations are common. Forcing the child or the youngster with *social phobia* to engage in social interactions can only lead to negative outcome. Younger children may respond to this pressure with increased anxiety and further withdrawal. While older children and adolescents may become embarrassed silent and may become oppositional since the experience in which they are forced in will be disturbing (Kroneberger & Meyer, 2001)

In addition to these critical features for a diagnosis of *social phobia* to be made it is necessary that the level of distress produced by the symptoms of *social phobia* interferes with the child' functioning in academic domain and social relationships. Symptoms must persist for at least 6 months (APA, 2000).

Associated Features

Children with social phobia have been reported to present a series of associated features such as, having inadequate social skills, having low levels of self-esteem being overly sensitive to criticism and perfectionistic (Bernstein, 1990). They often appear, to have lack of assertiveness, to be submissive in relations, to be lacking in self-confidence and be withdrawn (Last, 1989; Walters & Inderbitzen, 1998). Moreover, they are often viewed by their peers as targets of ridicule, isolation, and aggression (Davidson, Hughes, George, & Blazer, 1993; Walters & Inderbitzen, 1998).

As mentioned above, a higher level of anxiety as well as fearfulness is a well established associated feature of social phobia. Importantly, higher levels of fearfulness an anxiety in children with *social phobia* were reported not only in comparison to general population, but also in comparison to children with other anxiety disorders (Last, Francis & Strauss, 1989; Strauss & Last, 1993).

Not surprisingly, academic underachievement is often reported as an associated feature of social phobia. It is believe that the social avoidance of children with social phobias often results into impairment of their academic functioning. Their school performance is impaired maybe due to problems such as test anxiety, failure to participate in classroom activities as well as failure to join academic groups. For instance it has been reported that over time children with *social phobia* gradually experience diminished educational accomplishments (Velting & Albano, 2001). Frequently these social fears are assumed to result in school refusal (Last & Strauss, 1990) which may need to be treated itself.

The inability of children and adolescents with social phobia to entail in successful social interactions, intertwined with their deficits in social skills as well as their social avoidance often prevents them from dating, making friends, participating in sports, and joining social groups. In effect, adolescents with *social phobia* meet age-specific developmental challenges such as employment and dating later than their peers (Albano et al., 1996).

Social phobia has further been linked with increased levels of substance abuse. For instance, Sonntag and colleagues (2000) reported prevalence of smoking in 31.5% of the adolescents with *social phobia*, in 26.1% of the adolescents with one social fear but no diagnosis of *social phobia* and in 15.4% of adolescents with neither social phobia nor social fear. Nelson and colleagues (2000) also reported that *social phobia* and depression in youths was associated with elevated risk for *alcohol use* disorder. Importantly, it has been reported that *social phobia* typically precedes *substance use* disorder. For instance, Wittchen and colleagues (1999) reported that in their sample of youth aged 14-24 years, *social phobia* preceded *substance use* disorder 85.2% of the time. Although the mechanism that links *social phobia* to *substance abuse* is yet to be determined it has been argued that often adolescents self-medicate their symptoms of anxiety, with some of them reaching drug abuse and dependence (Albano & Detweiler, 2001).

Apart from *substance abuse*, several empirical reports (e.g. Davidson et al., 1993; Nelson, Grant, Bucholz, Glowinski, Madden, Reich& Heath, 2000) showed *social phobia* to be associated with elevated risk for suicidal ideation, suicide plan, and suicide attempt. The link of *social phobia* with suicidal behaviour however is not well established since there have been studies reporting no evidence of link between *social phobia* and elevated risk for suicide (Strauss, Birmaher, Bridge, Axelson, Chiappetta, Brent, & Ryan, 2000; Pawlak, Pascual-Sanchez, Rae, Fischer, & Ladame, 1999). Despite these contradictory findings, in clinical practice it is vital to consider possible suicidal ideation in adolescents with anxiety disorders including *social phobia* (e.g. Albano, et al., 2003). Good clinical practice needs to take into consideration that some adolescents under the enormous social and evaluative stress may consider suicide.

Despite the cumulative evidence on associated features of social phobia in the child and the youth most empirical data are cross-sectional. Therefore issues of causality are not elucidated. The development of associated features needs to be studies from the very initial stages of the child's development and require explicit longitudinal validation.

Epidemiology

The prevalence of childhood *social phobia* is still unclear. Epidemiological studies reveal a wide range of prevalence varying from 2 to 7% with most studies reporting figures to be at around 1 - 4% (e.g. Anderson, Williams, McGee & Silva, 1987; Beidel & Morris, 1995; Benjamin, Costello,& Warren, 1990; Fergusson, Horwood & Lynskey, 1993; Essau et al., 1999; Essau, Conradt, & Petermann, 2000).

In this variance on prevalence estimates factors such as age, gender, race, ethnicity, assessment instruments, methods of combination of data between parent reports and child reports as well as the employed diagnostic criteria and time seem to be implicated. With respect to age several investigations for instance report *social phobia* to be diagnosed during adoesecence rather than earlier (e.g. Essau et al 1999; Velting & Albano 2001). This finding however does not necessarily mean that prevalence is higher in adolescence. It might be that many children with *social phobia* are not referred until the disorder shows more adult-like features, or deteriorates.

As far as gender is concerned several investigations report equal prevalence in males and females; while some evidence suggests that it is more prevalent in girls relative to boys (e.g. Essau et al 1999; MCGee, & Stanton, 1990). These findings however is uncertain whether they reveal higher prevalence in girls or simply that boys are less likely to report their social anxiety due to socialization practices, or that boys are less likely to be referred for treatment when they present features of *social phobia*.

With respect to race several investigations report *social phobia* to have higher prevalence in Caucasians (e.g. Beidel et al., 1999; Straus, & Last, 1993) while other studies report higher rates in African-Americans relative to Caucasians (Compton, Nelson & March, 2000). Still a third line of evidence suggests a lack of racial differences (Ferrell, Beidel, & Turner, 2004). However, these findings may simply reflect clinic-referred adolescents and not those who are community based. Indeed, Compton and colleagues (2000) reported that *community-based* Caucasian children were more likely to endorse symptoms of *social phobia* and not social anxiety, whereas African-American children were more likely to endorse symptoms of *social anxiety* and not *social phobia*.

As far as diagnostic criteria and time is concerned it seems that prevalence rates increase with time as well as with the refinements in the diagnostic criteria. For instance, it has been reported that diagnosis of *social phobia* based on parents reports increased when switching from *DSM-III-R* (18% of the sample) to *DSM-IV* (40% of the sample) criteria (Kendall & Warman, 1996). It seems that across time prevalence rates will increase as our knowledge about childhood *social phobia* increases as well as diagnostic criteria become more sensitive to the children's unique characteristics.

While relatively uncommon in the *general population*, social phobia is one of the more common principal diagnoses in children who present for treatment at specialized clinics (Albano, 1996; Chapman, Mannuza, & Fyer, 1995; Last et al., 1992; Vasey, 1995). For instance it has been reported that among children referred to an anxiety disorders clinic, almost 20% met DSM criteria for a diagnosis of *social phobia* (Last et al., 1992). Thus, *social phobia* does not seem to be infrequent among children referred for anxiety related problems.

Further, it is believed that *social phobia* may be underreported and undertreated in children since, like many of the internalising disorders, the symptoms may not be easily recognized as evidence of a psychological disorder (Albano, DiBartolo, Heimberg & Barlow, 1995).

A notable point in relation to prevalence rates and future direction of research is that the data primarily derive from Caucasian and African-American children. Further investigations are needed to look into prevalence rates across other cultures and factors implicated in the possible variance in prevalence rates across these cultures. Beyond culture effect, developmental epidemiological studies are needed to determine prevalence patterns, as well as factors implicated in prevalence across developmental stages.

Comorbidity

Social Phobia rarely occurs alone and most frequently it is comorbit to another anxiety disorder (*APA*, 1994, Chavira & Stein, 2005). Last and colleagues (1992) reported that almost 87% of children with *social phobia* had at some time met criteria for an additional anxiety disorder. The anxiety disorders found most often were *overanxious disorder* (48% of the cases), *simple phobia* (41%) and *separation anxiety disorder* (26%). In a further clinical sample of children and adolescents, 27,3 % of those diagnosed with *generalized anxiety disorder* and 4,5% of those diagnosed with *separation anxiety disorder* also received a *social phobia* diagnosis (see Bernstein & Borchardt, 1991).

Although a further anxiety disorder is the most common comorbid diagnosis (Verdouin & Kendal, 2003), concurrence has further been reported with somatoform disorders (41.2%), substance use disorder (23.5%), agoraphobia (23.5%) and obsessive-compulsive disorder (15.3%) (Essau et al., 1999, Essau et al., 2000).

Overlap with depressive disorders is also not uncommon. For instance approximately 56% of the children diagnosed with *social phobia* at some time were reported to meet criteria for *depressive disorder* (Last et al., 1992).Beidel and colleagues (1999) postulated that childhood *social phobia* often precedes dysphoric mood. This contention is supported by empirical findings which suggest that (a) anxiety disorder symptomatology usually precedes diagnosis of depression (Brady & Kendall, 1992; Kovacs, Gatsonis, Paulauskas, & Richards, 1989), (b) children with *social phobia* are typically reported to be younger than adolescents with dysphoria (Epkins, 1996), and (c) *social phobia* precedes depression 81.6-100.0% of the time in adolescents and young adults with *social phobia* (Essau et al., 2000; Wittchen, Stein, & Kessler, 1999).

Comorbitity of *social phobia* with disruptive disorders is not high, but it is not uncommon. For instance approximately 8% of the children diagnosed with *social phobia* were reported to show evidence of some sort of *disruptive behavior disorder* (Last et al., 1992). Several case reports showed evidence of masking of *social phobia* by a *disruptive disorder* (e.g. Friman, 1996). This line of findings is particularly important for their significant clinical implications. Importantly when *social phobia* symptoms were addressed disruptive behaviours decreased to near-zero rates (Friman, 1996).

Etiology

At present little is known about the specific etiology of *social phobia*. Nonetheless, while we know relatively little regarding the specific factors that result in *social phobias*, it seems likely that many of the factors assumed to contribute to other anxiety disordered may be implicated.

Several investigations stressed out the importance of biological predisposition, but data are preliminary. Empirical studies reported that mothers of children with anxiety disorders such as *social phobia* meet criteria for anxiety disorders at higher degree relative to the general population (e.g. Bernstein & Borchardt, 1991). For instance it has been reported that *anxiety disorder* in both parents is related to diagnosis of *social phobia* in 36% of their offsprings, compared to 12.5% if one parent has *anxiety disorder* and 0% if none of the parents has an *anxiety disorder* (Merikangas, Avenevoli & Dierker, 1999). These data however are preliminary and it is yet unclear the extent to which they reflect genetic or environmental conditions, since disintegrating genetic predispositions and environmental influences is extremely difficult.

Some studies have suggested the possible role of temperament variables such as *behavioral inhibition* (reflected in increased arousal and negative responses to new and novel situations) as a contributor to this disorder (Husain & Cantwell, 1991). This increased arousal in response to novel situations places the child at risk to avoid early social encounters and failure to establish health social relationships. Out of these difficulties anxiety develops and increases following ineffective attempts of the child to successfully engage in social situations. The child in his attempt to reduce his anxiety, withdraws. This withdrawal acts as a reinforcer for the reduction of his anxiety with effect the child to enter a vicious cycle of withdrawal and progressively become more and more socially isolated.

At a cognitive level the child gradually develops negative expectations from social encounters and selective attention to one's behaviour during these social encounters (Albano et al., 1995).

Parents often behaviourally reinforce the child' s predisposition by unintentionally reinforcing social phobic responses of the child by providing a secondary gain to the child's phobic response (Kroneberger & Meyer, 2001).

Several environmental conditions, such as isolated families, chronic medical conditions, loss of significant other, often moves of the family, insecure attachments, strong differences from the majority culture could contribute in escalation of the unsuccessful social experiences of the inhibited child.

Nonetheless, despite the findings with respect to aetiology of *social phobia* at present the interaction of the various factors is not well understood and appears to be multifaceted (Rabian & Silverman, 1995). Future investigations need to address closely the interplay of genetic and environmental factors implicated in the development of *social phobia* and the plausible different interplay of these factors in the genesis and the development of *social phobia*.

Developmental Course

Most empirical evidence suggests that although *social phobia* can occur during early childhood it typically emerges in early adolescence (11.3 years) (e.g. Davidson et al., 1993; Last et al., 1992; Vasey, 1995). The finding that *social phobia* is more common in adolescence may reflect the developmental age-related social fears in nonclinical child and adolescent populations. It is in adolescence that anxieties about school and social activities increase (King, 1995; Strauss, & Last, 1993).

Social phobia sometimes appears to be an outgrowth of a history of social inhibition or shyness. It has been reported that increased anxious/withdrawn behaviour at age 8 was predictive of increased *social phobia* in young adulthood and adolescents (Goodwin, Fergusson, & Horwood, 2004)

Velting and Albano (2001) postulated that *social phobia* can be viewed within the context of development of normative factors. For instance, infants as young as 6-months of age display separation anxiety and stranger anxiety. However, the self-conscious emotions which are closely linked to *social phobia* do not developed until later. It has been argued that the ability to see oneself as a social object and feel embarrassment emerges at the age of around 4 -5 years. The capacity to successfully adopt the perspective of the others and be concerned about others' possible negative evaluation does not emerge until the age of 8. By late childhood early adolescence the youngster is considered to have developed the cognitive "*prerequisites*" for *social phobia* (i.e. self-consciousness, self-awareness perspective-taking). The combination of the cognitive readiness along with increased social demands such as the increased requirements from the social environment to perform tasks that have social-evaluative component (e.g. speak in class, engage in group activities, perform in sports or music, responsibility for initiating and arranging social activities placed on behalf of the parents etc) results in the development of social fears.

Since adolescence is a period which is characterised by a substantial degree of social anxieties an important issue that needs to be taken into consideration is to determine when the adolescent displays clinical features of *social phobia*. For instance in a community sample of adolescents aged 12 to 17 it has been reported that approximately 51% reported at least one social fear (Essau et al., 1999). Among these youngsters, however only a small percentage would be expected to meet criteria or develop the disorder later. Consequently when determining between normal and psychopathological *social phobias* is important to remember features that differentiate between the presence of *social fears* and the clinical diagnosis of *social phobia* which predetermines significant distortion in the individual's functioning.

The clinical course of *social phobia* varies significantly based on the possible stress in the environment (APA, 1994), on the presence of possible positive social experiences as well as on temperamental characteristics. Although there is still very little research on the presence of resilience factors, for some youngsters with *social phobia* symptoms show spontaneous remission. For instance it has been reported that a positive social experience with peers can potentially result into spontaneous remission (Husain & Cantwell, 1991). Further research however is needed to examine the plausible interactive factors implicated in spontaneous remission.

Although for some youngsters symptoms will show spontaneous remission, for most youngsters symptoms persist into adulthood. Research indicates that children with *social phobia* are at a high risk for developing major depression (Last et. al, 1992) and substance abuse disorders (Kessler, Foster, Saunders, & Stang, 1995). As such, *social phobia* tends to have a chronic course and individuals rarely recover (Davidson et al., 1993).

Consequently the disorder often continues into and throughout adulthood with the expression of symptoms often fluctuating with the levels of stress experienced by the individual. (Davidson et al., 1993; Last et al., 1992; Vasey, 1995. Entering into adulthood *social phobia* is associated with increased suicide attempts, poor medical health, lack of social support, poor occupational performance, and antisocial behavior in general (Davidson et al., 1993; Rapee, 1995). Thus, when left untreated the potential consequences of *social phobia* are broad, impacting the emotional, occupational, and social functioning of the individual in the long-term.

Treatment

For the treatment of *social phobia* in the child and the youth several psychosocial approaches have been found useful. These approaches include primarily cognitive-behavioural methods such as cognitive restructuring (to modify maladaptive self-statements and appraisals that can contribute to anxiety/avoidance), desensitisation (to decrease anxiety responses in specific social situations), as well as modeling and operant approaches for teaching social skills and increasing social interactive behaviors.

The empirical literature reporting on the efficacy of psychosocial treatment approaches for childhood *social phobia* has expanded markedly in the past decade (Cartwright-Hatton, Roberts, Chitsabesan, Fothergill, & Harrington, 2004) and includes several reports of the long-term maintenance of treatment gains (Beidel, Turner, Young, & Paulson, 2005; Kendall, Safford, Flannery-Schroeder, & Webb, 2004). Reviews on the treatment outcome literature (see Silverman, Pina & Viswesvaran, 2008) have documented that when *social phobia* is the primary diagnosis, no treatment meets criteria of a *well-established* treatment based on the criteria established by Chambless and Hollon, (1998). Nonetheless, Group Cognitive Behavior Therapy (GCBT), Individual Cognitive Behavior Therapy (ICBT), GCBT with Parents and Social Effectiveness Training for children (SET-C) each were reported to meet criteria for *probably efficacious* (see Silverman et al., 2008). School-based GCBT and school-based modified SET-C for *social phobia* were classified as experimental treatments (Silverman et al., 2008).

The CBT which met criteria for *probably efficacious* treatment incorporates key elements of cognitive behaviour therapy (i.e. cognitive challenging and graded exposures, relaxation) but weight is placed on social skills training, including handling of difficult social situations. The SET-C, (Beidel, Turner & Morris, 2000) which also met criteria for *probably efficacious* treatment targets the child's fears and incorporates child and parent education, social skills training, *in vivo* exposures and peer generalisation. Importantly follow up modifications of the SET-C (Masia, Klein, Storch, & Corda, 2001; Baer & Garland, 2005) resulted in less positive findings. For instance the modified SET-C (Baer & Garland 2005) excluded Beidel's et al. peer generalization sessions and contingent reinforcement procedures resulting into poorer treatment outcome. This finding illustrates the necessity that future investigations need to focus on the relative contribution of specific treatment components. Currently, which components are necessary or sufficient is unknown, although, based on meta-analyses conducted with adult outcome studies, some form exposure seems to be a vital element.

In addition, little attention has been given to the efficacy of specific treatment components in relation to developmental considerations. For instance, Spence, Donovan, & Brechman-Toussaint (2000) reported that young children with *social phobia*, aged 7-9 years, could not quite easily apprehend the concept of "*cognitive challenging*", therefore this treatment component was reduced for young children. Consequently, future investigations need to address the utility of including each treatment component in treatment taking into consideration the child's developmental stage.

Beyond the empirical literature reporting on the efficacy of psychosocial treatment approaches for childhood *social phobia* , research has begun to accumulate that sheds light on the effectiveness of pharmacological interventions. Psychopharmacological treatment has been acknowledged as a promising treatment modality (McClellan & Werry, 2003; Pine, 2002), but findings reporting on the efficacy of this treatment must still be considered preliminary (Hudson, Deveney, & Taylor, 2005). In fact, few randomised psychopharmacological studies have reported on the efficacy of psychopharmagological treatment approaches on childhood anxiety disorders (Birmaher, Axelson, Monk, Kalas, Clark, Ehmann , Bridge, Heo, & Brent 2003; Wagner, Berard, Stein, Wetherhold, Carpenter, & Perera, 2004). Further, as few studies have directly compared psychosocial approaches with psychopharmacological treatment (Cartwright-Hatton et al., 2004), very little is known about the relative efficacy of these interventions.

Of further potential concern is our lack of knowledge on treatment outcome among ethnic minorities. Several studies reported a less favorable attitude toward treatment for mental health problems in ethnic minorities (Kazdin, 1980; Tarnowksi, Rasnake, Mulick, & Kelly, 1989). Similarly in a study of childhood *social phobia*, ethnic minority parents were found to be less favorable towards pharmacological intervention relative to Caucasian parents (Chavira, Stein, Bailey, & Stein, 2003). Ethnic differences in the perception and utilization of mental health treatments seems to be the outcome of several factors such as the possible stigma attached to mental health treatment among ethnic minorities (Lin, Inui, Kleinman, & Womach, 1982), the fear of possible institutionalization (Takeuchi, Bui, & Kim, 1993) and the lack of culturally sensitive treatment approaches (Pederson, 2004). Given that ethnic minorities are typically underrepresented in clinical trials (Evelyn, Toigo, Banks, Pohl, Gray, & Robins, 2001), future investigations need to evaluate the degree to which the factors involved in treatment outcome differentially affect ethnic minorities as well as other diverse populations.

Conclusion

Although once a neglected disorder, *social phobia* in the child and the youth has in the past two and a half decades received increased attention by empirical investigations. Nonetheless, despite the increase in the empirical investigations, still little is know about the interplay of the factors implicated in the aetiology, developmental course of the disorder, as well as on empirically validated methods of treatment. Further, most studies report data on Caucasian and African American children with very few studies reporting data from other cultures as well as addressing whether *social phobia* is differentially presented across cultures and determine whether cultural issues are implicated in the aetiology, developmental course and treatment outcome of the disorder.

References

Albano, A. M. (1995). Treatment of social anxiety in adolescents. *Cognitive and Behavioural Practice, 2*, 271-298.

Albano, A. M., & Charpita, B. F., & Barlow, D. H. (2003). Childhood anxiety disorders. In E. J. Mash & R. A. Barkley (Eds.), *Child psychopathology* (2nd ed.). New York: Guilford Press.

Albano, A. M., Chorpita, B. E, & Barlow, D. H. (1996). Childhood anxiety disorders. In T. Mash & M. Barkley (Eds.), *Child psychopathology*. New York: The Guilford Press.

Albano, A.M., & Detweiler, M.F. (2001). The developmental and clinical impact of social anxiety and social phobia in children and adolescents. In S.G. Hofmann & P.M. DiBartolo (Eds.), *From social anxiety to social phobia: Multiple perspectives* (pp. 162–178). Needham Heights, MA: Allyn and Bacon.

Albano, A.M., Chorpita, B.F., & Barlow, D.H. (2003). Childhood anxiety disorders. In E.J. Mash & R.A. Barkley (Eds.), *Child psychopathology* (2nd.ed.) (pp. 279- 329). New York: Guilford

Albano, A.M., DiBartolo, P.M., Heimberg, R.G.,&Barlow, D.H. (1995). Children and adolescents: Assessment and treatment. In R.G. Heimberg, M.R. Liebowitz,, D.A. Hope, & F.R. Schneier (Eds.), *Social phobia: Diagnosis, assessment, and treatment* (pp. 387–425). New York: Guilford.

American Psychiatric Association. (1980). *Diagnostic and statistical manual of mental disorders third edition.* Washington, DC: Author.

American Psychiatric Association. (1987). *Diagnostic and statistical manual of mental disorders third edition. Text Revision.* Washington, DC: Author.

American Psychiatric Association. (1994). *Diagnostic and statistical manual of mental disorders, fourth edition.* Washington, DC: Author.

American Psychiatric Association, (2000). *Diagnostic and statistical manual of mental disorders, fourth edition. Text Revision.* Washington, DC: American Psychiatric Association.

Anderson, J. C., Williams, S., McGee, R., & Silva, P.A. (1987). DSM-III disorders in pre-adolescent children. *Archives of General Psychiatry, 44*, 69-76.

Baer, S. & Garland, E.J. (2005) Pilot study of community-based cognitive behavioral group therapy for adolescents with social phobia. *Journal of Developmental & Behavioral Pediatrics*, June, 2005

Beidel, D. C., Turner, S. M., & Morris, T. L. (2000). Behavioral treatment of childhood social phobia. *Journal of Consulting and Clinical Psychology, 68*, 1072-1080.

Beidel, D. C., Turner, S. M., & Morris, T.L. (1999). Psychopathology of childhood social phobia. *Journal of the American Academy of Child and Adolescent Psychiatry, 38*, 630-646.

Beidel, D., & Morris, T. L. (1995). Social phobia. In J. March (Ed.), *Anxiety disorders in children and adolescents*. New York: Guilford.

Benjamin, R. S., Costello, E. J., & Warren, M. (1990). Anxiety disorders in a pediatric sample. *Journal of Anxiety Disorders, 4*, 293-316.

Bernstein, G. A., & Borchardt, C. M. (1991). Anxiety disorders of childhood and adolescence: A critical review. *Journal of the American Academy of Child and Adolescent Psychiatry, 30*, 519–532.

Bernstein , G. A. (1990). Anxiety disorders. In B. D.Garfinkel, G. A. Carlson, & E.B. Weller (Eds.), Psychiatric disorders of childhood and adolescence (pp. 64-83). Philadelphia, PA: W.B. Saunders Company.

Birmaher, B., Axelson, D.A., Monk, K., Kalas, C., Clark, D.B., Ehmann, M., Bridge J., Heo, J & Brent, D.A. (2003). Fluoxetine for the treatment of childhood anxiety disorders. *Journal of the American Academy of Child and Adolescent Psychiatry, 42(4)*, 415–423.

Brady, E.U., & Kendall, P.C. (1992). Comorbidity of anxiety and depression in children and adolescents. *Psychological Bulletin, 111*, 244–255.

Cartwright-Hatton, S., Roberts, C., Chitsabesan, P., Fothergill, C. & Harrington, R. (2004). Systematic review of the efficacy of cognitive behaviour therapies for childhood and adolescent anxiety disorders. *British Journal of Clinical Psychology, 43(4)*, 421–436.

Chambless, D. L., & Hollon, S. D. (1998). Defining empirically supported therapies. *Journal of Consulting and Clinical Psychology, 66*, 7–18.

Chapman, T. F., Mannuzza, S., & Fyer, A. J. (1995). Epidemiology and familial studies of social phobia. In R. G. Heimberg, M. R. Liebowitz, D. A. Hope, & F. R. Schneier, *Social phobia: diagnosis, assessment, and treatment* (pp. 21–40). New York: Guilford Press.

Chavira, D. A., & Stein, M. B. (2005). Childhood social anxiety disorder: From Understanding to treatment. *Child and Adolescent Psychiatric Clinics of North America, 14*, 797-818.

Chavira, D. A., Stein, M. B., Bailey, K., & Stein, M. T. (2003). Parental opinions regarding treatment for social anxiety disorder in youth. *Journal of Developmental & Behavioral Pediatrics, 24(5)*, 315–322.

Compton, S.N., Nelson, A.H., & March, J.S. (2000). Social phobia and separation anxiety symptoms in community and clinical samples of children and adolescents. *Journal of the American Academy of Child and Adolescent Psychiatry, 39*, 1040–1046.

Davidson, J. R. T., Hughes, D.L., George, L.K., & Blazer, D. G. (1993). The epidemiology of social phobia: Findings from the Duke Epidemiological Catchment Area Study. *Psychological Medicine, 23*, 709-718.

Epkins, C.C. (1996). Affective confounding in social anxiety and dysphoria in children child, mother, and father reports of internalizing behaviors, social problems, and competence domains. *Journal of Social and Clinical Psychology, 15*, 449–470.

Essau, C. A., Conradt, J. & Petermann, F.(1999). Frequency and comorbidity of social phobia and social fears in adolescents. *Journal of Anxiety Disorders, Vol. 14, No. 3*, pp. 263–279,

Essau, C.A., Conradt, J., & Petermann, F. (1999). Frequency and comorbidity of social phobia and social fears in adolescents. *Behaviour Research and Therapy, 37*, 831–843.

Essau, C.A., Conradt, J., & Petermann, F. (2000). Frequency, comorbidity, and psychosocial impairment of anxiety disorders in German adolescents. *Journal of Anxiety Disorders, 14*, 263–279.

Evelyn, B., Toigo, T., Banks, D., Pohl, D., Gray, K., Robins, B., et al. (2001). Participation of racial/ethnic groups in clinical trials and race-related labeling: a review of new molecular entities approved 1995–1999. *Journal of the National Medical Association, 93(12)*, 18S–24S.

Fergusson, D.M., Horwood, J.,& Lynskey, M.T. (1993). Prevalence and comorbidity of DSM-III-R diagnoses in a birth cohort of 15 year olds. *Journal of the American Academy of Child and Adolescent Psychiatry, 32*, 1127–1134.

Ferrell, C.B., Beidel, D.C., & Turner, S.M. (2004). Assessment and treatment of socially phobic children: A cross cultural comparison. *Journal of Clinical Child and Adolescent Psychology, 33*, 260–268.

Francis, G., Last, C. G., & Strauss, C. C. (1992). Avoidant disorder and social phobia in children and adolescents. Journal of the American Academy of Child and Adolescents. *Journal of the American Academy of Child and Adolescent Psychiatry, 31*, 1086-1089.

Friman, P.C. (1996). Social Phobia Obscured by Disruptive Behavior Disorder: A Case Study. *Clinical Child Psychology and Psychiatry, 1(3)* 399-407.

Fyer, A.J., Mannuza, A.S., Chapman, T.F., Liebowitz, M.R. and Klein, D.F. (1993) A direct interview study of social phobia. *Archives of General Psychiatry 50*, 286-293.

Goodwin, R. D., Fergusson, D. M., & Horwood, L. J. (2004). Early anxious/withdrawn behaviours predict later internalising disorders. *Journal of Child Psychology and Psychiatry, 45*, 874-883.

Hudson, J. L., Deveney, C., & Taylor, L. (2005). Nature, assessment and treatment of generalized anxiety disorder in children. *Pediatric Annals, 34(2)*, 97–106.

Husain, S. A., & Cantwell, D.P. (1991). Fundamentals of child and adolescent psychopathology. Washington, DC: American Psychiatric Press.

Kazdin, A. E. (1980). Acceptability of alternative treatments for child deviant behavior. *Journal of Applied Behavioral Analysis, 13(2)*, 259–273.

Kendall, P.C., & Warman, M.J. (1996). Anxiety disorders in youth: Diagnostic consistency across DSM-III-R and DSM-IV. *Journal of Anxiety Disorders, 10*, 453–463.

Kessler, R.C., Foster, C.L., Saunders, W.B., & Stang, P.E. (1995). Social consequences of psychiatric disorders, I: Educational attainment. *American Journal of Psychiatry, 152*, 1026–1032.

Kovacs, M., Gatsonis, C., Paulauskas, S.L., & Richards, C. (1989). Depressive disorders in childhood. IV. A longitudinal study of comorbidity with and risk for anxiety disorders. *Archives of General Psychiatry, 46*, 776–782.

Kroneberger, W.G. & Meyer, R.G. (2001) Anxienty Disorders. In W.G. & R.G. Kroneberger (Eds) *The Child Clinician's Handbook* (pp. 206-270). Boston: Allyn & Bacon.

Last , C. G.(1989a). Anxiety disorders. In T.H. Ollendick & M. Hersen (Eds), *Handbook of child psychopathology* (2nd ed., pp. 219-227). New York: Plenum Press.

Last, C. G. (1989b). Anxiety disorders of childhood or adolescence. In C. G Last & M. Hersen (Eds.), *Handbook of child psychiatric diagnosis* (pp.-156-169). New York: John Wiley & Sons.

Last, C. G., Perrin, S., Hersen, M., & Kazdin, A. E. (1992). DSM-IIIR anxiety disorders in children: Sociodemographic and clinical characteristics. *Journal of the American Academy of Child and Adolescent Psychiatry, 31*, 1070–1076.

Last, C.G., Francis, G.,&Strauss, C.C. (1989). Assessing fears in anxiety-disordered children with the Revised Fear Survey Schedule for Children (FSSC-R). *Journal of Clinical Child Psychology, 18*, 137-141.

Lin, K. M., Inui, T. S., Kleinman, A. M., &Womach,W. M. (1982). Sociocultural determinants of the help-seeking behavior of patients with mental illness. *Journal of Nervous and Mental Disease,170 (2)*, 78–85.

Masia, C. L., Klein, R. G., Storch, E. A., & Corda, B. (2001). Schoolbased behavioral treatment for social anxiety disorder in adolescents: Results of a pilot study. *Journal of the American Academy of Child and Adolescent Psychiatry, 40*, 780–786.

McClellan, J. M., &Werry, J. S. (2003). Evidence-based treatments in child and adolescent psychiatry: an inventory. *Journal of the American Academy of Child and Adolescent Psychiatry, 42(12)*, 1388-1400.

McGee, R., & Stanton, W. (1990). Parent reports of disability among 13-year olds with DSM-III disorders. *Journal of Child Psychology & Psychiatry, 31*, 793-801.

Merikangas, K.R., Avenevoli, S., Dierker, L., & Grillon, C. (1999). Vulnerability factors among children at risk for anxiety disorders. *Biological Psychiatry, 46*, 1523-1535.

Nelson, E.C., Grant, J.D., Bucholz, K.K., Glowinski, A., Madden, P.A.F., Reich, W., & Heath, A.C. (2000). Social phobia in a population-based female adolescent twin sample: Co-morbidity and associated suicide-related symptoms. *Psychological Medicine, 30*, 797–804.

Pawlak, C., Pascual-Sanchez, T., Rae, P., Fischer, W., & Ladame, F. (1999). Anxiety disorders, comorbidity, and suicide attempts in adolescence: A preliminary investigation. *European Psychiatry, 14*, 132–136.

Pederson, P. B. (2004). The multicultural context of mental health. In: T. B. Smith (Ed.), Practicing multiculturalism: affirming diversity in counseling and psychology. USA: Pearson Education, Inc.

Pine, D. S. (2002). Treating children and adolescents with selective serotonin reuptake inhibitors: how long is appropriate? *Journal of Child and Adolescent Psychopharmacology, 12(3)*, 189–203.

Rabian, B., & Silverman, W. K. (2000). Anxiety disorders. In M. Herson & R. T. Ammerman (Eds.), *Advanced abnormal child psychology* (2nd ed). Mahwah, NJ: Lawrence Erlbaum Associates.

Silverman, W.K., Pina, A.A., & Viswesvaran, C. (2008). Evidence-Based Psychosocial Treatments for Phobic and Anxiety Disorders in Children and Adolescents. *Journal of Clinical Child & Adolescent Psychology, 37(1)*, 105–130, 2008.

Sonntag, H., Wittchen, H.-U., Hofler, M., Kessler, R.C., & Stein, M.B. (2000). Are social fears and DSM-IV social anxiety disorder associated with smoking and nicotine dependence in adolescents and young adults? *European Psychiatry, 15*, 67–74.

Spence, S. H., Donovan, C., & Brechman-Toussaint, M. (2000). The treatment of childhood social phobia: The effectiveness of a social skills training-based, cognitive-behavioral intervention, with and without parental involvement. *Journal of Child Psychology and Psychiatry, 41*, 713-726.

Standart, S., & Le Couteur, A. (2003). The quiet child: A literature review of selective mutism. *Child and Adolescent Mental Health, 8,* 154 -160.

Strauss, C. C., & Last, C. G. (1993). Social and simple phobias in children. *Journal of Anxiety Disorders, 7, 141-152.*

Strauss, J., Birmaher, B., Bridge, J., Axelson, D., Chiappetta, L., Brent, D., & Ryan, N. (2000). Anxiety disorders in suicidal youth. *Canadian Journal of Psychiatry, 45*, 739–745.

Takeuchi, D. T., Bui, K. T., & Kim, L. (1993). The referral of minority adolescents to community mental health centers. *Journal of Health and Social Behavior, 34(2)*, 153–164.

Tarnowski, K. J., Rasnake, L. K., Mulisk, J. A., & Kelly, P. A. (1989). Acceptability of behavioral treatments for self-injurious behavior. *American Journal of Mental Retardation, 93(5)*, 575-580.

Vasey, M. W. (1995). Social anxiety disorders. In A.R. Eisen, C.a. Kearney, & C.E. Schaefer (Eds.), *Clinical handbook of anxiety disorders in children and adolescents* (p.p.131-168). Northvale, NJ: Aronson.

Velting, O. N., & Albano, A. M. (2001). Current trends in the understanding and treatment of social phobia in youth. *Journal of Child Psychology and Psychiatry, 42*, 127-140.

Velting, O.N., & Albano, A.M. (2001). Current trends in the understanding and treatment of social phobia in youth. *Journal of Child Psychology and Psychiatry, 42*, 127–140.

Verduin, T. L., & Kendall, P. C. (2003). Differential occurrence of comorbidity within childhood anxiety disorders. *Journal of Clinical Child and Adolescent Psychology, 32,* 290–295.

Wagner, K. D., Berard, R., Stein, M. B., Wetherhold, E., Carpenter, D. J., Perera, P., Gee, M, Davy, K. & Machin, A., (2004). A multi-center, randomized, double-blind, placebo-controlled, trial of paroxetine in children and adolescents with social anxiety disorder. *Archives of General Psychiatry, 61(11),* 1153–1162.

Walters, K.S., & Inderbitzen, H.M. (1998). Social anxiety and peer relations among adolescents: Testing a psychobiological model. *Journal of Anxiety Disorders, 12*, 183–198.

Wittchen, H.-U., Stein, M.B. & Kessler, R.C. (1999). Social fears and social phobia in a community sample of adolescents and young adults: Prevalence, risk factors and co-morbidity. *Psychological Medicine, 29*, 309–323.

In: Social Phobia: Etiology, Diagnosis and Treatment
Editor: Clayton P. Axelby
ISBN 978-1-60692-159-3
© 2009 Nova Science Publishers, Inc.

Chapter VIII

THE RELATIONSHIP BETWEEN DEPRESSION AND IMPULSIVITY

Taiki Takahashi[1,*], Hidemi Oono[2] and Mark H. Radford[3]
[1]Department of Behavioral Science, Hokkaido University, N10 W7 Kita-ku, Sapporo, 060-0810 Japan;
[2]Department of Biological Psychiatry, Graduate School of Medicine, Tohoku University, 1-1 Seiryo-machi, Sendai, 980-0872 Japan;
[3]Symbiosis Group Limited, P.O. Box 1192, Milton, 4064 Australia.

ABSTRACT

Objective: Depression is often associated with social phobia. Several previous studies have reported that there are differences by sex in the risk factors for negative behavior, such as a suicide attempt. This study focused on the relationship between depression and impulsivity, a personality trait associated with negative behaviors, such as suicide, and possible sex differences on the relationship.

Method: 120 students from Hokkaido University and 20 psychiatric patients from Hokkaido University Hospital were included in the present study.

Results: The correlation between depressive tendency and self-reported impulsivity was higher in males than in females, and the correlation was significant only in male students.

Conclusion: Impulsivity may be a predictor of suicidal behavior. The results from the present study showed a strong correlation between depressive tendency and impulsivity only in males. Furthermore depressive tendency correlated with the sub-fators of impulsivity – *Attentional Impulsiveness* and *Nonplanning Impulsiveness*. It is possible that in males, depression leads to quick decisions being made (*Attentional Impulsiveness*), and a "present orientation" or a lack of "future consideration"

* Correspondence concerning this article should be addressed to: Taiki Takahashi, Telephone number: +81-11-706-3057; Fax number: +81-11-706-3066; E-mail: taikitakahashi@gmail.com. Institute for Department of Behavioral Science, Hokkaido University, Sapporo, Japan.

(*Nonplanning Impulsiveness*), then results in committing a suicidal behavior. Further studies are needed.

1. INTRODUCTION

1.1. Mental Health

Mental health is the one of the biggest issues in modern society. Terms such as "depression" and "impulsive murder" are heard frequently in most societies. The number of deaths by suicide is increasing in Japan. The Ministry of Health, Labor and Welfare has reported that there are more than 30,000 suicidal deaths a year (Ministry of Health, Labor and Welfare, 2003). This is three times the number of deaths due to traffic accidents. The number of suicide attempt is 10 times the number of actual suicides. These figures suggest that mental health has a great influence on people's lives, and society in general.

Certain psychiatric disorders, such as depression, have a significant impact on negative actions such as suicidal behavior. The aim of this study is to look at the connection between depression and impulsivity, a personality trait associated with suicide.

1.2. Depression

Almost all people experience being depressed at some time in their lives. For some, this depression can become more serious and result in a sense of constant sadness and nothingness. Depressed people can have various symptoms, most of which are measured by one of many of the depression questionnaires available. For example, in the *Beck Depression Inventory* (*BDI*, Beck et al., 1961), which is used to measure the severity of depression, symptoms evaluated include: *Mood, Pessimism, Sense of Failure, Lack of Satisfaction, Guilty Feeling, Sense of Punishment, Self-Hate, Self Accusations, Self Punitive Wishes, Crying Spells, Irritability, Social Withdrawal, Indecisiveness, Body Image, Work Inhibition, Sleep Disturbance, Fatigability, Loss of Appetite, Weight Loss, Somatic Preoccupation and Loss of Libido*. These symptoms describe a specific behavioral manifestation of depression (Beck et al., 1961).

In a study of 1,710 adolescents, Lewinsohn and colleagues (1993) reported that the risk of suicide increases with an increase in the number of risk factors present. The number of risk factors such as stressful events, self-consciousness, low social self-confidence, emotional reliance, reduced support from friends, conflicts with parents, hopelessness, recent suicide attempts by a friend, social desirability, and certain measures of health, increase significantly when combined with past suicide attempts (Lewinsohn et al., 1993). These risk factors are also associated with depression (Lewinsohn et al., 1993).

The risk factors for suicide are known to also include psychiatric disorders, especially depression (Pfeffer et al., 1988, Gould et al., 1998). Pfeffer and colleagues examined the factors associated with suicidal behavior in a sample of 200 adolescents aged 13-19 years. They reported that depressive disorders were the diagnoses positively associated with suicidal behavior and a significant predictor of suicidal behavior. Through regression analyses, they found that a large degree of variance for suicidal behavior was accounted for by a combination of risk factors including depression.

Gould and colleagues (1998) reported that the prediction of suicidal ideation or attempt is substantially improved with knowledge of one's diagnostic profile. In their study, if no information were available on an individual's mental state, the best available prediction of the occurrence of a suicide attempt would be 3.3 %. In the presence of depression, the attempt rate increases to 22 %. According to their study, depression is an important predictor of suicidal behavior, particularly in males (Gould et al., 1998).

Neurobiologically, depression has been associated with disruption of serotonergic activities in the brain and serotonin reuptake inhibitors are useful for psychopharmacological treatments of depression (Kutcher and Gardner, 2008). However, several studied have associated suicide with the intake of serotonin reuptake inhibitors (Marcinko, 2007). Thus, it is important to examine the relationship between depression and impulsive behavior such as suicide.

1.3. Impulsivity

In a study by Mann and colleagues (1999), it was found that patients with some form of psychiatric disorder scored much higher than those without a psychiatric disorder on an impulsivity factor, which is a risk factor for aggressive behaviors such as suicide (Davidson et al., 1980). This suggests a strong relationship between suicide and psychiatric disorders in general.

Impulsivity is supposed to have several domains in itself. Impulsivity, as a personality trait, can be measured with the *Barratt Impulsiveness Scale* (Patton et al., 1995). This scale measures three types of impulsivity: *Attentional* (not focusing on the task at hand), *Motor* (acting on the spur of the moment) and *Nonplanning* (not planning and thinking carefully).

In Mann and colleagues study (1999), it was reported that suicidal behavior had some relationship with impulsivity. Following admission to a university psychiatric hospital for evaluation and psychiatric treatment, Mann and colleagues recruited 347 consecutive patients, aged between 14 and 72 years for their study. Within these patients, 184 had made a previous suicide attempt, and 118 of these had made multiple suicide attempts. From the results, it was found that a trait factor, impulsivity, assessing lifetime externally directed impulsivity, was highly significant in distinguishing past suicide attempters from nonattempters with the same disorder including depression.

1.4. Aim and Hypothesis

As suggested above, psychiatric disorders, such as depression can cause some kinds of impulsive behavior. This fact suggests an important role for disorders, such as depression, in impulsive behavior which can result in suicide or suicide attempt.

Many studies that sought to discover the risk factors for negative behaviors such as suicide have recruited participants only from specific groups of people with similar backgrounds, for example age or area. Reinherz and colleagues (1995) examined nearly 400 young people, and reported that the early onset of major psychiatric disorder increased the risks for suicide by age 18. Dumais and colleagues (2005) studied 104 male suicide completers and 74 living depressed male subjects. They concluded that impulsive-aggressive personality disorders, and alcohol abuse or dependence, were two independent risk factors for suicide completion in major depression.

The approach of the following study was to look at a sample of people from a wide variety of backgrounds (i.e. both hospital patients and 'normal' university students) to examine the influence of depression on impulsivity. Results from such an investigation may improve our understanding of this important mental health topic.

The main aim of the present study was to investigate the relationship between depression and impulsivity.

Based on the results from previous studies, we hypothesized that

1) There is a correlation between depression and impulsivity; and

2) Depression and impulsivity are likely to be more strongly correlated in males than in females. This second prediction is based on the results from Silvana and colleagues' study (2005) that found depression to be a predictor of suicidal behavior particularly in males.

2. Study 1: University Students

2.1. Method

2.1.1. Participants

The participants consisted of 128 undergraduate students including 120 (65 males and 55 females) Japanese undergraduate students and eight (2 males and 6 females) foreign students from Hokkaido University. Only data from Japanese subjects were used for the analyses. Participants' ages ranged from 18 to 28 years (*Mean*=19.8, *S.D.*=1.50).

2.1.2. Measures

Beck Depression Inventory

To measure the degree of depression, the *Beck Depression Inventory* (*BDI*; Beck et al., 1961) was used. This scale consists of 21 items. Each item represents a category of symptoms and attitudes which describes a specific behavioral manifestation of depression. The statements are ranked to reflect the range of severity of symptoms from neutral to severe. Numerical values from 0 to 3 are assigned to indicate the degree of severity. The summed score for all items shows a subject's level of depression.

The *BDI* has been identified to have four primary factors and these have been labeled: *Disturbance of Mood*, *Feeling of Inhibition and Body Condition*, *Guilty Feeling*, and *Physiological Response* (Hayashi et al., 1991).

Reliability and validity for the *BDI* has been well established (e.g. Beck et al., 1988). The Japanese version was used in the present study (Hayashi, 1988).

The symptom-attitude categories are as follows:

1. Mood
2. Pessimism
3. Sense of Failure
4. Lack of Satisfaction
5. Guilty Feeling
6. Sense of Punishment
7. Self-Hate
8. Self Accusations
9. Self Punitive Wishes
10. Crying Spells
11. Irritability
12. Social Withdrawal
13. Indecisiveness
14. Body Image
15. Work Inhibition
16. Sleep Disturbance
17. Fatigability
18. Loss of Appetite
19. Weight Loss
20. Somatic Preoccupation
21. Loss of Libido

Barratt Impulsiveness Scale

The other questionnaire used in the present study was the Barratt Impulsiveness Scale (BIS; Barratt, 1959). This scale was designed to measure impulsivity as a personality trait. There are three main impulsivity sub-factors labeled: Attentional Impulsiveness, Motor Impulsiveness, and Nonplanning Impulsiveness. This scale consists of 30 items. All items are answered on a 4-point scale. The score for all items are summed, with a higher score indicating a higher level of impulsivity. To avoid a response set, selected items indicate non-impulsivity in this scale.

Reliability and validity for the BIS have been well established (e.g. Patton et al., 1995). The Japanese version (Someya et al., 2001) was used in the present study.

The Questionnaire for Demographic Data

In addition to the two scales above, demographic data about sex, age, and drinking and smoking habits were collected.

2.1.3. Procedure

The present study was done as a part of a larger study on risk–taking behavior, mood, stress and personality correlates. Participants were recruited from two undergraduate classes at Hokkaido University. All measures on this study were given to students to complete during their class.

2.1.4. Statistical Analysis

All statistical procedures were conducted using the SAS system for Windows V8 (the SAS institute Inc.). Significance level was set at 5%.

2.2. Results

2.2.1. Depression

To know the severity of depression for participants, the *Beck Depression Inventory* scores are shown. As Table 1 shows, within the student sample, there was no sex difference in their level of depression. Although the mean *BDI* score was higher in females than in males, this difference was not significant in a *t*-test analysis ($t(118)$=-0.52, *n.s.*).

Table 1. Means and standard deviations for *BDI* total score

	All (n=120) *Mean (S.D.)*	Males (n=65) *Mean (S.D.)*	Females (n=55) *Mean (S.D.)*
BDI	12.23 (1.50)	11.88 (8.45)	12.64 (7.56)

No statistically significant sex differences were found for the *BDI* sub-factor scores. Females had higher scores on *Feeling of Inhibition and Body Cognition*, *Guilty Feeling* and *Physiological Response*. On the other hand, males had a higher score on *Disturbance of Mood*. However, these differences were not significant in *t*-test analyses (*Disturbance of Mood* $t(118)$=0.16, *n.s.; Feeling of Inhibition and Body Condition* $t(113)$=-1.36, *n.s.; Guilty Feeling* $t(114)$=-0.11, *n.s.; Physiological Response* $t(117)$=-0.69, *n.s.*). Means and standard deviations for *BDI* sub-factors are shown in Table 2.

Table 2. Means and standard deviations for each sub-factor of the *BDI*

	All (n=120) *Mean (S.D.)*	Males (n=65) *Mean (S.D.)*	Females (n=55) *Mean (S.D.)*
Disturbance of Mood	4.81 (4.14)	4.86 (4.57)	4.74 (3.62)
Feeling of Inhibition and Body Condition	1.58 (1.93)	1.35 (1.89)	1.83 (1.97)
Guilty Feeling	3.67 (2.23)	3.65 (2.21)	3.69 (2.28)
Physiological Response	1.34 (1.13)	1.28 (1.26)	1.42 (0.98)

2.2.2. Impulsivity

The results for impulsivity are similar to those obtained for depression. While female student scores on the *Barratt Impulsiveness Scale* were a little higher than male scores on all sub-factors, these results were not statistically significant (total score $t(103)=-1.65$, *n.s.*, *Attentional Impulsiveness* $t(112)=-0.92$, *n.s.*, *Motor Impulsiveness* $t(110)=-1.67$, *n.s.*, *Nonplanning Impulsiveness* $t(109)=-1.52$, *n.s.*). Means and standard deviations for *BIS* total score and sub-factors are shown in Tables 3 and 4.

Table 3. Means and standard deviations for BIS total score

	All (*n*=120) *Mean (S.D.)*	Males (*n*=65) *Mean (S.D.)*	Females (*n*=55) *Mean (S.D.)*
BIS	68.58 (10.97)	67.05 (9.71)	70.40 (12.13)

Table 4. Means and standard deviations for each sub-factor of the *BIS*

	All (*n*=120) *Mean (S.D.)*	Males (*n*=65) *Mean (S.D.)*	Females (*n*=55) *Mean (S.D.)*
Attentional Impulsiveness	19.89 (3.96)	19.58 (3.83)	20.25 (4.10)
Motor Impulsiveness	23.02 (4.18)	22.43 (3.95)	23.71 (4.38)
Nonplanning Impulsiveness	25.68 (5.03)	25.03 (4.73)	26.44 (5.31)

2.2.3. Correlation between Depression and Impulsivity

In order to examine the relationship between depression and impulsivity, correlational analyses were conducted. It was found that depression was positively correlated with impulsivity only in males (Table 5). The males' correlation coefficient was $r=0.44$, and this result was significant at 1% level, whereas in the female student sample the correlation coefficient was $r=0.06$ and this was not significant (Figure 1 and 2).

Table 5. Correlation coefficients between the *BDI* and *BIS* total scores

All (*n*=120)	Males (*n*=65)	Females (*n*=55)
0.27**	0.44***	0.06 *n.s.*
**$p<.01$ ***$p<.001$		

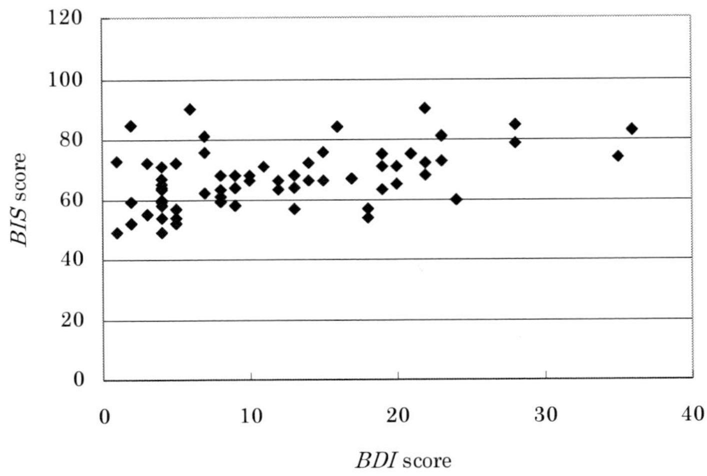

Figure 1. Correlation between *BDI* and *BIS* in males.

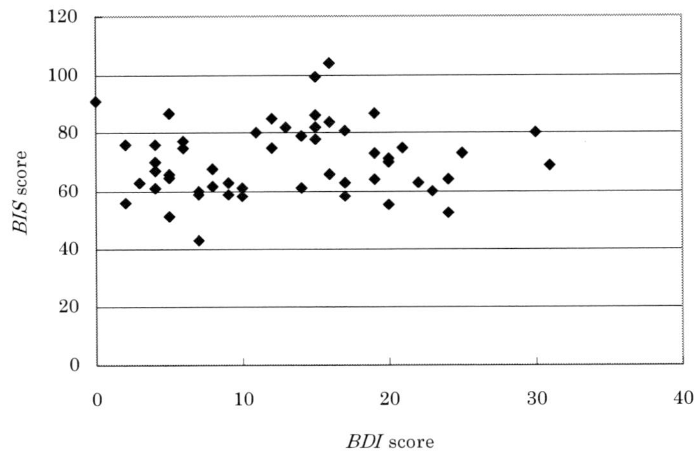

Figure 2. Correlation between *BDI* and *BIS* in females.

When we looked at the correlations between the *BDI* score and each sub-factor of the *BIS* (Table 6), we found significant correlations for only male participants in all sub-factors, except for *Motor Impulsiveness.* The correlation coefficient for *Attentional Impulsiveness* was r=0.47 in males and was r=0.17 in females and the for *Nonplanning Impulsiveness* was r=0.34 in males and r=0.06 in females. Both were significant only in males.

Table 6. Correlation coefficients between *BDI* total score and each sub-factor of *BIS*

	All (n=120)	Males (n=65)	Females (n=55)
Attentional Impulsiveness	0.35***	0.47***	0.17 *n.s.*
Motor Impulsiveness	0.12 *n.s.*	0.23 *n.s.*	-0.05 *n.s.*
Nonplanning Impulsiveness	0.22*	0.34**	0.06 *n.s.*

*p< .05 **p< .01 ***p< .001.

2.2.4. Discussion

Results for the student sample, did not show any sex differences in the levels of depression and impulsivity, but did show some support for our hypothesis that depression and impulsivity are likely to be more strongly correlated in males than in females. The correlation coefficient was significant only in males, and it was high (r=0.44 in males, versus r=0.06 in females).

3. STUDY 2: DEPRESSED PATIENTS

3.1. Method

3.1.1. Participants

Participants consisted of 20 (12 males and 8 females) psychiatric patients of Hokkaido University Hospital. Their ages ranged from 27 to 72 years (*Mean*=48.5, *S.D.*=13.60).

3.1.2. Measures

The questionnaires used in this study were same as Study 1 for university students, which were the *Beck Depression Inventory*, the *Barratt Impulsiveness Scale* and a demographic sheet.

3.1.3. Procedure

The present study was done as a part of a larger study on mood disorder and impulsivity. Participants were psychiatric inpatients and outpatients of Hokkaido University Hospital, and signed a consent form explaining the intention of this study. Measures on this study were given to the patients at the time of the interview with the doctor. Patients were requested to answer the questionnaires at their home and return them at the next interview.

3.1.4. Statistical Analysis

All statistical procedures were conducted using the SAS system for Windows V8 (the SAS institute Inc.). Significance level was set at 5%.

3.2. Results

3.2.1. Depression

Severity of depression for patient participants is indicated by *Beck Depression Inventory* scores (see Table 7). For patients, *t*-test analyses showed no sex difference ($t(14.4)=0.29$, *n.s.*), a result similar to that found with the student sample in study 1. However, the mean *BDI* total score was higher in male patients than in female patients, the opposite to what was found in study 1, as shown in Table 7.

Table 7. Means and standard deviations for *BDI* total score

	All (*n*=20) *Mean (S.D.)*	Males (*n*=12) *Mean (S.D.)*	Females (*n*=8) *Mean (S.D.)*
BDI	11.80 (8.24)	12.25 (8.23)	11.12 (8.77)

When we look at each sub-factor score of the *BDI*, female patients had higher scores on; *Disturbance of Mood* and *Physiological Response* (see Table 8). The higher score on *Disturbance of Mood* was opposite to that found in the student sample, where males were higher. But these differences were also found not to be significant.

Table 8. Means and standard deviations of each sub-factor of the *BDI*

	All (*n*=20) *Mean (S.D.)*	Males (*n*=12) *Mean (S.D.)*	Females (*n*=8) *Mean (S.D.)*
Disturbance of Mood	4.25 (3.51)	4.16 (3.56)	4.37 (3.66)
Feeling of Inhibition and Body Condition	2.85 (2.78)	3.08 (3.08)	2.50 (2.39)
Guilty Feeling	2.50 (2.37)	3.33 (2.19)	1.25 (2.19)
Physiological Response	1.40 (1.27)	1.00 (0.85)	2.00 (1.60)

3.2.2. Impulsivity

As with the results for depression, significant sex differences for impulsivity were found. As Table 9 shows, male patients had higher *BIS* score than female patients. The only exception was that female patients had a higher score on *Nonplanning Impulsiveness* (total score $t(14.4)=0.29$, *n.s.*, *Attentional Impulsiveness* $t(12.2)=0.56$, *n.s.*, *Motor Impulsiveness* $t(17.7)=0.63$, *n.s.*, *Nonplanning Impulsiveness* $t(15.5)=-0.48$, *n.s.*). Means and standard deviations for *BIS* total score and sub-factor scores are shown in Tables 9 and 10.

Table 9. Means and standard deviations for *BIS* total score

	All (*n*=20) *Mean (S.D.)*	Males (*n*=12) *Mean (S.D.)*	Females (*n*=8) *Mean (S.D.)*
BIS	57.50 (10.97)	59.25 (11.38)	54.88 (10.49)

Table 10. Means and standard deviations for each sub-factor of the *BIS*

	All (*n*=20) *Mean (S.D.)*	Males (*n*=12) *Mean (S.D.)*	Females (*n*=8) *Mean (S.D.)*
Attentional Impulsiveness	15.90 (2.43)	16.17 (2.17)	15.50 (2.88)
Motor Impulsiveness	18.00 (3.78)	18.41 (4.23)	17.38 (3.16)
Nonplanning Impulsiveness	23.60 (3.91)	23.25 (4.05)	24.13 (3.91)

3.2.3. Correlation between Depression and Impulsivity

Correlational analyses were conducted in order to examine the relationship between depression and impulsivity. Despite some moderately high positive correlation coefficients, the results from the correlational analyses were not significant in both males and females. This might be because the number of patient participants was extremely small compared to the number of student participants (see Tables 11 and 12).

Again, looking at the correlation coefficients between *BDI* total score and each sub-factor of the *BIS,* males had higher correlations than females in the two of the three factors - *Attentional Impulsiveness* and *Motor Impulsiveness*. But both correlations failed to reach significance.

Table 11. Correlation coefficients between the score of *BDI* and *BIS*

All (n=20)	Males (n=12)	Females (n=8)
0.42 *n.s.*	0.50 *n.s.*	0.50 *n.s.*

Table 12. Correlation coefficients between *BDI* total score and each sub-factor of *BIS*

	All (n=20)	Males (n=12)	Females (n=8)
Attentional Impulsiveness	0.08 *n.s.*	0.10 *n.s.*	0.03 *n.s.*
Motor Impulsiveness	0.34 *n.s.*	0.42 *n.s.*	0.29 *n.s.*
Nonplanning Impulsiveness	0.11 *n.s.*	0.13 *n.s.*	-0.49 *n.s.*

3.2.4. Discussion

Within the patient participants, we did not find significant sex differences in correlations, with the correlation coefficient being r=0.50 in both males and females. There is a possibility that this finding is due to a weakness in the present study, relating to the small size of the patient sample.

4. Comparison between Students and Patients

4.1. Depression

To examine the differences between students and patients in depression and impulsivity, t-test analyses were conducted in this study. Regarding depression, there are no significant difference although, contrary to expectation, students had slightly higher scores on the *BDI* than patients ($t(25.4)=-0.21$, *n.s.*). The means and standard deviations for *BDI* are shown in Table 13 below.

To examine the main effects of sex and participant group (students versus patients) and the interaction on depressive tendency, the ANOVA analysis was conducted. However, there were no significant main effects and interaction ($F(3, 136)=0.22$, *n.s.*).

Table 13. Means and standard deviations for *BDI* total score

	All (*n*=140) *Mean* (*S.D.*)	Students (*n*=120) *Mean* (*S.D.*)	Patients (*n*=20) *Mean* (*S.D.*)	*t* (*df*)
BDI	12.16 (8.02)	12.23 (8.02)	11.80 8.24	-0.21 (25.4) *n.s.*

4.2. Impulsivity

T-test Analyses were conducted to look at the difference in impulsivity as well as depression. Student scores on the *BIS* were higher than patient scores. It was found that students were significantly more impulsive than patients ($t(25.7)$=-4.18, $p< .001$).

Table 14. Means and standard deviations for *BIS*

	All (*n*=140) *Mean* (*S.D.*)	Students (*n*=120) *Mean* (*S.D.*)	Patients (*n*=20) *Mean* (*S.D.*)	*t* (*df*)
BIS	67.00 (11.60)	68.58 (10.97)	57.50 (10.97)	-4.18 (25.7) ***

***$p< .001$.

To examine the main effects of sex and participant group (students versus patients) and the interaction on impulsivity, the ANOVA analysis was conducted. There were no significant main effects and interaction ($F(3, 136)$=1.62, *n.s.*) except the main effect of group ($F(3, 136)$=17.70, $p< .001$).

4.3. Discussion

No difference in depression level between the student (normal) and patient samples were found. It is possible that patients are responding to treatment, and so that they currently feel less depressed than before. If this is so then it may be important to examine only patients who have yet to receive treatment.

Regarding the result that patients were less impulsive than students, the difference in the participant numbers could be partly responsible. The other possible reason for this result might be due to age. The student participants were adolescents, and this may be why students reported being more impulsive than patients. The student participants' ages ranged from 18 to 28 years with a mean age of 19.8 years. On the other hand the patient participants' ages ranged from 27 to 72 years, with a mean age of 48.5 years. There are many studies that have reported that age is negatively correlated with impulsivity (e.g. Mobini et al., 2006). It has also been found that impulsivity decreases with age (Mobini et al, 2006). More patient participants are needed before any further conclusions can be made.

5. General Discussion

The purpose of the present study was to investigate the relationship between depression and impulsivity. The results provide tentative support our general hypotheses – i.e. there is a correlation between depression and impulsivity, and that depression and impulsivity are more strongly correlated in males than in females.

The correlation analyses conducted between level of depression (as measured by the *BDI*), and level of impulsivity (as measured by *BIS*) showed stronger correlations in males than in females in student samples.

Within the student sample particularly, the males' correlation coefficient was strong. The correlation coefficient was significant at 1% level in males whereas it was not significant in females. When we looked at the correlations between the *BDI* score and each sub-factor of the *BIS*, we only found significant correlations for male student participants, except for *Motor Impulsiveness*. The correlation coefficient for *Attentional Impulsiveness* and *Nonplanning Impulsiveness* was also high in males, and both were significant only in males. In the study for the factor structure of *BIS* by Stanford and colleagues (1995), *Attentional Impulsiveness* involved making quick cognitive decisions, and *Nonplanning Impulsiveness* was characterized as a "present orientation" or a lack of "future consideration". Both *Attentional* and *Nonplanning Impulsiveness* factors are composed of items that refer to the absence of enough prospects for the future. A possible reason why there was no correlation between *BDI* score and *Motor Impulsiveness*, which is defined as a form of action, might be because this study used self-report questions, and not actual actions, to measure impulsive behavior.

Because the correlations coefficients between *BDI* score and *BIS* scores in the student sample were high, we expected the results with a patient sample to also support our hypotheses. However there were no significant correlations within patients. A number of factors may have influenced this result. In particular, the number of patient participants was perhaps not enough. In the present study, with cooperation from Hokkaido University Hospital, psychiatric inpatients and outpatients were recruited. At the time of the initial clinical interview, the doctor explained the intention of this study to the patients and then handed out the questionnaires. The patients were instructed to return the completed questionnaire during the next visit. Because of their illness, they were also told they could stop completing the questionnaire if it became too much trouble. As a result, in the end, only 20 patients submitted all questionnaires.

Despite the patient participant results, in general the hypotheses were supported by the results from this study. In other words, there is a correlation between depression and impulsivity. The more depressed a participant, the more impulsive, especially in males.

It has been reported that impulsivity is an important component of suicidal behavior (Mann et al., 1999). The results of the present study are consistent with the report that depression is associated with suicide behavior, particularly in males (Fennig et al., 2005).

In general, males are more likely to respond to frustration and stress with anger and hostility than females. Males have a tendency to externalize their pain in the form of behavioral problems, problems with the law, and drug abuse, all behaviors associated with impulsivity. By contrast, females tend to internalize their suffering and pain and to manifest their internal pain as anxiety, depression, and/or some form of psychosomatic symptoms (Rich et al., 1992).

Depression is associated with various 'uncomfortable' symptoms, which include negative feelings such as frustration, stress, suffering and pain. This fact may be able to help explain the results from the present study. When males are depressed, they externalize their suffering of/from depression in the form of impulsive behavior. Thus, in males, impulsivity may be more likely to be manifested under conditions of strong affect such as depression. Whereas in females, depressive affect tends to be internalized. As suicide is sometimes said to be an 'impulsive' behavior, it can be said that depression can be a predictor of suicide, particularly in males (Fennig et al., 2005).

There are limitations in the present study. First, the number of patient participants was not enough. The small sample size can reduce the chance of any potential differences reaching significance. Second, the number of participants in the two groups - students and patients, differed widely. In the comparison study, *t*-test analyses were conducted. The difference in the sample numbers for each group could influence the analyses. Third, this study used self-report measures that are often associated with potential response biases. There is likely to be some gaps between actual behavior and self-evaluation.

In general, our hypothesis was supported in the present study, but further research, addressing the issues outlined above are needed before any conclusive comments can be made.

REFERENCES

Baca-Garcia E, Diaz-Sastre C, Resa EG, Blasco H, Conesa DB, Oquendo MA, Saiz-Ruiz J, Leon J. (2005). Suicide Attempts and Impulsivity. *European archives of psychiatry and clinical neuroscience*, *255*, 152-156.

Beck AT, Ward CH, Mendelson M, Mock J, Erbaugh J. (1961). An Inventory for Measuring Depression. *Archives of General Psychiatry*, *4*, 53-63.

Davidson JA, Montgomery I. (1980). Impulsive Suicidal Behavior. *Journal of Clinical Psychology*, *36*, 90-94.

Dumais A, Lesage AD, Alda M, Rouleau G, Dumont M, Chawky M, Roy M, Mann JJ, Benkelfat C, Turecki G. (2005). Risk factors for Suicide Completion in Major Depression: A case-Control Study of Impulsive and Aggressive Behaviors in Men. *American Journal of Psychiatry, 162, 2116-2124.*

Gould MS, King R, Greenwald S, Fisher P, Schwab-Stone M, Kramer R, Frisher AJ, Goodman S, Canino G, Shaffer D. (1998). Psychopathology associated with suicidal ideation and attempts among children and adolescents. *Journal of the American Academy of Child and Adolescent Psychiatry*, *37*, 915-923.

Hayashi K, Takimoto T. (1991). The examination of Beck Depression Inventory (version 1978) and the link between depression and self-efficacy. *Annual Report of Shiraume Gakuen University*, *27*, 43-52.

Kutcher S and Gardner DM (2008) Use of selective serotonin reuptake inhibitors and youth suicide: making sense from a confusing story. *Current Opinion in Psychiatry, 21*:65-69.

Lewinsohn PM, Rohde P, Seeley JR. (1993). Psychosocial characteristics of adolescents with a history of suicide attempt. *Journal of the American Academy of Child and Adolescent Psychiatry, 32*, 60-68.

Mann JJ, Waternaux C, Gretcher LH, Malone KM. (1999). Toward a clinical model of suicidal behavior in psychiatric patients. *American Journal of Psychiatry*, 156, 181-189.

Marcinko, D (2007) Antidepressants and suicidality: the basis of controversies. *Psychiatria Danubina 19(3)*:238-240.

Mobini S, Pearce M, Grant A, Mills J, Yeomans MR. (2006). The Relationship between Cognitive Distortions, Impulsivity, and Sensation Seeking in a Non-clinical population sample. *Personality and Individual Differences, 40*, 1153-1163.

Pfeffer CR, Newcorn J, Kaplan G, Misruchi MS, Plutchik R. (1998). Suicidal behavior in adolescent psychiatric inpatients. *Journal of the American Academy of Child and Adolescent Psychiatry*, *27*, 357-361.

Reinherz HZ, Giaconia RM, Silverman AB, Friedman A, Pakiz B, FrostAK, Cohen E. (1995). Early Psychosocial Risks for Adolescent Suicidal Ideation and Attempts. *Journal of the American Academy of Child and Adolescent Psychiatry*, *34*, 599-611.

Rich AR, Kirkpatric-Smith J, Bonner RL, Jans F. (1992). Gender Differences in the Psychosocial Correlates of Suicidal Ideation Among Adolescents. *Suicide and Life-Threatening Behavior, 22*, 364-373.

Silvana F, Keren G, Zalsman G, Weizman A, Shmuel F, Apter A. (2005). Effect of gender on suicidal attempters versus nonattempters in an adolescent inpatient unit. *Comprehensive Psychiatry*, *46*, 90-97.

Someya T, Sakado K, Sek, T, Kojima M, Reist C, Tang SW, Takahashi S. (2001). The Japanese version of the Barratt Impulsiveness Scale, 11th version (BIS-11): its reliability and validity *Psychiatry and Clinical Neurosciences, 55*, 111-114

Stanford MS, Barratt ES. (1995). Factor structure of the Barratt Impulsiveness Scale. *Journal of Clinical Psychology*, *51*, 768-774.

In: Social Phobia: Etiology, Diagnosis and Treatment
Editor: Clayton P. Axelby
ISBN 978-1-60692-159-3
© 2009 Nova Science Publishers, Inc.

Chapter IX

TEMPERAMENTAL ANTECEDENTS OF SOCIAL PHOBIA: THE CASE OF BEHAVIORAL INHIBITION

Matilda E. Nowakowski and Louis A. Schmidt*
Department of Psychology, Neuroscience and Behaviour, McMaster University, Canada

ABSTRACT

Behavioral inhibition is defined as a consistent style of responding toward novel situations, individuals, and objects with wariness, distress and avoidance and is experienced by about 10% of typically developing children (Garcia-Coll, Kagan, & Reznick, 1984). Although behavioral inhibition is a normal variant of behavioral style, research has shown that behaviorally inhibited children are at an increased risk for a variety of internalizing problems, including anxiety disorders (Kagan & Snidman, 1999; Schwartz, Snidman, & Kagan, 1999). In the present chapter, we provide a review of the studies conducted to date that have investigated the role of behavioral inhibition in the development of anxiety disorders, with a specific focus on social phobia. We review studies that have used both clinical and non-clinical samples as well as a variety of methods and designs, including retrospective, cross-sectional and longitudinal. We suggest that behavioral inhibition by itself is not sufficient for the development of social phobia. Rather, it is the interaction of behavioral inhibition and environmental factors such as social stressors, parenting, and attachment that place an individual at an increased risk for developing social phobia. We propose a diathesis-stress model for the role of behavioral inhibition in the development of social phobia, with a need for future research to further investigate the stressors and protective factors that interact with behavioral inhibition. We conclude the chapter with a discussion of clinical implications.

* Correspondence concerning this chapter should be addressed to: Dr. Louis A. Schmidt, Department of Psychology, Neuroscience & Behaviour, McMaster University, Hamilton, Ontario, L8S 4K1 Canada; fax: 905-529-6225; email: schmidtl@mcmaster.ca.

INTRODUCTION

With a lifetime prevalence rate of 13% (Kessler et al., 1994), social phobia is the most common anxiety disorder in today's society. Given that social phobia results in serious functional impairment in key areas such as education, relationships and occupation (Turner, Beidel, Dancu, & Keys, 1986), it is essential that individuals with the disorder are properly diagnosed and treated. Even more critical is research investigating early risk factors for the development of social phobia so that preventive treatments can be applied before the disorder manifests itself. One early risk factor for the development of social phobia is a temperamental style known as behavioral inhibition.

In the present chapter, we present evidence for a link between early childhood behavioral inhibition and later anxiety disorders, with a special focus on social phobia. The chapter is divided among five sections. We first provide a brief overview of behavioral inhibition (Section 1) and social phobia (Section 2), including behavioral and physiological similarities (Section 3). We then review the studies that have been conducted to date investigating the relation between childhood behavioral inhibition and later development of social phobia (Section 4). We conclude the chapter with a discussion of clinical implications and future directions for research in the area of temperamental antecedents of social phobia (Section 5).

BEHAVIORAL INHIBITION

The study of temperament has a long and rich history dating back to 2 A.D. when Galen, a Greek physician, proposed the first scientific theory of temperament. Galen suggested that individual differences in temperament were determined by the balance of four different humors or fluids in the body: *flegma*, *chole*, *malanchole*, and *sanguis* (Galen, 170 A.D.). Although the modern study of temperament no longer views the balance between body fluids as determining individuals' reactions to the world, contemporary temperament theory still has a link to Galen's theory, with its focus on the identification of biological explanations for temperament.

Despite the long history of temperament, it was the work of Thomas and Chess in the 1950's that revitalized this area of research. Up to this time, the *zeitgeist* was such that biology and environment were viewed as mutually exclusive and any deviances in children's behaviors were believed to be due to poor environmental factors, especially inadequate parenting (Thomas & Chess, 1977). The work of Thomas and Chess brought a more balanced perspective to children's deviant behaviors by moving the focus away from placing complete blame on mothers and instead viewing biology as playing an important role in temperament. Through their New York Longitudinal Study, Thomas and Chess (1963, 1977) identified nine categories of temperament that they believed explained the variability seen in how individuals respond to various situations: activity level, rhythmicity/regularity, adaptability, threshold of stimulation, intensity of reaction, quality of mood, distractibility, and attention span and persistence. Thomas and Chess focused on the stylistic quality of behavior (i.e., the how of behavior) rather than the content of behavior (i.e., the what of behavior; Thomas & Chess, 1977).

The work of Thomas and Chess (1977) spawned a surge of research in the area of temperament, with many researchers using Thomas and Chess' theory of temperament as a starting point to the development of their own theories, most of which differed in the number and type of categories that were viewed as defining temperament (see Goldsmith et al., 1987, for a summary of the different definitions and conceptualizations of temperament). Despite the variability among researchers in the conceptualization of temperament, most agree that temperament is comprised of early appearing traits that are stable across time and place and that determine an individual's patterns of responding to environmental stimuli (Bates, 1986). Although temperament is viewed as having a genetic basis, most researchers agree that as an individual develops, his/her temperament can be modified within limits by his/her interactions with the environment (Buss & Plomin, 1984, Chess & Thomas, 1984; Goldsmith & Campos, 1982).

One of the most studied theories of temperament, especially as it relates to risk factors for psychopathology, is based on a model of approach and withdrawal by Jerome Kagan and his colleagues. In a series of studies beginning in the mid-1980s, Kagan and his colleagues described individual variation in children's responses to novel situations (Garcia-Coll et al., 1984; Kagan, Reznick, Clarke, Snidman, & Garcia-Coll, 1984; Kagan, Reznick, & Gibbons, 1989; Kagan, Reznick, & Snidman, 1987, 1988; Kagan, Reznick, Snidman, Gibbons, & Johnson, 1988; Reznick, Kagan, Snidman, Gersten, Baak, & Rosenberg, 1986). Kagan and his research group found that some children responded to novel social and nonsocial situations with fear and wariness while other children approached these situations with positive affect and high rates of exploratory behaviors. Based on these observations, two mutually exclusive categorizations of children were developed to describe individual differences in temperament: behaviorally inhibited and behaviorally uninhibited (Garcia-Coll et al., 1984). Between 10 to 15% of Caucasian children meet the criteria for behavioral inhibition (Kagan et al., 1988).

The evaluation of children as behaviorally inhibited or uninhibited was completed by observing children's responses at 2 years of age to a variety of age-appropriate social and nonsocial situations, including an unfamiliar adult and a robot that talked and walked (Garcia-Coll et al., 1984), completion of cognitive tasks with an unfamiliar experimenter and interaction with an unfamiliar peer in a play setting at 4 years of age (Kagan et al., 1984), engaging in a number of risk-taking behaviors such as walking on a beam or crawling through a tunnel at 5 ½ years of age (Reznick et al., 1986), and interacting in a play group consisting of 8 to 10 same-aged, same-sex peers at 7 ½ years of age (Kagan et al., 1988). Behaviors characteristic of inhibition in these situations were withdrawal, high rates of fretting and crying, long latencies to approach the object or individual, long latencies to communicate verbally, high levels of proximity to the mother, high levels of on looking behaviors, and high rates of facial expressions of distress (Garcia-Coll et al., 1984). In looking for early indicators of behavioral inhibition during the first year of life, Kagan and Snidman (1991) found that children who at 4 months of age showed high levels of motor activity and fretting in response to visual and auditory stimuli were significantly more likely to be rated as behaviorally inhibited at 9 and 14 months of age compared to children who at 4 months of age showed low levels of motor activity and fretting in response to the stimuli.

In addition to the observed behavioral characteristics that define both groups, researchers have also found a number of physiological correlates at baseline and in response to challenge situations that distinguish both groups. Kagan and colleagues (1988) found that in response to cognitive stress, behaviorally inhibited children had higher increases in heart rate, skeletal muscle tension, and pupillary dilations. More recent research has shown that at rest, behaviorally inhibited individuals have greater relative right frontal EEG activity as infants (Calkins, Fox, & Marshall, 1996), children (Fox et al., 1995; Fox, Henderson, Rubin, Calkins, & Schmidt, 2001), and adults (Schmidt, 1999), high and more stable heart rates (Kagan et al., 1984; Kagan et al., 1987, 1988, Reznick et al., 1986; Scarpa, Raine, Venables, & Mednick, 1997), and elevated basal morning cortisol (Kagan et al., 1988; Schmidt et al., 1997) as children than uninhibited individuals. The same psychophysiological and neuroendocrine patterns are seen in behaviorally inhibited children in response to challenge situations, such as the presentation of fear-eliciting videos in 4-year olds (Theall-Honey & Schmidt, 2006), and the completion of a task meant to evoke self-presentation anxiety in 7 year olds (Schmidt, Fox, Schulkin, & Gold, 1999). These psychophysiological and neuroendocrine patterns in response to stress still appear in behaviorally inhibited and shy adults (Schmidt, 1999; Schmidt & Fox, 1994).

The aforementioned physiological characteristics are associated with behavioral inhibition but, at this point in time, it is not possible to state whether they are correlates of the behavioral characteristics of behavioral inhibition or if they are biological precursors to the development of behavioral inhibition. One theory that has been proposed is that the behavioral and physiological responses that characterize behaviorally inhibited individuals and distinguish them from behaviorally uninhibited individuals are due to differences in the response of the amygdala brain area to novelty. In a recent study, Schwartz and colleagues (2003) used functional magnetic resonance imaging (fMRI) to study differences in amygdala activity in response to novel stimuli in young adults who at 2 years of age were classified as either behaviorally inhibited or uninhibited. The authors found that in response to novel faces, the behaviorally inhibited group had significantly more activity in the left and right amydala compared to the behaviorally uninhibited group while there were no differences between the groups in response to familiar faces (Schwartz, Wright, Shin, Kagan, & Rauch, 2003). Although these results need to be interpreted with caution given that amygdala activity was measured at one time point thus making it impossible to determine whether this pattern of activity was present throughout development, these findings do provide preliminary evidence for the hypothesis that differences in amygdala activity may be one of the key biological factors that underlie the two temperamental categories. We have recently replicated the findings by Schwartz et al. (2003) using event-related fMRI in young adults who were classified as contemporaneously temperamentally shy (Beaton, Schmidt, Schulkin, Antony, Swinson, & Hall, 2008).

Given the behavioral and psychophysiological characteristics of behavioral inhibition, and the findings that variations in behavioral inhibition are implicated as having a role in the later development of internalizing and externalizing disorders (Kaufman & Kagan, 2005), the question of the stability of behavioral inhibition is essential. The longitudinal studies conducted by Kagan and colleagues suggest that behavioral inhibition is moderately stable.

At age four, there was moderate stability of behavioral inhibition from 21 months, with those children who had high and stable resting heart rates when completing cognitive tests at 21 months of age more likely to still be behaviorally inhibited at age four than those with low and variable resting heart rates. Children who were behaviorally inhibited at age 4 were more cautious when playing with an unfamiliar child both when the child had the same temperamental style, and a different temperamental style, and showed higher latencies and greater resistance towards approaching and going through a tunnel (Kagan et al., 1984). At 5 ½ years of age, 78% of the children who were classified as behaviorally inhibited at 21 months were still behaviorally inhibited. The behaviorally inhibited children spent more time looking at their peers during free play and at the examiner when completing the testing and were more likely to show caution when placed in a situation that involved risk-taking (Reznick et al., 1986). At 7 ½ years of age, 75% of the children who were originally identified as behaviorally inhibited at 21 months of age still showed behaviors characteristic of inhibition, including a higher latency to speak and overall lower frequencies of verbalization with the examiner as well as maintaining a greater distance between themselves and other unfamiliar children during free play (Kagan et al., 1988). The children who showed extreme behavioral inhibition scores at 21 months of age were more likely to still be behaviorally inhibited at 7 ½ years of age, while those children who changed their style were those who had less extreme behavioral inhibition scores. When the children were again seen at 13 years of age, the quality of the behaviors of the children who were rated as behaviorally inhibited at 7 ½ years of age had not changed and two-thirds of the children who had been rated as behaviorally inhibited at 7 ½ years of age were still rated as behaviorally inhibited (Schwartz et al., 1999). In sum, behavioral inhibition is moderately stable throughout the preschool and school ages years, with more extreme levels of behavioral inhibition related to higher levels of stability.

Social Phobia

Social phobia is characterized by a persistent and extreme fear of one or more situations that involve interactions with unfamiliar individuals and the possibility of evaluation and scrutiny by others (APA, 2000). The situations that individuals with social phobia find distressing can be divided into two categories: performance and social (Morris, 2001). Performance situations are ones where the individual is expected to do something in front of others, such as giving a speech, reading out loud, or engaging in some type of athletic activity. On the other hand, social situations are ones where the individual is expected to interact with others, such as meeting new people and initiating conversations (Morris, 2001). Individuals with social phobia will either avoid or endure distressing levels of anxiety in one or both of these types of situations.

Social phobia is the third most prevalent disorder after depressive disorder and alcohol dependence (Kessler et al., 1994). Although there is variability in the reported prevalence rate due to the use of different diagnostic tools and the assessment of different populations, the US National Comorbidity Survey found that the lifetime prevalence of social phobia, as defined by the 3rd edition of the Diagnostic and Statistical Manual (DSM), is 13.3% (Kessler et al., 1994). The mean age of diagnosis appears to be at 15 years of age (Schneier, Johnson, Hornig, Liebowitz, & Weissman, 1992), although social phobia can be diagnosed as early as 8 years of age (Beidel & Turner, 1998). A diagnosis after 25 years of age is rare. Social phobia is associated with significant functional impairment across a number of domains, including social, educational, and occupational, especially if not identified and treated (Turner et al., 1986).

Starting with the 4th edition of the DSM, social phobia has been dichotomized into two subtypes: generalized social anxiety disorder and specific social anxiety disorder. Specific social anxiety disorder is characterized by extreme fear of one or a few specific situations while generalized social anxiety disorder is defined by extreme fear of most social and performance situations. Generalized social anxiety disorder has an earlier age of onset, greater functional impairment and higher rates of comorbidity (Bruch & Heimberg, 1994; Turner, Beidel, & Townsley, 1992). Given the high prevalence rate of social phobia, its early age of onset, and its association with serious functional impairment, the identification of early risk factors for social phobia is crucial.

Researchers have suggested a number of factors that may increase children's risk for social phobia, including genetics (i.e., having a parent with social phobia or another anxiety disorder), overprotective and over controlling parenting, and temperament (see Elizabeth, King & Ollendick, 2004 and Elizabeth et al., 2006, for reviews). However, it is beyond the scope of this chapter to present a comprehensive review of the literature on each of the aforementioned risk factors. Accordingly, we will focus on temperament, specifically behavioral inhibition, as a risk factor for the development of social phobia.

Similarities between Behavioral Inhibition and Social Phobia

Researchers have identified a number of behavioral and physiological similarities between behavioral inhibition and social phobia. From a behavioral perspective, both children with behavioral inhibition and individuals with social phobia show wariness and the tendency to exhibit high latencies to approach and verbalize with unfamiliar individuals (Beidel, Turner, & Morris, 1999; Henderson, 1997). Some researchers have also found psychophysiological similarities between behaviorally inhibited individuals and individuals with social phobia. For example, a number of studies have found that individuals with social phobia, much like behaviorally inhibited individuals, show higher heart rates in response to a social stressor (Davidson, Marshall, Tomarken, & Henriques, 2000; Johansson & Ost, 1982, but not Edelmann & Baker, 2002). Given these behavioral and physiological similarities, it is not surprising that for the last two decades, researchers have investigated the link between behavioral inhibition and anxiety disorders, with a special focus on social phobia.

BEHAVIORAL INHIBITION AS A PRECURSOR TO SOCIAL PHOBIA

Much of the research investigating the relation between behavioral inhibition and anxiety disorders has utilized three independent samples of children. Two of these samples involve clinical, cross-sectional populations of children whose parents had a diagnosis of panic disorder with agoraphobia (PDAG) with or without major depression (Rosenbaum et al., 1988; Rosenbaum et al., 2000). The third sample is a nonclinical longitudinal sample of children identified as behaviorally inhibited at 21 months of age and followed through childhood to 7 years of age (Garcia-Coll et al., 1984).

In a series of studies initiated twenty years ago, Rosenbaum and his research group (1988) investigated the link between behavioral inhibition and anxiety disorders. The researchers used a sample of 56 children between the ages of 2 and 7 years whose parents were classified into one of the following groups: panic disorder with or without agoraphobia (PDAG), major depressive disorder (MDD), PDAG and MDD, or psychiatric control (no PDAG or MDD but receiving treatment for a different disorder such as substance abuse or generalized anxiety disorder; Rosenbaum et al., 1988). Children between the ages of 2 and 7 years were classified as behaviorally inhibited and not behaviorally inhibited based on age-appropriate laboratory protocols (Rosenbaum et al., 1988). Maternal interviews were conducted when the children were 4 years of age or older to assess the children for internalizing and externalizing problems (Biederman et al., 1990). Offspring of parents with PDAG with or without MDD had significantly higher rates of behavioral inhibition (84.6% and 70%, respectively) compared to offspring of parents who had no MDD or PDAG (15.4%; Rosenbaum et al., 1988). Compared to the children who were uninhibited, the behaviorally inhibited children had higher rates of multiple anxiety disorders (22.2% versus 0%) and overanxious disorder (27.8% versus 0%; Biederman et al., 1990) at a mean age of 5 ½ years. In a 3-year follow up, Biederman and colleagues (1993) found that the behaviorally inhibited children again had higher rates of multiple anxiety disorders and overanxious disorder. This series of studies suggests that in children at risk for future psychiatric difficulties, the presence of behavioral inhibition acts to increase the risk for anxiety disorders in general. It is important to note that all of the children were at an increased risk for psychopathology due to the presence of panic disorder and major depressive disorder in their parents. However, only the children who were also behaviorally inhibited went on to develop anxiety disorders, suggesting that behavioral inhibition acts as an additional risk factor on top of parental psychopathology.

More recent work by Rosenbaum and his research group using a cross-sectional methodology and a clinically derived sample of over 250 children suggests a specific link between behavioral inhibition and social phobia (Biederman et al., 2001; Hirshfeld-Becker et al., 2007). Children between the ages of 21 months and 6 years of age were observed in the laboratory in a number of age-appropriate tasks. Based on their performance on these tasks, they were classified as behaviorally inhibited or uninhibited (Rosenbaum et al., 2000). When the children were 6 years of age, the mothers were interviewed to assess the children for any internalizing or externalizing disorders (Biederman et al., 2001). Children whose parents had comorbid PDAG and MDD had a significantly higher rate of behavioral inhibition (29%)

than children whose parents did not have PDAG and MDD (12%; Rosenbaum et al., 2000). This association between parental PDAG and MDD and behavioral inhibition in the child was not explained by a variety of psychosocial factors that are often associated with familial psychiatric illnesses, including socioeconomic status, family intactness, number of siblings, gender, birth order, and conflict (Hirshfeld-Becker, Biederman, Faraone, Segool, Buchwald, & Rosenbaum, 2004). The behaviorally inhibited children had significantly higher rates of social anxiety disorder (which was comprised of social phobia and avoidant disorder; 17% versus 5%) and significantly higher rates of disruptive disorders (6% versus 20%) compared to the uninhibited children at a mean age of 6 years (Biederman et al., 2001).

In a 5-year follow-up study during which the children were an average age of ten years, there were no significant differences between the behaviorally inhibited and uninhibited children in terms of overall rates of anxiety, mood, and disruptive disorders (Hirshfeld-Becker et al., 2007). Children classified as behaviorally inhibited, however, were significantly more likely to have a lifetime rate of social anxiety disorder (28%) compared to uninhibited children (14%) and were more likely to have a new onset diagnosis of social phobia than uninhibited children (22% versus 8%; Hirshfeld-Becker et al., 2007).

The series of studies conducted by Rosenbaum and his research group suggest that children at risk for psychopathology due to a parental diagnosis of panic disorder with major depressive disorder are at an increased risk for the development of future anxiety disorders, especially social phobia. The specificity of the relation between behavioral inhibition and social phobia is brought into question due to the fact that in the first series of studies behavioral inhibition was found to be a general risk factor for anxiety disorders while in the more recent studies it was found to be a specific risk factor for social phobia.

There are two possible explanations for these differences. First, the larger sample size in the recent studies gave the researchers more power to detect group differences across different disorders. In the first series of studies, there were only 18 children who were behaviorally inhibited (Rosenbaum et al., 1988) while in the most recent studies there were 84 children who were behaviorally inhibited (Rosenbaum et al., 2000). Second, in the first series of studies, the 3rd edition of the revised Diagnostic and Statistical Manual (DSM-III-R; APA, 1987) was used as a basis for diagnosing children. Despite the fact that the DSM-III-R does provide criteria for diagnosing children with social phobia, children were rarely diagnosed as such and were more likely to be diagnosed with avoidant disorder or overanxious disorder (Mancini, 2001). It was not until the 4th edition of the DSM that the diagnosis of social phobia in children became more common. Consequently, none of the children were diagnosed with social phobia in the early work of Rosenbaum and his research group (1990), but behaviorally inhibited children had significantly higher rates of overanxious disorder. This result suggests that the differences between the earlier and more recent studies in the relation between behavioral inhibition and anxiety disorders may be more a reflection of the use of differing diagnostic tools rather than actual differences in the disorders.

The relation between behavioral inhibition and anxiety disorders has also been assessed using Kagan's original sample of 41 typically developing children identified as behaviorally inhibited and uninhibited at 21 months of age (Garcia-Coll et al., 1984). Children were classified into 4 groups (stable and unstable behaviorally inhibited and stable and unstable behaviorally uninhibited) based on whether they retained their original classification at 21 months of age and behaviorally inhibited or uninhibited profiles at the follow-up assessments conducted at 4, 5 ½, and 7 years of age (Hirshfeld et al., 1992). The parents of the children who were identified as stable behaviorally inhibited had significantly higher rates of multiple childhood anxiety disorders, childhood avoidant disorders, and continuing anxiety disorder, defined as an anxiety disorder that developed during childhood and continued into adulthood (Hirshfeld et al., 1992). In addition, those children identified as stable behaviorally inhibited had significantly higher rates of anxiety disorders, multiple anxiety disorders and phobic disorder compared to the other 3 groups at 7 ½ years of age. Furthermore, at 7 ½ years of age, regardless of the stability of behavioral inhibition, children who were behaviorally inhibited had significantly higher rates of multiple anxiety disorders and phobic disorder compared to behaviorally uninhibited children (Biederman et al., 1993) while at 13 years of age behaviorally inhibited children had significantly higher rates of generalized social anxiety disorder compared to behaviorally uninhibited children (Schwartz et al., 1999). Based on the study of typically developing children not selected for any familial history of psychiatric disorders, it appears that behavioral inhibition may be a risk factor for anxiety disorder, especially if the behavioral inhibition remains constant throughout development. That is, children who are consistently behaviorally inhibited during the first 7 years of post-natal life may be at an increased risk for the development of an anxiety disorder.

With the exception of the follow-up study when the children were 13 years of age, the studies conducted on Kagan's sample of typically developing children appear to suggest that behavioral inhibition is a general risk factor for the development of an anxiety disorder. A closer examination of the studies, however, provides some evidence that the risk may be specific to social phobia. The children in the studies were not assessed specifically for social phobia. However, the majority of the phobic disorders with which the children who were behaviorally inhibited endorsed at higher rates than behaviorally uninhibited children were phobias of social situations, such as fear of standing up and speaking in front of the class, fear of crowds, and fear of being called on in class (Biederman et al., 1990). Consequently, this provides preliminary evidence of a specific association between behavioral inhibition and social phobia in typically developing children.

The specificity of the relation has been further supported by a retrospective study by Mick and Telch (1998) in which retrospective reports of childhood behavioral inhibition were significantly related to diagnoses of social phobia but not generalized anxiety disorder in a sample of undergraduate students. Furthermore, a number of studies have parsed the definition of behavioral inhibition into two categories and have found a significant, specific relation between behavioral inhibition and social phobia (Hayward, Killen, Kraemer, & Taylor, 1998; van Amerigen, Mancini, & Oakman, 1998). Kagan's original definition of behavioral inhibition encompassed a wariness and fearfulness towards both social and nonsocial situations (Garcia-Coll et al., 1984; Kagan et al., 1984). Given that social phobia is defined as an extreme fear of social situations that involves unfamiliar individuals (APA, 2000), it is possible that the relation between behavioral inhibition and social phobia would be clearer if there was a distinction made between fearfulness toward social and nonsocial situations. Reznick and his colleagues (1992) investigated this idea by decomposing behavioral inhibition into two distinct categories: fearfulness and social withdrawal. These two categories are defined, respectively, as a general fearfulness toward nonsocial situations and a fear toward social and school situations. To date, two studies have found significant specific relations between behavioral inhibition and social phobia parsing the concept of behavioral inhibition into these two categories.

Hayward and colleagues (1998) studied over 2000 typically developing adolescents with a mean age of 15 years. The adolescents completed a retrospective measure of behavioral inhibition and were assessed for the presence of social phobia and depression. The social avoidance scale significantly predicted the onset of social phobia during adolescence while the fearfulness scale was significantly associated with both social phobia and depression. Furthermore, those individuals who were rated high on both social avoidance and fearfulness had a 4 times greater risk for the development of social phobia compared to individuals who did not have either of these two features (Hayward et al., 1998).

Similar results have been reported by van Ameringen and colleagues (1998) using a sample of 225 patients who presented at an anxiety clinic with one of the following primary diagnoses: social phobia, panic disorder with or without agoraphobia, and obsessive compulsive disorder. The authors found that patients with social phobia scored significantly higher than patients with one of the other primary diagnoses on the social avoidance subscale of the retrospective behavioral inhibition measure, thus suggesting that the social avoidance subscale is the strongest predictor of social phobia (van Ameringen et al., 1998).

There are a number of methodological differences between the studies discussed above. These include: 1) different samples, including clinical and non-clinical samples of children, adolescents, and adults; 2) different study designs, including longitudinal, cross-sectional, and retrospective; and 3) varying methods for the assessment of behavioral inhibition, including direct observation and retrospective self-report. Despite these methodological differences, the findings from the studies do converge to suggest a relation between behavioral inhibition and social phobia. Although some have suggested that behavioral inhibition may be a general risk factor for psychopathology given that past studies have found significant relations between behavioral inhibition and depression (Kochanska, 1991; Muris, Meesters, & Spinder, 2003; Muris, Merckelbach, Wessel, & van de Ven, 1999; Neal, Edelmann, & Glachan, 2002; Reznick, Hegeman, Kaufman, Woods, & Jacobs, 1992), this hypothesis has been challenged by Muris and colleagues (2001) and Gladstone and colleagues (2005).

Structural equation modeling illustrated that the relation between behavioral inhibition and depression was indirect such that behavioral inhibition was directly related to the development of anxiety, which then increased the risk for the development of depression (Muris, Merckelbach, Schmidt, Gadet, & Bogie, 2001). In a study of one-hundred eighty-nine adults with major depressive disorder, retrospective measures of childhood behavioral inhibition revealed that individuals with high levels of behavioral inhibition were significantly more likely to meet the diagnostic criteria for social phobia compared to individuals with depression who had low levels of behavioral inhibition even when factors such as retrospectively reported parental control, neuroticism and extroversion were taken into consideration (Gladstone, Parker, Mitchell, Wilhelm, & Malhi, 2005). Furthermore, there were no differences in depression severity between individuals who reported high and low levels of childhood behavioral inhibition (Gladstone et al., 2005). Accordingly, a review of the current literature does appear to point toward a direct relation between behavioral inhibition and social phobia.

Despite this relation, however, it is important to remember that behavioral inhibition is not required for the development of social phobia. Consistent with the concept of equifinality, there are a number of developmental pathways that can lead to the same outcome. With regards to social phobia, the factors that are involved in the development of social phobia, include parenting, parental personality, familial characteristics, traumatic childhood experiences, and peer relationships (see Elizabeth et al., 2004; Elizabeth et al., 2006; Manassis, Hudson, Webb, & Albano, 2004, for reviews). Not only do these factors individually determine the mental health of the developing child, but they also interact with one another creating multiplicative effects of risk and resiliency.

It is also important to keep in mind that, consistent with the idea of multifinality, the same developmental pathways can lead to different outcomes. This idea is clearly seen in the research on the link between behavioral inhibition and social phobia, as the presence of behavioral inhibition is not a guarantee for the later development of social phobia. For instance, in the study by Biederman and colleagues (2001), only 17% of behaviorally inhibited children developed social phobia by age 5 to 6 years while in the study by Schwartz and colleagues (1999), 33% of behaviorally inhibited children developed social phobia by 13 to 14 years of age. Thus, although behavioral inhibition, especially if it is consistently present throughout development or is present in offspring who are at risk due to parental diagnoses of panic disorder, can increase the risk for social phobia, it is not a perfect predictor of social phobia. The question that remains to be answered is what factors interact with behavioral inhibition to determine whether and how behavioral inhibition leads to the development of social phobia.

To the best of our knowledge, only two studies to date have attempted to answer this question (Brozina & Abela, 2006; Muris & Meesters, 2002). Using retrospective measures of behavioral inhibition and attachment in a sample of 280 young adolescents aged 11 to 15 years of age, Muris and Meesters (2002) found that behavioral inhibition and attachment style were interrelated such that high levels of behavioral inhibition were associated with insecure attachment while low levels of behavioral inhibition were associated with secure attachment. Further, self-report measures of anxiety and depressive disorders revealed that both behavioral inhibition and attachment style were significantly related to anxiety symptoms and accounted for unique proportions of the variance associated with anxiety symptoms. Although we cannot deduce causation from the results due to the correlational nature of the study, the results do suggest that mother-child interactions and temperament provide unique contributions to the development of social phobia. Consequently, a child who is insecurely attached with his/her mother and who is behaviorally inhibited may have an increased risk for the development of social phobia than a child who only has one of these risk factors (i.e., only behavioral inhibition or only insecure attachment).

Using a short-term prospective design, Brozina and Abela (2006) investigated changes in anxious and depressive symptoms in a sample of over 300 children in grades 3 though 6 over a 6-week period. The authors found that only children who were behaviorally inhibited (as determined through self-report) and reported high levels of daily stressors had increased anxiety symptoms at the 6-week follow-up assessment. Children who were behaviorally inhibited and reported low levels of daily stressors as well as children who were not behaviorally inhibited regardless of the reported level of daily stressors had decreased levels of anxious symptoms. There were no relations between behavioral inhibition and daily stressors in predicting depressive symptoms (Brozina & Abela, 2006). These results provide preliminary evidence that a combination of behavioral inhibition and life stressors may place children who are behaviorally inhibited at an increased risk for anxiety.

To further ascertain this relation, studies with longer follow-up periods and more specific assessments of anxiety (i.e., distinguishing between the different types of anxiety disorders) need to be completed. As well, as discussed by Brozina and Abela (2006), future studies need to look at other possible risk factors that may interact with behavioral inhibition to determine social anxiety, including but not limited to, parental pressures to socialize, negative learning experiences, insecure attachment, and failed social relationships. Research into possible resiliency factors would also greatly strengthen this area of knowledge.

Clinical Implications and Conclusion

Based on the research to date, it is not entirely clear whether behavioral inhibition is a risk factor for social phobia or an early manifestation of the disorder. Despite this ambiguity in the actual relation, what is clear is that behavioral inhibition can be reliably measured early in life before the diagnosis of social phobia and is a sign of a statistically increased risk for the future development of social phobia (Hirshfeld-Becker, Biederman, Calltharp, Rosenbaum, Farone, & Rosenbaum, 2003). Thus, the link between behavioral inhibition and social phobia has implications for the manner in which social phobia is identified and treated. Hirshfeld-Becker and colleagues (2007) discussed a number of implications for the findings that behavioral inhibition is a risk factor for social phobia. First, children who show behavioral inhibition early in life (especially if there is a parental history of panic disorder or if the children remained behaviorally inhibited throughout development) should be monitored for signs of social phobia or social and educational impairment. Second, parents of behaviorally inhibited children should also be monitored for the presence of anxiety disorders, given that parents of behaviorally inhibited children do have an elevated risk for anxiety disorders, and these disorders can have a negative impact on the parenting experience of the child. Third, given the unique challenges that behaviorally inhibited children experience in novel situations, their parents should be educated on parenting approaches to enable them to empathize with the distress that their children experience while at the same time encouraging their children to gradually face their fears rather than rewarding avoidance behaviors. Even more, behaviorally inhibited children may benefit from short-term preventive cognitive behavioral therapy to learn the skills necessary to cope with their emotions and to learn strategies to help them face difficult situations. By identifying those children who are especially at risk for the development of social phobia, we can implement preventive measures to prevent them from developing social phobia as well as monitor their mental health development to ensure that if they do develop social phobia, it is identified and treated at an early stage to prevent functional impairment.

In order to increase the precision with which we can identify individuals at risk for social phobia based on behavioral inhibition, there is a need for future research to further ascertain and expand on this relation. Much of the research that has been done to date has used retrospective questionnaire approaches, asking individuals to self-report on their level of childhood behavioral inhibition. More studies that use a longitudinal approach and objectively derived behavioral measures, although understandably costly and time-consuming, would add credibility and strength to the findings. Second, there is variability across studies in the type of questionnaires that are used to assess behavioral inhibition and to determine diagnoses. Creating "gold standard" assessment questionnaires would facilitate comparisons across studies. Third, past studies have often used either general measures of anxiety (i.e., not differentiating among the anxiety disorders) or included a measure of functional impairment, using number of anxiety disorders as an outcome measure. Although there certainly are commonalities in the presentation, functional impairment, and treatment of anxiety disorders, differentiating among anxiety disorders is crucial to gain a further understanding of the specificity of the relation between behavioral inhibition and social phobia. Fourth, recent studies have suggested that the relation between behavioral inhibition and social phobia may be specific to fearfulness toward social situations and not towards nonsocial situations. The specificity of the relation needs to be further investigated and ascertained with the use of longitudinal studies. Lastly, as discussed above, it is essential that more studies investigate behavioral inhibition from a diathesis-stress approach, working to identify what factors interact with behavioral inhibition to increase the risk or resiliency for social phobia in children with behavioral inhibition.

In conclusion, the research to date appears to converge on a specific relation between behavioral inhibition and social phobia. Although more research needs to be conducted to identify the mechanism(s) by which behavioral inhibition increases risk for social phobia, it is clear that behavioral inhibition is a risk factor for social phobia. As such, behaviorally inhibited children should be monitored for the development of social phobia to allow early identification and treatment, if necessary, to prevent serious functional impairment.

ACKNOWLEDGEMENTS

The writing of this chapter was supported by a Predoctoral Scholarship from the Social Sciences and Humanities Research Council (SSHRC) of Canada awarded to the first author under the direction of the second author and Operating Grants from SSHRC and the Natural Sciences and Engineering Research Council (NSERC) of Canada awarded to the second author.

REFERENCES

American Psychiatric Association. (1987). *Diagnostic and statistical manual of mental disorders* (3rd ed., Revised (DSM-III-R). Washington, DC: American Psychiatric Press.

American Psychiatric Association. (2000). *Diagnostic and statistical manual of mental disorders* (4th ed., Text Revision (DSM-IV-TR). Washington, DC: American Psychiatric Press.

Bates, J.E. (1986). The measurement of temperament. In R. Plomin & J. Dunn (Eds), *The study of temperament: Changes, continuities and challenges* (pp. 1-11). Hillsdale, NJ: Erlbaum.

Beaton, E.A., Schmidt, L.A., Schulkin, J., Antony, M.M., Swinson, R.P., & Hall, G.B. (2008). Different neural responses to stranger and personally familiar faces in shy and bold adults. *Behavioral Neuroscience, 122*, 704-709.

Beidel, D.C., & Turner, S.M. (1998). *Shy children, phobic adults: Nature and treatment of social phobia.* Washington, DC: American Psychological Association.

Beidel, D.C., Turner, S.M., & Morris, T.L. (1999). Psychopathology of childhood social phobia. *Journal of the American Academy of Child and Adolescent Psychiatry, 38*, 643-650.

Biederman, J., Hirshfeld-Becker, D.R., Rosenbaum, J.F., Herot, C., Friedman, D., Snidman, N., Kagan, J., & Faraone, S.V. (2001). Further evidence of association between behavioral inhibition and social anxiety in children. *American Journal of Psychiatry, 158*, 1673-1679.

Biederman, J., Rosenbaum, J.F., Bolduc-Murphy, E.A., Faraone, S.V., Chaloff, J., Hirshfeld, D.R., & Kagan, J. (1993). A 3-year follow-up of children with and without behavioral inhibition. *Journal of the American Academy of Child and Adolescent Psychiatry, 32*, 814-821.

Biederman, J., Rosenbaum, J.F., Hirshfeld, D.R., Faraone, S.V., Bolduc, E.A., Gersten, M., Meminger, S.R., Kagan, J., Snidman, N., & Reznick, S. (1990). Psychiatric correlates of behavioral inhibition in young children of parents with and without psychiatric disorders. *Archives of General Psychiatry, 47*, 21-26.

Brozina, K., & Abela, J.R.Z. (2006). Behavioral inhibition, anxious symptoms, and depressive symptoms: A short-term prospective examination of a diathesis-stress model. *Behaviour Research and Therapy, 44*, 1337-1346.

Bruch, M.A., & Heimberg, R.G. (1994). Differences in perceptions of parental and personal characteristics between generalized and nongeneralized social phobics. *Journal of Anxiety Disorders, 8*, 155-168.

Buss, A.H., & Plomin, R. (1984). *Temperament: Early developing personality traits.* Hillsdale, NJ: Erlbaum.

Calkins, S.D., Fox, N.A., & Marshall, T.R. (1996). Behavioral and physiological antecedents of inhibited and uninhibited behavior. *Child Development, 67*, 523-540.

Chess, S., & Thomas, A. (1984). *Origins and evolution of behavior disorders.* New York: Brunner/Mazel, Inc.

Davidson, R.J., Marshall, J.R., Tomarken, A.J., & Henriques, J.B. (2000). While a phobic waits: Regional brain electrical and autonomic activity in social phobics during anticipation of public speaking. *Biological Psychiatry, 47*, 85-95.

Edelmann, R.J., & Baker, S.R. (2002). Self-reported and actual physiological responses in social phobia. *British Journal of Clinical Psychology, 41*, 1-14.

Elizabeth, J., King, N., & Ollendick, T.H. (2004). Etiology of social anxiety disorder in children and youth. *Behavior Change, 21*, 162-172.

Elizabeth, J., King, N., Ollendick, T.H., Gullone, E., Tonge, B., Watson, S., & Macdermott, S. (2006). Social anxiety disorder in children and youth: A research update on aetiological factors. *Counselling Psychology Quarterly, 19*, 151-163.

Fox, N.A., Henderson, H.A., Rubin, K.H., Calkins, S.D., & Schmidt, L.A. (2001). Continuity and discontinuity of behavioral inhibition and exuberance: Psychophysiological and behavioral influences across the first four years of life. *Child Development, 72*, 1-21.

Fox, N.A., Rubin, K.H., Calkins, S.D., Marshall, T.R., Coplan, R.J., Porges, S.W., Long, J.M., & Stewart, S. (1995). Frontal activation asymmetry and social competence at four years of age. *Child Development, 66*, 1770-1784.

Garcia-Coll, C., Kagan, J., & Reznick, S. (1984). Behavioral inhibition in young children. *Child Development, 55*, 1005-1019.

Gladstone, G.L., Parker, G.B., Mitchell, P.B., Wilhelm, K.A., & Malhi, G.S. (2005). Relationship between self-reported childhood behavioral inhibition and lifetime anxiety disorders in a clinical sample. *Depression and Anxiety, 22*, 103-113.

Goldsmith, H.H., Buss, A.H., Plomin, R., Rothbart, M.K., Thomas, A., Chess, S., Hinde, R.A., & McCall, R.B. (1987). Roundtable: What is temperament? Four approaches. *Child Development, 58*, 505-529.

Goldsmith, H.H., & Campos, J.J. (1982). Toward a theory of infant temperament. In R.N. Emde & R.J. Harmon (Eds.), *The development of attachment and affiliative systems*. New York: Plenum.

Hayward, C., Killen, J.D., Kraemer, H.C., & Taylor, B.C. (1998). Linking self-reported childhood behavioral inhibition to adolescent social phobia. *Journal of the American Academy of Child and Adolescent Psychiatry, 37*, 1308-1316.

Henderson, L. (1997). Mean MMPI profile of referrals to a shyness clinic. *Psychological Reports, 80*, 695-702,

Hirshfeld-Becker, D.R., Biederman, J., Calltharp, S., Rosenbaum, E.D., Faraone, S.V., & Rosenbaum, J.F. (2003). Behavioral inhibition and disinhibition as hypothesized precursors to psychopathology: Implications for pediatric bipolar disorder. *Biological Psychiatry, 53*, 985-999.

Hirshfeld-Becker, D.R., Biederman, J., Faraone, S.V., Segool, N., Buchwald, J., & Rosenbaum, J.F. (2004). Lack of association between behavioral inhibition and psychosocial adversity factors in children at risk for anxiety disorders. *American Journal of Psychiatry, 161*, 547-555.

Hirshfeld-Becker, D.R., Biederman, J., Henin, A., Faraone, S.V., Davis, S., Harrington, K., & Rosenbaum, J.F. (2007). Behavioral inhibition in preschool children at risk is a specific predictor of middle childhood social anxiety: A five-year follow-up. *Journal of Developmental and Behavioral Pediatrics, 28*, 225-233.

Hirshfeld, D.R., Rosenbaum, J.F., Biederman, J., Bolduc, E.A., Faraone, S.V., Snidman, N., Reznick, S.J., & Kagan, J. (1992). Stable behavioral inhibition and its association with anxiety disorder. *Journal of the American Academy of Child and Adolescent Psychiatry, 31*, 103-111.

Johansson, J., & Ost, L.G. (1982). Perception of autonomic reactions and actual heart rate in phobic patients. *Journal of Behavioral Assessment, 4*, 133-143.

Kagan, J., Reznick, S.J., Clarke, C., Snidman, N., & Garcia-Coll, C. (1984). Behavioral inhibition to the unfamiliar. *Child Development, 55*, 2212-2225.

Kagan, J., Reznick, S.J., & Gibbons, J. (1989). Inhibited and uninhibited types of children. *Child Development, 60*, 838-845.

Kagan, J., Reznick, J.S., & Snidman, N. (1987). The physiology and psychology of behavioral inhibition in children. *Child Development, 58*, 1459-1473.

Kagan, J., Reznick, S.J., & Snidman, N. (1988). Biological bases of childhood shyness. *Science, 240*, 167-171.

Kagan, J., Reznick, S.J., Snidman, N., Gibbons, J., Johnson, M.O. (1988). Childhood derivatives of inhibition and lack of inhibition to the unfamiliar. *Child Development, 59*, 1580-1589.

Kagan, J., & Snidman, N. (1991). Infant predictors of inhibited and uninhibited profiles. *Psychological Science, 2*, 40-44.

Kagan, J. & Snidman, N. (1999). Early childhood predictors of adult anxiety disorders. *Biological Psychiatry, 46*, 1536-1541.

Kaufman, S.E., & Kagan, J. (2005). Infant predictors of kindergarten behavior: The contribution of inhibited and uninhibited temperament styles. *Behavioral Disorders, 30*, 331-347.

Kessler, R.C., McGonagle, K.A., Zhao, S., Nelson, C.B., Hughes, M., Eshelman, S., Wittchen, H., & Kendler, K.S. (1994). Lifetime and 12-month prevalence of DSM-III-R psychiatric disorders in the United States. *Archives of General Psychiatry, 51*, 8-19.

Kochanska, G. (1991). Patterns of inhibition to the unfamiliar in children of normal and affectively ill mothers. *Child Development, 62*, 250-263.

Manassis, K., Hudson, J.L., Webb, A., & Albano, A.M. (2004). Beyond behavioral inhibition: Etiological factors in childhood anxiety. *Cognitive and Behavioral Practice, 11*, 3-12.

Mancini, C. (2001, May). *Social phobia in children and adolescents*. Canadian Psychological Association Bulletin, Retrieved May 14 2008 from: http://ww1.cpa-apc.org:8080/Publications/Archives/Bulletin/2001/May/Social.asp

Mick, M.A., & Telch, M.J. (1998). Social anxiety and history of behavioral inhibition in young adults. *Journal of Anxiety Disorders, 12*, 1-20.

Morris, T.L. (2001). Social phobia. In M.W. Vasey, & M.R. Dadds (Eds), *Anxiety disorders in children and adolescents* (2nd ed., pp. 59-70), New York: Guildford Press.

Muris, P., & Meesters, C. (2002). Attachment, behavioral inhibition, and anxiety disorder symptoms in normal adolescents. *Journal of Psychopathology and Behavioral Assessment, 24*, 97-106.

Muris, P., Meesters, C., & Spinder, M. (2003). Relationships between child- and parent-reported behavioral inhibition and symptoms of anxiety and depression in normal adolescents. *Personality and Individual Differences, 34*, 759-771.

Muris, P., Merckelbach, H., Schmidt, H., Gadet, B., & Bogie, N. (2001). Anxiety and depression as correlates of self-reported behavioral inhibition in normal adolescents. *Behavior Research and Therapy, 39*, 1051-1061.

Muris, P., Merckelbach, H., Wessel, I., & van de Ven, M. (1999). Psychopathological correlates of self-reported behavioral inhibition in normal children. *Behaviour Research and Therapy, 17*, 575-584.

Neal, J.A., Edelmann, R.J., & Glachan, M. (2002). Behavioral inhibition and symptoms of anxiety and depression: Is there a specific relationship with social phobia? *British Journal of Clinical Psychology, 41*, 361-374.

Reznick, J.S., Hegeman, I.M., Kaufman, E., Woods, S.W., & Jacobs, M. (1992). Retrospective and concurrent self-report of behavioral inhibition and their relation to adult mental health. *Developmental Psychopathology, 4*, 301-321.

Reznick, S.J., Kagan, J., Snidman, N., Gersten, M., Baak, K., & Rosenberg, A. (1986). Inhibited and uninhibited children: A follow-up study. *Child Development, 57*, 660-680.

Rosenbaum, J.F., Biederman, J., Gersten, M., Hirshfeld, D.R., Meminger, S.R., Herman, J.B., Kagan, J., Reznick, S., & Snidman, N. (1988). Behavioral inhibition in children of parents with panic disorder and agoraphobia: A controlled study. *Archives of General Psychiatry, 45*, 463-470.

Rosenbaum, J.F., Biederman, J., Hirshfeld-Becker, D.R., Kagan, J., Snidman, N., Friedman, D., Ninberg, A., Gallery, D.J., & Faraone, S.V. (2000). A controlled study of behavioral inhibition in children of parents with panic disorder and depression. *American Journal of Psychiatry, 157*, 2002-2010.

Scarpa, A., Raine, A., Venables, P.H., & Mednick, S.A. (1997). Heart rate and skin conductance in behaviorally inhibited Mauritian children. *Developmental Psychobiology, 30*, 127-140.

Schmidt, L.A. (1999). Frontal brain electrical activity in shyness and sociability. *Psychological Science, 10*, 316-320.

Schmidt, L.A. & Fox, N.A. (1994). Patterns of cortical electrophysiology and autonomic activity in adults' shyness and sociability. *Biological Psychology, 38*, 183-198.

Schmidt, L.A., Fox, N.A., Rubin, K.H., Sternberg, E.M., Gold, P.W., Smith, C.C., & Schulkin, J. (1997). Behavioral and neuroendocrine responses in shy children. *Developmental Psychobiology, 30*, 127-140.

Schmidt, L.A., Fox, N.A., Schulkin, J., & Gold, P.W. (1999). Behavioral and psychophysiological correlates of self-presentation in temperamentally shy children. *Developmental Psychobiology, 35*, 119-135.

Schneier, F.R., Johnson, J., Hornig, C.D., Liebowitz, M.R., & Weissman, M.M. (1992). Social phobia: Comorbidity and morbidity in an epidemiologic sample. *Archives of General Psychiatry, 49*, 282-288.

Schwartz, C.E., Snidman, N., & Kagan, J. (1999). Adolescent social anxiety as an outcome of inhibited temperament in childhood. *Journal of the American Academy of Child and Adolescent Psychiatry, 38*, 1008-1015.

Schwartz, C.E., Wright, C.I., Shin, L.M., Kagan, J., & Rauch, S.L. (2003). Inhibited and uninhibited infants 'grown up': Adult amygdalar response to novelty. *Science, 20*, 1952-1953.

Theall-Honey, L.A., & Schmidt, L.A. (2006). Do temperamentally shy children process emotion differently than non-shy children? Behavioral, psychophysiological, and gender differences in reticent preschoolers. *Developmental Psychobiology, 48*, 187-196.

Thomas, A., & Chess, S. (1977). *Temperament and development.* New York, NY: Brunner/Mazel, Inc.

Thomas, A., Chess, S., Birch, H.G., Hertzig, M.E., & Korn, S. (1963). *Behavioral inhibition in early childhood.* New York, NY: New York University Press.

Turner, S.M., Beidel, D.C., Dancu, C.V., & Keys, D.J. (1986). Psychopathology of social phobia and comparison to avoidant personality disorder. *Journal of Abnormal Psychology, 95*, 389-394.

Turner, S.M., Beidel, D.C., & Townsley, R.M. (1992). Social phobia: A comparison to specific and generalized subtypes and avoidant personality disorder. *Journal of Abnormal Psychology, 101*, 326-331.

Van Ameringen, M., Mancini, C., & Oakman, J.M. (1998). The relationship of behavioral inhibition and shyness to anxiety disorder. *The Journal of Nervous and Mental Disease, 186*, 425-431.

In: Social Phobia: Etiology, Diagnosis and Treatment
Editor: Clayton P. Axelby
ISBN 978-1-60692-159-3
© 2009 Nova Science Publishers, Inc.

Chapter X

SOCIAL ANXIETY DISORDER: ETIOLOGY, DIAGNOSIS, AND TREATMENT

Kelsey C. Collimore and Gordon J. G. Asmundson**[*]**
Department of Psychology, University of Regina, Regina, Saskatchewan, Canada.

ABSTRACT

Social anxiety disorder (SAD; also called social phobia) is characterized by an intense and persistent fear of one or more social or performance situations (e.g., public speaking, dating situations). People with SAD typically present with significant levels of distress and impairment, and greatly fear being judged negatively by others, or acting in a way that might be embarrassing. SAD has the lowest overall remission rate of all the major anxiety disorders (Massion et al., 2002), and is the fourth most common psychiatric disorder (Kessler, Berglund, Demler, Jin, & Walters, 2005). The purpose of this chapter is to provide an overview of the clinical features of SAD, and to highlight issues related to assessment and treatment. First, we discuss diagnostic and descriptive characteristics of SAD, including a discussion on the epidemiology and course of the disorder. Second, we review etiological factors contributing to SAD, with a specific focus on environmental, genetic, and cognitive and behavioural processes. Third, we discuss assessment instruments and strategies, including information on clinical interviews and self-report measures. Fourth, we review empirically-supported treatments (e.g., cognitive-behavioural therapy) for SAD. Fifth, we note emerging trends in relatively unexplored issues pertaining to SAD. We conclude with a summary and a brief outline of issues that warrant future research attention.

[*] Correspondence concerning this article should be addressed to: Gordon J. G. Asmundson, Ph.D., Anxiety and Illness Behaviours Laboratory, Department of Psychology, University of Regina, Regina, Saskatchewan, S4S 0A2. Tel: (306) 347-2415; Fax: (306) 585-4854; E-mail: gordon.asmundson@uregina.ca.

INTRODUCTION

Social anxiety is the tendency to be anxious, nervous, or feel uncomfortable in social situations. People with high levels of social anxiety typically fear being judged negatively by other people, or acting in way that might be embarrassing (Antony & Swinson, 2000). The magnitude of social anxiety can differ from person to person, with some individuals experiencing mild (i.e., tolerable or manageable) anxiety in social situations, and others finding their fear completely overwhelming. Some people may be uncomfortable in formal situations (e.g., meetings), but more comfortable in casual situations (e.g., parties) or vice versa (Hofmann, Heinrichs, & Moscovitch, 2004). Moreover, some individuals experience social anxiety in only select social situations, while others may be socially anxious in most or all social situations (Hofmann et al., 2004). In this chapter, we will discuss (a) diagnostic and descriptive features of social anxiety, (b) etiological factors contributing to social anxiety, (c) assessment strategies, (d) empirically-supported treatments, and (e) emerging research trends. We conclude with a summary and suggestions for future research.

DIAGNOSTIC AND DESCRIPTIVE FEATURES

Clinically significant expressions of social anxiety may develop into Social Anxiety Disorder (SAD; American Psychiatric Association [APA], 2000). SAD, also called social phobia, is defined by an intense and persistent fear of one or more social or performance situations (e.g., parties, formal speaking, participating in meetings). The most common fears involve possible scrutiny by others and fear of acting in a way that is embarrassing or humiliating. When exposed to the feared social situation, individuals with SAD almost always experience extreme anxiety, which may take the form of a panic attack. Individuals with SAD recognize that their fears in social situations are excessive or unreasonable. Nevertheless, the feared social situations are avoided or endured with intense anxiety or distress. To be diagnosed with SAD, the individual must find the fear markedly distressing or associated with interference in daily functioning. In persons younger than 18 years, symptoms must be present for at least six months. Finally, the anxiety symptoms cannot be due to the direct physiological effects of a substance or general medical condition, or better accounted for by another mental disorder. SAD, generalized subtype is specified if the individual is fearful of almost all social situations (APA, 2000). The generalized subtype affects approximately 50% of individuals suffering from SAD (Mannuzza et al., 1995) and is associated with poorer overall functioning and higher levels of depression (Boone et al., 1999; Tran & Chambless, 1995).

SAD has a lifetime prevalence of 7 to 13.3% (Furmark, 2002), and is the fourth most common psychiatric disorder following major depressive disorder, alcohol abuse, and specific phobia (Kessler et al., 2005). In the National Comorbidity Survey Replication, lifetime prevalence rate of SAD was 12.1%, and current (i.e., past 12 months) prevalence rate of SAD was 7.1% (Kessler et al., 2005). Similar prevalence rates for SAD have been found in other western nations, such as Australia and Canada (Iancu et al., 2006). Higher prevalence rates of SAD are found among women than among men (Kessler et al., 2005; Ruscio et al.,

2008); however, in clinical settings, prevalence rates between men and women are comparable or greater among men (APA, 2000; Barlow, 2002). SAD is present in countries that differ from western nations, such as Iran (Mohammadi, Ghanizadeh, Mohammadi, & Mesgarpour, 2006), although the presentation of SAD may differ across cultures (APA, 2000). For example, in Eastern cultures, Taijin Kyofusho is a form of SAD wherein the individual believes they make others feel uncomfortable (Matsunaga, Kiriike, Matsui, Iwasaki, & Stein, 2001; Stein & Stein, 2008).

Onset of SAD generally occurs during early to mid-teenage years (age 10 to 13) with most individuals reporting onset before age 18 (Nelson et al., 2000; Otto et al., 2001). SAD is often continuous and chronic (Rapee & Spence, 2004), and has the lowest overall remission rate of all major anxiety disorders (Massion et al., 2002).

ETIOLOGY

The causal mechanisms of SAD are not yet fully understood; however, empirical findings suggest that both genetic and environmental factors (e.g., negative life events) are implicated in its development (Rapee & Spence, 2004). A considerable amount of research has been conducted on maintenance factors for SAD (e.g., cognitive and behavioural processes), which has lead to effective treatments. Below we provide an overview of models that have been posited to explain the development and maintenance of SAD.

Diathesis-stress Model of SAD

Diathesis-stress models have been proposed to explain the development of anxiety disorders, including SAD (e.g., Barlow, 2002; Rapee & Spence, 2004). This model suggests that environmental factors interact with preexisting vulnerabilities (i.e., psychological and biological vulnerabilities) that lead to the development of emotional disorders (Barlow, 2002). Accordingly, it is plausible that several potential pathways and risk factors might eventually lead to the development of SAD (Rapee & Spence, 2004). Individuals with SAD may differ in their genetic makeup and life experiences that contributed to the development of the disorder. Furthermore, these etiological factors are probably not specific to SAD; rather, a particular combination of risk factors (i.e., diatheses) likely leads to SAD following one or more stressors. According to the model, genetic factors predispose an individual towards a given level of social anxiety. Environmental factors (e.g. parenting behaviour, aversive social outcomes, adverse life events) then influence changes in social anxiety expression.

There is evidence supporting the postulates of the diathesis-stress model for SAD. Support for a genetic component for SAD has come from several twin studies (e.g., Kendler, Neale, Kessler, Heath, & Eaves, 1992; Nelson et al., 2000). Concordance rates for generalized SAD in a sample of 2163 female twin pairs were approximately 24% in monozygotic (MZ) twins and 15% in dizygotic (DZ) twins (Kendler et al., 1992). This supports a significant genetic contribution to generalized SAD, with a heritability estimate of

30% (i.e., 30% of the differences observed between people were directly attributed to genetic differences between them). In a follow-up study, a larger genetic contribution to SAD was found (50%) when unreliable diagnostic interviews were statistically controlled (Kendler, Karkowski, & Prescott, 1999).

There is also empirical support for the role of negative life events as risk factors for developing SAD (Bandelow et al., 2004; Chartier, Walker, & Stein, 2001; Kessler, Davis, & Kendler, 1997; Magee, 1999). For example, sexual assault by a relative and marital conflict (e.g., verbal aggression) are uniquely associated with the onset of SAD (e.g., Magee, 1999), and divorce and sexual abuse are associated with the onset of anxiety disorders in general (Kessler et al. 1997). Persons with SAD also report higher rates of exposure to trauma compared to persons with obsessive-compulsive disorder (Fontanelle et al., 2007), and elevated rates of sexual and/or physical abuse relative to those with panic disorder (David, Giron, Mellman, 1995). In addition, persons with SAD report a significantly higher number of childhood risk factors relative to those without SAD, including childhood physical and sexual abuse, family violence, parental history of psychopathology, a history of no close personal relationship with an adult, dropping out of school, and juvenile justice system involvement (Bandelow et al., 2004; Chartier et al., 2001; Zhang, Ross, & Davidson, 2004).

Cognitive-behavioural Model of SAD

Cognitive-behavioural approaches to SAD, which describe cognitive and behavioural processes underlying social anxiety, explain how SAD is maintained over time. According to the most popular cognitive-behavioural model of SAD (Clark & Wells, 1995), cognitive processes contribute to the maintenance of social anxiety. People with excessive social anxiety have dysfunctional beliefs and assumptions about themselves and other people. For example, they demonstrate a strong motivation to make a positive impression on other people, and they believe that they are likely to act in a way that is perceived as inept or inappropriate. Another common belief of people with excessive social anxiety is that their behaviour in social situations will lead to catastrophic consequences (e.g., rejection, loss of status). Behaviourally, these beliefs and assumptions manifest into increased self-focused attention and a decrease in outward attention on other people and their surroundings. People with excessive social anxiety also use safety behaviours (e.g., avoiding eye contact, avoiding social situations) that are intended to prevent feared consequences. Hofmann (2007) recently presented a comprehensive cognitive-behavioural model of SAD. According to this model, people with SAD have unrealistic social standards and have difficulty selecting attainable social goals. In addition, such individuals tend to overestimate negative consequences associated with social situations, lack confidence in their social skills, and feel that they have little control over their emotional reactions.

Consistent with the cognitive-behavioural model, research suggests that people with excessive social anxiety are more likely to attend to and recall social threat information (e.g., see Williams, Mathews, & MacLeod, 1996). They are also more likely to overestimate the probability of negative social consequences and to exaggerate the costs associated with negative social outcomes, relative to healthy controls and persons with other anxiety disorders (Foa, Franklin, Perry, & Herbert, 1996; Gilboa-Schechtman, Franklin, & Foa, 2000; McManus,Clark, & Hackmann, 2000). It is beyond the intent and scope of this paper to comprehensively review the research stimulated by the cognitive-behavioural model of SAD. Interested readers are referred to recent reviews by Heinrichs and Hofmann (2001) and Schultz and Heimberg (2008).

ASSESSMENT

There are several different methods that can be used for the assessment of SAD. Most commonly, these include clinician-administered structured clinical interviews and self-report questionnaires. Below, we highlight details of specific assessment methods that may be useful in the context of assessing SAD. It is important to note, however, that in clinical practice, there may be several different purposes of the assessment process. Accordingly, different assessment strategies and tools may be used depending on the function of the assessment (Antony & Rowa, 2005). For example, the purpose of the assessment might be to establish a diagnosis of SAD, to measure the severity of social anxiety symptoms, or to measure treatment outcome [for a more comprehensive review of the functions of assessment see Antony and Rowa (2005)]. Thus, in determining which assessment tool or strategy to use, it is important to consider the purpose of the assessment.

We recommend the use of clinician-administered structured clinical interviews to establish a diagnosis of SAD. The Structured Clinical Interview for DSM-IV (SCID-IV; First, Spitzer, Gibbon, & Williams, 1996; 1997) or the Anxiety Disorders Interview Schedule (ADIS-IV; Brown, Di Nardo, & Barlow, 1994; Di Nardo, Brown, & Barlow, 1994) can be used for this purpose. Such interviews lead to more accurate and reliable diagnoses than unstructured clinical interviews (Miller, 2001; Miller, Dasher, Collins, Griffiths, & Brown, 2001). The SCID also provides a comprehensive assessment of a range of Axis I disorders (e.g., mood disorders, somatoform disorders, eating disorders), allowing for the assessment of comorbid conditions.

Comprehensive assessment of social anxiety also includes consideration of several other details (which may be assessed through a more traditional clinical interview). An evaluation of personal history may help to identify any learning experiences that may have contributed to the onset, development, and course of social anxiety. An examination of current living circumstances (e.g., environmental and family factors) will help to determine any significant life stressors that might contribute to the maintenance of social anxiety. It is also important to identify specific features of social anxiety (e.g., dysfunctional beliefs, anxiety cues and triggers, overt and subtle avoidance behaviours, physical symptoms, social skills deficits). These salient features may be useful for effective treatment planning. Finally, as with all mental disorders, it is important that patients receive a medical workup to ensure that any organic pathology or other identifiable physical factors do not account for the anxiety symptoms.

There are several self-report measures that can be used to assess the severity and intensity of excessive social anxiety. These measures provide supplementary information that can be useful for the assessment of social anxiety symptoms. Below, we provide brief descriptions of some of the most commonly used measures.

Fear of Negative Evaluation scale (FNE; Watson & Friend, 1969). The FNE assesses concerns with social-evaluative threat. The original scale comprised 30 items that were rated as either True or False. Existing research suggests that the FNE is a better measure of social anxiety symptoms, rather than SAD (see Orsillo, 2001). The shorter version – the Brief Fear of Negative Evaluation Scale (BFNE, Leary, 1983) – is also commonly used. We recommend using a revised version of the scale, the BFNE-II (Carleton, McCreary, Norton, & Asmundson, 2006), which is comprised of 8 items each rated on a 5-point Likert scale ranging from 0 (*not at all characteristic of me*) to 4 (*extremely characteristic of me*). In this version, revisions were made to remove a methodological factor stemming from the four reverse-worded items (see recommendations by Taylor, 1993). The BFNE-II has been found to have good psychometric properties (Carleton et al., 2006; Carleton, Collimore, & Asmundson, 2007).

Social Avoidance and Distress scale (SAD; Watson & Friend, 1969). The SAD was initially developed with the FNE, and was designed to measure two other aspects of social-evaluative anxiety — social avoidance and social distress. Social avoidance is defined as active avoidance of social situations, whereas social distress is defined as the experience of negative emotions during or in anticipation of social situations. The SAD continues to be used in its original format (i.e., dichotomous true-false answer format), despite the advantages of Likert response formats (see Velicer, DiClemente, & Corriveau, 1984). Watson and Friend (1969) reported good convergent validity for the SAD. More recently, the SAD has demonstrated good internal consistency and test-retest reliability in an undergraduate sample of Chinese students (Chun-zi, Xiao-ling, Fan, & Luo-chu, 2003), and good construct validity and test-retest reliability in an adolescent Spanish-speaking sample (Garcia-Lopez, Olivares, Hidalgo, Beidel, & Turner, 2001). Further investigation is needed to evaluate the psychometric properties of the SAD scale.

Social Interaction Anxiety Scale (SIAS; Mattick & Clarke, 1998) and *Social Phobia Scale* (SPS; Mattick & Clarke, 1998; 1989). The SIAS and the SPS are two widely used self-report measures that were designed to be administered together. The SIAS assesses fears of social interaction situations (e.g., having a conversation), whereas the SPS assesses fear of performance situations or observation (e.g., public speaking). The SIAS and SPS are comprised of 19 and 20 items respectively, each rated on a 5-point Likert scale ranging from 0 (*not at all characteristic or true of me*) to 4 (*extremely characteristic or true of me*). The scales demonstrate good validity (Brown et al., 1997; Mattick & Clark, 1998), excellent internal consistency, and test-retest reliability (Heimberg, Mueller, Holt, Hope, & Liebotwitz, 1992; Mattick & Clark, 1998). In addition, the SIAS and SPS show discriminant validity between patients with SAD versus healthy controls and patients with other anxiety disorder diagnoses (Heimberg et al., 1992). Recently, initial empirical support was found for the use of shortened versions of the SIAS and SPS across both clinical and undergraduate samples (Carleton et al., 2008; in press).

Social Phobia Inventory (SPIN; Connor et al., 2000). The 17-item SPIN is a measure of fear, avoidance, and physiological arousal associated with SAD. Each item is rated on a 5-point Likert scale ranging from 0 (*not at all*) to 4 (*extremely*), and respondents indicate how much they have been bothered in the past week. The SPIN has been found to have strong psychometric properties (i.e., internal consistency, test-retest reliability, convergent validity, construct validity, discriminant validity; Antony, Coons, McCabe, Ashbaugh, & Swinson, 2006; Connor et al., 2000).

Social Phobia and Anxiety Inventory (SPAI; Turner, Beidel, Dancu, & Stanley, 1989). The SPAI assesses somatic, cognitive, and behavioural symptoms of SAD. The scale contains an embedded agoraphobia (AG) scale, in addition to the social phobia (SP) scale. The AG scale was included to remove variance that that is not entirely due to social-evaluative anxiety. The SPAI is comprised of 45-items, and 21 items contain additional sub-items, for a total of 109 items. The SPAI has demonstrated excellent psychometric properties (Peters, 2000; Turner et al., 1989). An abbreviated version of the SPAI, the SPAI-23 (Roberson-Nay, Strong, Nay, Beidel, & Turner, 2007), was recently developed and correlates highly with the original measure and similarly with other measures of social anxiety.

EMPIRICALLY SUPPORTED TREATMENTS

Psychosocial Interventions

There are several empirically-supported psychosocial interventions for SAD. The most promising come from a cognitive-behavioural therapy (CBT) perspective and include (a) psychoeducation, (b) cognitive strategies, (c) exposure-based strategies, (d) social skills training, and (e) applied relaxation (see Rodebaugh, Holaway, & Heimberg, 2004; Turk, Coles, & Heimberg, 2002). These can be delivered in either an individual format or in a group format.

Psychoeducation

This involves providing information about the nature of anxiety and, more specifically, SAD. Additional topics include providing patients with a simplified cognitive-behavioural model to help explain the etiology and processes underlying SAD, the three component model of anxiety (i.e., thoughts, behaviours, and emotions), and the costs and benefits of overcoming SAD. Psychoeducation might take place in the treatment session (e.g., through didactic presentations), or can be provided through readings (e.g., short handouts) or videos.

Cognitive Strategies

Cognitive strategies (i.e., cognitive restructuring) involve examining evidence for the veracity of anxious beliefs, interpretations, and predictions relative to alternatives. The use of these strategies is based on the idea that thoughts about feared social situations contribute to the experience of anxiety (Beck & Emery, 1985). The two main types of cognitive distortions are probability overestimation and catastrophic thinking (Antony & Swinson, 2000). In probability overestimation, individuals with SAD overestimate the likelihood that something negative will happen. It is a prediction that the individual believes will come true, despite the likelihood being relatively low (e.g., everyone will think that I am stupid). Catastrophic thinking involves overestimating how terrible, unbearable, or unmanageable, a negative outcome would be (e.g., *It would be awful if I looked anxious throughout my presentation*). In order to challenge probability overestimation, the therapist and the patient can collaboratively examine evidence both supporting and disconfirming the distorted thought. Similarly, to challenge catastrophic thinking, the therapist can help the patient put the "catastrophe" into perspective by asking questions such as, "What if (the catastrophic thought) did happen?", "Would it matter in the future?" [see Heimberg and Becker (2002) or Hope, Heimberg, Juster, and Turk, (2000) for a more detailed explanation of cognitive strategies for SAD].

Exposure-based Strategies

Situational exposures are behavioural exercises wherein an individual gradually enters (and confronts) feared social situations (e.g., giving a presentation, eating or drinking in front of other people, meeting new people). Exposure-based strategies are based on the assumption that the patient must fully experience the feared social situation in order to change emotional (i.e., anxiety) and behavioural (i.e., escape/avoidance) symptoms (Foa & Kozak, 1986). In order for exposures to be most effective, patients should stay in the feared social situation until they experience a significant reduction in their anxiety symptoms (see Beiling, McCabe, & Antony (2006), Heimberg & Becker (2002), and Hope et al. (2000) for a more detailed description of exposure-based strategies for SAD). Exposure-based strategies for SAD might also include role plays, where the individual can practice a situation before the actual exposure.

Social Skills Training

The purpose of social skills training for people suffering from SAD is to help them improve their conversational and social skills. Examples of social skills targeted include nonverbal communication (e.g., eye contact, tone of voice), assertiveness training, and presentation skills. The inclusion of social skills training is justified according to the skills deficit model of SAD (e.g., Curran, 1977; Twentyman & McFall, 1975), which assumes that social anxiety develops due to inadequate interaction skills. It is noteworthy, however, that evidence supporting social skills deficits in persons with SAD is inconsistent (Rapee & Lim, 1992; Stopa & Clark, 1993; van Dam-Baggen & Kraaimaat, 2000). As such, social skills training may be included in treatment depending on the needs of the patient.

Applied Relaxation

There is some evidence for the use of progressive muscle relaxation (PMR; Berstein, Borkovec, & Hazlett-Stevens, 2000), in combination with gradual exposure-based strategies, in the treatment of SAD. Patients learn PMR and are encouraged to practice using such strategies during their daily activities and subsequently when entering feared social situations (Ost, 1987). Notably, empirical evidence suggests that PMR alone is insufficient to treat SAD (e.g., Alstrom, Norlund, Persson, Harding, & Ljungqvist, 1984).

Pharmacotherapies

Randomized controlled trials show that various medications can also be useful in reducing social anxiety, including selective serotonin reuptake inhibitors [e.g., paroxetine (Paxil), sertraline (Zoloft), fluoxetine (Prozac), fluvoxamine (Lovox), and citalopram (Celexa)], dual serotonin-norepinephrine reuptake inhibitors [e.g., venlafaxine (Effexor)], and monoamine oxidase inhibitors [e.g., phenelzine (Nardil)] (Davidson, 2003; Fedoroff & Taylor, 2001; Stein, Ipser, & Balkom, 2004). Although an effective treatment for SAD, recent research suggests that phenelzine may be associated with unpleasant side effects, interact with other medications, and also interact with foods containing tyramine (e.g., cured meats, wine, aged cheese, soy sauce; Antony & Swinson, 2000). As a result, selective serotonin reuptake inhibitors and serotonin-norepinephrine reuptake inhibitors are more frequently used and better tolerated (although these drugs may also be associated with side effects).

Combining Psychosocial Interventions with Pharmacotherapies

A number of studies comparing pharmacotherapy to CBT have shown that both treatment approaches are effective for the treatment of SAD (Gould, Buckminster, Pollack, Otto, Yap, 1997; Heimberg et al., 1998; Stein & Stein, 2008). Studies comparing CBT, pharmacotherapy, and a combination of CBT and pharmacotherapy have found mixed results. Blomhoff and colleagues (2001) compared sertraline, exposure therapy, a combination of sertraline and exposure therapy, and placebo in a primary care setting. Both sertraline and the combination of sertraline and exposure therapy were more efficacious than placebo, with the combination therapy being the most effective. At 1-year follow-up, patients who received exposure continued to show improvements whereas patients who received sertraline and the combination treatment did not (and showed some deterioration; Haug et al., 2003). Another large-scale study compared fluoxetine, CBT (i.e., 14-week group treatment involving psychoeducation, cognitive restructuring, social skills training, and in vivo exposure), a combination of fluoxetine and CBT, placebo, and a combination of placebo and CBT (Davidson et al., 2004). Posttreatment, patients receiving any of the four active treatments were more improved than those receiving placebo, and the treatments did not differ in terms of efficacy. In a large scale study that remains to be published, Heimberg (2003) reported that combined treatment of phenelzine and cognitive-behavioural had a modest benefit over either treatment alone and placebo..Recent research also suggests that D-cycloserine, a glutamatergic agent, is useful for augmenting psychosocial interventions for SAD (Hofmann, Pollack, & Otto, 2006; Hofmann et al., 2006).

EMERGING TRENDS AND UNEXPLORED ISSUES IN SAD

There are a number of unexplored research issues that are currently emerging in the literature. These include trends exploring SAD comorbidity [e.g., comorbid posttraumatic stress disorder (PTSD) and depression], the issue of which component of CBT is most effective, and self-help approaches for SAD. Here, we briefly describe and expand upon each of these important issues.

Research findings consistently demonstrate high levels of anxiety disorder comorbidity (Kessler, Chiu, Demler, & Walters, 2002). Recently, there has been a growing interest in co-occurring SAD and PTSD (Hofmann, Litz, & Weathers, 2003; Zayfert, DeViva, & Hofmann, 2005). The existing research indicates higher levels of SAD among PTSD populations, with prevalence rates ranging from 4 to 46% in civilian samples (Green, Lindy, Grace, & Leonard, 1992; Zayfert et al., 2005; Zayfert, Becker, Unger, & Shearer, 2002), and 12 to 32% in veteran samples (e.g., Orsillo, Heimberg, Juster, & Garrett, 1996; Orsillo et al., 1996). Possible suggested factors implicated in co-occurring SAD and PTSD include shame (Orsillo, Heimberg, et al., 1996), guilt (Zayfert et al., 2005), depression (Kashdan, Frueh, Knapp, Hebert, & Magruder, 2006), and trauma type (Collimore, Asmundson, Taylor, Jang, & Carleton 2008), although investigations into this co-occurrence are still in their infancy.

SAD is also highly comorbid with depressive disorders (Kessler et al., 1994); however, the relationship between SAD and depression remains largely unexplored. There is evidence that SAD is consistently associated with the onset of subsequent depression (e.g., Beesdo et al., 2007), but the mechanisms underlying this co-occurrence are unclear. Future research investigating how treatments for SAD might be adapted to address comorbid depression are warranted. Indeed, pre-treatment depression scale scores have been found to be the most significant predictor of treatment outcome (Chambless, Tran, & Glass, 1997). In one study, SAD patients who were more depressed were less likely to improve on measures of anxiety relative to SAD patients who were less depressed. In contrast, other studies suggest that comorbid mood disorders have little influence on the rate of SAD treatment outcome (Turner, Beidel, Wolff, Spaulding, & Jacob, 1996).

Which component of CBT is most effective for the treatment of SAD has yet to be determined. Several studies have examined the relative effects of the treatment components (i.e., behavioural exposure, cognitive restructuring, a combination of behavioural exposure and cognitive restructuring, social skills training, and applied relaxation; Clark, Ehlers, Hackmann, et al., 2006; Federoff & Taylor, 2001; Feske & Chambless, 1995; Gould et al., 1997; Taylor, 1996). Across meta-analytic investigations, each of the treatment strategies demonstrate moderate to large effect sizes relative to wait-list controls. However, according to a recent study, cognitive restructuring strategies are a critical component of SAD treatment (Clark et al., 2006). These results are in line with previous findings which showed that combination treatments including cognitive restructuring and behavioural exposure, but not cognitive restructuring alone, exposure alone, or social skills training, was more effective than placebo (Taylor, 1996). In contrast, earlier findings have demonstrated no differences between behavioural exposure and combined exposure and cognitive restructuring (Feske & Chambless, 1995), and that exposure is most effective whether administered alone or in combination with cognitive strategies (Gould et al., 1997). These mixed findings suggest that future research efforts should continue to examine the efficacy of CBT treatment components for SAD.

The role of self-help approaches in SAD has not yet fully been explored. To our knowledge, there has been only one study evaluating the efficacy of pure self-help (e.g., written materials for SAD) versus a combination of self-help and five group therapy sessions (Rapee, Abbott, Baillie, & Gaston, 2007). Posttreatment, 20% of patients in the pure self-help group no longer met criteria for a diagnosis of SAD; however, treatment gains decreased at three months follow-up (i.e., 6% without a diagnosis of SAD). At 3-months follow-up, self-help augmented with group therapy was more effective than wait-list controls and was not significantly different from group therapy (22-26% without a diagnosis of SAD). A number of investigations have also emerged on the use of computer-assisted or internet-based approaches to self-help (e.g., Andersson et al., 2006; Carlbring et al., 2007). Together, these data suggest that computer-based approaches are promising and may lead to a reduction in social anxiety symptoms. Future research studies using more controlled designs are needed.

Conclusion

SAD is one of the most prevalent mental health conditions resulting in significant distress and impairment for those afflicted (Rapee & Spence, 2004). Why one person develops SAD, while others do not, is not yet fully understood but many etiological factors (e.g., environmental, genetic) have been implicated and supported empirically. Research findings suggest that effective treatments for SAD have been developed and include both psychosocial interventions and pharmacotherapies. Below we highlight a number of specific research directions that await investigation.

- Specific studies related to the causal mechanisms of SAD, including additional research on environmental and genetic factors.
- Further empirical exploration of Axis I comorbidity in SAD, including PTSD and depressive disorders. Existing research suggests that depressive disorders are more likely to develop subsequently to the onset of SAD. Future research on the temporal sequence of co-occurring SAD and PTSD is warranted.
- Continued investigation of which components of CBT are most effective for the treatment of SAD (i.e., dismantling studies).
- Additional research on the role of self-help approaches in the treatment of SAD, including computer and internet-based approaches. The preliminary research regarding the application of such approaches in this context is promising.
- Further examination of the application of psychosocial interventions to culturally-diverse patients with SAD and other special populations (e.g., the elderly, persons with developmental disabilities).

References

Alstrom, J. E., Nordlund, C. L., Persson, G., Harding, M., & Ljungqvist, C. (1984). Effects of four treatment methods on social phobic patients not suitable for insight-oriented psychotherapy. *Acta Psychiatrica Scandinavica, 70*, 97–110.

American Psychiatric Association. (2000). *Diagnostic and statistical manual of mental disorders* (4th ed. text rev.). Washington, DC: Author.

Andersson, G., Carlbring, P., Holmstrom, A., Parthan, E., Furmark., T., Nilsson-Ihrfelt, E., Burman, M., & Ekselius, L. (2006). Internet-Based Self-Help With Therapist Feedback and In Vivo Group Exposure for Social Phobia: A Randomized Controlled Trial. *Journal of Consulting and Clinical Psychology, 74*, 677-686.

Antony, M. M., Coons, M. J., McCabe, R. E., Ashbaugh, A. R., & Swinson, R. P. (2006). Psychometric properties of the Social Phobia Inventory: Further evaluation. *Behaviour Research and Therapy, 44*, 1177-1185.

Antony, M. M., & Rowa, K. (2005). Evidence-based assessment of anxiety disorders in adults. *Psychological Assessment, 17*, 256-266.

Antony, M. M., & Swinson, R. P. (2000). *The shyness and social anxiety workbook: Proven techniques for overcoming your fears*. Oakland, CA: New Harbinger Publications.

Bandelow, B., Charimo Torrente, A., Wedekind, D., Broocks, A., Jajak, G., & Ruther, E. (2004). Early traumatic life events, parental rearing styles, family history of mental disorders, and birth risk factors in patients with social anxiety disorder. *European Archives of Psychiatry and Clinical Neuroscience, 254*, 397-405.

Barlow, D. H. (2002). *Anxiety and its disorders: The nature and treatment of anxiety and panic*. New York: The Guilford Press.

Beck, A. T., & Emery, G. (1985). Anxiety *disorders and phobias: A cognitive perspective*. New York: Basic Books.

Beesdo, K., Bittner, A., Pine, D. S., Stein, M. B., Hofler, M., Lieb, R., & Wittchen, H-U. (2007). Incidence of social anxiety disorder and the consistent risk for secondary depression in the first three decades of life. *Archives of General Psychiatry, 64*, 903-912.

Beiling, P. J., McCabe, R. E., & Antony, M. M. (2006). *Cognitive-Behavioural therapy in groups*. New York: The Guilford Press.

Berstein, D. A., Borkovec, T. D., & Hazlett-Stevens, H. (2000). *New directions in progressive relaxation training: A guidebook for helping professionals*. Westport, CT: Praeger.

Blomhoff, S., Haug, T. T., Hellstrom, K., Holme, I., Humble, M., Madsbu, H. P., & Wold, J. E. (2001). Randomised controlled general practice trial of sertraline, exposure therapy and combined treatment in generalized social phobia. *British Journal of Psychiatry, 179*, 23–30.

Boone, M. L., McNeil, D. W., Masia, C. L., Turk, C. L., Carter, L. E., Ries, B. J., & Lewin, M. R. (1999). Multimodal comparisons of social phobia subtypes and avoidant personality disorder. *Journal of Anxiety Disorders, 13*, 271-292.

Brown, T. A., Di Nardo, P. A., & Barlow, D. H. (1994). *Anxiety Disorders Interview Schedule for DSM–IV (ADIS-IV)*. Boulder, CO: Graywind.

Brown E. J., Turovsky, J., Heimberg, R. G., Juster, H. R., Brown, T. A., & Barlow D. H. (1997). Validation of the social interaction anxiety scale and the social phobia scale across the anxiety disorders. *Psychological Assessment, 9*, 21-27.

Carlbring, P., Gunnarsdottir, M., Hedensjo, L., Andersson, G., Ekselius, L., & Furmak, T. (2007). Treatment of social phobia: Randomised trial of internet-delivered cognitive-behavioural therapy with telephone support. *British Journal of Psychiatry, 190*, 123-128.

Carleton, R. N, Collimore, K. C, & Asmundson, G. J. G. (2007). Construct validity of the BFNE -II. *Journal of Anxiety Disorders, 21*, 131-141.

Carleton, R. N., Collimore, K. C., Asmundson, J. G., McCabe, R. E., Rowa, K., & Antony, M. M. (in press). Refining and validating the social interaction anxiety scale and the social phobia scale. *Depression and Anxiety*.

Carleton, R. N., McCreary, D., Norton, P. J., & Asmundson, G. J. G. (2006). The brief fear of negative evaluation scale, revised. *Depression & Anxiety, 23*, 297-303.

Chambless, D. L., Tran, G. Q., & Glass, C. R. (1997). Predictors of response to cognitive-behavioral group therapy for social phobia. *Journal of Anxiety Disorders, 11*, 221–240.

Chartier, M. J., Walker, J. R., & Stein, M. B. (2001). Social phobia and potential childhood risk factors in a community sample. *Psychological Medicine, 31*, 307-315.

Chun-zi, P., Xiao-ling, Fan, & Luo-chu, Li. (2003). The validity and reliability of social avoidance and distress scale in Chinese students. *Chinese Journal of Clinical Psychology, 11*, 279-281.

Clark, D. M., Ehlers, A., Hackmann, A., McManus, F., Fennel, M., Grey, N., Waddington, L., & Wild, J. (2006). Cognitive therapy versus exposure and applied relaxation in social phobia: A randomized controlled trial. *Journal of Consulting and Clinical Psychology, 74,* 568–78.

Clark, D. M. & Wells, A. (1995). A cognitive model of social phobia. In R. Heimberg, M. Liebowitz, D.A. Hope, & F. R. Schneier (Eds.), *Social phobia: Diagnosis, assessment and treatment* (pp. 69–93). New York: Guilford Press.

Collimore, K. C., Asmundson, G. J. G., Taylor, S., Jang, K. L., & Carleton, R. N. (2008). Social Anxiety and Trauma: Exploring Environmental and Genetic Influences. In R. N. Carleton (Chair), *Predilections for posttraumatic distress: Exploring cognitive, environmental, and genetic diatheses for PTSD.* Symposium presentation at the 28th annual meeting of the Anxiety Disorders Association of America, Savannah, Georgia.

Conner, K. M., Davidson, J. R. T., Churchill, L. E., Sherwood, A., Foa, E., & Wesler, R. H. (2000). Psychometric properties of the social phobia inventory SPIN. *British Journal of Psychiatry 176*, 379-386.

Curran, J. P. (1977). Skills training as an approach to the treatment of heterosexual-social anxiety: A review. *Psychological Bulletin, 84*, 140–157.

David, D., Giron, A., & Mellman, T. A. (1995). Panic-phobic patients and developmental trauma. *Journal of Clinical Psychiatry, 56*, 113-117.

Davidson, J. R. T. (2003). Pharmacotherapy of social phobia. *Acta Psychiatrica Scandinavica, 108 Suppl 417*, 65-71.

Davidson, J. R. T., Foa, E. B., Huppert, J. D., Keefe, F. J., Franklin, M. E., Compton, J. S., Zhao, N., Connor, K. M., Lynch, T. R., & Gadde, K. M. (2004). Fluoxetine, comprehensive cognitive behavioral therapy, and placebo in generalized social phobia. *Archives of General Psychiatry, 61*, 1005-1013.

Di Nardo, P. A., Brown, T. A., & Barlow, D. H. (1994). *Anxiety Disorders Interview Schedule for DSM–IV: Lifetime version*. Boulder, CO: The Psychological Corporation.

Fedoroff, I. C., & Taylor, S. T. (2001). Psychological and pharmacological treatments of social phobia: A meta-analysis. *Journal of Clinical Psychopharmacology, 21*, 311–324.

Feske, U., & Chambless, D. L. (1995). Cognitive behavioral versus exposure only treatment for social phobia: A meta-analysis. *Behavior Therapy, 26*, 695–720.

First, M. B., Spitzer, R. L., Gibbon, M., & Williams, J. B. W. (1996). *Structured Clinical Interview for DSM–IV Axis I Disorders: Patient edition* (SCID-I/P, Version 2.0). New York: New York State Psychiatric Institute.

First, M. B., Spitzer, R. L., Gibbon, M., & Williams, J. B. W. (1997). *Structured Clinical Interview for DSM–IV Axis I Disorders (SCID-I): Clinician version*. Washington, DC: American Psychiatric Press.

Foa, E. B., & Kozak, M. J. (1986). Emotional processing of fear: Exposure to corrective information. *Psychological Bulletin, 99*, 20-35.

Foa, E. B., Franklin, M. E., Perry, K. J., & Herbert, J. D. (1996). Cognitive biases in generalized social phobia. *Journal of Abnormal Psychology, 105*, 433–439.

Fontenelle, L. F., Domingues, A. M., Souza, W. F., Mendlowicz, M. V., de Menezes, G. B., Figueira, I. L., & Versiani, M. (2007). History of trauma and dissociative symptoms among patients with obsessive-compulsive disorder and social anxiety disorder. *Psychiatric Quarterly, 78*, 241-250.

Furmark, T. (2002). Social phobia: Overview of community surveys. *Acta Psychiatrica Scandinavica, 105*, 84-93.

García-Lopez, L. J., Olivares, J., Hidalgo, M. D., Beidel, D. C., & Turner, S. M. (2001). Psychometric properties of the social phobia and anxiety inventory, the Social Anxiety Scale for Adolescents, the Fear of Negative Evaluation Scale, and the Social Avoidance and Distress Scale in an adolescent Spanish-speaking sample. *Journal of Psychopathology and Behavioral Assessment, 23*, 51-59.

Gilboa-Schechtman, E., Franklin, M. E., & Foa, E. B. (2000). Anticipated reactions to social events: differences among individuals with generalized social phobia, obsessive compulsive disorder, and nonanxious controls. *Cognitive Therapy and Research, 24*, 731–746.

Gould, R. A., Buckminster, S., Pollack, M. H., Otto, M., & Yap, L. (1997). Cognitive-behavioral and pharmacological treatment for social phobia: A meta-analysis. *Clinical Psychology: Science and Practice, 4*, 291–306.

Green, B. L., Lindy, J. D., Grace, M. C., & Leonard, A. C. (1992). Chronic posttraumatic stress disorder and diagnostic comorbidity in a disaster sample. *The Journal of Nervous and Mental Disease, 180*, 760-766.

Haug, T. T., Blomhoff, S., Hellstrom, K., Holme, I., Humble, M., Madsbu, H. P., & Wold, J. E. (2003). Exposure therapy and sertraline in social phobia: 1-year follow-up of a randomised controlled trial. *British Journal of Psychiatry, 182*, 312–318.

Heimberg, R. G. (2003, March). Cognitive-behavioral and psychotherapeutic strategies for social anxiety disorder. In M. R. Liebowitz (Chair), *Beyond shyness: Recognition, diagnosis, and treatment for social anxiety disorder*. Symposium presented at the annual meeting of the Anxiety Disorders Association of America, Toronto, Ontario, Canada.

Heimberg, R. G., & Becker, R. E. (2002). *Cognitive-behavioral group therapy for social phobia: Basic mechanisms and clinical strategies*. New York: Guilford Press.

Heimberg, R. G., Liebowitz, M. R., Hope, D. A., Schneier, F. R., Holt, C. S., Welkowitz, L. A., Juster, H. R., Campeas, R., Bruch, M. A., Cloitre, M., Fallon, B., & Klein, D. F. (1998). Cognitive-behavioral group therapy versus phenelzine in social phobia: 12-week outcome. *Archives of General Psychiatry, 55*, 1133–1141.

Heimberg, R. G., Mueller, G. P., Holt, C. S., Hope, D. A., & Liebowitz, M. R. (1992). Assessment of anxiety in social interaction and being observed by others: The social interaction anxiety scale and the social phobia scale. *Behaviour Therapy, 23*, 53-75.

Heinrichs, N., & Hofmann, S. G. (2001). Information processing in social phobia: A critical review. *Clinical Psychology Review, 21*, 751-770.

Hofmann, S. G. (2007). Cognitive factors that maintain social anxiety disorder: A comprehensive model and its treatment implications. *Cognitive Behaviour Therapy, 36*, 193-209.

Hofmann, S. G., Heinrichs, N., & Moscovitch, D. A. (2004). The nature and expression of social phobia: Toward a new classification. *Clinical Psychology Review, 24*, 769-797.

Hofmann, S. G., Litz, B. T., & Weathers, F. W. (2003). Social anxiety, depression, and PTSD in Vietnam veterans. *Journal of Anxiety Disorders, 17*, 573-582.

Hofmann, S. G., Meuret, A. E., Smits, J. A. J., Simon, N., Pollack, M. H., Eisenmenger, K., Shiekh, M., & Otto, M. W. (2006). Augmentation of exposure therapy with D-cycloserine for social anxiety disorder. *Archives of General Psychiatry, 63*, 298–304.

Hofmann, S. G., Pollack, M. H. & Otto, M. W. (2006). Augmentation treatment of psychotherapy for anxiety disorders with D-Cycloserine. *CNS Drug Reviews, 12*, 208-217.

Hope, D. A., Heimberg, R. G., Juster, H. R., & Turk, C. L. (2000). *Managing social anxiety: A cognitive-behavioral therapy approach*. San Antonio, TX7 Psychological Corporation.

Iancu, I., Levin, J., Hermesh, H., Dannon, P., Poreh, A., Ben-Yudah, Y., Kaplan, Z., Maron, S., Kotler, M. (2006). Social phobia symptoms: Prevalence sociodemographic correlates, and overlap with specific phobia symptoms. *Comprehensive Psychiatry, 47*, 399–405.

Kashdan, T. B., Frueh, B. C., Knapp, R. G., Hebert, R., & Magruder, K. M. (2006).

Social anxiety disorder in veterans affairs primary care clinics. *Behaviour Research and Therapy, 44,* 233-247.

Kendler, K. S., Karkowski, L. M., & Prescott, C. A. (1999). Fears and phobias: Reliability and heritability. *Psychological Medicine, 29*, 539-553.

Kendler, K. S., Neale, M. C., Kessler, R. C., Heath, A. C., & Eaves, L. J. (1992). The genetic epidemiology of phobias in women: The interrelationship of agoraphobia, social phobia, situational phobia, and simple phobia. *Archives of General Psychiatry, 49*, 273-281.

Kessler, R. C., Berglund, P., Demler, O., Jin, R., & Walters, E. E. (2005). Lifetime prevalence and age-of-onset distributions of DSM-IV disorders in the National Comorbidity Survey Replication. *Archives of General Psychiatry, 62*, 593-602.

Kessler, R. C., Chiu, W. T., Demler O., Walters, E. E. (2002). Prevalence, severity, and comorbidity of 12-month DSM-IV disorders in the National Comorbidity Survey Replication. *Archives of General Psychiatry, 62*, 617-627.

Kessler, R. C., Davis, C. G., & Kendler, K. S. (1997). Childhood adversity and adult psychiatric disorder in the US National Comorbidity Survey. *Psychological Medicine, 27*, 1101-1119.

Kessler, R. C., McGonagle, K. A., Zhao, C. B., Nelson, M., Hughes, S., Eshleman, H. U., et al. (1994). Lifetime and 12-month prevalence of DSM-III-R psychiatric disorders in the United States: Results from the National Comorbidity Survey. *Archives of General Psychiatry, 51*, 8-19.

Leary, M. R. (1983). A brief version of the Fear of Negative Evaluation Scale. *Personality and Social Psychology Bulletin 9*, 371-375.

Magee, W. J. (1999). Effects of negative life experiences on phobia onset. *Social Psychiatry and Psychiatric Epidemiology, 34*, 343-351.

Mannuzza, A., Schneier, F., Chapman, T., Leibowitz, M., Klein, D., & Fyer, A. (1995). Generalized social phobia: Reliability and validity. *Archives of General Psychiatry, 52*, 230-237.

Massion, A. O., Dyck, I. R., Shea, M. T., Phillips, K. A., Warshaw, M. G., & Keller, M. B. (2002). Personality disorders and time to remission in generalized anxiety disorder, social phobia, and panic disorder. *Archives of General Psychiatry, 59*, 434-440.

Matsunaga, H., Kiriike, N., Matsui, T., Iwasaki, Y., Stein, D. J. (2001). Taijin Kyofushc: a form of social anxiety disorder that responds to serotonin reuptake inhibitors? *International Journal of Neuropsychopharmacology, 4*, 231–37.

Mattick, R.P., & Clarke, J.C. (1989). Development and validation of measures of social phobia scrutiny fear and social interaction anxiety. *Unpublished manuscript.*

Mattick, R. P., & Clarke, J. C. (1998). Development and validation of measures of social phobia scrutiny fear and social interaction anxiety. *Behaviour Research and Therapy, 36*, 455-470.

McManus, F., Clark, D. M., & Hackmann, A. (2000). Specificity of cognitive biases in social phobia and their role in recovery. *Behavioural and Cognitive Psychotherapy, 28*, 201–209.

Miller, P. R. (2001). Inpatient diagnostic assessments: 2. Interrater reliability and outcomes of structured vs. unstructured interviews. *Psychiatry Research, 105*, 265–271.

Miller, P. R., Dasher, R., Collins, R., Griffiths, P., & Brown, F. (2001). Inpatient diagnostic assessments: 1. Accuracy of structured vs. unstructured interviews. *Psychiatry Research, 105*, 255–264.

Mohammadi, M. R., Ghanizadeh, A., Mohammadi, M., & Mesgarpour, B. (2006). Prevalence of social phobia and its comorbidity with psychiatric disorders in Iran. *Depression and Anxiety, 23*, 405–11.

Nelson, E. C., Grant, J. D., Bucholz, K. K., Glowinski, A., Madden, P. A. F., Reich, W., & Heath, A. C. (2000). Social phobia in a population-based female adolescent twin sample: Co-morbidity and associated suicide-related symptoms. *Psychological Medicine, 30*, 797-804.

Orsillo, S. M. (2001). Measures for social phobia. In M. M. Antony, S. M. Orsillo, & L. Roemer (Eds.), *Practitioner's guide to empirically based measures of anxiety*. New York: Kluwer Academic/Plenum.

Orsillo, S. M., Heimberg, R. G., Juster, H. R., & Garrett, J. (1996). Social phobia and PTSD in Vietnam veterans. *Journal of Traumatic Stress, 9*, 235-252.

Orsillo, S. M., Weathers, F. W., Litz, B. T., Steinberg, H. R., Huska, J. A., & Keane, T. M. (1996). Current and lifetime psychiatric disorders among veterans with war zone-related posttraumatic stress disorder. *The Journal of Nervous and Mental Disease, 184*, 307-313.

Ost, L. G. (1987). Applied relaxation: Description of a coping technique and review of controlled studies. *Behaviour Research and Therapy, 25*, 397–409.

Otto, M. W., Pollack, M. H., Maki, K. M., Gould, R. A., Worthington, J. J., Smoller, J. W., & Rosenbaum, J. F. (2001). Childhood history of anxiety disorders among adults with social phobia: Rates, correlates, and comparisons with patients with panic disorder. *Depression and Anxiety, 14*, 209-213.

Peters, L. (2000). Discriminant validity of the Social Phobia and Anxiety Inventory (SPAI), the Social Phobia Scale (SPS), and the Social Interaction Anxiety Scale (SIAS). *Behaviour Research and Therapy, 38*, 943–950.

Rapee, R. M., & Lim, L. (1992). Discrepancy between self- and observer ratings of performance in social phobics. *Journal of Abnormal Psychology, 101*, 728–731.

Rapee, R. M., & Spence, S. H. (2004). The etiology of social phobia: Empirical evidence and an initial model. *Clinical Psychology Review, 24*, 737-767.

Rapee, R. M., Abbott, M. J., Baillie, A. J., & Gaston, J. E. (2007). Treatment of social phobia through pure self-help and therapist-augmented self-help. *British Journal of Psychiatry, 191*, 246-252.

Rickels, K., Mangano, R., & Khan, A. (2004). A double-blind, placebo-controlled study of a flexible dose of venlafaxine ER in adult outpatients with generalized social anxiety disorder. *Journal of Clinical Psychopharmacology, 24*, 488-496.

Roberson-Nay, R., Strong, D. R., Nay, W. T., Beidel, D. C., & Turner, S. M. (2007). Development of an abbreviated Social Phobia and Anxiety Inventory (SPAI) using item response theory: The SPAI-23. *Psychological Assessment, 19*, 133-145.

Rodebaugh, T. L., Holaway, R. M., Heimberg, R. G. (2004). The treatment of social anxiety disorder. *Clinical Psychology Review, 24*, 883-908.

Ruscio, A. M., Brown, T. A., Chiu, W. T., Sareen, J., Stein, M. B., & Kessler, R. C. (2008). Social fears and social phobia in the USA: results from the National Comorbidity Survey Replication. *Psychological Medicine, 35*, 15–28.

Schultz, L.T. & Heimberg, R.G. (2008) Attentional focus in social anxiety disorder: Potential for interactive processes, *Clinical Psychology Review, 00*, 000-000.

Stein D. J., Ipser, J. C., Balkom, A. J. (2004). Pharmacotherapy for social phobia. *Cochrane Database Systematic Reviews, 4*, CD001206.

Stein, M. B., & Stein, D. J. (2008). Social anxiety disorder. *Lancet, 371*, 1115-1125.

Stopa, L., & Clark, D. M. (1993). Cognitive processes in social phobia. *Behaviour Research and Therapy, 31*, 255–267.

Taylor, S. (1996). Meta-analysis of cognitive-behavioral treatments for social phobia. *Journal of Behavior Therapy and Experimental Psychiatry, 27*, 1–9.

Taylor, S. (1993). The structure of fundamental fears. *Journal of Behavior Therapy and Experimental Psychiatry, 24*, 289-299.

Tran, G. Q., & Chambless, D. L. (1995). Psychopathology of social phobia: Effects of subtype and of avoidant personality disorder. *Journal of Anxiety Disorders, 9*, 489-501.

Turk, C. L., Coles, M., & Heimberg, R. G. (2002). Psychotherapy for social phobia. In D. J. Stein, & E. Hollander (Eds.), *Textbook of anxiety disorders* (pp. 323–339). Washington, DC7 American Psychiatric Press.

Turner, S. M., Beidel, D. C., Dancu, C. V., & Stanley, M. A. (1989). An empirically derived inventory to measure social fears and anxiety: The Social Phobia and Anxiety Inventory. *Psychological Assessment, 1*, 35– 40.

Turner, S. M., Beidel, D. C., Wolff, P. L., Spaulding, S., & Jacob, R. G. (1996). Clinical features affecting treatment outcome of social phobia. *Behaviour Research and Therapy, 34*, 795–804.

Twentyman, C. T., & McFall, R. M. (1975). Behavioral training of social skills in shy males. *Journal of Consulting and Clinical Psychology, 43*, 384-394.

van Dam-Baggen, R., & Kraaimaat, F. (2000). Group social skills training or cognitive group therapy as the clinical treatment of choice for generalized social phobia? *Journal of Anxiety Disorders, 14*, 437-451.

Velicer, C. C., Diclemente, C. C., & Corriveau, D. P. (1984). Item format and the structure of the personal orientation inventory. *Applied Psychological Measurement, 8*, 409-419.

Watson, D., & Friend, R. (1969). Measurement of social-evaluative anxiety. *Journal of Consulting and Clinical Psychology, 33,* 448-457.

Williams, J. M. G., Mathews, A., & MacLeod, C. (1996). The emotional stroop task and psychopathology. *Psychological Bulletin, 120*, 3-24.

Zayfert, C., Becker, C. B., Unger, D. L., & Shearer, D. K. (2002). Comorbid anxiety disorders in civilians seeking treatment for posttraumatic stress disorder. *Journal of Traumatic Stress, 15*, 31-38.

Zayfert, C., DeViva, J. C., Hofmann, S. G. (2005). Comorbid PTSD and social phobia in a treatment-seeking population: An exploratory study. *The Journal of Nervous and Mental Disease, 193*, 90-101.

Zhang, W., Ross, J., & Davidson, J. R. T. (2004). Social anxiety disorder in callers to the Anxiety Disorders Association of America. *Depression and Anxiety, 20*, 101-106.

In: Social Phobia: Etiology, Diagnosis and Treatment
Editor: Clayton P. Axelby
ISBN 978-1-60692-159-3
© 2009 Nova Science Publishers, Inc.

Chapter XI

COGNITIVE-BEHAVIOURAL THERAPY AND EMOTIONAL WORK FOR PATIENTS WITH SOCIAL PHOBIA

Lucia Romo*, Cindy Legauffre, Sonia Marquez, Stéphanie Bailleux, Stéphanie Mille and Yael Lerfel
Paris X-Nanterre University, France ;
Louis Mourier University Hospital (Colombes), France.

1. INTRODUCTION

Social anxiety disorders or social phobia are irrational, disabling fears of humiliation in social situations. This disorder is defined as an overwhelming and disabling fear of scripting, and embarrassment in social situations, which leads to the avoidance of potentially pleasurable and meaningful activities. Usually, studies show an incidence rate of 14.4% [1]. Although this disorder affects 1 to 18% of the general population in France, few clinical epidemiologic studies have been conducted on social phobia in France [2].

Social phobia are marked by extreme anxiety, fear and avoidance of social situations which involve social interactions with other people, or performance and evaluation such as speaking or eating in front of others [3].

Among the situations avoided by people with such phobia, we find: being teased or criticized, being the centre of attention, being watched or observed while doing something, having to speak in public, meeting people with authority, eating, talking or making phone calls in public.

People with social anxiety disorders usually recognize that their fears are irrational, but they cannot help feeling fearful and allowing their fears to affect the way they conduct their lives; social phobia can start during childhood when children avoid eye contact, speak

* Correspondence concerning this article should be addressed to: Lucia Romo, mail: lucia.romo@wanadoo.fr.

inaudibly or fidget and tremble and often do not want to go to school. However, we will discuss this disorder in adults only.

In a study in France (1) involving 952 psychiatric in- or out-patients with a primary diagnosis of social phobia, according to DSM-IV criteria, the average duration of social anxiety disorders was shown to be 12 years. A major depressive disorder was found in 47.7% of the sample, the prevalence of agoraphobia was even higher (49,2%), alcohol-dependence affected 10,6% of the patients and substance abuse 12,7%. About 15% of the patients with a history of suicide attempts and suicide risk were present.

The psychosocial impact and the alteration of quality of life was high, and the quality of life was found to be poorer than in other anxiety disorders, with respect to childhood, friends, partner and health [4,5,6].

Social learning within the family environment appears to be related to the presence of anxiety disorders. Temperamental factors were involved.

People with this disorder have a tendency to negatively evaluate aspects of their own performance, or to interpret the response of others as a form of criticism.

Biased information processing contributes to the aetiology and maintenance of social anxiety [7].

The risk in social anxiety disorders is often associated with alcohol use disorders and cannabis dependence, whereas other anxiety and mood disorders do not, according to a study made with 1709 adolescents who were followed for 30 years [8]. In adolescents, social phobia were associated with the subsequent regular and hazardous use of alcohol, in a 4-year follow-up.

2. TREATMENT

The psychological treatments for social phobia include: social skills training, exposure therapy, cognitive treatment (social skills training plus cognitive modification), and exposure to anxiety management and rational emotive therapy, self-instruction and training, and symptom prescription with reframing.

Cognitive-behaviour therapy (CBT) for social phobia has been shown to be efficient and specific. Educational supportive group therapy, placebo pills, placebo plus self-exposure and "flouxetine" plus self-exposure produce less change in symptoms [9].

Two studies insist on the importance of social skills training (SST) with methods used for acquiring basic and specific social skills, such as: modelling, behaviour rehearsal, successive approximation, and homework assignments [10].

In psychiatric patients with generalized social phobia, economic evaluation has demonstrated that the ratio between cost and benefit for CBT is positive, and that such treatment should therefore be more accessible to the population [11,12].

3. The Groups

Our groups take place twice a year, and can accept up to eight participants. For diagnosis we also used diagnostic interviews with avoidance situations.

3.1. Evaluations

All participants were evaluated using the following instruments:

1) Beck depression inventory » (BDI-13) with 13 diverse criteria: sadness, pessimism, defeat, dissatisfaction, fault, disgust with oneself, suicidal tendencies, withdrawal, indecision, negative modification of self-image, difficulties at work, tiredness and loss of appetite. These items fall into 3 subgroups, which are: negative consideration of oneself; the outside world and the future; slow-down and somatic disorders [13].
2) Spielberger Trait/State Anxiety inventory (STAI): this is an adapted Beck anxiety inventory with a Y "State" shape. It is divided into two parts with 40 items: the first part estimates the state of anxiety (YA) and the second estimates the anxiety stroke (YB). The anxiety state corresponds to the anxiety felt by the subject at some point in time, whereas the anxiety stroke corresponds to the normal anxious tendency [14].
3) Beck's anxiety inventory comprises a list of 21 anxiety symptoms. These items correspond to the main symptoms of Panic Confusion and Generalized Anxiety, according to the DSM III-R. By virtue of its contents, its brevity, the ease with which items can be assigned, and its frequent quotation, Beck's Anxiety Inventory turns out to be a well-adapted tool for clinical psychology [15].
4) The Liebowitz Social Anxiety Scale (LSAS) is based on a questionnaire with 24 items, whose aim is to assess the range of social interactions and performance situations that individuals with social phobia may fear and/or avoid. It is also a popular measurement tool used in research, to evaluate the efficiency of various social anxiety disorder treatments [16].
5) The Assertiveness Rating Scale of Rathus estimates self-assertion with a global note, based on 30 items. This scale is sensitive to therapeutic change, but does not distinguish between assertion and aggressivity [17].
6) The TAPIS is the « social interaction self statement test » of Glass, based on 30 items used to estimate the frequency of facilitative thoughts (positive thoughts) or inhibitive thoughts (negative thoughts) in a hetero-social relationship. The negative scale predicts social anxiety [18].
7) The self esteem inventory of Coopersmith (SEI) was designed to measure evaluative attitudes of oneself in the social, family, personal and professional domains, using 58 items. A lying scale is included [19].
8) The Automatic Thoughts Questionnaire (ATQ) of Hollon and Kendall, with 30 items, estimates the negative contents of the patient's inner monologue. The

identification of negative automatic thoughts helps with their modification, over a period of time [20].

9) The FSS III is the « Fear Survery Schedule" of Wolpe and Lang, based on 89 items. It helps to identify a patient's fears and is very commonly used in CBT because it enables the evolution of phobic symptomatology to be estimated. Five categories are evaluated: irrational fears of non human objects, fear of social or inter-personal situations, various manifestations of agoraphobia or claustrophobia, fears of injuries and surgical intervention, or of general illness and risky events [21].
10) The Emotionality Activity Sociability (EAS) *questionnaire* is a measurement tool for the evaluation of temperament, developed by Buss and Plomin. It is based on a temperamental dimensions model, proposed by the authors in the same year, and includes Emotionality (variations in the propensity to be easily or intensely upset or annoyed), Activity (variations in pace, vigour and persistence) and finally Sociability (variations in the provision to get closer to others). In the EAS questionnaire, emotionality comprises 3 sub-dimensions: fear, sadness and anger [22].
11) The Mindfulness Attention Awareness Scale (MAAS) was proposed by Brown and Ryan in 2003; it allows mindfulness to be measured, and assesses individual differences in the frequency of mindful states over time. The MAAS is focused on the presence or absence of attention and awareness, related to what is happening in the present, rather than on attributes such as acceptance, trust, empathy, gratitude, or various other characteristics which have been associated with mindfulness. The MAAS is a 15-item self-report instrument with a single factor [23].
12) The *20-item Toronto Alexithymia Scale* (TAS-20) self-reporting questionnaire was proposed by Taylor. It is by far the most popular measure of alexithymia, because it is a well-validated and consistent data-collection device. The subject assesses his/her degree of agreement or disagreement with a statement, on a 5-point Likert scale. The answers are grouped into three factors: difficulty in identifying feelings and distinguishing them from bodily sensations (F1), difficulty in describing feelings to others (F2), and externally oriented thinking (F3) [24].
13) In 1990 Lane, Quinland, Schwartz and Walker developed the Levels of Emotional Awareness Scale (LEAS) in an attempt to measure emotional awareness, which is based on a new cognitive-developmental model of emotional experience. This scale is a performance measure of an individual's ability to put feelings into words. The LEAS poses evocative interpersonal situations and elicits descriptions of the emotional responses to their self and to others, which are then scored using specific structural criteria. It comprises twenty hypothetical vignettes or 'scenes', which are presented to the subject in order to elicit his/her emotional self response or response to others [25].

3.2. Group Functioning

This group works with self-esteem: self-esteem means that a person can recognize his/her rights to make a decision about what should be done, in any situation, with respect to the rights of others.

Session 1: We work with the participants' communication style: passive, assertive and aggressive communications, and with simulated problematic social situations, automatic thinking, emotions and "adapted beliefs".

PASSIVE	ASSERTIVE	AGGRESSIVE
Jeer at rights ⇔ doesn't respect me	Does respect his rights and respect the rights of others ⇔ Equal to everybody	Jeer at others' rights. ⇔ Take advantage of others
Goals out of reach	Reach goals without hurting anybody	Achieve goals which hurt other people
Frustrated, unhappy, offended, anxious	Self confidence, self reliance	Is on the defensive, denigrating, humiliating others
Inhibited, dominated	Expressive	Explosive
Allow others to choose for oneself ⇔ Hold back on one's opinion	Choose for oneself ⇔ Express one's own opinion	Choose for others ⇔ impose one's opinion on others

An effective communication presents a message: clear, accurate, direct, concrete, relevant, warm, analyses the other's position, verbal and non-verbal components. The individuals observe and evaluate their behaviour.

Session 2: In the second work session we introduce active listening, which is characterized by face to face situations involving the persons who are affected by phobia: adaptive non verbal communication (from shaking one's head to nodding), banishment of absent-mindedness, making a difference between open and closed questions, reformulation, reflecting on one's feelings ...

Definitions of "empathic" assertion: firstly, the individual listens to elements which can be true in the dialogue of the person he/she is speaking to, in order to reformulate his/her reasons or what he/she has understood to be his opinions, giving his/her own opinion. All with each of the following possible scenarios:

Apathy (neglect emotions) => indifference

Aversion (avoidance or confrontation) => aggressively

Sympathy (stick to emotions) => compassion

Empathy (understand emotions) => understanding.

We work with the management of emotions towards others.

Concerning the emotions needed for this form of management, we need to: identify present emotions, facilitate the expression of emotions, take emotions into account.

In each session, there is homework for the participants.

Session 3: Fight against social anxiety: diminish feelings of incompetence. When confronted by social fears, learn not to confuse those things we are incapable of doing with the non-recognition of one's own capabilities.

The techniques we use include: making a social fears list, lengthy and progressive exposure to anxious situations, and learning relaxation.

Self-verbalisation is important, using sentences spoken to one self without being totally conscious.

"I will not be able to do it", self-verbalisation before, during and after situations. And the homework involves: how to use positive self-verbalisation instead.

Session 4: Work with the initiation and maintenance of a conversation, and with open conversation: sufficient adjustment of the interpersonal approach; open corporal posture: remaining in front of the person, without one's hand in front of the mouth, looking him/her in his/her eyes. Work with assertion in dialogue: keep listening, ask open questions, ask questions using the information given by the other person, provide information about oneself.

The patient needs to accurately re-evaluate his/her objectives: choose the appropriate instant, formulate any request clearly and briefly, become involved (use "I"), acknowledge the positions of the other person; persist with the 'scratched record' technique; search for a compromise or suggest other solutions. If all these methods fail, the individual should verbalize his/her disappointment. The homework deals with the risk associated with a situation, where to start a dialogue, and the risk of a request or refusal situation.

In the 5th session we work with criticism: the objective is to describe the relevant behaviour: describe the consequences for oneself (material, emotional), search for a possible solution, and establish more sincere relations, using the following guidelines: be brief, use neither direct nor indirect accusations, use the first person ("I") and talk about your feelings and what you don't like (concretely). Explain how, in concrete terms, the other person's behaviour affects your life and your feelings; clearly indicate the behaviour which you would like the other person to adopt in the future by making useful suggestions and mentioning the positive consequences related to his acceptance of such a change, find a compromise.

Work with negative beliefs: arbitrary interference, selective abstractions, dichotomous thoughts, minimalisation, maximalisation, over-generalisation, and personalization ...

The difficulty experienced in attempting to achieve efficient assistance is that of specifying graduated and repeatable tasks, because social situations are unpredictable and variable. The other difficulty is related to prolonged exposure (due to the brevity of many social situations) [26], although the CBT group techniques are particularly effective in dealing with the principal symptoms of social phobia, and with other symptoms such as general anxiety, depression and self-esteem [27].

In the 6th session we work with beliefs and congratulations. With congratulations it is important not only to formulate a compliment, but also to know how to accept one from others. One cannot assume that others know how we feel.

The exercise consists in: formulating compliments in terms of personal feelings rather than facts "I really like your T-shirt" rather than "It is a nice T-Shirt". The subject is encouraged to choose the specific aspects he/she likes, and not to disclaim or refuse compliments which are addressed to him/her.

If he/she does not share the opinion of others, remaining positive and answering politely allows others to know that he/she appreciates their compliments. The exercise is conducted, as for the other sessions, in the form of role-playing.

4. Emotion

Researchers' interest in emotions is increasing, because several theorists have argued that social anxiety is, in some ways, an extreme manifestation of an adaptive response which has evolved to promote an individual's sensitivity to the disapproval of others [28].

With this disorder, biological or psychological vulnerabilities to experiences of anxiety interact with real-life events, which involve social interaction or performance.

Some authors [29] suggest that individuals with social phobia can display non-verbal behaviour characteristic of anxiety. The expressed emotions (EE) construct may be relevant to CBT treatment for social phobia: people with this disorder feel safe, and may be particularly vulnerable to the effects of criticism and hostility [30]. Some other authors suggest that expressed emotions and criticism have an influence in cognitive behavioural therapy. In addition, the typical early maladaptive scheme is involved [31,32].

Recent studies suggest the specific importance of diminishing positive experiences to depression, and suggest that this same affective profile is consistent with social anxiety [33]. These authors have evaluated the temporal relationship between social anxiety and positive emotions in students, and found that social anxiety may become particularly problematic in the presence of chronic, rigid tendencies to manage emotional experiences and the situations which elicit them. These individuals inhibit the expression of positive and negative emotions, and can function with strong emotional reactions. They also have a tendency to suppress emotions (an avoidance-based lifestyle).

Our work with emotions takes the form of a workshop spread over several weeks. For the prevention of anxiety and depression, one example is the targeted intervention in a population with an elevated risk of depression or anxiety symptoms [8]. At the beginning of the course, the emotional psychotherapy process is based on exposure therapy [34]. In social phobia, there are basic signs which presage a positive outcome: fear is activated physiologically as well as by verbal self-report, there is a gradual reduction in these reactions through exposure to fearful stimuli, and there is a reduction in the level of initial reaction to these stimuli from one session to the next.

Emotional processing has not traditionally been an important part of cognitive therapy, but has often been a range of suggestions for ways in which emotions and emotional arousal can be used as a form of therapy.

The first step of Acceptance and Commitment Therapy is for the individual to allow and accept, rather than fear, without avoiding negative emotions [35]. In addition, strong evidence has been found [35] for the effectiveness of emotional validation and soothing, as part of the treatment for borderline personalities. Empathy appears to be particularly important when a person is learning to self-soothe and restore his/her emotional equilibrium.

Empirical support for mindfulness based cognitive therapy of depression focuses on a form of awareness of internal processes [37], which allows an individual to gain distance and perspective on his/her acceptance, for example, of depressive and anxious emotions as normal phenomena. In summary, these authors contend that anxiety disorders are best understood as problems of emotional regulation [34].

In the case of social phobia, and in some cases of generalized anxiety disorders, emotional experiences that become dysfunctional and generate deregulation may help in improving both the conceptualization and the treatment of complicated anxiety disorders, such as Generalized Anxiety Disorder (GAD).

The Emotion Regulation Therapy [38] recommended for GAD can be used for the treatment of social phobia; it consists in twenty 50 to 60 minute sessions, over a 16 week period.

Phase 1: psychoeducation monitoring and developmental history (four weekly sessions): functional patterns of anxiety, and emotions in past and current situations, self- monitoring.

Phase 2: four weekly sessions: skills training in somatic awareness and adaptive emotion regulation.

Phase 3: Two sessions a week, for a period of 4 weeks: thematic experimental exposure (application of skills during exposure to emotionally evocative themes).

Phase 4, final session: progress review, future goals/relapse prevention, and termination processing.

In a different study dealing with emotional processing in social phobia [39], based on the use of prosodic rather than facial information, the authors revealed enhanced identification of sad and fearful voices, and decreased identification of happy voices, in individuals with social phobia, compared to healthy control subjects.

This work on emotion is important when using other's expressed emotions (EE) as predictors, among the various factors related to cognitive behavioural therapy outcome [40]. People with social phobia feel safe, and they are therefore likely to have extended periods of contact with a restricted number of people. Social phobia is also associated with acute sensitivity to embarrassment and shame, resulting in over-involvement, which enables avoidance behaviour. The efficacy of CBT is uncertain in this context.

These authors led a group with 4 to 6 participants and two co-therapists, who compared a CBT group (restructured skills were practiced during behavioural exposure exercises) with an Exposure Therapy group (performances were compared using videotapes). In the CBT group working alliance: a therapeutic board was set up, and an agreement was found between client and therapist concerning the tasks and goals [41]. Encouragement is important during sessions, for patients who fear negative evaluations when they engage in risk-taking therapeutic tasks. We have evaluated the results of the working alliance with that of the Working alliance Inventory (WAI), the Helpfulness Scale of Elliot and the measure of emotional processing [cit op 32]. These evaluations need to be complemented with physiological measurements, and be extended to samples of greater size. Studies of western patients show that the achieved reduction in social anxiety disorder symptoms is similar to that achieved in other European countries and the USA [42].

The aim of the present study was to introduce emotional aspects, and the relationship between cognitive emotion regulation strategies and depressive symptoms, by comparing them with strategies such as: rumination, catastrophizing, self-blame, blame of others and acceptance, positive refocusing, and planning reappraisal. These comparisons also placed the individuals' development, which differs between early adolescents and elderly people, into perspective.

The classification scheme of affect-regulation strategies, diversion, distraction, disengagement, confrontation (affect directed situation), acceptance. And a link with coping: usually refers to people's ways of dealing with negative events in their life, regardless of whether affect occurs or is registered by the cognitive system [43]. The coping responses are associated with anticipatory social anxiety [44], and the anticipatory processing is associated with instruments such as STA, BDI and self-evaluative thoughts (association between social anxiety and anticipatory processing).

Highly socially anxious individuals produced significantly less positive autobiographical memories when faced with a future stressful event, and these individuals were more likely to report negative feelings and thoughts about themselves and less likely to report positive self-evaluative thoughts.

5. Emotional Work in our Groups

We completed the above-described sessions with six sessions on the topic of emotional regulation, where we addressed emotions with the Mindfulness Cognitive-Behavioural Therapy (MBCT) and Acceptance and Commitment Therapy (ACT) techniques.

The study of emotion and the practice of psychotherapeutical methods which facilitate emotional development have always been central to psychotherapy, and are becoming more compelling to clinicians of all theoretical orientations.

Without describing the details of these sessions, we summarise their content as being restricted essentially to the main emotions (anger, sadness, joy, surprise, fear, distaste, guilt, shame and interest).

We supplied the participants with an informative paper about depression and emotions.

We then carried out the "guest house" exercise, using the MBCT approach. The work was spread over two sessions dealing with positive and negative emotions, with a distribution of leaflets on emotions and an emotions register, and a sketch presenting the relationship between emotions, behaviour and cognitive processes.

In each session there was homework, the register and a brief exercise in meditation, in accordance with the MBCT approach.

In sessions 3 and 4, we worked on negative emotions, and their description: usefulness of these emotions and life experiences recounted by patients.

In sessions 5 and 6, we worked on positive emotions: their definition and usefulness, and we used the LEAS Scale.

Experiences were related by patients, and ways to develop these positive emotions were discussed. The patients completed a list of situations and associated thoughts.

We completed all sessions with an exercise in MBCT meditation. In the final session, a progress report was prepared in which we presented an informative bibliography and set meeting dates for the follow-up (after one, three and six months).

6. Review Studies

The review study of social anxiety disorders is largely described in the literature [45], however even the best treatment may have non responders, corresponding to approximately 1/6 of individuals for the CBT group [3]. In this case, the treatment focusing on emotional regulation, for example the Dialectical Behavior Therapy of M Linehan, is an interesting alternative.

Several studies concerning social anxiety disorders, such as [9] describing the meta-analysis of a randomized placebo-controlled trial in adult anxiety disorders using CBT, found CBT to be efficient for adults with this disorder; or the large effect size in a review of meta-analysis [46]. Also, over the long term, the positive effects of social phobia treatment CBT were maintained [47]. A study based on three methodologically rigorous meta-analyses of the treatment of social phobia found size effects for CBT, ranging from 0.74 up to 1.06, with the greatest size effect obtained from treatment with behavioural exposure components.

In addition, virtual reality technologies are an alternative to standard exposure in social phobia, especially since studies have demonstrated its usefulness in dealing with the fear of public speaking. The outcome of the CBT group and virtual reality therapy are similar (no statistically significant difference) [48].

In addition, the Mindfulness-based stress reduction (MBSR) program applied to patients with social phobia was compared to the CBT group, showing that: the social anxiety scores for patients and therapists were lower than the response and remission rates, although two CBT and MBSR interventions were comparable in terms of improving mood and quality of life [49].

In another review [50], qualitative CBT resulted in better improvements, at the time of post treatment and follow-up, than the supportive group, and improvement was maintained at the time of a 5 year follow-up.

In addition, relaxation is important in fighting the physiological affects of social anxiety. The combination of both medication and psychological treatment (attention focus training and task concentration training (TCT), have similar effects to exposure [51].

An Intrapsychic-Biological Matrix Model: within the intrapsychic-biological matrix the cognitive schema (core beliefs) are affective, and within the neurobiological matrix they are defensive processes, temperamental dispositions and neurobiological underpinnings. When the system is poorly integrated, symptoms of emotional deregulation, impairment of self esteem and cognitive distortions create anxiety and depressive symptoms [52].

The group can be guided by an individual worker: we use a leader or someone from the hierarchy as a flexible guide in our planning, enabling the individuals to meet their goals and increase their expectations, until their goals are finally met. This group also prevents anxiety and depression. Social phobias are often associated with unipolar depression, which is one of the most common psychological disorders in adulthood and adolescence.

The group is useful for individuals with social anxiety, who are less likely to be engaged in interactions, speak less, have reduced eye contact and endeavour to exit interactions rapidly [53]. These individuals are likely to have fewer sources of social support, and fewer social interactions than individuals without social phobia. The manifestation of extreme anxiety is probably more central to disruptions in social interactions.

7. Discussion

After completing the CBT session groups for social phobia, with the inclusion of CBT and emotional aspects, we noticed that the group sessions helped decrease anxiety and depression, but had no effect on the recognition and expression of emotions. Regarding social phobia, the results have led to an improvement in terms of depression and anxiety, and also to an increase in self-esteem.

We have focused more strongly on group dynamics than on quantitative results, and have demonstrated the evolution of the emotional aspects of these groups (with the integration of other approaches such as ACT and MBCT), which consolidate the therapeutic alliance with these patients.

The authors plan to continue this research, with this type of group, in order to adapt their therapeutic protocol to other disorders such as depression and alcohol-dependency.

References

[1] Weiller, E., Bisserbe, J.C., Boyer, P., Lepine, J.P. & Lecrubier, Y. (1996). Social phobia in general health care: an unrecognised undertreated disabling disorder. *British Journal of Psychiatry, 168*(2), 169-74.

[2] Pélissolo, A., Huron, C., Fanget, F., Servant, D., Stiti, S., Richard-Berthe, C. & Boyer P. (2006). Les phobies sociales en psychiatrie : caractéristiques cliniques et modalités de prise en charge (étude phoenix). *Encephale, 32*(1 Pt 1), 106-112

[3] Liebowitz, M.R., Heimberg, R.G., Schneir, F.R., Hope, D.A., Holt, C.S., Welkowitz, L.A. & all. (1999). Cognitive behavioral group therapy vs phenelzine therapy for social phobia: long term outcome. *Depression and anxiety, 10,* 89-98

[4] Bech P. & Angest J. (1996). Quality of life in anxiety and social phobia, *international clinical psychopharmacology, 11*(supl 3), 97-100

[5] Beidel, D.C., Turner, S.M. & Morris, T.L. (1999). Psychopathology of childhood social phobia. *Journal of the American Academy of Child and Adolescent Psychiatry, 38*(6), 643-650.

[6] Neal, J.A. & Edelmann, R.J. (2003). The etiology of social phobia: toward a developmental profile. *Clinical Psychology Review, 23*(6), 761-786.

[7] Schofield, C.A., Coles, M.E. & Gibb, B E. (2007). Social anxiety and interpretation biases for facial displays of emotion: emotion detection and ratings of social cost. *Behaviour research and therapy, 45*(12), 2950-2963

[8] Buckner, J.D., Schmidt, N.B., Lang, A.R, Small, J.W, Schlauch, R.C. & Lewinsohn, P.M. (2008). Specificity of social anxiety disorder as a risk factor for alcohol and cannabis dependence. *Journal of Psychiatric Research, 42*(3):230-9

[9] Hofmann, S.G. & Smits, J. (2008). cognitive behavioural therapy for adult anxiety disorder: a meta-analysis of randomized placebo-controled trials. *Journal of clinical psychiatry, 5*

[10] Van Dam-Baggen, R. & Kraaimaat, F.W. (20002); Group Social Skills Training or Cognitive Group Therapy as the Clinical Treatment of Choice for Generalized Social Phobia? *Journal of Anxiety Disorders, 14(* 5), 437-451(15)
[11] Herbert, J.D., Gaudiano, B.A., Rheingold, A.A., Myers, V.H., Dalrymple, K. & Nolan, E.M. (2005). Social skills training augments the effectiveness of cognitive behavioral group therapy for social anxiety disorder. *Behavior therapy, 36(*2), 125-138
[12] Roberge, P., Marchand, A., Reinharz, D., Marchand, L., & Cloutier, K. (2004). Évaluation économique de la thérapie cognitive-comportementale des troubles anxieux. *Psychologie canadienne, 45*(3), 202-218.
[13] Beck, A.T., Steer, R. & Garbin, M. (1988). Psychometric properties of the Beck depression inventory : twenty-five years of research. *Clinical Psychology Review*, 8(1), 77- 100.
[14] Oei, T.P., Evans, L., & Crook, G.M. (1990). Utility and validity of the STAI with anxiety disordered patients. *British Journal of Clinical Psychology, 29*(4), 429-432.
[15] Beck, A.T.; Epstein, N. & Brown, G. (1998) An inventory for measuring clinical anxiety: Psychometric properties. *Journal of Consulting and Clinical Psychology, 56*(6), 893-897
[16] Liebowitz, M.R. (1987). social Phobia. *Modern Problems in Pharmacopsychatry, 22,* 141-173
[17] Rathus, S.A. (1973). A 30-item schedule for assessing assertive behavior. *Behavior therapy, 4*(3), 398-406
[18] Glass, Carol, R., Merluzzi, T.V., Biever, J.L. & Larsen, K.H. (1982). Cognitive assessment of social anxiety: Development and validation of a self-statement questionnaire. *Cognitive Therapy and Research,6,* 37-45
[19] Coopersmith, S. (1959). A method for determining types of self-esteem. *The Journal of Abnormal and Social Psychology, 59*(1), 87-94
[20] Hollon, S.D. & Kendall, P.C. (1980). Cognitive self statements in depression: development of an automatic thoughts questionnaire. *Cognitive therapy and research,4*, 383-395
[21] Landy, F.J., & Gaup, L.A. (1971). A factor analysis of the Fear Survey Schedule-III. *Behaviour Research and Therapy, 9*, 89-93
[22] Bydlowski, S., Corcos, M., Paterniti, S., Guilbaud, O., Jeammet, P. & Consoli, S.M. (2002). French validation study of the levels of emotional awareness scale. *Encephale, 28*(4), 310-320
[23] Brown, K.W. & Ryan, R.M. (2003). The benefits of being present: The role of mindfulness in psychological well-being. *Journal of Personality and Social Psychology*, *84*, 822-848.
[24] Taylor, G.J., Bagby, R.M. & Parker, J.D. (2003). The 20-Item Toronto Alexithymia Scale. IV. Reliability and factorial validity in different languages and cultures. *Journal of Psychosomatic research*, *55*(3), 277-283.
[25] Lane, R.D., Quinlan, D.M., Schwartz, G.E., Walker, P.A. & Zeitlin, S.B. (1990). The levels of emotional awareness scale: a cognitive-developmental measure of emotion. *Journal of personality assessment*, *55*(1-2):124-134.

[26] Ponniah, K. & Hollon, S.D. (2007). Empirically supported psychological interventions for social phobia in adults: a qualitative review of randomized controlled trials. *Psychological Medicine, 38*(1), 3-14

[27] Camart, N., André, C., Trybou, V., Bourdel, M.C. (2006). Evaluation des effets à court terme d'une thérapie cognitivo-comportementale de groupe dans la phobie sociale : résultats aupres de soixante patients. *Encephale, 32*(6 Pt 1), 1011-1018.

[28] Barlow, D.H (1988). *Anxiety and its disorders*. New York: Guildford Press

[29] Marcus, D.K. & Wilson, J.R. (1996). Interpersonal perception of social anxiety: A Social relation analysis. *Journal of social and Clinical psychology, 15* , 471-487

[30] Clark, D.M (1997). Panic desorder and social phobia. In: Clark, D.M. & Fairburn, C.G., Oxford University press. *Science and practice of cognitive behavior therapy*. New York; 1997; 119-153

[31] Young, J.E. (1990). *Cognitive therapy for personality disorders: A schema –focused approach*. Sarasota: Professional resource exchange, 1990,1994

[32] Young, J.E. & Klosko, J.S. (1993). R*einventing your life*, USA: penguin books

[33] Kashdan, T.B. & Breen, W.E. (2008). Social anxiety and positive emotions: a prospective examination of a self-regulatory model with tendencies to suppress or express emotions as a moderating variable, *Behaviour Therapy, 39*(1), 1-12

[34] Whelton, W.J. (2004). Emotional processes in psychotherapy: Evidence across therapeutic modalities. *Clinical Psychology and Psychotherapy, 11*, 58-71.

[35] Blackledge, J.T. & Hays, S.C. (2001). emotion regulation in acceptance and commitment therapy. In session: *Psychoterapy in practice, 57*, 243-255

[36] Linehan, M.M. (1993). *Cognitive-behavioural traitment of borderline personality disorder*. New York, Guildford press

[37] Segal, Z.V, Williams M.G, Teasdale J.D. (2002) Mindfulness-Based Cognitive Therapy for Depression. New York : The Guilford Press

[38] Mennin, D.S. (2006). emotion regulation therapy: an interactive approach to traitement persistant anxiety disorder. *journal of contemporary psychotherapy, 36*, 95-105

[39] Quadflieg, S., Wendt, B., Mohr, A., Miltner, W.H., Straube, T. (2007). Recognition and evaluation of emotional prosody in individuals with generalized social phobia: a pilot study. *Behaviour research and therapy, 45*(12), 3096-3103

[40] Fogler, J.M., Tompson, M.C., Steketee, G. & Hofmann, S.G. (2007). Influence of expressed emotion and perceived criticism on cognitive-behavioral therapy for social phobia, *behavior research and therapy, 45*(2), 235-249

[41] Hayes, S.A., Hope, D.A., VanDyke, M.M. & Heimberg, R.G. (2007). Working alliance for clients with social anxiety disorder: relationship with session helpfulness and within-session habituation. *Cognitive Behavioral Therapy, 36*(1), 34-42.

[42] Chen, J., Nakano, Y., Ietzugu, T., Ogawa, S., Funayama, T., Watanabe, N., Noda, Y. & Furukawa, T.A. (2007). Group cognitive behavior therapy for Japanese patients with social anxiety disorder: preliminary outcomes and their predictors. *BMC Psychiatry, 10*, 7-69

[43] Parkinson, B. & Tottferdell, P. (1999). classifiying affect-regulation strategies. *cognition and emotion, 13*(3), 277-303

[44] Vassilopoulos, S.P. (2008). Coping strategies and anticipatory processing in high and low socially anxious individuals. *Journal of Anxiety Disorders, 22*(1), 98-107

[45] Rodebaugh, T.L., Holaway, R.M. & Heimberg, R.G. (2004). The treatment of social anxiety disorder. *Clinical Psychology Review, 24*(7), 883-908.

[46] Butler, A.C., Champman, J.E., Forman, E.M. & Beck, A.T. (2006). the empirical status of cognitive behavioural therapy: A review of meta- analisis. *clinical psychologie review, 26*, 17-31

[47] Gould, R.A. & Johnson, M.W. (2001). *Comparative effectiveness of cognitive-behavioral treatment and pharmacotherapy for social phobia: Meta-analytic outcome.* In Hoffmann SG,

[48] Klinger, E., Bouchard, S., Légeron, P., Roy, S., Lauer, F., Chemin, I. & Nugues, P. (2005). Virtual reality therapy versus cognitive behavior therapy for social phobia: a preliminary controlled study. *Cyberpsychology and Behaviour, 8*(1), 76-88.

[49] 49 Koszycki, D., Benger, M., Shlik, J. & Bradwejn, J. (2007). Randomized trial of a meditation-based stress reduction program and cognitive behavior therapy in generalized social anxiety disorder. *Behaviour Research and Therapy, 45*(10), 2518-2526

[50] Rowa, K. & Antony, M.M. (2005). Psychological treatments for social phobia, *Canadian Journal of Psychiatry, 50*, 308-316

[51] Norton, P.J. & Price, E.C. (2007). A meta-analytic review of adult cognitive-behavioral treatment outcome across the anxiety disorders. *The Journal of Nervous and Mental Disease, 195*(6), 521-531

[52] Magnavita, J.J. (2006). The centrality of emotion in unifying and accelerating psychotherapy, *Journal of Clinical Psychology, 62*(5), 585-96

[53] Leary, M. & Kowalski, R.M. (1995). *Social anxiety*. New York, Guildford press.

In: Social Phobia: Etiology, Diagnosis and Treatment
Editor: Clayton P. Axelby
ISBN 978-1-60692-159-3
© 2009 Nova Science Publishers, Inc.

Expert Commentary

SOCIAL PHOBIA AND SCHIZOPHRENIA: A BRIEF REVIEW

Jean Kim[1] and Phillip J. Seibell[2]
[1]Weill Medical College of Cornell University, White Plains, NY, USA;
[2]Mount Sinai School of Medicine, New York, NY, USA.

ABSTRACT

Several studies have described high rates of comorbidity between the anxiety disorders and schizophrenia. Social anxiety disorder (SAD) also known as social phobia is arguably the anxiety disorder that occurs with the highest frequency among patients with schizophrenia. Despite this correlation, the connection between the two disorders remains poorly studied in the literature. This brief review will examine the current literature and attempt to clarify the hypotheses regarding how social anxiety and schizophrenia are related. The connection may be a primary one, relating to a biological/genetic or phenomenological connection between schizophrenia/psychotic symptoms and social phobia, or a secondary one, relating to a psychological connection where social phobia develops in response to the damaging consequences of coping with schizophrenia and its social sequelae. There may also be a connection to prodromal symptoms of schizophrenia and its own social sequelae during childhood and adolescence. Treatments such as anti-anxiety pharmacology and CBT that target this particular comorbidity have shown good efficacy in preliminary studies. Neurobiological studies of SAD and schizophrenia both examine the dopaminergic system of the brain and may show some connection in terms of its relationship to perceptions of social behavior and interpersonal threat and judgment and even paranoia. More studies are warranted to clarify the timing and nature of the relationship between the two disorders over the full course of schizophrenia.

INTRODUCTION AND EPIDEMIOLOGY

Several studies have demonstrated high levels of comorbidity between the anxiety disorders and schizophrenia. In particular, social anxiety disorder (SAD), also known as social phobia, appears to have the highest rates of comorbidity among the anxiety disorders with schizophrenia, with rates ranging from 8-36% in sample populations in several different studies (Cosoff 17% in 100 inpatients, Tibbo: 13.3%, Goodwin 8.2%, Pallanti 36%, Voges 32%).

Despite this high rate of comorbidity, SAD remains sparsely studied in the research literature in the schizophrenic population. Abnormalities in social relatedness have been well-described in schizophrenia and psychotic spectrum disorders. There are some superficial similarities between social anxiety and schizophrenia in terms of symptomatology: both involve social withdrawal, isolation, feelings that others judge or perceive them in a negative fashion that can veer into paranoia. However, schizophrenia is a much more severe, progressive condition with concomitant hallucinations and frank delusions and apathy/avolition, whereas patients with SAD alone do not have these symptoms.

Also, the social distress symptoms associated with SAD tend to be more situational, whereas with schizophrenia, they may be part of a chronic system of social misinterpretation related possibly to cognitive deficits from the illness. There have also been some studies examining whether stress and emotional reactivity can affect the course of psychosis, or if the cognitive impairments of schizophrenia are part of a separate, more insidious pathway. Overall, the relationship between the two conditions could illuminate elements of the etiology of the two conditions, and could help clarify and target which specific behaviors and cognitions stem from psychosis and which from anxiety. Accordingly, treatments could be customized to a more appropriate extent.

Several studies indicate that anxiety and social phobia comorbidity lead to poorer outcomes and a more severe clinical course for patients with schizophrenia. Pallanti et al. (2004) noted higher rates of suicide attempts, social decline, and decreased quality of life in an outpatient population. There were also higher rates of substance abuse among the patients with comorbid SAD. Lysaker (2007) confirmed poorer outcomes with increased anxiety and schizophrenia. Braga (2005) conducted a study of 53 outpatients and also found increased problems with global functioning and work/education and social/romantic life with comorbid social phobia/schizophrenia, although no disruption of family life functioning (which seems typical of the more isolative nature of these conditions) and no increase in suicidality in this particular study. Huppert (2001) also noted overall worse quality of life for patients with both schizophrenia and anxiety comorbidity. SAD was the most prevalent anxiety disorder in this sample population.

There is some controversy over the exact nature of this comorbidity and its phenomenology, with 3 typical hypotheses to explain the relationship of social phobia and schizophrenia:

A. Biological/Phenomenological: Is social anxiety an intrinsic part of schizophrenic pathology? Is there a biological or phenomenologic link between the two conditions? Are social anxiety symptoms part of psychotic symptomatology?

B. Psychological: Has social anxiety developed in response to the trauma/shame/difficulty of schizophrenia or its associated symptoms that affect social relationships?
C. Prodromal: Was social anxiety a syndrome that developed as part of or in response to prodromal symptoms that preceded the patient's first break? (In some ways this hypothesis still ends up boiling back down to hypotheses A vs. B, primary biology and/or phenomenology vs. secondary reactive psychology)

Hypothesis A: Primary (Biological/Phenomenological) Connection

With regard to Hypothesis A (a primary connection between social anxiety and schizophrenia), studies have offered variable results. Some studies have indicated the possibility of a phenomenological connection between symptoms of psychosis (especially negative symptoms of schizophrenia) and associated symptoms of social anxiety. This connection may explain the high rates of comorbidity, and may also allude to the other dimension of this primary connection, a biological/genetic link between the two syndromes. Other studies examining overall stress/emotional reactivity factors in schizophrenia have alluded to this connection as well, although little clear evidence of such a link exists thus far in the literature.

Penn et al. (1994) analyzed the relationship between the positive and negative symptoms of schizophrenia in 38 inpatients, in an attempt to clarify the issue of a phenomenologic link between psychotic symptoms and social anxiety. He found an association between self-reported social anxiety symptoms and positive symptoms of schizophrenia, but not with objectively observed social anxiety-related behaviors during role play evaluation. Conversely, he found an association with social anxiety-related behaviors in the role play (such as alterations in speech rate and fluency) and negative symptoms of schizophrenia. The study noted some limitations in its ability to distinguish the cause and effect relationship between the visible anxiety symptoms and negative symptoms (such as affective flattening and speech latency). So the exact nature of the association remained unclear from this study, although some association was clearly present.

Seedat et al. (2007) noted that there are difficulties in making diagnostic distinctions between some of the symptom criteria between social anxiety and schizophrenia (which might have been an obfuscating issue with the Penn study). He felt that symptoms like social withdrawal and freezing of affect could appear with either condition (particularly negative symptoms of schizophrenia) and would not help distinguish the true etiology of those symptoms. This overlap might argue against a true phenomenologic link between the two syndromes.

Freeman (2008) tried to examine more closely these phenomenologic distinctions between social anxiety and paranoia in their recent study. 250 people who did not meet criteria for full psychiatric disorders were given various questionnaires after observing certain social situations in a virtual reality subway ride setting. Interestingly, they found that in many cases, there were no significant differences in people's self-report of anxiety, depression, worry and interpersonal sensitivity in those who reported social anxiety versus paranoid symptoms. However, the reported presence of perceptual anomalies (which were likely harbingers of psychotic spectrum symptoms) correlated more highly with paranoia scales as opposed to social anxiety scales, and vice versa as well (higher social anxiety reports did not correlate with the presence of perceptual anomalies.) This study seems to corroborate the ongoing challenge in differentiating the contribution of anxiety to social phobic versus paranoid symptoms in people, since there is some overlap in anxiety's contribution to both states of mind. But the Freeman study also seems to corroborate the other evidence that points to the classic phenomenologic distinctions between the two disorders, related to the presence or absence of hallucinations or other frank perceptual anomalies.

Azorin (2007) noted an increase in the severity of manic psychosis amongst bipolar patients with comorbid SAD. They also noted increased rates of SAD in patients with psychotic mania, younger ages of onset, and higher rates of drug use. While bipolar is of course a different disorder, the association between increased social phobia and specifically psychotic periods of mania is interesting and may point to a primary association between psychosis and social phobia.

In terms of clearer biological or genetic connections between social phobia and schizophrenia, there is a little more potential evidence in this direction. Fogelson et al. (2007) noted higher levels of avoidant PD in relatives of patients with schizophrenia relative to control families (9.4% vs 2% control, and 5% ADHD). It is already well known that cluster A PDs occur at higher rates in these families, and this study controlled for the presence of those other cluster A PDs. This increase in familial rates of avoidant PD would seem to indicate that perhaps avoidant PD and its sister condition social phobia are possibly somewhere on the schizotypy spectrum, and share some sort of genetic link.

Hypothesis B: Psychological Connection

Traditional distinctions between avoidant and schizoidal spectrum disorders have hinged on the concept of seeking out relationships versus lack of awareness or interest in them. However, several studies have noted that this distinction to be more complex in clinical actuality, as patients with schizophrenia describe feelings akin to social anxiety/ avoidant phenomena even due to or despite the other social impairments created by the negative symptoms of schizophrenia.

Birchwood's 2006 study of 79 patients (unclear if they were inpatient or outpatient) with first-break psychosis went on to postulate that Hypothesis B, a secondary, psychologically-induced relationship between schizophrenia and social anxiety, was more likely. This study found high levels of self-perceived shame amongst first-break schizophrenics with social anxiety, and a correlation with improved insight and depression. This population would be particularly vulnerable to such feelings, given the new trauma and adjustment to a difficult, life-altering diagnosis and its associated stigma. (The other possibility though is that they are not as affected as yet by the social indifference and withdrawal that occurs with progressive negative symptoms in more advanced stages of the illness.) This study postulated that there was a high correlation between the associated negative cognitions of SAD and this shame-inducing setup of first-break psychosis. This study did not find a direct correlation between levels of psychosis and symptoms of SAD, further supporting their view of Hypothesis B relative to A.

Voges in 2005 also noted increased levels of negative self-statements and cognitions apart from negative symptoms in schizophrenics with social phobia in his 2006 survey of 60 first-break outpatients, confirming Birchwood's findings with regards to the contribution of negative self-perception, and controlling for the presence of negative symptoms (although again, this is an early-stage schizophrenic population). This study again points more towards psychological origins of social phobia in this schizophrenic population, especially in the vulnerable early stages of the illness.

Pallanti's 2004 study of outpatients with schizophrenia also found that there were higher levels of insight and avoidance related behaviors in the patients with comorbid social phobia and schizophrenia, which would also correlate with the idea that awareness of the illness and its sequelae might lead to an increase in social phobia psychologically. He found that an increase in negative symptoms seemed to correlate with a decrease in insight and avoidance-related behaviors, which seems to contradict Penn's findings in some fashion. Accordingly, he felt that negative symptoms or primary psychosis led to more detachment-style behaviors which could be confused with social phobia versus the actual interpersonal sensitivity/avoidant features which went along with true social phobia in schizophrenics. However, anxiety induced by stress also seemed to increase levels of paranoia, which might indicate that social anxiety might exacerbate positive symptoms. It remains unclear if this connection is a psychologically induced one like Hypothesis B, or a biological one like Hypothesis A with anxiety having a direct connection to psychosis.

Hypothesis C: Prodromal Connection

Little has been investigated with regard to Hypothesis C, and Bogels in 2004 indicated that an associated potential area of investigation would be to examine levels of stranger anxiety in infants and any future correlation with social phobia or other conditions. Social phobia already remains a highly prevalent condition amongst adolescents and young adults per Wittchen's community survey. A few studies (Tien and Eaton 1992, Dworkin 1994) did seem to indicate an increased (nearly 3.5 times) risk of children/teens with social phobia developing schizophrenia relative to normal controls. Another possibility is that the premorbid symptoms of schizophrenia cause social awkwardness and behaviors and difficulties with peers that result in later development of social phobia, and can possibly lead to higher vulnerability when a first break does occur.

Treatment

Given the high level of comorbidity, social phobia in schizophrenia ought to be adequately treated with more targeted therapies that address social phobia in both social skills/CBT related realms, and with anxiety disorder psychopharmacology. A couple studies indicated the positive effects of targeted CBT in this population. Halperin's 2000 CBT trial population showed improvement in all measures of social skills training, and even improvement in secondary depression ratings amongst 20 patients enrolled in 6 weeks of group CBT relative to a control group (waiting list). The CBT in this study particularly focused on social exposure training and support. This study indicates that social skills might be again a core reactive issue that exacerbates social anxiety in this population, and targeting this issue can alleviate these symptoms. Kingsep also did a group CBT study (incorporating more primary anxiety and stress management and relaxation training) in 2003 with similarly positive results, showing that general coping skill training can also help.

In terms of psychopharmacologic interventions, Pallanti noted in another study that fluoxetine helped patients with social phobia and schizophrenia improve their social phobia symptoms, even if their primary psychotic symptoms did not show much change (again, pointing more to Hypothesis B, with the social phobia as a distinct condition apart from psychotic phenomena). He also noted a possible link between atypical antipsychotics (particularly clozapine) and exacerbation of social phobia, which has also been noted with OCD (Eales and Layeni). Serotonin blockade related phenomena may be responsible, given social phobia's h/o response to SSRIs and shared neurobiology with other anxiety disorders. Pallanti also interestingly postulated though that the increase could also be related to alleviation of psychotic symptoms and improved insight with clozapine (known to be the most effective antipsychotic) specifically, leading to increased awareness and expectation that then leads to social anxiety. Other possible pharmacologic interventions include benzodiazepines, which have been shown to improve other anxiety disorders like panic disorder in patients with schizophrenia (Kahn), and other antidepressants like the SNRIs or MAOIs (less practical due to drug interactions and dietary restrictions).

Neurobiology

In terms of neurobiology, some studies still seem to point towards the possibility of a Hypothesis A link, with abnormalities in dopaminergic transmission in social phobia, apart from the presence of schizophrenia, that are not found in other anxiety disorders. Potts showed decreased basal ganglia volume on MRI in patients with social phobia. Tiihonen showed decreased dopamine reuptake site densities. Schneier showed decreased dopamine receptor binding sites on PET scan in social phobics. Stein noted increased rates of social phobia in patients with Parkinson's Disease who are well-known to have hypodopaminergic transmission in the basal ganglia. Liebowitz noted that MAOIs have been shown to be more effective than TCAs in social phobia. Increased social phobia has been seen in patients with Tourette's syndrome on Haldol (Mikkelsen). However, other dopaminergic enhancing agents have not been known to provide effective treatment in social phobia (Spollen). Also the affected binding sites in the imaging studies thus far appear to be different than those involved in schizophrenia, and lower dopamine binding has not been shown as a finding in schizophrenia (Laruelle). Still, there seems to be some correlation between social behavior and levels of striatal dopamine binding, which were found to be decreased in monkeys that demonstrated subordinate, social phobia style behaviors (Grant). Perhaps there are still similarities or connections between social phobia and schizophrenia in terms of neurobiological mechanisms that perceive interpersonal threat and judgment, and paranoia. On the other hand, the two illnesses could be neurogenetically distinct entities with their own specific relationships to the dopaminergic system in the brain.

Conclusions

Overall, more studies are warranted to clarify the etiology and phenomenology of social phobia in schizophrenia, as the evidence thus far remains equivocal in terms of demonstrating whether there is a primary biological association between the two conditions and/or a link to psychosis and positive or negative symptoms, or if the higher rates of social phobia relate more to the devastating psychological impact and secondary sequelae of the impaired social functioning of schizophrenia. More controlled studies that examine all stages of schizophrenia and all phases of symptomatology relative to social phobia can help elucidate the relationship between the two disorders. More neurobiological and neuroimaging studies are needed to refine our understanding of the contribution and specifics of dopamine transmission abnormalities in either condition, and lead to better sites for pharmacologic action. Advances in social skills training and psychotherapies that address the shame and stigma and negative cognitions associated with the illness itself and its social sequelae are ongoing; CBT has provided an effective means to help this population. Greater clarification of the relationship between social phobia and schizophrenia will help enhance and promote more targeted and effective therapies for both disorders, and improve overall outcomes for this highly comorbid set of conditions.

References

Azorin J-M, et al. Is psychosis in DSM-IV mania due to severity? The relevance of selected demographic and comorbid social-phobic features. *Acta Psychiatr Scand* (2007) 115: 29-34.

Birchwood M, et al. Social anxiety and the shame of psychosis: A study in first episode psychosis. *Behaviour Research and Therapy* (2006) 45:1025-1037.

Bogels SM, Tarrier N. Unexplored issues and future directions in social phobia research. *Clinical Psychology Review* (2004) 24:731-736.

Braga RJ, et al. Anxiety disorders in schizophrenia. *Comprehensive Psychiatry* (2004) 45: 460-468.

Braga RJ, et al. Anxiety disorders in outpatients with schizophrenia: prevalence and impact on the subjective quality of life. *Journal of Psychiatric Research* (2005) 39: 409-414.

Cassano GB, et al. Occurrence and clinical correlates of psychiatric comorbidity in patients with psychotic disorders. *Journal of Clinical Psychiatry* (1998) 59: 60-68.

Cosoff SJ, Hafner RJ. The prevalence of comorbid anxiety in schizophrenia, schizoaffective and bipolar disorder. *Australian and New Zealand Journal of Psychiatry* (1998) 32: 67-72.

Dworkin RH, et al. Childhood precursors of affective vs. social deficits in adolescents at risk for schizophrenia. *Schizophrenia Bulletin* (1994) 20: 453-480.

Eales MJ, Layeni AO. Exacerbation of obsessive-compulsive symptoms associated with clozapine. *British Journal of Psychiatry* (1994) 164:687-8.

Emsley RA, et al. Depressive and anxiety symptoms in patients with schizophrenia and schizophreniform disorder. *Journal of Clinical Psychiatry* (1999) 60: 747-751.

Fogelson DL, et al. Avoidant personality disorder is a separable schizophrenia-spectrum personality disorder even when controlling for the presence of paranoid and schizotypal personality disorders: the UCLA family study. *Schizophrenia Research* (2007) 91: 192-199.

Freeman D, et al. What makes one person paranoid and another person anxious? The differential prediction of social anxiety and persecutory ideation in an experimental situation. *Psychological Medicine* (2008) 4: 1-12.

Freeman MP, et al. The comorbidity of bipolar and anxiety disorders: prevalence, psychobiology and treatment issues. *Journal of Affective Disorders* (2002) 68:1-23.

Goodwin RD, et al. Anxiety and substance use comorbidity among inpatients with schizophrenia. *Schizophrenia Research* (2003) 61: 89-95.

Grant KA, et al. Effect of social status on striatal dopamine D2 receptor binding characteristics in cynomolgus monkeys assessed with positron emission tomography. *Synapse* (1998) 29:80-83.

Halperin S, et al. A cognitive-behavioural, group-based intervention for social anxiety in schizophrenia. *Australian and New Zealand Journal of Psychiatry* (2000) 34: 809-813.

Huppert JD, et al. Quality of life in schizophrenia: contributions of anxiety and depression. *Schizophrenia Research* (2001) 51: 171-180.

Kahn JP, et al. Adjunctive alprazolam for schizophrenia with panic anxiety: clinical observation and pathogenetic implications. *American Journal of Psychiatry* (1988) 145: 742-4.

Kessler RC, et al. Social phobia subtypes in the National Comorbidity Survey. *American Journal of Psychiatry* (1998) 155: 613-619.

Kingsep P, et al. Cognitive behavioural group treatment for social anxiety in schizophrenia. *Schizophrenia Research* (2003) 63: 121-129.

Laruelle M. Imaging dopamine transmission in schizophrenia. *Q J Nucl Med* (1998) 42: 211-221.

Lecrubier Y. Schizophrenia and anxiety disorders. www.ipap.org/schiz (Mar 2006).

Marcin MS, et al. The neurobiology of social anxiety disorder: the relevance of fear and anxiety. *Acta Psychiatr Scand* (2003) 108:51-64.

Pallanti S, et al. Social anxiety in outpatients with schizophrenia: a relevant cause of disability. *American Journal of Psychiatry* (2004) 161: 53-58.

Pallanti S, et al. The emergence of social phobia during clozapine treatment and its response to fluoxetine augmentation. *Journal of Clinical Psychiatry* (1999) 60: 819-823.

Pallanti S, et al. Social anxiety and premorbid personality in paranoid schizophrenics treated with clozapine. *CNS Spectrums* (2000) 9:29-43.

Penn DL, et al. Social anxiety in schizophrenia. *Schizophrenia Research* (1994) 11: 277-284.

Pilkonis PA, Feldman H. Social anxiety and psychiatric diagnosis. *Journal of Nervous and Mental Disease* (1980) 168: 13-18.

Potts NLS, et al. Magnetic resonance imaging in social phobia. *Psychiatric Research* (1994) 52: 35-42.

Schneier FR, et al. Low dopamine D2 receptor binding potential in social phobia. *American Journal of Psychiatry* (2000) 157: 457-459.

Seedat S, et al. Measuring anxiety in patients with schizophrenia. *Journal of Nervous and Mental Disease* (2007) 195: 320-324.

Spollen JJ. Schizophrenia and social anxiety disorder. http://www.medscape.com/viewarticle/457030, 2003.

Strakowski SM, et al. Comorbidity in psychosis at first hospitalization. *American Journal of Psychiatry* (1993) 150: 752-757.

Tanner RJ, et al. Implicit views of the self in social anxiety. *Behaviour Research and Therapy* (2006) 44: 1397-1409.

Tibbo P, et al. Prevalence and relationship to delusions and hallucinations of anxiety disorders in schizophrenia. Depression Anxiety (2003) 17: 65-72.

Tien AY, Eaton WW. Psychopathologic precursors and sociodemographic risk factors for the schizophrenia syndrome. *Archives of General Psychiatry* (1992) 49: 37-46.

Tiihonen J, et al. Dopamine reuptake site densities in patients with social phobia. *American Journal of Psychiatry* (1997) 154: 239-242.

Voges M, Addington J. The association between social anxiety and social functioning in first episode psychosis. *Schizophrenia Research* (2005) 76: 287-292.

Wetherell JL, et al. Anxiety symptoms and quality of life in middle-aged and older outpatients with schizophrenia and schizoaffective disorder. *Journal of Clinical Psychiatry* (2003) 64:1476-1482.

Wittchen H-U, et al. Social fears and social phobia in a community sample of adolescents and young adults: prevalence, risk factors and co-morbidity. *Psychological Medicine* (1999) 29: 309-323.

In: Social Phobia: Etiology, Diagnosis and Treatment
Editor: Clayton P. Axelby
ISBN 978-1-60692-159-3
© 2009 Nova Science Publishers, Inc.

Chapter XIII

NEWSPAPER ADVERTISEMENT RECRUITMENT OF THE SUBJECTS WITH SOCIAL ANXIETY DISORDER AND ITS RELATIONSHIP TO TAIJIN-KYOFUSHO

Toshihiko Nagata[1,*], Hisashi Yamada[1], Chiho Yoshimura[1], Hisato Matsunaga[1], Hidehiro Fukuhara[1], Irene van Vliet[2] and Nobuo Kiriike[1]

[1]Department of Neuropsychiatry, Osaka City University Medical School, 1-4-3 Asahimachi, Abunoku, Osaka 545-8585, Japan;
[2]Department of Psychiatry, Leiden University Medical Center, Leiden, the Netherlands.

ABSTRACT

Japan is well-known as the country of taijin kyofusho (TKS), but it remains unclear whether TKS rather than social anxiety disorder (SAD) is still predominant, even in clinical settings. Subjects consisted of 11 responders to a newspaper advertisement (ad-responders) and 103 self-referrals with SAD. All subjects underwent SCID-I and II (Structured Clinical Interview-DSM-IIIR Axis I Disorders and Personality Disorders) in addition to evaluation of basic background demographics. Ad-responders were significantly older and more likely to have finished university, be married, have better occupational (academic) function, to have later a onset of SAD and they were less likely to have lifetime comorbidity of major depression than self-referrals. In addition, ad-responders tended to be less likely to have TKS offensive subtype than self-referrals. Although limited by the small sample size, the results suggested the hidden presence of

* Correspondence concerning this article should be addressed to: Department of Neuropsychiatry, Osaka City University Medical School, 1-4-3 Asahimachi, Abunoku, Osaka 545-8585, Japan. Phone +81-6-6645-3821; Fax +81-6-6636-0439; Email address: toshi@med.osaka-cu.ac.jp (T. Nagata).

untreated and undiagnosed middle-aged patients with SAD, and that the presence of TKS offensive subtype might be skewed.

Keywords: anxiety disorders, taijin-kyofusho, social anxiety disorder, prevalence, cross-cultural comparison.

Introduction

Social anxiety disorder (SAD) is a psychiatric condition in which patients experience fear in social situations, often accompanied by somatic symptoms such as blushing, sweating and trembling. Patients fear a negative evaluation by others and therefore try to avoid social situations. In the late 1960s, Marks [1,2] described "social phobia" as a minor subtype of phobia in the West. Two decades later SAD was still labeled as "a neglected anxiety disorder" in Western countries [3]. Nowadays, almost four decades after Marks' work, SAD became well recognized as a treatable disorder and is treated using selective serotonin reuptake inhibitors (SSRIs) or cognitive behavioral therapy (CBT) [4].

Table 1. Proposed diagnostic criteria for taijin-kyofusho (TKS)

A. At least one of the following features: (1) Fear of blushing in the presence of others (2) Fear of stiffening of facial expression, of trembling of the head, hands, feet, or voice, of sweating while facing with others (3) Fear of physical deformities being noticed (4) Fear of emitting body odours (5) Fear of line-of-sight becoming uncontrollable (6) Fear of uncontrollable flatus in the presence of others
B. Either of the following two, because of the above fear(s) (1) Fear of being looked at (noticed) by others (2) Fear of offending or embarrassing others*
C. At most points during the course of the disorder, the person recognizes that the fear is excessive or unreasonable.
D. The fear(s) interferes significantly with the person's normal routine, occupational (academic) functioning, or social activities or relationships, or there is marked distress about having the fear(s)
E. The symptoms must have been present for at least one year. In individuals under age 18 years, the duration should have been at least 6 months

*A diagnosis of TKS offensive subtype requires the patient to meet criterion B(2).

Conversely, in Japan, taijin kyohusho (TKS) had been described as the predominant type of "Neurose" by Shoma Morita since the 1930s [5]. TKS is also characterized by fear in and avoidance of social situations. In addition, two subtypes have been described: the 'typical' subtype, characterized by one's fear of being noticed; and the 'offensive' subtype (as indicated by criteria B2 in Table 1), characterized by one's fear of offending or embarrassing others because of 'his or her body, its parts or its functions, appearance or odor, facial expressions or movements [6,7].

Although these 'offensive type' (B2) type cases are bordering on psychosis, former Japanese authorities [8,9] insisted that their prognosis was different from that of psychosis, and that these cases should be considered in the context of Neurose. Only patients with TKS, especially offensive type, rather than SAD, seem to visit psychiatrists in Japan [8,9]. As a result, TKS offensive type was listed as a culture-bound syndrome in the DSM diagnostic system [10]. However, we have the impression that these descriptions were skewed by the views of a few "Neurose" treatment specialists because we have recently experienced the usual SAD cases more frequently than these former psychiatrists insisted [7].

In February 2002, patients suffering from SAD were recruited for participation in a double blind study using an advertisement that ran in three major newspapers in Japan. This was the first use of newspaper advertisements for recruiting psychiatric subjects in Japan probably because of the stigma attached to psychiatric disorders. The same psychiatrists at the same institute ran both standard clinical psychiatric services and the treatment trial for SAD. Thus, there was an opportunity to compare clinical features between responders to the newspaper advertisement and self-referrals. We hypothesized that the rate of TKS offensive subtype would be lower among responders to a newspaper advertisement than among self-referrals because TKS offensive subtype in Japan might be as rare as in Western countries.

METHOD

Subjects

Subjects consisted of 11 responders to the newspaper advertisement (ad-responders) and 103 consecutive self-referred (self-referrals) patients with SAD according to DSM-IV criteria [10]. The Japanese version [11] of the Structured Clinical Interview for DSM-IIIR Axis I Disorders, Patient Edition (SCID-I) [12] was used for diagnosis. The section on anxiety disorders was modified to establish a DSM-IV diagnosis based on the modification by Stein and Hazen [13]. In addition, item C of the DSM-IV diagnostic criteria for SAD was expanded to read, "At most points during the course of disorder, the person recognizes that the fear is excessive or unreasonable," in order to include the TKS offensive type patients in the current study [7].

A full-page advertisement recruiting participants for a double-blind, placebo-controlled study of fluvoxamine for SAD ran in the three major newspapers on February 24, 2002, in the Kansai area (one of nine areas in Japan). In Japan, most households subscribe to home delivery of a newspaper, and thus newspaper advertisements are a very useful way of recruitment. Readers who considered participating in the current double-blind study, were asked to contact the "call center." Receptionists at the call center made an appointment at the institute nearest to their home, among nine sites in Kansai, after screening for social anxiety by asking a few questions concerning subjects such as anxiety relating public speaking or talking with authority figures. Participants were not screened regarding TKS symptoms. Both ad-responders and self-referrals lived in the area of the University Hospital. Thirteen subjects were referred from the call center, all with generalized SAD. Two could not be included in the double-blind study because of concurrent alcohol abuse (in one subject) and refusal to withdraw from current medication (benzodiazepine in both subjects). These two subjects also did not appear at follow-up appointments. Therefore, eleven subjects entered the current study. All patients provided written informed consent before entering the study.

Nation wide, 265 SAD patients enrolled in this double-blind study. There are no records how many people totally contacted the call center because all private information regarding these individuals was destroyed to maintain confidentiality after closing the call center on March 9, 2002.

Measurements

All subjects underwent a direct (face-to-face) 2- to 3-hour in-depth assessment conducted by T. N. or H. Y. on the third or fourth consultation. However, this assessment was not performed when patients were too tense to have a long interview. In such cases, the interview was re-scheduled after recovery from the condition. The assessment included the Japanese version [11] of the Structured Clinical Interview for DSM-III-R (SCID-p) [12] and personality disorders (SCID-II) [14]. All Axis I disorders other than SAD were based on the DSM-III-R (American Psychiatric Association, 1987).

The presence of TKS was determined using the proposed diagnostic criteria for TKS (Table 1) as proposed in our previous study [6,7]. "Hikikomori," defined as complete withdrawal from society for more than 6 months, is a recent social problem in Japan [15].

The Japanese version of the Liebowitz Social Anxiety Scale (LSAS) [6,16] has only been used recently, and thus not all of the subjects in this study completed the LSAS. The number of subjects who completed the LSAS is shown in Table 2.

Statistics

Fisher's exact test or independent t-test with Levene's test for equality of variances were performed to compare between responders to the advertisement (ad-responders) and self-referrals (SPSS for Windows, Chicago, IL). Because of the exploratory nature of this study, alpha was set at 0.05.

Results

Ad-responders were significantly older, significantly more likely to be married, and were significantly less impaired in functioning than self-referrals, as is shown in Table 2. Ad-responders also tended to be men, to have been educated for more years, to be full-time workers, and had less frequently attempted suicide or turned to "hikikomori" than self-referrals. Onset of SAD in ad-responders was significantly later than in self-referrals.

However, there were no significant differences in the rate of generalized SAD or LSAS score between the two groups. There were no significant differences in the rates of TKS offensive type (as indicated B2 type) between ad-responders and self-referrals.

In terms of lifetime comorbidity including dysthymia, bipolar I, panic disorder, agoraphobia, simple phobia, obsessive compulsive disorder, alcohol abuse, alcohol dependence, there were no significant differences between the two groups. Only lifetime comorbidity of major depressive disorder was significantly more frequent in self-referrals than in ad-responders. In addition, there were no significant differences in rate of comorbid personality disorders.

Table 2. Comparison of demographic backgrounds between ad-responders and self-referrals

		Ad-responder	Self-referral	X^2/t/Fisher (p)
N		11	103	
Age (years)		41.8 (12.7)[a]	28.0 (9.6)	4.4 (<.001)
Men		9 (82%)	54 (52%)	(.11)
Education (years)		14.7 (2.2)	13.3 (2.5)	1.8 (.07)
Marital Status	Single	6 (55%)	94 (91%)	18.0 (<.001)
	Married	5(46%)	6 (6%)	
	Divorced	0	3 (3%)	
Employment status	Full time	9 (82%)	51 (50%)	4.4 (.11)
	Part time	0	11 (11%)	
	Unemployed	2 (18%)	41 (40%)	
Global Assessment of Function[b]		65.5 (11.3)	54.3 (14.3)	2.5 (.01)
"Hikikomori" (%)		0	18 (18%)	(.21)
Suicide attempt (%)		0	20 (19%)	(.21)
Onset of SAD (years)		16.4 (7.6)	12.9 (4.6)	2.2 (.03)
Generalized type		8 (73%)	89 (86%)	(.21)
LSAS		78.9 (17.9)	86.3 (26.7)[c]	0.8(.38)
TKS offensive type		5 (46%)	61 (59%)	(.52)
Onset of TKS (years)		18.4(8.3)	17.0(3.9)	0.4(.78)
Lifetime comorbidity				
Major depressive disorder		2 (18%)	60 (58%)	.02
Dysthymia		3 (27%)	18 (18%)	.42
Avoidant personality disorder		8(73%)	90(87%)	.18

LSAS: Liebowitz Social Anxiety Scale, [a] Mean and Standard deviation, [b] Axis V of DSM-IV, [c] not all the self-referrals (87/103, 84%) competed the LSAS

Discussions

The current study suggests that self-referral SAD patients in Japan are different from the SAD patients (ad-responders) who responded to a newspaper advertisement, in terms of age, marital status, employment status, and lifetime comorbidity of major depressive disorder, although prevalence differences of TKS failed to reach significance. The rate of lifetime comorbid depression in self-referrals was located at the high end, and that in ad-responders at the low end of the range in previous studies in Western countries [17]. In addition, 18% of self-referrals had a housebound lifestyle for more than 6 months (hikikommori) which draw public concerns in Japan [15], although no ad-responders had such a history.

Why were ad-responders much different from self-referrals in terms of current age and current social adaptation? To the best of our knowledge, no previous studies have compared self-referral and ad-responder SAD subjects. Miller et al. [18] compared newspaper advertisement and consultation referral subjects with Major Depressive Disorder (MDD). They found no significant differences in gender, age, educational levels, marital and employment status, age of onset of first MDD episode, or number of other previous psychiatric diagnosis. However, SAD differs from MDD in terms of the gap between prevalence rate and treatment seeking rate [19]. In the multivariate model, having social anxiety was associated with a 2.8 times greater risk of being afraid of what others might think or say about one seeking treatment [20]. Therefore, there seems to be a significant barrier to seek treatment for SAD especially among the community [19]. The current study show the hidden presence of middle-aged patients with SAD who never seek treatment in Japan. It is part of the symptoms of the disease that SAD patients show low treatment-seeking behaviors [21].

In the current study, 59% of self-referrals and 46% of ad-responders had TKS of the offensive type. In addition, no ad-responders had fears regarding physical deformity, body odor, or flatus (not significantly differed between two groups), although body odor is one of the most prototypal concerns among the offensive type [8,9]. The results of the current study raise the question why TKS offensive type used to be the predominant prototype of "Neurose" in Japan. There are several explanations for this. First, the diagnostic threshold of SAD can be very different depending on the socio-cultural background and social value. Shyness has been recognized as a desirable property in Japanese culture since a long time ago [22]. How much shy persons are accepted differs even among Western countries [23]. East Asian Countries share similar social values regarding shyness and self-restriction (rather than self-assertiveness). Interestingly, in Shanghai, China, shy students achieved higher grades and their leadership was more admired than that of usual students [24]. In the 1970s when Japanese "Neurose" researchers were interested in TKS [8,9], the atmosphere was similar to that in Shanghai. Mild cases did not meet the diagnostic threshold because of that atmosphere, and could survive without any help from mental health professionals. Only extremely severe case with "Neurose" used to visit psychiatrists. Thus, we could speculate that only severe SAD patients who had fear of giving offense, e.g. TKS offensive type, visited psychiatrists in the 1970s.

However, social values have drastically changed in the last ten years. People did not need to speak anything other than "Yes" or "OK" in meetings or conferences especially toward superiors, just a decade ago. Recently, the economic bubble has burst, and the Japanese labor style, such as lifetime employment, the seniority-based wage system, and one union in one company, has changed dramatically. The recent economic depression damaged the security of middle-aged patients with SAD. Moreover, people must undergo job interviews more than once, because of the breakdown of lifetime employment. This is also suggested by the results of Dingemans et al. (2001), showing that men with a high educational level tended to seek more help because more impairment in functioning at work. Self-assertiveness and self-promotion have become much more important in the current Japanese socio-cultural background. When SAD patients reach the middle age, they cannot survive without the help of mental professionals. As a result, they might seek treatment by responding to a newspaper advertisement for a double-blind study.

The second reason is sampling bias, e.g. Berkson's Effect [25], also suggested by the current results. There were the possibilities that TKS offensive type might not be the predominant type of "Neurose" even in the 1970s, and that mild TKS patients might abandon seeking treatment. TKS cases tend not to visit just any psychiatric clinics, but rather to visit Japanese Morita therapists or psychiatrists interested in treating "Neurose" [8,9,26]. Moreover, Morita therapy was available at only a few particular university hospitals and clinics in Japan [26], although the theory of Morita itself was well-known and accepted by most Japanese psychiatrists. In contrast to the understanding of TKS in Western countries, the distribution of prototypal TKS patients was considerably skewed. In addition, stigma toward the psychiatric service in Japan was extremely severe, although this has recently been reducing. The number of psychiatric private practice clinics in Japan has doubled last ten years [27], and the rate of increase of psychiatric clinics is the highest among all outpatient clinics. Therefore, we must consider the sampling bias known as Berkson's bias [25] in the phenomenology of TKS, suggested by the differences in the clinical profiles between ad-responders and self-referrals.

Limitations of the current study include the small sample size among ad-responders, sampling bias, and it being not a community survey. Even with these limitations, the current study suggests the possibility that the view of TKS might suffer from a sampling bias [25] and that an atmosphere of Confucian values such as respecting elderly people might contribute to the clinical profiles of TKS (also SAD) and the Japanese labor system. In addition, the current results suggest that psychiatric disorders, especially SAD, must be understood from the viewpoint of socio-cultural context. In our experiences with generalized SAD patients, they usually suffer offensive anxiety. However, they only admit the presence of these symptoms when they are asked. Further study, including a community survey, regarding both SAD and TKS in Western countries is warranted.

REFERENCES

[1] Marks IM, Gelder MG. Different ages of onset in varieties of phobia. *American Journal of Psychiatry* 1966; 123: 218-21.

[2] Marks IM. The classification of phobic disorders. *British Journal of Psychiatry* 1970; 116: 377-86.

[3] Liebowitz MR, Gorman JM, Fyer AJ, Klein DF. Social phobia. Review of a neglected anxiety disorder. *Archives of General Psychiatry* 1985; 42: 729-36.

[4] Bandelow B, Stein DJ. *Social anxiety disorder*. Marcel Dekker, New York, 2004.

[5] Maeda F, Nathan JH. Understanding taijin kyofusho through its treatment, Morita therapy. *Journal of Psychosomatic Research* 1999; 46: 525-30.
[6] Nagata T, Oshima J, Wada A, Yamada H, Iketani T, Kiriike N. Open trial of milnacipran for Taijin Kyofusho in Japanese patients with social anxiety disorder. *International Journal of Psychiatry in Clinical Practice* 2003; 7: 107-112.
[7] Nagata T, van Vliet I, Yamada H, Kataoka K, Iketani T, Kiriike N. An open trial of paroxetine for the "offensive subtype" of taijin kyofusho and social anxiety disorder. *Depression and Anxiety* 2006; 23: 168-74.
[8] Kasahara Y, Fujinawa A, Sekiguchi H, Matsumoto M. *Fear of eye-to-eye confrontation and fear of emitting bad odors (in Japanese).* Igaku Shoin, Tokyo, 1972.
[9] Yamashita I. *Taijin-Kyofu (in Japanese).* Kanahara, Tokyo, 1977.
[10]American Psychiatric Association. *Diagnostic and statistical manual of mental disorders (4th ed.).* American Psychiatric Press, Washington, DC, 1994.
[11]Takahashi S, Hanada K, Ono Y. *Japanese version of SCID DSM-III-R.* Igaku-shoin, Tokyo, 1992.
[12]Spitzer R, Williams J, Gibbon M, First M. *Structured Clinical Interview for DSM-III-R - Patient edition(SCID-P, Version 1.0).* American Psychiatric Press, Washington, DC, 1990.
[13]Stein MB, Hazen AL. *Modified version of Structured Clinical Interview for DSM-IV(SCID-P).* Anxiety Disorders Research Program, University of California, San Diego, San Diego, 1995.
[14]Spitzer R, Williams J, Gibbon M, First M. *Structured Clinical Interview for DSM-III-R - Personality Disorders (SCID-II, Version 1.0).* American Psychiatric Press, Washington, DC, 1990.
[15]Watts J. Public health experts concerned about "hikikomori". *Lancet* 2002; 359: 1131.
[16]Liebowitz MR. Social phobia. *Modern Problems of Pharmacopsychiatry* 1987; 22: 141-73.
[17]Stein MB, Fuetsch M, Muller N, Hofler M, Lieb R, Wittchen HU. Social anxiety disorder and the risk of depression: a prospective community study of adolescents and young adults. *Archives of General Psychiatry* 2001; 58: 251-6.
[18]Miller CA, Hooper CL, Bakish D. A comparison of patients with major depressive disorder recruited through newspaper advertising versus consultation referrals for clinical drug trials. *Psychopharmacology Bulletin* 1997; 33: 69-73.
[19]Olfson M, Guardino M, Struening E, Schneier FR, Hellman F, Klein DF. Barriers to the treatment of social anxiety. *American Journal of Psychiatry* 2000; 157: 521-7.
[20]Ollendick TH, Hirshfeld-Becker DR. The developmental psychopathology of social anxiety disorder. *Biological Psychiatry* 2002; 51: 44-58.
[21]Dingemans AE, van Vliet IM, Couvee J, Westenberg HG. Characteristics of patients with social phobia and their treatment in specialized clinics for anxiety disorders in the Netherlands. *J Affect Disord* 2001; 65: 123-9.
[22]Benedict R. *Chrysanthemum and the Sword : Patterns of Japanese Culture.* Meridian Books, Cleveland, 1967.
[23]Kerr M, Lambert WW, Ben DJ. Life course sequalae of childhood shyness in Sweden: Comparision with United States. *Development and Psychology* 1996; 32: 1100-1105.

[24]Chen X, Rubin KH, Li B. Social and school adjustment of shy and aggressive children in China. *Development and Psychopathology* 1995; 7: 337-349.

[25]Berkson J. Limitation of the application of fourfold table analysis to hospital data. *Biometric Bulletin* 1946; 2: 47-53.

[26]Ushijima S. *Pathology of personality and psychotherapy; Psychoanalysis, Morita therapy, and Psychiatry (in Japanese)*. Kongo Publishing, Tokyo, 2004.

[27]Nikkei Medical. Weather report depending on the department. *Nikkei Medical* 2005: 46-47.

In: Social Phobia: Etiology, Diagnosis and Treatment
Editor: Clayton P. Axelby
ISBN 978-1-60692-159-3
© 2009 Nova Science Publishers, Inc.

Chapter XIV

SOCIAL ANXIETY SECONDARY TO A GENERAL MEDICAL CONDITION

Erguvan T. Ozel-Kizil
Ankara University School of Medicine, Department of Psychiatry, Turkey.

ABSTRACT

Disfiguring physical diseases like acne, psoriasis, essential tremor, cervical dystonia, hemifacial spasm, stuttering etc. may cause significant social embarrassment which leads to social avoidance and decreases the quality of life. Previous research on social anxiety secondary to chronic medical diseases clearly demonstrates the importance of this condition, since the rates they reported were considerably higher than the rates of primary social anxiety disorder in general population. However, previous research mainly examined the prevalance of secondary social anxiety and clinical characteristics or the treatment of secondary social anxiety were not clearly identified. This chapter reviews previous literature about social anxiety secondary to disfiguring diseases like hyperkinesias, stuttering and dermatological diseases.

1. INTRODUCTION

Social anxiety disorder may also develop secondary to chronic medical diseases which cause significant disfigurement [1]. Actual overlap of social anxiety disorder and the physical illness is a great challange for the patient. Leary and Kowalski pointed out that social anxiety can be a pervasive and persistent experience for individuals with physical anomalies [2]. However, in the Diagnostic and Statistical Manual for Mental Disorders-IV (DSM-IV) social anxiety related to a general medical condition like stuttering or trembling in Parkinson's disease, is excluded from the diagnosis of social anxiety disorder [3]. Although some previous findings have supported the notion that social anxiety secondary to a medical condition might be similar to social anxiety disorder in terms of its clinical characteristics including treatment response, these patients receive the diagnosis of "Anxiety Disorder Not Otherwise Specified" [1,3,4]. This procedure may lead to the failure of identifying social anxiety disorder in patients with other medical conditions, therefore might preclude these patients from receiving the treatment they need and limit further research. Such an approach, which somewhat normalizes social anxiety related to a physical disease, is also contradictory to the concept of classical psychosomatics, that is interested in psychological/mental problems secondary to a physical disease or in physical diseases which are exacerbated by psychological/mental problems. By contrast with DSM-IV, International Statistical Classification of Diseases and Related Health Problems 10th Revision (ICD-10) does not preclude the diagnosis of social phobia related to physical diseases [5]. However, studies investigating social anxiety in patients with physical diseases mainly used DSM-IV criteria A-G disregarding the criterion H, which stipulated that social anxiety should not be related to a medical condition [6-9].

Data validating social anxiety secondary to a chronic medical disease are scarce. Previous research mainly examines the prevalence of social anxiety disorder in some medical conditions, but social anxiety which develops secondary to the physical disease was not clearly identified in all of these studies. Secondary social anxiety was generally studied in patients with stuttering, dermatological diseases like acne vulgaris and especially in movement disorders like essential tremor and cervical dystonia [6-15]. All of these disorders which cause secondary social anxiety are also known to be exacerbated by stress and this leads to a vicious circle in the natural course of the disease.

Previous data upon social anxiety in physical diseases points out that the severity of social anxiety was not associated with the objective severity of the disease, but it was associated with the patient's perception of the severity of the disease [7,9,10,12,16]. Moreover, one of the common findings in previous research is that the degree of social anxiety is higher especially in younger patients with a disfiguring physical disease [9,12]. In a recent study by Klieger and Johnson, there was score inflation in the Social Phobia and Anxiety Inventory due to underlying medical conditions especially among college men and women. The most frequent underlying medical conditions were reported as stuttering (2.8%), acne (2.4%), dry mouth (2.1%), obesity (.9%), and scars (.9%)[17].

In this chapter, previous literature about secondary social anxiety in diseases like hyperkinesias, stuttering and dermatological diseases will be reviewed in the light of the clinical characteristics and probable risk factors. In addition, some important points for future research will be highlighted.

2. Social Anxiety in Patients with Hyperkinesias

Secondary social anxiety has been mostly studied in hyperkinesias like essential tremor, cervical dystonia and hemifacial spasm. All of these disorders cause chronic and socially embarrassing involuntary movements. The earliest study on this subject was carried out by Schneier et. al. In this study, the overall prevalence of DSM-IV social anxiety disorder in patients with essential tremor was reported as 32.7%. The H criterion in DSM-IV social anxiety disorder was disregarded and temporal relationship between the social anxiety and essential tremor was evaluated. When primary vs. secondary social anxiety were compared in terms of clinical characteristics; they found that patients with secondary social anxiety reported a later age of onset (51 vs 8.8 years of age), greater fear and avoidance of eating, drinking, and writing in public. Also the patients with secondary social anxiety had more severe tremor and tremor-related disability. Moreover, in all essential tremor cases severity of social phobia symptoms and tremor independently contributed to disability. The authors suggested that essential tremor patients with secondary social anxiety might benefit from beta blockers and benzodiazepines instead of antidepressant medication [8]. In another study, Topcuoglu et. al. reported social anxiety frequency of 42.2% in patients with essential tremor, but there was no difference in terms of tremor severity between patients with and without social anxiety. However, tremor-related functional disability was also higher in patients with social anxiety [10].

In a large sample of patients with cervical dystonia (n=116), a high frequency (48%) of DSM-IV social anxiety was also reported [7]. The authors examined the temporal relationship between social anxiety and spasmodic torticollis and classified social anxiety as reactive or not. In 80% of the patients with cervical dystonia social anxiety was reactive. Depressive coping and the extent of body image dissatisfaction were the predictive factors of social anxiety, while clinical variables like the severity or the duration of dystonia were not associated [7].

In a recent comparison study of ours, we found no difference in terms of the frequency or the severity of secondary social anxiety in patients with hyperkinesias like essential tremor(n=20), cervical dystonia(n=20) and hemifacial spasm(n=20). In this study patients were asked about the onset of social anxiety symptoms and the hyperkinesias, as well as their attribution of social anxiety/ avoidance to the symptoms of hyperkinesias in order to differentiate secondary vs. primary social anxiety. A total of 16 patients (26.7 %) had social anxiety secondary to hyperkinesias. Consistent with previous data, the severity of social anxiety was not associated with the severity or the duration of the hyperkinesias, but with younger age and depression [9].

Psychiatric disorders, especially anxiety disorders frequently occur in patients with Parkinson's Disease [18], which is also a highly disabling and disfiguring movement disorder due to the presence of resting tremor, bradykinesia and Parkinsonian posture. In a small sample(n=16), Stein et. al. reported a social anxiety frequency of 29% in patients with Parkinson's disease [19]. A patient with Parkinson's disease who met critera for social phobia was reported and in this patient 12 week group sessions of cognitive- behaviour therapy resulted with improvement of social anxiety symptoms [20]. A study suggesting striatal dopaminergic dysfunction in patients with social anxiety disorder [21] also supported the relationship between Parkinson's disease and social anxiety, however there is no further evidence of a clinical or biological link between these disorders.

3. Social Anxiety in Patients with Stuttering

Stuttering is a speech disorder in which the normal flow of speech is disrupted by repetitions or prolongations of sounds, syllables or words or by inability to start a word. Stuttering was closely associated with anxiety; some suggested that anxiety was the main cause of stuttering and some suggested that it was a precipitating/aggravating factor in stuttering. However, the nature of their relationship was not clearly identified [22].

Stein et. al. found clinically significant social anxiety in 7 of 16 stutterers seeking speech therapy and all of these patients identified social anxiety as an important source of role impairment. Three of them reported to be attended to cognitive-behavioral group therapy and benefited from this intervention [23].

Kraaimaat et. al. investigated social anxiety by the Inventory of Interpersonal Situations in a large sample of patients with stuttering (n=89) [24]. Although their previous work did not support the notion of social anxiety as an essential part of stuttering [25], in the latter study 50% of the stutterers had scores within the range of a group of highly socially anxious psychiatric patients.When compared to controls, the patients with stuttering displayed significantly higher levels of emotional tension or discomfort in social situations and reported a significantly lower frequency of social responses [24].

4. Social Anxiety in Patients with Dermatological Disease

Acne vulgaris, the most common dermatological disease, usually occurs in adolescence or early adulthood, during which people generally keen on their physical appearance. Therefore, the patients of acne are vulnerable for psychological problems like anxiety, depression, suicidal ideation, psychosomatic symptoms and social dysfunctioning [26-30]. Most of the previous studies found that the clinical severity of acne was not associated with patient perception or the severity of psychological symptoms [16,31,32].

There is much data about psychological problems seen in acne vulgaris patients, however only a few mainly investigated social anxiety. In a comparison study by Khan et. al., ICD-10 social anxiety was more frequent in acne patients (34%) as compared to patients with seborrhic skin problems(10%). In this study patients were between 13-25 years of age and the patients with acne, especially the females, had higher frequency of depression (38%) [33]. A recent study by Yolac Yarpuz et. al. also reported that social anxiety, social withdrawal and depression as well as general anxiety and negative automatic thoughts were higher and self-esteem was lower in patients with acne vulgaris (n=83). However, they found no relationship between psychological symptoms and gender. Psychological symptoms were negatively correlated with age and education in the patient group, but they were not correlated with the severity of acne or acne localization. The patients rated their symptoms more severely than the clinicians, but their ratings were not correlated with their psychological symptoms, either [12].

In another study Loney et. al. found that acne-related social anxiety had negative effects on the quality of life which was defined by sport/exercise participation in this group of patients [34].

Psoriasis is a highly disfiguring and debilitating dermatological disease that is characterized by red skin plaques. A high frequency of these patients were reported to be exposed to explicit social rejection due to their physical appearance [35]. Previous literature points out the presence of high levels of anxiety and depression as well as high fear of negative evaluation in these patients [36,37,38,39]. Leary et. al. examined the factors that contribute to the psychological and social dysfunctioning of patients with psoriasis. They found that disease severity and fear of negative evaluation significantly predicted perceptions of being stigmatized, interpersonal discomfort, stress over others' reactions, distress regarding the observable symptoms of the disease, the degree to which psoriasis interfered with the patients' lives, and patients' quality of life [37]. Another study that investigated the effects of psoriasis on quality of life in a large sample of patients with psoriasis (n=141) pointed out that psoriasis was most relevant for quality of life for those patients whose condition was visible on their face and hands and who reported a high fear of negative evaluation [38]. In this study, authors also examined the effects of past experiences and found that current quality of life, fear of negative evaluation and anxiety symptoms were related to the nature of previous experiences. Although these studies examined fear of negative evaluation which is an important component of social anxiety, there is only one study which investigated secondary social anxiety in psoriasis patients (n=32). In this study, Ozguven et. al. reported that psoriasis patients with skin lesions at the exposed parts of the body (e.g. face, hand,arm,leg etc.) had higher social anxiety and depression levels than controls and there was a correlation between social anxiety levels and the clinical severity of psoriasis [39].

Koo et. al. reported high prevalance of social anxiety disorder in patients with alopecia areata, but secondary social anxiety was not specifically addressed in that study [40].

5. Conclusion

Disfiguring physical diseases like acne, psoriasis, essential tremor, cervical dystonia, hemifacial spasm etc. may cause significant social embarrassment which leads to social avoidance and decreases the quality of life. Previous research on social anxiety secondary to chronic medical diseases clearly demonstrates the importance of this condition, since the rates they reported were considerably higher than the rates of primary social anxiety disorder in general population [41,42].

Moreover, in these studies the patients were mainly under treatment, so secondary social anxiety would be even more frequent and more severe in untreated patients.

Management of social anxiety and depressive coping style in these patients is necessary in adjunct to the treatment of the primary disease, since secondary social anxiety is associated with the patient’s perception/expression of the severity of the disease, but not with the objective severity of the disease. However, there is no study investigating the treatment of social anxiety related to physical diseases. In a study by Stein et. al., three of the stutterers with social anxiety were reported to be benefited from cognitive-behavioral therapy [23] and there is a case report of a patient with Parkinson's disease whose social anxiety symptoms were improved after a 12-week cognitive-behavioural psychotherapy [20].

In addition, little is known about the clinical characteristics of social anxiety secondary to physical diseases. Only a few disease groups were studied in detail, although there are many disfiguring diseases causing significant distress in social interaction. For instance, Berk et. al. reported higher levels of social anxiety in adult patients with oral-facial clefts than their unaffected siblings [43]. Two recent studies reported high prevalances of social phobia in bariatric patients(18%; n=294) attending a presurgical psychological consultation and in patients with coeliac disease(70%; n=40) [44,45]. However, these studies did not address whether social anxiety was related to the primary disease or not.

In conclusion, we should refer to the presence of a social anxiety disorder related or secondary to the existing physical disease. Therefore, revision of the criteria for social anxiety disorder in future diagnostic systems like DSM-V, based on current evidence is necessary. This would provide recognition and management of this condition, as well as a basis for future research.

References

[1] Oberlander EL, Schneier FR, Liebowitz MR. Physical disability and social phobia. *J Clin Psychopharmacol* 1994;14:136–43.

[2] Leary MR, Kowalski RM. *Social anxiety*. New York: Guilford Press,1995.

[3] *American Psychiatric Association Diagnostic and Statistical Manual of Mental Disorders*, 4th ed. American Psychiatric Association, Washington D.C., 1994.

[4] George MS, Lydiard RB. Social phobia secondary to physical disability. A review of benign essential tremor and stuttering. *Psychosomatics* 1994;35:520–3.

[5] World Health Organisation. The ICD-10 classification of mental and behavioural disorders. *Clinical descriptions and diagnostic guidelines*. Geneva: World Health Organisation, 1992.

[6] Stein MB, Baird A, Walker JR. Social phobia in adults with stuttering. *Am J Psychia*try 1996;153:278–80.

[7] Gündel H, Wolf A, Xidara V, Busch R, Ceballos-Baumann AO.Social phobia in spasmodic torticollis. *J Neurol Neurosurg Psychiatry* 2001; 71:499–504.

[8] Schneier FR, Barnes LF, Albert SM, Louis ED. Characteristics of social phobia among persons with essential tremor. *J Clin Psychiatry* 2001;62: 367-372.

[9] Ozel-Kizil ET, Akbostanci MC, Ozguven HD, Atbasoglu EC.Secondary social anxiety in hyperkinesias. *Mov Disord* 2008 Apr 15;23(5):641-5.

[10] Topcuoglu V, Bez Y, Sahin Bicer D, Dib H, Kuscu MK, Yazgan C, Ince Gunal D, Goktepe E. Social phobia in essential tremor. *Turk Psikiyatri Derg* 2006;17(2):93-100.

[11] Devrimci-Özgüven H, Kudakçı N, Boyvat A. Secondary social anxiety in patients with psoriasis. *Turk Psikiyatri Derg* 2000;11(2):121-126.

[12] Yolac Yarpuz A, Demirci Saadet E, _anlı H, Devrimci-Özgüven H. Social anxiety in acne vulgaris patients and relationship with clinical variables. *Turk Psikiyatri Derg* 2008 Spring;19(1):29-37.

[13] Wenzel T, Schnider P, Wimmer A, et al: Psychiatric comorbidity in patients with spasmodic torticollis. *J Psychosom Res* 1998;44:687–690.

[14] Lauterbach EC, Freeman A., Vogel RL. Differential DSM-III Psychiatric Disorder Prevalence Profiles in Dystonia and Parkinson's Disease. *J Neuropsychiatry Clin Neurosci Winter* 2004; 16: 29-36.

[15] George MS, Lydiard RB. Social phobia secondary to physical disability. A review of benign essential tremor (BET) and stuttering. *Psychosomatics* 1994;35:520–3.

[16] Mosam A, Vawda NB, Gordhan AH, Nkwanyana N, Aboobaker J.Quality of life issues for South Africans with acne vulgaris. *Clin Exp Dermatol* 2005 Jan;30(1):6-9.

[17] Klieger DM, Johnson HK.The social phobia and anxiety inventory: problem of underlying medical conditions. *Psychol Rep* 2007 Dec;101(3 Pt 1):697-706.

[18] de Rijk C, Bijl RV. Prevalence of mental disorders in persons with Parkinson's disease. *Ned Tijdschr Geneeskd* 1998 Jan 3;142(1):27-31.

[19] Stein MB, Heuser IJ, Juncos JL, Uhde TW. Anxiety disorders in patients with Parkinson's disease. *Am J Psychiatry* 1990;147: 217-220.

[20] Heinrichs N, Hoffman EC, Hofmann SG. Cognitive-behavioral treatment for social phobia in Parkinson's disease: A single-case study. *Cogn Behav Pract.* 2001;8(4):328-335.

[21] Tiihonen J, Kuikka J, Bergström K, Lepola U, Koponen H, Leinonen E.Dopamine reuptake site densities in patients with social phobia. *Am J Psychiatry* 1997 Feb;154(2):239-42.

[22] Menzies RG, Onslow M, Packman A. Anxiety and stuttering: Exploring a complex relationship. *Am J Speech-Language Pathology* 1999; 8: 3–10.

[23] Stein MB, Baird A, Walker JR. Social phobia in adults with stuttering. *Am J Psychiatry* 1996 Feb;153(2):278-80.

[24] Kraaimaat FW, Vanryckeghem M, Van Dam-Baggen R. Stuttering and social anxiety. *J Fluency Disord* 2002 Winter;27(4):319-30.

[25] Kraaimaat FW, Janssen P, van Dam-Baggen R. Social anxiety and stuttering. *Percept Mot Skills* 1991 Jun;72:766.

[26] Gupta MA, Gupta AK. Depression and suicidal ideation in dermatology patients with acne, alopecia areata, atopic dermatitis and psoriasis. *Br J Dermatol.* 1998 Nov;139(5):846-50.

[27] Gupta MA, Gupta AK. The psychological comorbidity in acne. *Clin Dermatol* 2001; 19: 360–363.

[28] Niemeier V, Kupfer J, Gieler U. Acne vulgaris--psychosomatic aspects. J *Dtsch Dermatol Ges.* 2006 Dec;4(12):1027-36.

[29] Tan JK. Psychosocial impact of acne vulgaris: evaluating the evidence. *Skin Therapy Lett* 2004 Aug-Sep;9(7):1-3, 9.

[30] Picardi A, Mazzotti E, Pasquini P. Prevalence and correlates of suicidal ideation among patients with skin disease. *J Am Acad Dermatol* 2006 Mar;54(3):420-6.)

[31] Niemeier V, Kupfer J, Demmelbauer-Ebner M, Stangier U, Effendy I, Gieler U.Coping with acne vulgaris. Evaluation of the chronic skin disorder questionnaire in patients with acne. *Dermatology* 1998;196(1):108-15.

[32] Uslu G, Sendur N, Uslu M, Savk E, Karaman G, Eskin M.Acne: prevalence, perceptions and effects on psychological health among adolescents in Aydin, Turkey. *J Eur Acad Dermatol Venereol* 2008 Apr;22(4):462-9. Epub 2007 Dec 20.

[33] Khan MZ, Naeem A, Mufti KA. Prevalence of mental health problems in acne patients. *J Ayub Med Coll Abbottabad* 2001 Oct-Dec;13(4):7-8.

[34] Loney T, Standage M, Lewis S. Not just 'skin deep': psychosocial effects of dermatological-related social anxiety in a sample of acne patients. *J Health Psychol.* 2008 Jan;13(1):47-54.

[35] Ginsburg IH, Link BG. Psychosocial consequences of rejection and stigma feelings in psoriasis patients. *Int J Dermatol* 1993; 32: 587-591.

[36] Devrimci-Ozguven H, Kundakci TN, Kumbasar H, Boyvat A.The depression, anxiety, life satisfaction and affective expression levels in psoriasis patients. *J Eur Acad Dermatol Venereol* 2000 Jul;14(4):267-71.

[37] Leary MR, Rapp SR, Herbst KC, Exum ML, Feldman SR.Interpersonal concerns and psychological difficulties of psoriasis patients: effects of disease severity and fear of negative evaluation. *Health Psychol* 1998 Nov;17(6):530-6.

[38] Kent G, Keohane S. Social anxiety and disfigurement: the moderating effects of fear of negative evaluation and past experience. *Br J Clin Psychol* 2001 Mar;40(Pt 1):23-34.

[39] Ozguven HD, Kudakci N, Boyvat A. Secondary social anxiety in patients with psoriasis. *Turk Psikiyatri Derg* 2000;11(2):121-126.

[40] Koo JY, Shellow WV, Hallman CP, Edwards JE.Alopecia areata and increased prevalence of psychiatric disorders. *Int J Dermatol* 1994 Dec;33(12):849-50.

[41] Wacker HR, Müllejans R, Klein KH, Battegay R. Identification of cases of anxiety disorders and affective disorders in the community according to ICD-10 and DSM-III-R by using the Composite International Diagnostic Interview (CIDI). *Int J Methods Psychiatr Res* 1992; 2: 91-100.

[42] Magee WJ, Eaton WW, Wittchen HU, Mc Gonagle KA, Kessler RC. Agoraphobia, simple phobia and social phobia in the National Comorbidity Survey. *Arch Gen Psychiatry* 1996; 53: 159-168.

[43] Berk NW, Cooper ME, Liu YE, Marazita ML.Social anxiety in Chinese adults with oral-facial clefts. *Cleft Palate Craniofac J* 2001 Mar;38(2):126-33.

[44] Rosik CH. Psychiatric symptoms among prospective bariatric surgery patients: rates of prevalence and their relation to social desirability, pursuit of surgery, and follow-up attendance. *Obes Surg* 2005 May;15(5):677-83.

[45] Addolorato G, Mirijello A, D'Angelo C, Leggio L, Ferrulli A, Vonghia L, Cardone S, Leso V, Miceli A, Gasbarrini G Social phobia in coeliac disease. *Scand J Gastroenterol* 2008;43(4):410-5.

INDEX

A

B

C

D

E

H

I

J

K

L

M

N

Q

R

S

T

U

V

W

Y

Z